D0878449

DOMINANCE

Other Football Titles from Brassey's

Playing Hurt: Treating and Evaluating the Warriors of the NFL
by Pierce E. Scranton, Jr., M.D.

Pro Football Prospectus: 2002
by Sean Lahman and Todd Greanier

Blue Ribbon College Football Yearbook: 2002 Edition
Edited by Chris Dortch

Football's Most Wanted: The Top 10 Book of the Great Game's Outrageous Characters, Fortunate Fumbles, and Other Oddities
by Floyd Conner

DOMINANCE

the BEST SEASONS *of* PRO FOOTBALL'S GREATEST TEAMS

EDDIE EPSTEIN

Foreword by Mel Kiper, Jr.

Brassey's, Inc.
WASHINGTON, D.C.

Library of Congress Cataloging-in-Publication Data

Epstein, Eddie.

Dominance : the best seasons of pro football's greatest teams / Eddie Epstein.– 1st ed.

p. cm.

ISBN 1-57488-466-2

1. Football teams–History–20th century. 2. Football teams–United States–Statistics. I. Title

GV954 E67 2002

796.332'06–dc21

2002008092

Printed in Canada on acid-free paper

Brassey's, Inc.
22841 Quicksilver Drive
Dulles, Virginia 20166

Cover photo courtesy of Transcendental Graphics
Cover design by Jesse Marinoff Reyes
Text design by Pen & Palette Unlimited.

First Edition

10 9 8 7 6 5 4 3 2 1

For the beautiful love of my life, Vikki

Contents

Photographs

Foreword

Mel Kiper, Jr., ESPN football analyst

Over the years, I've found that in life you really only have–if you are fortunate–one or two true friends that you can count on. For my wife Kim and me, Eddie Epstein is a friend that we hold in the highest regard.

When I first met Eddie about 10 years ago, I knew him as Doctor Baseball. He has an uncanny ability to evaluate baseball players and teams, often using his own sophisticated methods, but he also just has a feel for the game in addition to encyclopedic knowledge about its history. I always thought he would end up as a successful major league general manager. Maybe he still will, as teams that are struggling couldn't find a more qualified person to make them competitive.

However, over time I learned that Eddie is much more than a baseball guy. He's also very knowledgeable about football, with a keen eye for talent. When you combine that ability with his knowledge of history and his wizardry with math, I strongly believe that he could be a valued executive with an NFL organization. In fact, if I were an owner or GM, he would be one of my first hires.

I gravitate to purists when it comes to football or other sports, and Eddie has few peers in this regard. He's dedicated, passionate, energetic, and confident; that last trait is a key in the entire equation. Folks, if you don't have strength in your convictions, any evaluation or scouting report that you provide isn't worth the paper it's written on. Eddie will give you a firm, unwavering assessment that is based on hours of study and research.

With all this in mind, I can't think of anyone more qualified to provide an in-depth analysis of the greatest teams in NFL history. You will no doubt learn a great deal about football, about what makes great teams tick, and you will know that Eddie left no stone unturned in his effort.

Acknowledgments

I want to thank Chris Kahrl at Brassey's for believing in this project and Keith Law for being the catalyst. Dave Schoenfield and Joe Lago of ESPN.com have been advocates of my work, and I am very appreciative. Many thanks to Bob Valvano and Andy Elrick of ESPN Radio. I really enjoy the Fridays. Bob Gain, Calvin Hill, Brent Jones, Lenny Moore, and Jerry Vainisi were very gracious in allowing me to interview them. Vince Bagli and Bernie Miklasz were great sources of information and encouragement. I am indebted to Pete Palmer for providing me with the raw data I needed to make this book possible. The PR departments of the Browns, Colts, Packers, Dolphins, Steelers, Bears, 49ers, Redskins, and Rams were very courteous and most helpful. In particular, Dino Lucarelli of the Browns and Will Norman of the Redskins went above and beyond the call of duty. My life would be far less plentiful if it weren't for my family: my mother, Ann, my sisters, Debbie and Rose, my niece, Jennifer, and my "brothers," Gary and Brad. I love you all.

Introduction

Football is not about statistics. Football is about guts and character and playing through pain, sacrificing your body for the good of the team. You can't measure how good a player is by his numbers, and the only number that matters for a team is how many wins they have.

OK, who said that? Actually, the above quote is just me combining hundreds of player remarks heard over the years. There is, without doubt, a lot of validity in those sentiments. Unlike baseball, which is primarily a game of trained reflex and muscle memory, football is a game of emotional and physical intensity.

A football player is far more dependent on his teammates for success than is a baseball player. It's easy to recognize a productive baseball player on even the worst team; it can be difficult to know how good a football player is because one has to consider the quality of the players surrounding him. Obviously, football is also far more of a "team" game because of the sheer number of players involved. For example, the Chicago Bears added Dick Butkus *and* Gale Sayers to their team in 1965. Both are universally acclaimed as being among the greatest players of all time. They played together for five years (not counting Sayers's injury-riddled comeback attempts in 1970 and 1971). What was Chicago's record in those five years? 29–38–3. It's difficult to imagine a baseball team with Babe Ruth and Lefty Grove finishing under .500 for a five-year period. In Steve Young's second NFL season (as a member of Tampa Bay), his passer rating was 65.5 and his team's record was 2–14. The very next year, in limited duty with San Francisco, his passer rating was 120.8; in his second season as the 49ers' starter, Young's rating was 107.0 and San Francisco's record was 14–2. Of course, there was a learning process involved, but just as obviously a football player's production and recognition are, in large part, a function of his teammates.

All that being said, I felt that when it came to evaluating *teams* a systematic and numerical approach could work. I believe I can measure a team's dominance and greatness, to a large degree if not completely, using some of the same techniques that Rob Neyer and I applied to baseball teams in

Baseball Dynasties. The most important concept was using the idea of standard deviation to measure how a team dominated its contemporaries. (Standard deviation is a measure of the dispersion, or spread, of a set of numbers.)

A brief digression, if I may: until recently, buyers of sports books primarily purchased baseball and golf titles. The market for baseball books, in particular, has been diverse. Football has now acquired a history that it lacked 20 or 30 years ago, a history that makes a book like this possible. The popularity of books such as *When Pride Still Mattered,* David Maraniss's wonderful biography of Vince Lombardi, shows that a quality football book will be successful. This really should come as no surprise given football's unquestioned status as the most popular sport in America.

Let me quickly add that the focus in this book is on the period from 1950 to the present. In that year, unlimited substitution was made a permanent part of pro football, forever changing the way teams were organized. We have all heard of the toughness of "two-way" players, and that is no doubt the case, as one can only imagine what it was like to slog away on a professional football field for 60 minutes on offense and defense. I felt that it was an intractable "apples and oranges" problem to compare teams from the free-substitution era to teams from the two-way era. A less important, but not insignificant reason I use 1950 as our beginning is because that was the first year after the merger between the National Football League and the All-America Football Conference. The merger brought the Browns, who played in the NFL title game in each of their first six seasons after the merger, and 49ers into the NFL. (The merger with AAFC also brought the Baltimore Colts to the NFL, but that franchise—not to be confused with the later Colts' teams discussed elsewhere—folded after one miserable season in 1950.)

I must inject a disclaimer. I am not suggesting in this book that the 1955 Browns can be directly compared to the 1999 Rams. I determined teams for inclusion in the book by using methods that measure how much a team dominated its competition in a particular season or seasons, not how they would do if placed in a different era. Although starting at 1950 gives me some framework for comparison, pro football has changed quite a bit since then.

One change has been in the sheer size (and speed) of players. Dick Vermeil noticed a marked difference in player size and speed after being out of the NFL "only" 15 years; imagine how players have changed over the last 50 years. (See "The Coach: Dick Vermeil" in the 1999 Rams' chapter.)

In *The Sports Encyclopedia: Pro Football,* there are no players in 1950 with a listed weight of 300 pounds. The highest listed weight is Cleveland's Chubby

Grigg at 280 pounds. Even granting that Grigg and others (like Detroit's Les Bingaman) may have fudged on their weights, there were not a lot of 300-pounders. Bob Davis of the Pittsburgh Steelers is listed as a 5–11, 195-pound *defensive end.*

In the *NFL 2000 Record & Fact Book,* I counted 281 players with listed weights of 300+ pounds on the 31 veteran rosters, about nine per team. I probably even missed some, but you get the point.

Roster size has also changed dramatically. In 1950, the active player limit was 32; in 2000, it was 45, not including the "emergency" quarterback. This change in roster size has allowed teams to substitute not just with separate offense and defense "platoons" but also by situation. In the early 1950s, even though free substitution was permitted, many players played on both offense and defense simply because teams didn't always have enough players for separate offensive and defensive units. Today, many players don't play on every down because, for example, their job is to play in the "jumbo" package on offense (a short-yardage/goal-line unit) but not on the "quad" package (a four wide-receiver set). Without larger rosters, this type of situation substitution would be impossible.

As for actual strategy, the early 1950s saw NFL offenses open up and rely more on the passing game than ever before. The Browns added timing routes and sideline passes to the passing game; the Rams added the flanker. (What the Browns did was really the foundation for today's West Coast offense.) Defenses countered by changing from five-man lines to four-man lines, which created the position of middle linebacker. They also used variations of the Umbrella defense (called the umbrella because the secondary formed a dome shape in coverage) created by Giants head coach Steve Owen to counteract the Browns' passing game. The zone defense was developed to keep offenses from exploiting mismatches in man-to-man coverage. And teams still had trouble keeping Cleveland out of the end zone, not to mention the championship game.

As defenses adjusted, partly due to the "new" trend of putting most of the best athletes on defense, and with the success of Lombardi's Packers, the 1960s saw a shift back to the running game. That trend continued into the 1970s. The change in the position of the hashmarks in 1972, placing them close together near the center of the field, meant defenses no longer had the advantage of having a "short" side of the field. In the first two seasons after the merger (1970 and 1971), there were seven 1,000-yard runners. In the first two seasons after the repositioning of the hashmarks, there were 15. Ironically, the hashmarks were moved primarily to help the passing game.

With more sophisticated pass coverages and quicker defensive players, NFL offenses ran more, threw less, and scored fewer points. In 1977, rushing yards actually exceeded passing yards and scoring was at its lowest since 1942 (17.2 points per game per team). The following year, the league made the first of a series of rules changes designed to open the game by making it easier to throw the football—changes such as liberalizing the blocking rules for offensive lineman and creating the five-yard zone after which a receiver could not be touched. By 1985, NFL teams gained 16 yards passing for every 10 rushing yards, and scoring was up to 21.5 points per team/game. In 2000, the ratio was 18 passing yards for every 10 rushing yards, and teams still averaged over 20 points per game (20.7).

No doubt some of the change in NFL strategy in the '80s and '90s occurred because of the tremendous success of one team: the San Francisco 49ers. In the Bill Walsh offense, the pass was primary and the 49ers would throw on any down. His teams were well schooled in the "pick" play where one receiver would obstruct his teammate's defender. This play was soon common throughout the league. The 49ers were also adept at finding the "dead" areas between zones, and the entire pass offense was well-coordinated and rehearsed at an unprecedented level.

While a few teams today try a version of the Lombardi approach—controlling the game by running the football and relying on a dominant defense—most teams use the pass as the main method of moving the ball. The influence of Bill Walsh is everywhere, or should I say Paul Brown? Football strategy is always evolving, a series of moves and countermoves. However, true shifts in tactics usually occur when some team has been extraordinarily successful, and those teams always have exceptional players. Maybe that's the real constant in football or in any team sport.

Now, as for this book, it differs from *Baseball Dynasties* in a few ways. The most obvious difference is the subject, plus, *Dominance* is more restrictive in terms of period of time covered. I focus on one specific season for this book. In *Baseball Dynasties,* the focus of the team chapters was one season, but it had to be a great season in the middle of great seasons. I didn't do that with this book because I wanted to be able discuss individual games, which is easier to do when using one season. Besides, none of the teams in the book are one-season wonders. In fact, such teams are more rare in football than they are in baseball.

The other difference in the two books is in the use of quotes and interviews—first person accounts. I think that football is more of an emotional experience than baseball, and I felt that more first person accounts would make the teams seem more real to the reader.

I applied some of the methods that have been used in the "new era" of baseball analysis to the study of football, which brings us back to standard deviations. Standard deviation is the most well-known number used to measure the dispersion, or difference, in a set of numbers. In other words, it is a measure of how much the numbers differ from each other, calculated using the "average" difference of each number from the mean of the group. (That's not the exact definition, but the exact definition uses terms like "sums of squares" that I don't want to use.) Take the following example:

Set #1: 1, 2, 3, 4, 5, 6, 7, 8, 9, 10
Set #2: 4, 7, 5, 6, 3, 8, 4, 7, 5, 6

The mean, or average, of these two sets of numbers is the same, 5.5. The first set, however, is more widely dispersed than the second set. The standard deviation of the first set is 2.9; the standard deviation of the second set is 1.5.

Here's another example:

Set #1: 14, 21, 38, 45, 57
Set #2: 31, 33, 35, 37, 39

Each set of numbers has the same mean or average, 35. Which set has the higher standard deviation? If you said Set #1, you're right.

In 1950, the standard deviation of points allowed for NFL teams was 98.8. In 1999, the standard deviation of points allowed was 61.0, even though the league average was higher. (In general, if one looks at two sets of numbers describing similar events, the standard deviation will be affected by the average. The higher the average, more likely than not, the standard deviation will be higher as well.) Forgetting for a moment the different league averages caused by schedules of different lengths, rule changes, and the like, this example illustrates something that happens over time. Without getting too involved in an esoteric discussion about the maturation of complex systems, generally, the differences among teams have gotten smaller as football has evolved. In an article I wrote for *Pro Football Revealed,* this "shrinking" of those differences was applied to the evaluation of the best passing seasons in NFL history. In 1950, the standard deviation of the NFL passing rating among teams was 14.6 points. In 1999, the standard deviation was just 10.5 points *and* the league average was much higher (77.1 compared to 52.9 in 1950). In other words, the differences between the best and worst passers, and all the passers in between, have gotten smaller through time.

Using standard deviations instead of just comparing teams to league averages seems like a good way to make comparisons across eras while considering the overall changes. Just as with baseball, no time period seems to dominate when ranking teams by standard deviations; that alone is strong evidence of the validity of this approach.

Now to the "technical" stuff. The number at the core of selecting these teams is called the Power Index. It is identical in concept to what we called the SD Score in *Baseball Dynasties,* although the Power Index uses more categories of performance. Besides, "Power Index" sounds more like a football statistic. Unlike the baseball book, where we just used runs scored and runs allowed, here I used points scored/allowed *and* yards gained/allowed. I felt that this would more thoroughly capture the performance of teams. And since there are more plays in a football game than there are plate appearances in a baseball game, using yards gained/allowed lets us use the fact that there are so many discrete game events in football. Using points scored and allowed allows us to at least partially capture the impact of special teams play and other "non-scrimmage" factors.

We'll use the 1958 Baltimore Colts as our example of how Power Index is calculated. They scored 381 points, allowed 203, gained 4,539 yards, and allowed 3,284. Here is how those numbers compare to the league average and standard deviations for that season:

1958 Colts		**League Average**	**Standard Deviation**	**Standard Deviations Above/Below the Average**
Points Scored:	381	271.1	50.7	+2.17
Points Allowed:	203	271.1	59.4	+1.15
Yards Gained:	4,539	3,859.2	434.2	+1.57
Yards Allowed:	3,284	3,859.2	513.0	+1.12
"Raw" Power Index				**+6.00**

The Colts scored 381 points, the NFL team average in 1958 was 271.1, and the standard deviation of points scored for NFL teams that season was 50.7. So 381 minus 271.1 is 109.9, and that number divided by 50.7 is 2.17, which means that the Colts' points scored total was 2.17 standard deviations above the league average. The Power Index is simply the sum of all of the differences from the league mean as measured by standard deviation in these four categories. (There is no error in the addition in the Colts' example; the numbers weren't rounded until the very end.) For a team that is worse than the league average in a category, its number of standard deviations from the league mean would be negative, a number like −0.63. The

Colts' points allowed total is less than the league average, but for the points allowed category, more is not better, which is why the Colts are shown to be 1.15 standard deviations better than the league average in points allowed. [(271.1 − 203) / 59.4 is 1.15.]

Besides the obvious difference in the number of games played by teams in the two sports, football teams also don't play the same *kind* of schedule as baseball teams play. Baseball teams play all the other teams in their league during the course of a season. That doesn't happen in football. Therefore, some adjustment has to be made to adjust a team's Power Index for strength of schedule. Thanks to the graciousness of Pete Palmer, I had the data for the collective records of every team's opponents going back to 1950. I made an adjustment based on the difference between the collective winning percentage of a team's opponents, not counting games against that team, and .500. The 1958 Colts' opponents had a collective winning percentage of .504; their Adjusted Power Index, abbreviated as API and meaning Power Index adjusted for strength of schedule, was +6.02.

If the math seems a bit intimidating, don't worry. The idea is to measure how much better a team was than its league in a given season. I do this by comparing its performance to the league average in four categories, while factoring in how team performances were distributed and the strength of the team's schedule.

In general, teams with a great Power Index were teams that really dominated their opposition. More specifically, mirroring SD Scores for baseball (where a figure of +3.00 or higher was the standard of excellence), a Power Index of +6.00 or higher is the mark of excellence for football. Remember, in baseball we used two components (runs scored and runs allowed), whereas in football I used four components (points scored, points allowed, yards gained, and yards allowed). *Twenty-two* teams since 1950 (excluding the strike years of 1982 and 1987) have had an Adjusted Power Index of +6.00 or higher. *Thirteen of those teams* won the Super Bowl (or NFL title in the pre-Super Bowl days, before 1966), although one of those 13 didn't win its division. Collectively, the record of those 22 teams was 271–56–1. This is the distribution by decade:

1950s 2 teams
1960s 4 teams
1970s 6 teams
1980s 3 teams
1990s 6 teams (not including the 2001 Rams)

This is the distribution of top Adjusted Power Indexes by percentile:

80th Percentile: +2.58 } 16.7% greater than or equal to +3.00
85th Percentile: +3.27
90th Percentile: +3.88 } 9.3% greater than or equal to +4.00
95th Percentile: +4.82 } 4.1% greater than or equal to +5.00; 1.9% greater than or equal to +6.00
99th Percentile: +6.61

While the frequency by decade is not quite as evenly distributed as in baseball, I still felt that the use of standard deviation is the best way to compare teams across eras. Of course, that's just my opinion; I could be wrong. (Dennis Miller?)

So you don't have to re-read this whole section if you want to refer back later, I'll try to squeeze the general criteria into one sentence. Ahem, the teams in this book were selected like this: they were the teams that won the Super Bowl (or pre-1966 NFL title), won their division (no Wild Cards in order to give some meaning to the regular season), and had an Adjusted Power Index of +6.00 or higher. While that didn't give me any discretion as to which teams were used, I felt it was a good way to balance all of the criteria I felt were important, among those were regular-season record and postseason performance. As it turned out, every team in the book also had an *un*adjusted Power Index of +6.00 or higher. Only one team, the 1992 Cowboys, got "adjusted" out of the book because their strength of schedule pushed their adjusted Index below +6.00.

The no Wild Card criterion excluded only one team, the 1997 Denver Broncos. The 1997 Broncos were an excellent team (12–4 record, +6.43 API); however, I felt that a team could not be considered as being among the very best of all time if it did not even win its own division. The regular season has to count for something. In 1997, the Chiefs won the AFC West with a 13–3 record. (It was close, though. The Broncos lost a 24–22 game to the Chiefs in the final seconds to give Kansas City the division title; Denver repaid them with a 14–10 win in the divisional playoffs—in KC, no less.)

What about the AFL? It is my strong opinion that the league was inferior to the NFL prior to the adoption of the common draft in 1967. In case you're wondering, the 1968 Jets had an API of +4.23, while the 1969 Chiefs had an API of +6.00, the best in the AFL. However, Kansas City was really a Wild Card team since it did not win its division—the Raiders won the AFL Western Division. The Chiefs were in the AFL playoffs because, for the only year of its 10-year existence, the league adopted a plan in which the second-place teams in each division made the playoffs.

Granted, that is a lot of criteria (and a lot of math), but in the end, I have selected what I truly feel are the 12 best NFL teams since 1950.

Glossary of Statistical Terms

I want to say up front that some of the material in this book has appeared, in one form or another, on ESPN.com. I occasionally contribute baseball and football material to the website and they graciously allowed me to use that material here.

This seems like the best place to bring up a few points regarding what is included in each chapter.

The head coach and quarterback of each team are profiled because I believe that they are the two people most responsible for the success or failure of a pro football team. In this day of the salary cap and free agency, one might consider adding the GM to that list.

When examining consecutive season streaks, like how many years the Tampa Bay Buccaneers had a below average Offense Power Index (OPI), I exclude the strike years of 1982 and 1987. I exclude 1982 because of the truncated and interrupted season and I exclude 1987 because 20 percent of the games that counted were played by replacement players.

Lastly, I take full responsibility for any errors, either of omission or commission. I was very careful with the work, but I'm only human.

Now to the abbreviations and notes:

Terms

OPI	Offense Power Index
DPI	Defense Power Index
API	Adjusted Power Index, adjusted means adjusted for strength of schedule; the sum of OPI and DPI
Att	Attempts, either pass attempts or rushing attempts
Avg	Average yards per carry, per reception, per kickoff/punt/interception return, per punt. With the exception of punting average, I decided to carry the averages out to two decimal places. The NFL shows average yards per pass attempt to two decimal places, but everything else to just one. I decided to carry just about everything to two.
Comp	Passes completed
Comp Ret	Pass completion percentage

FG	Field goals made
FGA	Field goals attempted
FG Pct	Field goal percentage
Lg Avg	League Average
Net (Rushing) Yards	For running backs only with 50 or more carries, their average per carry minus the NFL average multiplied by the number of carries. This is an attempt to measure quantity and quality. Example: In 1999, Marshall Faulk averaged 5.46 yards per rushing attempt on 253 carries. The 1999 NFL average per rush was 3.90. So 5.46 minus 3.90 is 1.56, 1.56 times 253 is about +395, which means that Faulk gained 395 more yards than a running back with the league average per carry would have gained in the same number of rushing attempts.
Opp	Opponent
Rating	NFL passing rating
Ret	Number of kickoff or punt returns
XP	Extra points made
XPA	Extra points attempted
XP Pct	Extra points percentage
Yds	Yards gained
YPA or Yds Per	Yards per pass attempt

Positions

LE	Left End
SE	Split End
TE	Tight End
C	Center
OG	Offensive Guard
LG	Left Guard
RG	Right Guard
OT	Offensive Tackle
LT	Left Tackle
RT	Right Tackle
QB	Quarterback
RB	Running Back
H-B	H-Back
WR	Wide Receiver
FL	Flanker
OE	Offensive End
RE	Right End
KR	Kick Returner
PR	Punt Returner
K	Kicker
P	Punter
MG	Middle Guard (Middle man on five-man defensive line)
DE	Defensive End
DT	Defensive Tackle
NT	Nose Tackle
LLB	Left Linebacker
MLB	Middle Linebacker
RLB	Right Linebacker
DB	Defensive Back
LCB	Left Cornerback
RCB	Right Cornerback
LS	Left Safety
RS	Right Safety
SS	Strong Safety
FS	Free Safety

Teams

Some cities, including Baltimore, Chicago, Los Angeles, and St. Louis, have had multiple franchises since 1950. Most people are probably familiar with the teams referred to in the various tables and charts, but just to be on the safe side, I'll include a list of team abbreviations:

ARI	Arizona Cardinals
ATL	Atlanta Falcons
BAL	Baltimore Colts
BAR	Baltimore Ravens
BUF	Buffalo Bills
CAR	Carolina Panthers
CHB CHI	Chicago Bears
CHC	Chicago Cardinals
CIN	Cincinnati Bengals
CLE	Cleveland Browns
DAL	Dallas Cowboys
DEN	Denver Broncos
DET	Detroit Lions
GB	Breen Bay Packers
HOU	Houston Oilers
IND	Indianapolis Colts
JAC	Jacksonville Jaguars
KC	Kansas City Chiefs
LA	Los Angeles Rams
LRD	Los Angeles Raiders
MIA	Miami Dolphins
MIN	Minnesota Vikings
NE	New England Patriots
NO	New Orleans Saints
NYG	New York Giants
NYJ	New York Jets
NYY	New York Yanks
OAK	Oakland Raiders
PHI	Philadelphia Eagles
PIT	Pittsburgh Steelers
SD	San Diego Chargers
SF	San Francisco 49ers
STC	St. Louis Cardinals
TB	Tampa Bay Buccaneers
TEN	Tennessee Oilers/Titans
WAS	Washington Redskins

Despite the fact that the NFL has only done this since 1972, I *always* count a tie as a half-win and a half-loss. That is why some of the winning percentages I show for pre-1972 teams/coaches won't match what's in *Total Football* or the *NFL Record & Fact Book.*

CHAPTER 1

1955 Cleveland Browns: 10 for 10

STARTING LINEUP – 1955 BROWNS

Offense		Defense	
LE	Darrel "Pete" Brewster	LE	Carlton Massey
LT	Lou Groza	LT	John Kissell
LG	Abe Gibron	MG	Bob Gain
C	Frank Gatski	RT	Don Colo
RG	Harold Bradley	RE	Len Ford
RT	Mike McCormack	LLB	Chuck Noll
RE	Dante Lavelli	RLB	Walt Michaels
FL	Ray Renfro	LCB	Warren Lahr
QB	Otto Graham	RCB	Don Paul
RB	Fred "Curly" Morrison	LS	Kenny Konz
RB	Ed Modzelewski	RS	Tommy James

The 1955 Browns were the last in a line of Cleveland teams that made the most remarkable run in pro sports history. Granted that their early success came in a league that may not have been the best pro league around, but 1955 marked the Browns' tenth season of existence *and* their tenth season playing in a championship game. Their regular season record in those 10 years was a mind-numbing 105–17–4 and they won a total of seven league championships, four in the All-America Football Conference and three in the National Football League.

Of course, if Otto Graham had made his first retirement stick, then the 1955 Cleveland Browns wouldn't have "happened." Graham had announced his retirement after the 1954 season, but when the Browns stumbled through training camp and the 1955 exhibition season, head coach Paul Brown convinced Graham to come back for one more season. Graham did, and the Browns made it 10 for 10 in 1955.

Coming into training camp, the big story, of course, was whether the Browns could make their way to the NFL title game without Otto Graham.

After losing three straight NFL championship games in 1951, 1952, and 1953, Graham and the Browns had won the NFL title in 1954 by revenging two title game losses to the Lions with a 56–10 rout of Detroit. That seemed like the perfect time for Graham to retire.

Reading this far, you already know that head coach Paul Brown talked Graham into returning for one more season. What you probably don't know is that Cleveland's 1955 1–5 exhibition record and opening-day loss to the Washington Redskins (who were 3–9 in 1954) left everyone still wondering if the Browns could make it 10 for 10, even with Graham. In the end, they did.

Team in a Box

Record: 9–2–1

The Browns lost their season opener to the surprising Washington Redskins, who would finish second in the Eastern Conference in 1955. After winning their first two games, the Redskins lost three of four games, including the rematch with the Browns, and never caught up.

Against Teams Over .500: 2–1–1, 100 points scored, 90 points allowed

This is probably the least impressive part of the 1955 Browns' résumé. Of the 12 teams in the book, only the 1999 Rams did less against teams with winning records. In the regular season, the Browns did not play either of the Western Conference teams with winning records (the Rams and the Bears).

Points Scored/Allowed: 349/218 (1955 NFL average: 250)

The Browns' point differential doesn't look impressive, but they were the only NFL team to score more than 300 points in 1955, and they also allowed the fewest points in the league. NFL team statistics were really "bunched up" in 1955, as no NFL team allowed more than 298 points. The standard deviation of points allowed was just 26.2, so the Browns were actually more than one standard deviation better than the league average.

Yards Gained/Allowed: 3,970/2,841 (1955 NFL average: 3,682)

Cleveland was the only team in the league to allow fewer than 3,000 total yards. The Browns had also yielded fewer than 3,000 yards in 1954.

Opponents' Record: 60–67–5, .473

(Not counting games against the Browns; ties counted as a half-win and a half-loss.)

Adjusted Power Index:

Offense: +3.30
Defense: +3.10
TOTAL: +6.41

The total is not a typo, as all statistics weren't rounded until the last calculation. Obviously, the 1955 Browns were a very balanced team. By this measure (the difference between Offense and Defense Power Index), the 1955 Browns, the 1972 Dolphins, and the 1996 Packers were the most balanced of the 12 teams in this book. The Browns are one of only six teams since 1950 with both an Offense and Defense Power Index of +3.00 or higher; the other five include the aforementioned Dolphins and Packers teams, as well as the 1973 Rams, the 1978 Cowboys, and the 1995 49ers.

Innovations/What You Should Know:

As outlined both in the introduction and in "The Coach: Paul Brown," the Browns of this era were responsible for numerous innovations, many of which are still used today. Brown was the first coach to make coaching a year-round job, to make use of position coaches, to require players to keep and produce a playbook, and the first to regularly quiz his players on formations, plays, and tendencies.

Cleveland's passing offense, the first to really use timing routes and sideline passes, was ahead of its time. It was, in reality, the foundation for today's West Coast Offense. Paul Brown has been credited with developing the draw play, in order to slow down the defensive pass rush, and the modern idea of the pass pocket, where Brown coached his offensive linemen to shield defenders out of the way instead of trying to move them. By 1955, the Browns' tenth season, none of these innovations were still new, but they were copied extensively and changed the way that pro football was played.

After 10 straight trips to their league's championship game, how much did Browns' tickets cost in 1956? The most expensive seat was . . . $4. Actually, after adjusting for inflation, that would be $26 in 2001. That's still pretty cheap for the most expensive seat.

Homegrown First-Round Picks:

For teams prior to the adoption of the common NFL/AFL draft in 1967, this category is not quite as meaningful. Nevertheless, here is the list:

DB Kenny Konz, 1951

Having just one homegrown first-round pick is unusual for a successful team, even for the 1950s. However, the college draft was much less a factor in building a team in that era than it would become later in pro football. (See "Pro Bowl Players.") The other 11 teams in this book had a total of 65 homegrown first-round picks on their rosters—about six per team.

The Browns, however, made two noteworthy first-round picks in the early 1950s. In 1953, they selected Doug Atkins in the first round. Atkins went on to a Hall-of-Fame career, primarily with the Chicago Bears, who acquired him in a trade with Cleveland after the 1954 season.

Cleveland selected Harry Agganis in the first round in 1952 as a future pick. Future picks allowed teams to draft a player who was four years out of high school even if he hadn't used up his college eligibility as in the case of a redshirt or a transfer. The player could be drafted as a future and signed a year later when he used up his college eligibility. Unfortunately for Agganis, his future was short. Agganis chose to play baseball instead of football and signed with the Boston Red Sox. In 1955, he developed pneumonia and seemed to be recovering when he died suddenly on July 27 of a pulmonary embolism, a blood clot in the lungs.

Pro Bowl Players:

OE Pete Brewster, DT Don Colo, C Frank Gatski, G Abe Gibron, OT/PK Lou Groza, DB Kenny Konz, DE Carlton Massey, LB Walt Michaels, RB Fred "Curly" Morrison.

In addition to the Browns' nine Pro Bowl players, OT Mike McCormack, QB Otto Graham, and eventual Hall of Fame DE Len Ford were named to many All-Pro teams such as the ones chosen by United Press and *The Sporting News.*

Of the 12 Cleveland players who received Pro Bowl and/or All-Pro recognition in 1955, only Konz, Massey (8th round, 1953), and Michaels (7th round, 1951) were drafted by the Browns in the NFL. Gatski, Graham, and Groza were AAFC veterans, as was Ford, although Ford had played for the Los Angeles Dons and not the Browns.

Colo and McCormack were acquired with three other players from the Colts on March 26, 1953, in what is still the largest trade in NFL history that didn't involve draft choices. Baltimore received 10 players, including Don Shula, in exchange for the five they sent to Cleveland. Brewster (Chicago Cardinals) and Morrison (Bears) were also obtained in trades. Gibron was selected in the draft of AAFC players whose teams were not included in the merger with the NFL; he had played for Buffalo.

Game-by-Game:

Sep. 25th WASHINGTON 27, BROWNS 17 AT CLEVELAND

After returning to the Browns only just before their last exhibition game, Otto Graham had a less than stellar day in the Redskins' upset of the defending NFL champions. Playing just the first half before being replaced by George Ratterman, Graham completed only 3 of 9 passes for 30 yards and threw 2 interceptions. If that game is removed from Graham's 1955 record, his passing rating is 101.3; his actual passing rating was 94.0.

Head coach Paul Brown thought the team was still adjusting to the return of Graham. Brown said after the game, "There is no doubt that Graham's late arrival made it difficult to get a good organization out there."

One bright spot for the Browns was Fred Morrison. He was a star at Ohio State who the Browns acquired before the 1954 season after four lackluster seasons with the Bears. He gained 117 yards on 15 carries; in his five previous seasons, including one with Cleveland, Morrison had averaged only 251 yards rushing per season.

Oct. 2nd BROWNS 38, SAN FRANCISCO 3 AT SAN FRANCISCO

Cleveland held the 49ers to just 139 yards of offense and 8 first downs and didn't look anything like the team that had lost its season opener. Graham had an efficient day, completing 7 of 11 passes for 140 yards with no interceptions. His passing complemented the Browns' effective running game, which gained 210 yards. Graham's counterpart, Y. A. Tittle, completed 7 of 15 passes for just 57 yards for San Francisco.

Oct. 9th BROWNS 21, PHILADELPHIA 17 AT CLEVELAND

Trailing 17–14 with just over three minutes left and the ball on their own 13-yard line, Otto Graham led the Browns to a game-winning touchdown. He rushed for 60 of the 87 yards on the last drive and two of his runs were key plays that set up the game winning TD pass to Dante Lavelli. On third-and-3 from his own 20, Graham faked a pass and ran 18 yards for a first down. After converting a fourth-and-6 from his own 42 on a 14-yard pass to Lavelli, Graham ran 36 yards to the Eagles' 8-yard line on a run/pass option to the right. For the day, he completed 16 of 21 passes for 223 yards with two touchdowns and no interceptions.

Lavelli got anxious waiting for the game-winning pass, "I thought the ball would never come down. It sort of hung in mid-air. My arms were quivering waiting for it." I don't think any NFL player today would use the word "quivering."

Oct. 16th BROWNS 24, WASHINGTON 14 AT WASHINGTON

In the rematch of the season opener, the Browns won a hard-fought defense-dominated game by forcing 5 turnovers and limiting Washington to 51 net yards passing. The two teams combined for only 392 yards gained.

Paul Brown thought his team was a little flat, "We didn't have much of a head of steam up [*sic*]. Maybe it was a natural letdown after being fired up for the last two games."

Oct. 23rd BROWNS 41, GREEN BAY 10 AT CLEVELAND

Cleveland demolished the Packers, particularly in the second half, outgaining them 454–161. This was the fourth straight game in which the Browns held an opponent to fewer than 200 yards of offense. Green Bay's only touchdown came on an Al Carmichael 100-yard kickoff return in the second quarter, which actually gave the Packers a brief 10–7 lead.

Curly Morrison led the Browns with 87 yards rushing on 17 carries, while Graham completed 7 of 12 passes for 187 yards. In the four games since his poor performance in the season opener, Graham completed 39 of 60 passes for 688 yards with 3 touchdowns and only 1 interception. Even for 1955, it was hard to lose when your quarterback averaged over 11 yards per pass attempt.

Oct. 30th BROWNS 26, CHICAGO CARDINALS 20 AT CHICAGO

(See "Elsewhere Around The NFL.")

On a rainy, dismal day in Chicago the Browns' running game enabled them to hold off the Cardinals. Ed Modzelewski ran for 116 yards on 27 attempts and Fred Morrison added 70 yards on 15 carries. The Browns had a 21–6 halftime lead that almost got away, perhaps in part due to their conservative offense in the second half (Graham attempted just 1 pass after halftime).

Late in the game several fights broke out, leading to the ejection of three players. I really enjoyed the way *Cleveland Plain Dealer* reporter Chuck Heaton described one of the fights: "Herschel Forester got the heave-ho after exchanging punches with Ollie Matson who also left by official request." The speedy Matson had gained 66 yards rushing on 9 carries before being tossed. Bob Gain was the third player ejected.

Nov. 6th BROWNS 24, NEW YORK 14 AT CLEVELAND

In what was really two games, George Ratterman rallied the Browns to victory after replacing an injured Otto Graham. Cleveland trailed 14–3 at halftime having been outgained 217 yards to 90. Graham suffered a concussion in the second quarter, but Ratterman had a great day, completing 10 of 15 passes for 163 yards and 2 touchdowns.

He also scored the Browns' last touchdown on a play that was suggested by Cleveland fullback Ed Modzelewski. On fourth-and-goal at the Giants' 4-yard line, Ratterman made a great fake to Modzelewski and then rolled to his right and scored the touchdown untouched. As Ratterman explained after the game, "Mo [Modzelewski] called that play. We had run three into the line without advancing much so he came up with the idea of faking a handoff and bootlegging it. We were the only ones who knew about it. Even our own players were surprised."

In the second half, Cleveland outgained New York 227 yards to five.

Nov. 13th PHILADELPHIA 33, CLEVELAND 17 AT PHILADELPHIA

Seven Browns' turnovers led to coughing up an early 17–0 lead. The defeat ended their winning streak at six games. The Eagles put the game away with a 17-point fourth quarter.

An injury to Browns' safety John Petitbon hurt Cleveland's offense and defense late in the game. How? Running back/wide receiver Ray Renfro was Petitbon's replacement and having to play both ways took him out of the passing game. In 1955, some players still had to play offense and defense because of the small roster size, just 33 players.

Nov. 20th BROWNS 41, PITTSBURGH 14 AT CLEVELAND

Fully recovered from a pulled leg muscle that had limited his production for three weeks, Fred Morrison ran for 140 yards on 17 carries as Cleveland cruised past Pittsburgh. The game was notable in that it marked the first time that the Modzelewski brothers had ever played against each other. After serving in the military for two years, the Browns' Ed (Big Mo) was traded by the Steelers to Cleveland before the 1955 season. Dick (Little Mo) was a defensive tackle for Pittsburgh. The two brothers had played together in high school near Pittsburgh, in college at the University of Maryland, and were almost teammates with the Steelers.

Nov. 27th BROWNS 35, NEW YORK 35 AT NEW YORK

The Giants' Ray Krouse blocked his second field goal of the day, a Lou Groza 21-yard attempt in the final seconds, to preserve the tie. Despite Otto Graham's highest yardage total in two years (319 yards passing, completing 17 of 31 attempts), two early Browns mistakes helped keep the Giants in the game. New York blocked a Horace Gillom punt after a bad snap, which led to the Giants' first touchdown. Graham then threw an interception deep in Giants' territory to end a long Cleveland drive without any points.

Ray Renfro and Darrell "Pete" Brewster each had over 100 yards receiving, combining for 10 catches, 237 yards, and 3 touchdowns.

Dec. 4th BROWNS 30, PITTSBURGH 7 AT PITTSBURGH

The Browns held the Steelers to just 123 yards of offense while running for 273 themselves (104 of those by Fred Morrison). Cleveland's easy win, combined with Washington's loss at home against the Giants, clinched the Eastern Conference title for the Browns and a tenth consecutive trip to their league's championship game.

Paul Brown admitted he had a few doubts about the team at the beginning of the season: "I can frankly say that we came farther than I thought we would at one stage of this thing . . . we had to make some changes in our system this season. We had a flanker out there just about all of the time and Curly Morrison gave us the big running threat at halfback." Brown also singled out Bob Gain and Chuck Noll (yes, *that* Chuck Noll) as players who had done well adapting to new roles.

Dec. 11th BROWNS 35, CHICAGO CARDINALS 24 AT CLEVELAND

Despite "nothing" to play for, Cleveland scored 21 points in the fourth quarter to come back from a 24–14 deficit and win the game. Otto Graham's 41-yard touchdown pass to Ray Renfro gave the Browns the lead for good midway through the fourth quarter.

NFL Championship:

Dec. 26th BROWNS 38, LOS ANGELES 14 AT LOS ANGELES

(See "Retirement Encore.")

Elsewhere Around the NFL:

Sep. 6th Among those released by the Pittsburgh Steelers this day is a hometown kid they had selected in the ninth round of the 1955 NFL draft. You may have heard of him: Johnny Unitas. Unitas was born and raised in Pittsburgh before attending the University of Louisville.

Unitas was cut without ever playing in a preseason game. Supposedly, Art Rooney's sons begged his father to make head coach Walt Kiesling keep Unitas. Kiesling's rationale for cutting Johnny U. was that he wasn't versatile. Unitas wasn't going to beat out Jim Finks, the team's incumbent, or 1953 first-round pick Ted Marchibroda. Unitas's competition was rookie Vic Eaton, who could punt, return punts, and play defensive back. Kiesling also didn't think Unitas was smart enough to play quarterback in the NFL.

In the NFL, everyone's path seems to cross at some point. Ted Marchibroda eventually ended up as the head coach of the Baltimore Colts in the post-Unitas era and was the first head coach of the Baltimore Ravens.

Nov. 27th After three losses to start what was supposed to be George Halas's last season as head coach ("Papa Bear" later returned as head coach in 1958), the Bears came into their game with the crosstown "rival" Cardinals on a six-game winning streak and in contention for the Western Conference title. The Cardinals were having another one of their usual seasons (3–5–1) for that period in their history. (Come to think of it, for most of their history.) On any given Sunday . . . the Cardinals trounced the Bears 53–14. The Cards didn't win either of their last two games and finished 4–7–1. The Bears finished 8–4, just a half game behind the Rams for the Western Conference title. The Bears beat Los Angeles in both meetings that year, but lost four games to teams that finished .500 or worse. Actually, while the Cardinals weren't very good during the 1950s, (33–84–3), and had just one winning season, they beat the Bears in six of their nine meetings between 1950 and 1955.

What Happened the Next Season:

Otto Graham finally made his retirement stick and the Browns learned how the other half lives in 1956, falling to a 5–7 record. The big decline came offensively; the Browns' Offense Power Index fell from +3.30 in 1955 to −2.42 in 1956. Not only is that one of the 10 worst year-to-year declines in Offense Power Index since 1950, it is *the* worst.

People have written about how the down year in 1956 was a cloud with a silver lining since the Browns were then in a position to draft Jim Brown in 1957. They did draft Brown, of course, but only after Pittsburgh head coach Walt Kiesling passed on Brown to take Len Dawson. Remember, Kiesling was the same guy who cut Johnny Unitas without ever letting him get into a preseason game. Not that Len Dawson was a bad player, but he didn't show his Hall-of-Fame talents until he hooked up with his college coach,

Hank Stram, in the AFL. (Dawson led Stram's Dallas Texans to the 1962 AFL championship, plus two more league titles—and two Super Bowl appearances—after the franchise became the Kansas City Chiefs in 1963.) What was Dawson's last NFL team before he joined the AFL? The Browns, of course. Paul Brown thought highly of the Ohio native and might have drafted Dawson out of Purdue in 1957 if he had still been on the board. It's really no surprise, then, that Dawson played for the Browns while Paul Brown was still head coach.

Retirement Encore

Michael Jordan didn't invent un-retiring. (Is that a word?) Otto Graham had retired after leading the Browns to the 1954 NFL title and to their ninth league championship game in nine seasons. No doubt, it seemed like the right time to leave for Graham.

What brought him back? The short answer is that Cleveland head coach Paul Brown asked Graham to return. As we've seen in today's NFL with Barry Sanders and Robert Smith, however, just being asked back is not always enough.

Although Paul Brown's image is that of a stoic tactician, the truth is that Brown did care about his players and they knew it. (See "The Coach: Paul Brown.") He had a warm spot for Graham and although there were times he didn't think so, Graham had a warm spot for Brown as well.

Graham's second and final farewell call was the 1955 NFL title game against the Los Angeles Rams. The Browns and Rams had played in the NFL Championship Game in both 1950 and 1951. The Browns won 30–28 in 1950 in an incredible game that has never gotten its due as one of the best ever. The Rams came back to win 24–17 in 1951 when Rams' head coach Joe Stydahar let quarterback Norm Van Brocklin out of his doghouse just in time for the QB to lead the Rams to the win; the deciding score was a 73-yard TD pass from Van Brocklin to Tom Fears less than a minute after the Browns had tied the score at 17 in the fourth quarter.

The 1955 Rams were led by coaching legend Sid Gillman, at the time a first-year head coach hired from the University of Cincinnati. Van Brocklin actually had an off year in 1955, but the Rams had a good running game led by Tank Younger and rookie Ron Waller. Younger, however, missed the title game with a hairline fracture of a neck vertebra.

In the first quarter, the teams swapped interceptions with Cleveland getting the only score on a Lou Groza field goal. About four minutes into the second quarter, Cleveland's Don Paul intercepted a Van Brocklin pass—one of seven interceptions the Browns would get—and ran it back 65 yards for a touchdown. The Rams answered with a 67-yard TD bomb from Van Brocklin to Skeets Quinlan, but the rest of the game, especially the second half, belonged to the Browns. Graham threw a 50-yard TD pass to Dante Lavelli right before halftime. Whether or not that took the air out of the Rams is hard to say, but they were not in the game in the second half.

Graham ran for two touchdowns in the third quarter and passed for another at the beginning of the fourth to put the game away at 38–7. The Rams scored a meaningless touchdown with a little over two minutes left to make the final score 38–14.

Graham completed 14 of 25 passes for 209 yards. Ed Modzelewski led the Browns with 61 yards rushing on 13 carries. Except for the bomb to Quinlan, Van Brocklin threw for just 99 yards on 10-of-24 passing.

Paul Brown attributed the 7 interceptions to the Browns' constant pressure on Van Brocklin (and backup Billy Wade, who tossed an INT into the total). As for Graham, Brown called him the "greatest" quarterback and conceded that he would be sadly missed in 1956. After the game Graham said, "Nothing would induce me to come back again." He did not un-retire this time.

We're Supposed to Go That Way

Although Otto Graham's retirement was a large factor, it couldn't have been the only reason for the historic decline in the offensive productivity of the Browns from 1955 to 1956. Graham's successor, George Ratterman, suffered a season-ending knee injury in the fourth game of the 1956 season. Ratterman's replacement, Babe Parilli, played three games until he suffered a shoulder injury. Desperate for a quarterback, the Browns signed Tom O'Connell who made it through the season. The next year, he set the NFL record for the highest average gain per pass attempt, 11.17 (1,229 yards on 110 attempts). The record is dubious because it only took 100 pass attempts to qualify for the passing title in those days. Cleveland was so impressed it got rid of O'Connell, who resurfaced in 1960 with the AFL Buffalo Bills.

As measured by Offense Power Index (OPI) the 1955–56 Browns suffered the largest one-season decline in offensive performance of any team since 1950. Cleveland's OPI dropped from +3.30 in 1955 to −2.42 in 1956, a decrease of 5.72. Here are the top five year-to-year declines in OPI since 1950:

	Team, Seasons	Year 1 W-L/OPI	Year 2 W-L/OPI	Decline
1.	Cleveland Browns, 1963–64	9–2–1/+3.30	5–7/−2.42	5.72
2.	Atlanta Falcons, 1973–74	9–5/+0.79	3–11/−4.86	5.65

Behind a good running attack and a decent season by quarterback Bob Lee, the Falcons were in the running for the playoffs in 1973 until late-season losses to Buffalo, which had a good team, and to St. Louis, which did not. The Falcons opened their season by scoring 62 points against the Saints and scoring 40 or more in three other games. They were also held to fewer than 10 points in four games.

The next year, with most of the same players, the offense was pitiful. Their −4.86 OPI is the third worst of any team since 1950. Atlanta quarterbacks threw just 4 touchdown passes the entire season and threw 31 interceptions. Since 1950, only the 1977 Buccaneers had a worse TD/INT ratio. Head coach Norm Van Brocklin was fired after eight games.

3.	New York Giants, 1963–64	11–3/+3.38	2–10–2/−2.07	5.45

This is simply a classic case of old age ruining a team. In particular, three key players—quarterback Y. A. Tittle, offensive tackle Jack Stroud, and wide receiver Frank Gifford—seemingly aged a decade in the course of one offseason. The injury to wide receiver Del Shofner, which effectively ended the productive part of his career, didn't help either.

Tittle's passing rating suffered an incredible decline. He had a tremendous 1963 season, setting an NFL record with 36 touchdown passes en route to a 104.8 rating. In 1964, his rating plummeted to 51.6. Take a look:

	Att	Comp	Yds	YPA	TD	Int
1963	367	221	3,145	8.57	36	14
1964	281	147	1,798	6.40	10	22

	Team, Seasons	Year 1 W-L/OPI	Year 2 W-L/OPI	Decline
4.	Houston Oilers, 1993–94	12–4/+2.35	2–14/−2.96	5.3

This was probably the first team to suffer from salary cap meltdown, although the "only" offensive player to be a cap casualty was quarterback Warren Moon. He refused to take a pay cut and instead of just releasing him and getting nothing, Houston traded Moon to Minnesota. Houston, in turn, did nothing on the field. Quarterbacks Cody Carlson, Billy Joe Tolliver, and Bucky Richardson simply couldn't move the team. The Oilers scored 142 fewer points in 1994 than in 1993 and gained 1,177 fewer yards.

Head coach Jack Pardee was fired after ten games with the team 1–9. Who succeeded him? He's still there . . . Jeff Fisher.

	Team, Seasons	Year 1 W-L/OPI	Year 2 W-L/OPI	Decline
5.	San Francisco 49ers, 1998–99	12–4/+4.62	4–12/−0.13	4.76

This is the most dramatic of the offensive meltdowns. The 49ers had set the standard for offensive excellence in the NFL for many years. From 1984–98, their average OPI was an incredible +3.29. Only about 4 percent of all teams since 1950 have had an OPI of +3.29 or better for *one season.*

Obviously, the big blow for San Francisco in 1999 was the loss of quarterback Steve Young. In the third game of the year (against Arizona), he suffered a concussion that ended his season and his career. Another important loss was Garrison Hearst, who was sidelined by a broken ankle and bone disease. Hearst had rushed for 1,570 yards and a 5.1 average per carry in 1998. He missed two entire seasons, but made a miraculous recovery and returned to the 49ers in 2001.

Bob Gain

Art Donovan was the first Baltimore Colt elected to the Hall of Fame. He was a defensive tackle on a successful team in the 1950s who played in five Pro Bowls. His on-field accomplishments are very similar to those of Bob Gain (for example, he also played in five Pro Bowls), who played on the defensive line for Cleveland from 1952 to 1964 (excluding his 1953 military assignment). The major difference is that Gain is not enshrined in Canton.

Before entering pro football, Gain was one of the best college players in history. While playing for Bear Bryant at the University of Kentucky (Bryant coached there from 1946 to 1953 before moving on to Texas A&M and then Alabama), Gain was a two-time All-American and won the Outland Trophy as the nation's best lineman in 1950. He was inducted into the College Football Hall of Fame in 1980.

He was Green Bay's first-round pick in 1951 (fourth overall, fifth if you count the bonus choice), but never played for the Packers. I had the privilege of speaking with Bob Gain about the 1955 Browns and his career. I asked him what happened with the Packers and he replied, "They asked me what would make me happy [on a contract]? I said $8,000 would do it; they offered me $7,000. Why did they ask me what would make me happy? I decided I wasn't going to play for Green Bay so I went to Canada."

The Canadian Football League (CFL) was also enjoying the fruits of the postwar economic recovery and signed some notable NFL draftees and veterans in the early and mid-1950s. For example, 1952 Heisman Trophy winner Billy Vessels—the Baltimore Colts' 1953 first-round pick—signed with Edmonton of the CFL and was named CFL Most Outstanding Player in 1953. Warren Moon and Doug Flutie were two later recipients of that award.

Gain played for Ottawa in 1951 and the Rough Riders (as opposed to the Saskatchewan Roughriders, that wasn't too confusing, eh?) won the Grey Cup. Green Bay then traded Gain and Walt Michaels to Cleveland in 1952. Michaels also played in five Pro Bowls after joining the Browns. It's no wonder the Packers were so bad for most of the 1950s.

"It was very good to join a successful team," Gain told me. "When you're winning, people put up with a lot more. To be on a losing team is pathetic. It's discouraging, it usually breeds contempt as people are pointing fingers." Actually, the Browns only had one losing season during Gain's career.

Although Gain hadn't played with the Browns in the AAFC, he was aware of the reputation that they carried over from that league that they were "soft," that they were playing "basketball with cleats." He said, "Everyone respected us and we were not all finesse; you couldn't win with just finesse. We had our share of headhunters."

Gain played for legendary coaches Paul Brown and Bear Bryant, but they were two different people in two very different situations. Other than results, the two men could not be compared, he said. About Brown, Gain added, "Paul never forgot his friends and I was friends with him until he died. He really did care about his players. He wasn't a drum beater and he didn't go crazy during the game. He motivated his players by needling them; he was a good needler."

Gain called 1955 a great season, most notable because it was Otto Graham's last season. Gain also singled out Frank Gatski and Abe Gibron as two players who had outstanding seasons; Gatski and Gibron were both Pro Bowl selections. Gain also said that 1955 was the year the Browns switched to the 4–3 as their base defense instead of the 5–2, which meant that Gain would have actually played some downs at what we would call today the middle linebacker position, in addition to playing on the line as a middle guard in a 5–2 and as a defensive tackle in a 4–3. Later in his career, Gain also played defensive end.

Bob Gain is an example of why I am not very interested in which players are in or out of the Hall of Fame in any sport. I don't know if Gain should be in or not, but I know that his credentials are equal to those of a fair number of enshrinees. I do know that the specific identities of the people on the selecting bodies has had way too much to do with which players get in and which don't. I can't imagine that the Hall of Fame selection process, which is done in person, is much different from the Veterans Committee of the Baseball Hall of Fame, which for many years was also done face-to-face. The Baseball Hall of Fame is filled with people elected by the Veterans Committee who were only enshrined in Cooperstown because their cronies were on the committee and they "persuaded" the other members to vote them in. Canton's record isn't much better.

That Championship Decade: 1946–1955

I just wanted to show the Browns' record and Power Indexes for each of their first 10 years, which include the AAFC. I did not adjust the AAFC Power Indexes for strength of schedule. That league had a balanced schedule where every team played two games against every other team in the league. I suppose I could have adjusted the Power Indexes for the fact that Cleveland didn't play itself, but that seemed silly. The adjustments wouldn't change the impressive magnitude of the Browns' Power Indexes.

AAFC

Year	Record	PF	PA	OPI	DPI	PI	Notes
1946	12–2	423	137	+3.50	+2.55	+6.05	Next best power index was +2.90.
1947	12–1–1	410	185	+3.21	+2.09	+5.29	
1948	14–0	389	190	+1.69	+3.89	+5.58	The 12–2 49ers had a +4.83 Power Index; only one other team was positive and their PI was +0.74.
1949	9–1–2	339	171	+2.27	+2.06	+4.33	

PF = Points Scored (For)
PA = Points Allowed
OPI = Offense Power Index
DPI = Defense Power Index
PI = Power Index
API = Adjusted Power Index

The Browns' four-year PI was +21.25, obviously the best in the AAFC. Their arch-rivals, the 49ers, had a four-year PI of +14.57.

NFL

Year	Record	PF	PA	OPI	DPI	API
1950	10–2	310	144	+0.28	+2.51	+2.78
1951	11–1	331	152	+0.90	+3.05	+3.95
1952	8–4	310	213	+2.54	+1.96	+4.51
1953	11–1	348	162	+2.08	+1.91	+3.98
1954	9–3	336	162	+1.49	+3.33	+4.82
1955	9–2–1	349	218	+3.30	+3.10	+6.41

For 1950–55, Cleveland's API was +26.45, again by far the best in the league. The Rams' 1950–55 API was +18.68.

The Coach: Paul Brown

Coaching Record (with Browns Only)

AAFC

	W	L	T	Pct	
1946	12	2	0	.857	AAFC Western Division title; AAFC champs
1947	12	1	1	.893	AAFC Western Division title; AAFC champs
1948	14	0	0	1.000	AAFC Western Division title; AAFC champs
1949	9	1	2	.833	AAFC champs
AAFC Total	**47**	**4**	**3**	**.898**	

NFL

	W	L	T	Pct	
1950	10	2	0	.833	NFL American Conference title; NFL champs
1951	11	1	0	.917	NFL American Conference title
1952	8	4	0	.667	NFL American Conference title
1953	11	1	0	.917	NFL Eastern Conference title

(continued next page)

NFL *(continued)*

	W	L	T	Pct	
1954	9	3	0	.750	NFL Eastern Conference title; NFL champs
1955	9	2	1	.792	NFL Eastern Conference title; NFL champs
1956	5	7	0	.417	
1957	9	2	1	.792	NFL Eastern Conference title
1958	9	3	0	.750	
1959	7	5	0	.583	
1960	8	3	1	.708	
1961	8	5	1	.607	
1962	7	6	1	.536	
NFL Total	**111**	**44**	**5**	**.709**	
CLE Total	**158**	**48**	**8**	**.757**	

I know I showed Cleveland's AAFC record elsewhere in the book; I just like looking at 47–4–3. For illustrative purposes, here are composite standings for the AAFC and for the NFL from 1950 through 1962:

AAFC: 1946–49

	W	L	T	Pct
CLE	47	4	3	.898
SF	38	14	2	.722
NYY	35	17	2	.667
LA	25	27	2	.481
BUF	23	26	5	.472
MIA/BAL	13	40	1	.250
CHI	11	40	3	.231
BKN ('46–'48)	8	32	2	.214

NFL: 1950–62

	W	L	T	PCT
CLE	111	44	5	.709
NYG	104	50	6	.669
DET	94	61	5	.603
CHB	92	65	3	.584
SF	83	73	4	.531
BAL ('53–'62)	62	61	1	.504
LA	77	78	5	.497
PHI	74	80	6	.481
PIT	74	82	4	.475
GB	71	87	2	.450
WAS	54	98	8	.363
CHC/STL	50	105	5	.328

Doing the profile for the head coaches in the book is the part I dreaded the most. Many of these men are legends about whom much has already been written. What can I write about Paul Brown (or Vince Lombardi or Tom Landry) that will add to the body of knowledge about him? So I tried to find what others had to say.

Otto Graham once stated, "Paul Brown ran the game from the sideline like a computer." Yet, Graham also recalled how Brown consoled him after he fumbled late in the 1950 NFL Championship Game, apparently ending Cleveland's chances. Brown put his arm around Graham's shoulder and said, "Don't worry, Ots. We're going to beat them anyway." Cleveland came back to win the game 30–28.

Cleveland's star defensive tackle Bob Gain's statement about Brown's loyalty runs contrary to his reputation as being cold. On the other hand, Cleveland quarterback Frank Ryan told a story about Brown grabbing him as he came off the field after throwing an interception. Brown kept asking Ryan, "Why, why, why?" When Ryan asked, "Why what?" Brown replied, "Why did you throw that interception at a time like this?"

While Brown's demeanor has faded from many people's memories, his innovations are still very much in use today. He hired the first full-time, year-round coaching staff, used films to grade players on every assignment in every game, developed playbooks and meticulous game plans based on scouting reports, and held intensive classroom sessions—including tests—for his team. Within a few years, all NFL teams were preparing the "Paul Brown" way.

Brown was fanatical about preparation, especially when compared to the pro standard that existed before his arrival. He once said, "I believe in being prepared. Football is war, you know. Wars are won by the army that's fit and ready. That's why I'm such a nut on the subject." Since I've never played pro football and never fought in a war, maybe I shouldn't say anything, but I don't see football as war; yet one can understand Brown's perspective as someone who lived through both world wars and coached football at the Great Lakes Naval Training Center during World War II.

As for the controversy surrounding Brown's dismissal... in the three years after Brown left, Cleveland compiled a 31–10–1 record, won two Eastern Conference titles, and the 1964 NFL championship. In Brown's last three years as head coach, Cleveland's record was 23–14–3 with no title game appearances. Looking at the move objectively, without considering the people involved and the current efforts to vilify Art Modell (who fired Brown) at every opportunity, it would be hard to say that the move didn't work. Even the greatest men can grow stale if left in the same situation for many years.

While I think Vince Lombardi was the greatest coach in pro football history, a very strong argument can be made that Paul Brown should hold that title. The success of his Cleveland teams is well documented here, but what some of you may not know is that he was an extremely successful high school coach in Ohio (supposedly his charges at Washington High in Massillon once went an entire season without punting) and Ohio State won the "national title" in 1942 with Brown as head coach. If one defines greatness as leaving an enduring mark on one's field, then Paul Brown was beyond great.

The Quarterback: Otto Graham

Year	Team	Att	Comp	Yds	TD	Int	YPA	Rating	Lg Avg	W	L	Pct
1950	CLE	253	137	1,943	14	20	7.68	64.7	52.9	10	2	.833
1951	CLE	265	147	2,205	17	16	8.32	79.2	55.6	11	1	.917
1952	CLE	364	181	2,816	20	24	7.74	66.6	55.7	8	4	.667
1953	CLE	258	167	2,722	11	9	10.55	99.7	53.6	11	1	.917
1954	CLE	240	142	2,092	11	17	8.72	73.5	61.7	9	3	.750
1955	CLE	185	98	1,721	15	8	9.30	94.0	57.1	9	2	.818
Total		**1,565**	**872**	**13,499**	**88**	**94**	**8.63**	**78.2**	**56.1**	**58**	**13**	**.817**

YPA = Yards Per Pass Attempt
Rating = Passer Rating
Lg Avg = League Passer Rating in that season
W, L, Pct = Team's Record in his starts

Do you want to see Graham's AAFC numbers? OK...

Year	Team	Att	Comp	Yds	TD	Int	YPA	Rating	Lg Avg	W	L	Pct
1946	CLE	174	95	1,834	17	5	10.54	112.1	55.4	12	2	.857
1947	CLE	269	163	2,753	25	11	10.23	109.2	64.5	12	1	.923
1948	CLE	333	173	2,713	25	15	8.15	85.6	64.2	14	0	1.000
1949	CLE	285	161	2,785	19	10	9.77	97.5	58.4	9	1	.900
Total		**1,061**	**592**	**10,085**	**86**	**41**	**9.51**	**99.1**	**60.9**	**47**	**4**	**.922**

No knock at Graham, but the comparison between his AAFC and NFL numbers are an indication of the relative strengths of the two leagues. Graham led the AAFC in passing rating in 1946, 1947, and 1949. He led the

Transcendental Graphics

Paul Brown, *right,* and Otto Graham

NFL in 1953 and 1955. I think it's impressive he led his league in both his first and last seasons. Few people today, however, know much about his background.

First, Otto Graham was a huge baby. No, he didn't cry or whine a lot; he weighed 14 pounds, 12 ounces at birth. The "average" baby weighs 7 pounds, 8 ounces at birth. Graham was born in Evanston, Illinois, home of Northwestern University. He attended NU where he played football, basketball, and baseball. Graham originally went to Northwestern on a basketball scholarship, but when head football coach Lynn "Pappy" Waldorf saw Graham rifling the ball in intramural football games, he "invited" Graham to play for him as well.

I think noting the multiple sports achievements is important because most people, when they think of Otto Graham at all, think of him as Paul Brown's robot quarterback. Yet he was a gifted athlete. According to one biography, Graham is the only college player to be named All-American in football and basketball in consecutive seasons. He was also a two-sport professional.

Graham played for the Rochester Royals in the National Basketball League (NBL) in the 1945–46 season; the Royals (now the Sacramento Kings by way of Cincinnati and Kansas City) won the league title that year. The NBL merged with the Basketball Association of America (BAA) in 1949 to form the NBA.

Cleveland head coach Paul Brown first noticed Graham in 1941. As Brown recalled later, "When I was coach at Ohio State, the only Big Ten game we lost was in 1941 to Northwestern, 14–7, and we lost it on a play where Graham ran left from the single wing, then threw back to his right to a man going away from him, right on target, for the winning touchdown. I asked myself, 'What kind of player is this?' He was the first man I picked for my Cleveland team."

After leaving Northwestern, Graham became a commissioned officer in the United States Navy Air Corps and served for two years. Paul Brown signed Graham to a personal services contract in 1945 while Otto was still an air cadet at Glenville Naval Base in Evanston. According to Graham, a big reason he signed was the contract called for him to be paid as long as the war lasted . . . $250 a month. Some of Graham's football salaries were: $7,500 in 1946, $12,000 in 1947, and $25,000 in his last year, 1955. The salary cap and its attendant manipulations make it difficult for a straight comparison of salaries, but using Brett Favre's 1999 base salary, without counting the pro-rated portion of his signing bonus that counted for cap purposes,

Favre made $268,750 per game. Even adjusting for inflation, that would be about $43,000 *per game* in 1955 dollars—almost twice as much as Graham made for the entire 1955 season.

Graham thought that two factors were paramount in the Browns' amazing success. The first was Paul Brown. The second was an esprit de corps (group spirit for those of you who don't know French) that Graham believed was rare even in his day. He said, "We didn't have petty jealousies. It didn't matter who got the credit, who made the headlines, or who scored. The important thing was, did you do a good job?"

After his retirement, Graham became athletic director and football coach at the United States Coast Guard Academy. For 10 seasons, he also coached the college All-Stars in their annual exhibition game against the defending NFL champions. He was head coach of the Washington Redskins for three years (1966–68). While Sonny Jurgenson enjoyed great success as his quarterback, the team had no winning seasons and was 17–22–3 in Graham's tenure. He was replaced in Washington by Vince Lombardi. Graham returned to the Coast Guard Academy, retiring in 1985.

I can't say that I'm an expert on Otto Graham and I don't want to turn this book into a steady stream of pandering, but it seems to me that Graham was one of the top five or six quarterbacks in NFL history. I guess that's not exactly going out on a limb since he was one of the four quarterbacks on the NFL's seventy-fifth anniversary team. That being the case, I doubt that many football fans today know much about him and there are certainly very few, if any, mentions of Graham by today's media. In his day, he probably wasn't given quite as much respect as he deserved because, unlike Graham, other quarterbacks called their own plays. Field generalship was an important part of the image of many of the successful quarterbacks of the 1950s like Bobby Layne and Johnny Unitas. Layne, and quarterbacks like Norm Van Brocklin, also had a clearly defined personality. In Layne's case, he had a joie de vivre—more French, this time meaning charisma—that Graham did not possess. Graham was, however, an outstanding passer, an excellent runner, and his team played in its league championship game *every year he was the quarterback.* Graham's football résumé is hard to match.

1955 Cleveland Browns Statistics

Passing

	Att	Comp	Comp Pct	Yds	Yds Per	TD	Int	Rating
Graham	185	98	53.0%	1,721	9.30	15	8	94.0
Ratterman	47	32	68.1%	504	10.72	6	3	116.5
Renfro	2	0	0.0%	0	0.00	0	0	39.6
Browns	**234**	**130**	**55.6%**	**2,225**	**9.51**	**21**	**11**	**98.3**
Opponents	323	126	39.0%	1,775	5.50	15	25	40.7
League Average			47.9%		6.62			57.1

Browns' passers were sacked 34 times for 275 yards in losses.
The Browns sacked their opponents 15 times for 123 yards in losses.

Two things jump out at me. One, the Browns' passing attack was so superior to their competition as to be almost unbelievable. Their passing rating was more than twice as good as their opposition and 72 percent better than the league average. Cleveland's average gain per pass attempt was 4 yards better than their opponents' and almost 3 yards better than the league average.

Two, the Browns didn't get after the passer. (Thanks to Pete Palmer for pre-1963 team sack totals.) It's hard to imagine that in today's NFL a team could average barely a sack a game and still have a great pass defense.

Rushing

	Att	Yds	Avg	Net Yards	TD
Morrison	156	824	5.28	+201	3
Modzelewski	185	619	3.35	−120	6
Bassett	38	174	4.58		3
Smith	37	142	3.84		1
Graham	68	121	1.78		6
Renfro	29	90	3.10		0
Jones	10	44	4.40		0
Petitbon	3	10	3.33		0
Ratterman	6	8	1.33		1
James	1	2	2.00		0
H. Ford	2	1	0.50		0
Gillom	1	−15	−15.00		0
Browns	**536**	**2,020**	**3.77**	**−120**	**20**
Opponents	351	1,189	3.39	−212	12
League Average			3.99		

As recounted in the game-by-game accounts in "Team in a Box," Fred "Curly" Morrison had not done much in his five prior seasons in the NFL. He didn't do much after this one, either; 1956 was his last season in the NFL. Yet Morrison did not disappear completely. As a CBS salesman in the early 1960s, he tried to put together a deal where CBS president William Paley would buy the Browns from Cleveland industrialist David Jones. That deal fell apart because Paley didn't want the appearance of impropriety as CBS and the NFL were about to strike a TV deal. Morrison then called a prominent TV agent in New York named Vincent Andrews about the sale. Andrews called a successful TV ad man to see if he would be interested. His name was Art Modell.

Receiving

	Rec	Yds	Avg	TD
Brewster	34	622	18.29	6
Lavelli	31	492	15.87	4
Renfro	29	603	20.79	8
Modzelewski	13	113	8.69	2
Morrison	9	185	20.56	0
Bassett	9	83	9.22	0
Jones	3	115	38.33	1
Smith	2	12	6.00	0
Browns	**130**	**2,225**	**17.12**	**21**
Opponents	126	1,775	14.09	15
League Average			13.82	

Ray Renfro led the league in average yards per catch and was tied for second in touchdown receptions. Compared to other years under Otto Graham the 1955 Browns didn't attempt as many passes, so, naturally, there weren't as many receptions to go around. Darrell Brewster finished just fourteenth in the league in catches.

Kickoff Returns

	Ret	YDS	Avg	TD
Smith	13	320	24.62	0
White	10	258	25.80	0
Bassett	7	151	21.57	0
Paul	5	109	21.80	0
Konz	3	66	22.00	0

(continued next page)

Kickoff Returns *(continued)*

	Ret	Yds	Avg	TD
Michaels	3	45	15.00	0
Browns	**41**	**949**	**23.15**	**0**
Opponents	50	1,220	24.40	1
League Average			23.07	

Punt Returns

	Ret	Yds	Avg	TD
Paul	19	148	7.79	1
Konz	17	138	8.12	0
H. Ford	4	15	3.75	0
White	2	28	14.00	0
Smith	1	5	5.00	0
Renfro	1	3	3.00	0
Browns	**44**	**337**	**7.66**	**1**
Opponents	37	186	5.03	1
League Average			5.63	

Only one NFL team (the Chicago Cardinals thanks to Ollie Matson) averaged over 10 yards per return, and five teams averaged less than 5 yards per return. Two teams, the Eagles and Steelers, had ridiculously low punt return averages: Philadelphia, 2.32; Pittsburgh, 1.91.

Interceptions

	Int	Yds	Avg	TD
Noll	5	74	14.80	1
Lahr	5	52	10.40	0
Konz	5	32	6.40	1
Paul	4	49	12.25	0
James	2	20	10.00	0
Petitbon	2	11	5.50	0
Michaels	1	25	25.00	1
Massey	1	24	24.00	0
Browns	**25**	**287**	**14.69**	**3**
Opponents	11	181	15.36	1

Only a warped mind like mine would find this noteworthy: this was the fifth consecutive season that Warren Lahr intercepted exactly 5 passes. He had a career total of 40.

As mentioned in the summary of the December 4 game against the Steelers that clinched the Eastern Conference title for the Browns, Chuck Noll was singled out by Paul Brown as a player who had done an excellent job adapting to a new role. Noll began his career with the Browns as a guard before switching to linebacker.

Turnovers

Turnovers Committed:	29
Turnovers Forced:	40
Turnover +/−:	+11

Cleveland's turnover margin was second best in the league behind Los Angeles. Of course, those were the two teams that played for the NFL championship in 1955.

Punting

	No	Avg
Gillom	58	41.2
Opponents	70	39.1
League Average		41.0

Horace Gillom was a terrific punter who led the NFL in punting average in 1951 and 1952. He spent his entire career with the Browns (1947–56).

Kicking

	XP	XPA	XP Pct	FG	FGA	FG Pct
Groza	44	45	97.8%	11	22	50.0%
Opponents	23	29	79.3%	7	15	46.7%
League Average			93.2%			46.0%

Leading Scorer:	Lou Groza, 77 Points
Leading Scorer, Non-Kicker:	Ed Modzelewski and Ray Renfro, 48 Points

1955 Cleveland Browns Roster

Head Coach	Paul Brown
QB	Otto Graham
QB	George Ratterman
RB/KR	Mo Bassett
RB	Henry Ford
RB/WR	Dub Jones
RB	Ed Modzelewski
RB	Fred "Curly" Morrison
RB/WR	Ray Renfro
RB/KR	Bob Smith
OE	Darrell Brewster
OE	Dante Lavelli
OE/DE/P	Horace Gillom
C	Frank Gatski
OG	Harold Bradley
OG	Herschel Forester
OG	Abe Gibron
OT/K	Lou Groza
OT	Mike McCormack
OT/DT	John Sandusky
DE	Len Ford
DE	Carlton Massey
DT	Don Colo
DT/MG/LB	Bob Gain
DT	John Kissell
DT/OT	Tom Jones
LB	Walt Michaels
LB	Chuck Noll
LB/C	Sam Palumbo
LB/RB	Pete Parini
LB/DE/OG	Chuck Weber
DB/RB	Tommy James
DB/PR	Kenny Konz
DB	Warren Lahr
DB/PR/KR	Don Paul
DB/RB	Johnny Petitbon
DB/KR	Bob White

Hall of Famers: Brown, Graham, Lavelli, Gatski, Groza, Ford, Noll (as a coach).

CHAPTER 2

1958 Baltimore Colts: The Game That Made the Game

Yeah, yeah, The Game. The Greatest Game Ever Played. The Game That Changed Pro Football. What you probably don't know is that many, if not most, of the players on the 1958 Baltimore Colts do *not* think that the 1958 NFL Championship Game was the greatest ever, or even the greatest they played *that year.*

STARTING LINEUP – 1958 COLTS

Offense		Defense	
LE (SE)	Raymond Berry	LE	Gino Marchetti
LT	Jim Parker	LT	Art Donovan
LG	Art Spinney	RT	Gene "Big Daddy" Lipscomb
C	Buzz Nutter	RE	Don Joyce
RG	Alex Sandusky	LLB	Bill Pellington
RT	George Preas	MLB	Don Shinnick
RE (TE)	Jim Mutscheller	RLB	Leo Sanford
FL/RB	Lenny Moore	LCB	Carl Taseff
QB	Johnny Unitas	RCB	Milt Davis
RB	L. G. Dupre	LS	Andy Nelson
RB	Alan Ameche	RS	Ray Brown

Colts Hall-of-Fame defensive end Gino Marchetti: "To me, the biggest game we played and the one I'll always remember most was not the '58 championship game, but the one on November 30 that year at Memorial Stadium when we clinched the western conference against the 49ers." The Colts rallied from a 20-point halftime deficit to win 35–27, clinching a spot in the NFL title game.

Johnny Unitas: "I've always felt that it [the championship game] wasn't a real good football game until the last two minutes, and then the overtime. . . . Just the fact that it was the first overtime in championship play and it happened in Madison Avenue's backyard, that was enough to make people feel they had seen something fantastic. They always forget that the month before, in the game we clinched the division and put us into the playoff, San Francisco has us down 27–7 at the half and we came back to beat 'em 35–27. That was a much better game."

Colts Hall-of-Fame back Lenny Moore: "I thought the best game we ever played as a team in my years with the Colts was the one when we were down 27–7 to the 49ers in '58 and came back to win."

Regardless of whether the championship game was the greatest game ever, it was certainly among the most important games in league history. Art Donovan thought so. "That's the game that put the league over the hump," Donovan said. "We were at the right place at the right time. Baseball was around, but people were tired of watching guys tightening their gloves and scratching their asses every time they swung. TV was ready for football." Don't hold back anything, Artie.

Giants Hall-of-Fame defensive end Andy Robustelli felt that the game, "really turned the country on to pro football. I don't think pro football was nearly as popular before that game as it was just after it."

Robustelli's comments notwithstanding, pro football was already popular before the 1958 title game. NFL attendance figures don't show any dramatic increase after 1958. NFL average attendance rose 4.6 percent from 1957 to 1958—from 42,169 to 44,109—and 4.5 percent from 1958 to 1959, to 46,091. Television ratings for NFL games actually declined in 1960 compared to 1959. Perception is often more important than reality, however, and the 1958 NFL Championship Game will always be perceived as the game that made pro football.

Entering the 1958 season, Colts' fans, coaches, and management were wondering if "this" would be the year. When he took over the team, head coach Weeb Ewbank had said it would take five years to build a winner, and even though he really just pulled the number out of the air, 1958 was his fifth season. Some, perhaps including Colts owner Carroll Rosenbloom, wanted to hold Ewbank to his "promise." The previous two seasons were considered disappointments to many: a 5–7 record in 1956 when a winning record was expected (after the Colts had finished 5–6–1 in 1955), and a 7–5 mark in 1957, including a blown 24-point lead in a 31–27 loss on October 30. That defeat cost the Colts a chance to at least tie for the Western Conference title.

The only real bump the Colts hit during the 1958 season (they got off to a 6–0 start) was an injury to Johnny Unitas that forced him to miss two games. Once he returned, Colts' fanatics realized that 1958 could be the year, and it was.

Team in a Box

Record: 9–3

The Colts started the year at 9–1. Their first loss of the year came on November 9 to the New York Giants (24–21) in a game Johnny Unitas watched from the bench due to an injury. They then lost the two games on their annual West Coast trip. All three defeats in 1958 were on the road.

Against Teams Over .500: 3–2, 151 Points Scored, 99 Points Allowed

Baltimore's record against .500 or better teams is nothing to be ashamed of, but it might be a little misleading given that the Colts lost to the Giants without Johnny Unitas and lost to the Rams after they had already clinched the conference title.

Points Scored/Allowed: 381/203 (1958 NFL Average: 271)

Only the 1950 and 1951 Rams scored more points in a season during the decade than the 1958 Colts. Of course, the Rams of that period were famous for their explosive offense and less-than-intimidating defense.

Baltimore's point differential, +178, was the third-best of the decade. The other four among the top five of the 1950s were four Browns' teams.

Yards Gained/Allowed: 4,539/3,284 (1958 NFL Average: 3,859)

The 1958 Colts averaged 378 yards of offense per game. Between 1959 and 1974, only one team averaged at least 375 yards gained per game—the 1965 49ers. The playing strategies, rules of the era, and the implementation of new defenses (see "Introduction") had a lot to do with the relative lack of offensive output in the 1960s and early 1970s. As teams moved back to running the football, it became more difficult to pile up high offensive yardage totals. Historically, teams average about 4 yards per rush and 7 yards per pass attempt. It doesn't take a math whiz to figure out what happens if you run more and pass less.

Since 1980, 38 teams have averaged at least 375 yards gained per game.

Opponents' Record: 64–63–5, .504

(Not counting games against the Colts; ties counted as a half-win and a half-loss.)

Adjusted Power Index:

Offense: +3.74
Defense: +2.28
TOTAL: +6.02

The popular image of the Colts as an explosive team that won primarily with its offense is consistent with the facts although the Colts' defense more than held its own. Baltimore's Power Index (OPI) ranks in the top 3 percent among all NFL teams since 1950, but their Defense Power Index (DPI) ranks in the top 10 percent, which is certainly a good performance.

The 1959 Colts' OPI was even better at +4.43, but their DPI was actually in the minus column: −0.30.

Innovations/What You Should Know:

In the NFL Films presentation of the 1958 NFL Championship Game, Raymond Berry said, "The best offense is one that is so balanced that the defense never knows if the next play is going to be a run or a pass." While the daring play-calling and ability of Johnny Unitas had much to do with the unpredictability and success of the Colts' offense, it's also true that the unique versatility of Lenny Moore had much to do with it as well. Moore was a potent weapon whether he was carrying the ball from scrimmage or catching the ball as a receiver. He was Marshall Faulk 40 years before Marshall Faulk.

A Gino Marchetti story by way of Weeb Ewbank, "We were having trouble once with a young player from Kent State. He was lining up against Gino in practice, and Gino was just going boom, boom–right by him. He told the kid, 'You're up too high. Get lower.' The guy got lower and Gino, with that powerful torso of his, gave him a fake and a shove and knocked the kid down and went by him. The coach told the kid to get even lower. This time Gino went straight at him, put his hands on the kid's shoulders and leap-frogged over him. The kid said, 'Now what do I do?' John Unitas was standing there watching. He said, 'You just applaud, that's all.'"

Homegrown First-Round Picks:

QB George Shaw (Bonus Choice), 1955; RB Alan Ameche, 1955; RB/WR Lenny Moore, 1956; OL Jim Parker, 1957; DB/KR Lenny Lyles, 1958.

The draft was much more of a hit-and-miss process in the 1950s than it is today, but the Colts certainly didn't waste their number one picks. Heisman Trophy winner Alan Ameche was a fine back whose career was short-circuited by an Achilles tendon injury in 1960, but can you imagine drafting players the caliber of Lenny Moore and Jim Parker in consecutive drafts? I'll write about Moore later; Parker was the first "pure" offensive lineman (a non-two-way player who played the O-line) elected to the Hall of Fame.

The bonus choice was a strange NFL practice that awarded the first pick in the draft by lottery, but each team could only get it once. For example, the Rams won the NFL title in 1951, but had the first selection in the draft in 1952 because they won the lottery for that year. Technically, the bonus pick was not considered the first pick for some reason, but when you picked first it was the first pick.

Pro Bowl Players:

RB Alan Ameche, WR Raymond Berry, DE Don Joyce, DT Gene "Big Daddy" Lipscomb, RB Lenny Moore, OT Jim Parker, QB Johnny Unitas.

The two defensive linemen on this team who went to the Hall of Fame, Art Donovan and Gino Marchetti, didn't play in the Pro Bowl in 1958, but the other two defensive linemen did. Donovan had been selected in each of the previous five seasons and this was the only Pro Bowl that Marchetti missed between 1955 and 1965; Marchetti broke his leg in the 1958 championship game. Marchetti and Unitas were each named to the Pro Bowl team 10 times during their respective careers.

Of the Pro Bowl players who were not first-round Colts picks, the Colts drafted Raymond Berry (twentieth round, 1954), acquired Big Daddy Lipscomb (Rams, 1955) and Don Joyce (Cardinals, 1954) on waivers and, of course, signed Johnny Unitas as a free agent in 1956 almost a year after he had been released by the Steelers.

Although he didn't play in the Pro Bowl, defensive back Andy Nelson received considerable All-Pro mention.

Game-by-Game:

Sep. 28th COLTS 28, DETROIT 15 AT BALTIMORE

The Colts scored 2 fourth-quarter touchdowns to win their opener and get a small measure of revenge against the defending NFL champion Lions. In their second meeting of 1957, the Colts opened up a 27–3 lead and led 27–17 with three minutes left. Detroit rallied to win 31–27 and Baltimore finished a game behind them (and San Francisco) in the NFL Western Conference. In this game, the Colts outgained the Lions 416 yards to 182 and had a 26–12 advantage in first downs.

Oct. 4th COLTS 51, CHICAGO BEARS 38 AT BALTIMORE

Lenny Moore scored 4 touchdowns in an incredible display of his talents as the Colts beat the Bears in a wild Saturday night game. Moore gained 71 yards rushing on 10 carries and caught 3 passes for 118 yards. (See "The Magnificent Mr. Moore.")

The Colts intercepted 5 passes, the first of five games this season in which they would get at least 4 interceptions. Intercepting passes was a key strength of the 1958–59 Colts. (See "Ballhawking Colts.")

Oct. 12th COLTS 24, GREEN BAY 17 AT GREEN BAY

Coming out a little flat after their big win against the Bears, the Colts trailed the Packers 17–0 six and a half minutes into the second quarter. A fluke interception—a low Bart Starr pass bounced off the foot of Packers end Billy Howton and into the hands of Colts safety Andy Nelson at the Green Bay 46—led to Baltimore's first touchdown. A "quick whistle" on a Johnny Unitas fumble in the fourth quarter helped Baltimore tie the game at 17. On the next series, Nelson intercepted a pass and ran 52 yards for the winning touchdown. Another interception, the second of the game by Colts linebacker Don Shinnick and the team's fourth of the day, secured the win.

Oct. 19th COLTS 40, DETROIT 14 AT DETROIT

In his game story, Cameron Snyder of *The Baltimore Sun* opined that it wasn't as easy a win as the score indicated. On the other hand, the Colts outgained the Lions 535 yards to 220. Baltimore scored 27 second-half points, 20 in the fourth quarter, to win going away after leading 13–7 at halftime. Johnny Unitas completed 11 of 17 passes for 221 yards and a touchdown; when a quarterback averages 13 yards per pass attempt, his team usually wins. Having Lenny Moore gain 136 yards rushing on 12 carries didn't hurt.

Colts offensive tackle George Preas never doubted the outcome, "I knew we could move the ball against them and I figured we could just score any time they scored."

Oct. 26th COLTS 35, WASHINGTON 10 AT BALTIMORE

Lenny Lyles's 101-yard kickoff return touchdown in the third quarter put the Redskins away for good. It was his second 100+ yard TD kickoff return of the season—Lyles ran one back 103 yards against the Bears on October 4th—making him the first player in NFL history with two 100+ yard TD kickoff returns in the same season. Lyles, a star running back at Johnny Unitas's alma mater—the University of Louisville—was known as the "Fastest Man in Football." In college, Lyles once ran a 9.4-second 100-yard dash; at the time, the world record was 9.3 seconds.

Washington scored on its first possession to lead 7–0, but after Weeb Ewbank made a defensive adjustment, Baltimore throttled the Redskins' offense the rest of the day.

Redskins owner George Preston Marshall, never a person with a lot of tact, gave at least one Colts player extra incentive for this game. He called Colts center Buzz Nutter a liar at a press conference the week before the game. That was in response to Nutter joking about having to hitchhike home after being released by the Redskins in 1953. You'd think Marshall would have learned his lesson from the 1940 NFL Championship Game. In case you don't know, Marshall called the Chicago Bears "crybabies" and "quitters" after Washington beat the Bears in a regular-season game that year. The psyched-up Bears got their revenge by obliterating the Redskins in record fashion, 73–0, in the NFL title game three weeks later.

Nov. 2nd COLTS 56, PACKERS 0 AT BALTIMORE

Although the Colts drubbed the hapless Packers, it was far from a great day for Baltimore, as Johnny Unitas suffered three broken ribs and a punctured lung when tackled by Packers' defensive back Johnny Symank. Part of the lore surrounding Unitas is that the Baltimore papers reported the next day that he would be out the rest of the season. However, in *The Baltimore Sun* the next day, one headline read "Unitas's Rib Injury Believed Not Serious" and reported that he would be available for the next game against the Giants.

For the first half of the season, the Colts outscored their opponents 234–94 and outgained them 2,438 yards to 1,403. This game was the third straight that the Colts outgained their opponent by more than 200 yards.

Nov. 9th NEW YORK 24, COLTS 21 AT NEW YORK

Even though the Colts played this game without Unitas, head coach Weeb Ewbank had a different reason for the loss. "There was only one thing wrong with our defense, that's tackling. We just didn't tackle." Subbing for Unitas, George Shaw threw for 239 yards and 3 touchdowns, but the Giants won on Pat Summerall's 28-yard field goal with three minutes left.

The loss meant that Ewbank's lucky suit, the one he had worn for the first seven games, was going to the cleaners. Someone asked Ewbank if he was giving up on the suit and he answered, "No, but I'm going to have the mud from one defeat removed from it. The mud from six victories can stay on."

Nov. 16th COLTS 17, CHICAGO BEARS 0 AT CHICAGO

Behind a defense that held the Bears to eight first downs and 161 total yards and 142 yards rushing in 26 attempts by Alan Ameche, Baltimore hung the first shutout on the Bears since 1946, a span of 148 games. Weeb Ewbank sounded much different than he did the previous week when talking about his defense, "Our defense was marvelous and I would say our deep secondary is 100 percent better than it was a year ago. But there is no defense like rushing the passer."

Nov. 23rd COLTS 34, LOS ANGELES 7 AT BALTIMORE

Wearing a protective corset-like wrap devised by trainer Eddie Block, Johnny Unitas returned to the starting lineup and completed 12 of 18 passes for 218 yards, 2 touchdowns, and no interceptions. A terrific game for a quarterback in the 1950s, especially for one who had suffered three broken ribs and a punctured lung three weeks before.

Former Rams great quarterback Bob Waterfield, by then an assistant coach, said this about Unitas: "He's the top quarterback in the league now. I think he is the best quarterback the league has had in some years."

The game was fairly even from the line of scrimmage, but the Colts forced 9 turnovers, including 4 interceptions.

Nov. 30th COLTS 35, SAN FRANCISCO 27 AT BALTIMORE

See beginning of chapter.

Dec. 6th LOS ANGELES 30, COLTS 28 AT LOS ANGELES

Johnny Unitas broke Cecil Isbell's NFL record for consecutive games throwing a touchdown pass. This was the twenty-fourth straight game for Unitas throwing at least one TD—and the streak was just barely past the halfway point. The streak, which he began as a rookie in 1956, would last until 1960 and reach 47 games. No other quarterback in NFL history has a streak longer than 30 games.

Dec. 14th SAN FRANCISCO 21, COLTS 12 AT SAN FRANCISCO

Johnny Unitas barely preserved his touchdown pass streak, throwing a 38-yard TD to tight end Jim Mutscheller with 1:39 left in the game. Otherwise, this was a lackluster performance by the Colts who made a season-low 13 first downs and gained less than 300 yards for only the second time all season. This was also the only regular season game in which Baltimore did not grab an interception.

Don't think that the Colts weren't aware of Unitas's streak. That was probably the only reason he played as much as he did in this game. On Baltimore's first possession, George Shaw was replaced by Unitas with the Colts at the 49ers' 3, but his fourth-down pass to Mutscheller was dropped in the end zone.

NFL Championship:

Dec. 28th COLTS 23, NEW YORK 17 (OT) AT NEW YORK

As far as I'm concerned, the key sequence that turned this into a close game came early in the third quarter. The Giants were forced to punt on their first possession of the second half. The Colts then drove down the field to a first-and-goal at the Giants' 3-yard line. Leading 14–3, another touchdown may have put the game away for Baltimore. Three runs into the line only got the ball to the Giants' 1-yard line. On fourth-and-goal the Colts went for it—Weeb Ewbank didn't have a lot of faith in kicker Steve Myhra. Unitas called a 428, a toss right to Ameche, who was supposed to throw an option pass to tight end Jim Mutschseller. Ameche heard the call as 28, a run with no pass, and didn't look up to see Mutscheller open in the end zone. Mutscheller, thinking the play was a pass to him, released early from his block so he could get into the end zone. Ameche was tackled for a 4-yard loss.

On second-and-5 from their own 10-yard line, Charley Conerley completed a pass to Kyle Rote at the Giants' 35; Rote broke a tackle and ran into Colts' territory but two Colts' tacklers forced Rote to fumble at the Baltimore 35. The ball rolled forward and New York's Alex Webster, trailing the play, picked up the ball at the Colts' 25-yard line and took it to the 1. Mel Triplett then ran for the touchdown. Instead of trailing 21–3, the Giants were down only 14–10.

Frank Gifford and all of the Giants will tell you that the turning point in the game came with about two minutes left when Gifford carried the ball on a third-and-4 from his own 40. Colts defensive end Gino Marchetti's leg was broken on the play when Colts defensive tackle Big Daddy Lipscomb fell on it. The Giants felt that, in the confusion after the injury, the ball was spotted incorrectly by the officials as short of the first down.

Johnny Unitas supposedly gambled on the winning drive in overtime when he threw a pass to Mutscheller with the Colts in "easy " field goal range inside the New York 10. Ewbank had given Unitas instructions to keep the ball on the ground. When Unitas threw the pass, Ewbank was upset. ("I liked to have crapped in my pants," he said later.) However, Ewbank had also told Unitas, "John, we were lucky to get the one field goal." Ewbank did not mince words: "I had no confidence in my kicker, Steve Myhra. He was just a bad place kicker. . . . I had coached Lou Groza at Cleveland. If Lou kicked ten times, his steps would leave the same marks in the dirt each time. If Myhra kicked twice, it looked like the chickens had been scratching in the dirt." Maybe the pass wasn't really a gamble.

Elsewhere Around the NFL:

Sep. 28th Lou Groza's field goal with 25 seconds left capped a 16-point fourth quarter as the Browns rallied to beat the Rams 30–27 in Los Angeles. The Rams finished the season 8–4, one game behind the Colts for the Western Conference title.

Nov. 9th In front of a Los Angeles Coliseum crowd of 95,082, the Rams crushed San Francisco 56–7—still the worst loss in 49ers' history. After three years as San Francisco head coach, former star quarterback Frankie Albert resigned after this season.

Dec. 14th In a must-win situation, a Giants' loss or tie would have given Cleveland the Eastern Conference title, New York beat the Browns 13–10 on an "impossible" 49-yard field goal in the snow by Pat Summerall. New York offensive coach Vince Lombardi told Summerall after the kick, "You know, you son of a bitch, you can't kick the ball that far."

New York's win set up a playoff game the following week against Cleveland. The Giants beat the Browns again (10–0) to advance to the NFL title game against the Colts.

What Happened the Next Season:

In 1959, the Colts' defense was not quite as effective, except for its amazing ability to intercept passes, but the offense stayed in high gear as the Colts repeated as Western Conference champs and NFL champs, once again defeating the Giants in the NFL Championship Game. This game, won by the Colts 31–16 at Baltimore, was summed up perfectly by Colts GM Don Kellett: "We didn't win easily, but we won convincingly." The Giants led the game 9–7 at the end of the third quarter, but the Colts made numerous big plays in the fourth quarter, including a 42-yard interception return for a touchdown by Johnny Sample.

Johnny Unitas had a phenomenal 1959 season, throwing 32 touchdown passes in just 12 games. That prorates to 43 touchdown passes in 16 games, and that doesn't take into account the numerous rule changes implemented since the late 1970s to help the passing game.

The Magnificent Mr. Moore

		Rushing						Receiving				
Year	G	Att	Yds	Avg	Lg Avg	TD	Rec	Yds	Avg	Lg Avg	TD
1	16	115	865	7.55	4.11	11	15	136	9.27	14.04	1
2	16	131	651	4.98	3.90	4	53	649	12.18	14.69	9
3	16	109	797	7.29	4.23	9	67	1251	18.76	14.49	9
4	16	121	563	4.64	4.22	3	63	1128	18.00	14.49	8
5	16	121	499	4.11	4.08	5	60	1248	20.80	14.42	12
6	15	105	741	7.04	4.22	8	56	832	14.86	14.35	9
Total	**95**	**702**	**4115**	**5.86**	**4.13**	**40**	**313**	**5244**	**16.74**	**14.41**	**49**

What would you think about a player who had compiled these above numbers? I hope you would think that's a hell of a player. This player scored 89 touchdowns from scrimmage in 95 games, had three consecutive 1,000-yard receiving seasons with a high per-catch average, and gained a lot of yards rushing with an exceptional average per carry. From the title of the article you can probably figure out that these numbers have something to do with Lenny Moore. What they represent are Moore's numbers from his first six seasons in the league, 1956–1961, prorated for a 16-game schedule.

In their wonderful book *The Pro Football Chronicle,* Dan Daly and Bob O'Donnell wrote, "Moore is a unique player in pro football history. He was an all-pro halfback and flanker wrapped into one. . . . If Moore isn't the greatest player, he's certainly one of the finalists." I don't think many people today appreciate just how special a player he was.

Joe Paterno, at the time an assistant coach at Penn State, advised during Moore's senior year, "Go tell Weeb Ewbank not to miss this guy because if he does, it will be the greatest mistake he ever made." The Colts picked Moore in the first round of the 1956 draft (from Penn State, obviously), eighth overall not counting the bonus selection. Some of the players drafted ahead of Moore that year were: Gary Glick (Pittsburgh), the aforementioned bonus selection, Art Davis (Pittsburgh) who played one year in the NFL, and Jack Losch (Green Bay) who also played just one year in the NFL.

I had the privilege of talking to Lenny Moore about the 1958 Colts.

Q: Was there some moment during the 1958 season when you first knew that the team was special?

Moore: No, not particularly. At the end of the 1957 season, we lost a game to the 49ers on a questionable play without which we might have made the title game. At the beginning of the 1958 season, we knew we were one of the best teams in the league and we felt we could beat any team on any given day.

Q: Where did you line up so that you could compile the numbers you did both running and receiving?

Moore: We usually used the split T with two backs behind the quarterback, but depending on the play I might line up at flanker, at wingback, or in the backfield.

Q: It seems like almost everyone on the 1958 Colts thinks that the game against San Francisco that clinched the Western Conference title was a better game than the more famous championship game. What do you remember about the 49ers game?

Moore: We were losing 27–7 at halftime and Weeb Ewbank simply told us at the half that while the defense hadn't played that poorly—they got a TD late in the half on a deflected pass and interception—we had to stop the 49ers and get the offense in gear. You have to remember that the 49ers had Y. A. Tittle, Joe Perry, and Hugh McElhenny in the backfield, so shutting them down for a half wouldn't be easy, but we did it.

Q: You scored the touchdown (a 73-yard run) that put the Colts ahead for good. What was the play?

Moore: I think the call was 38 Sweep, a sweep to the left. There was perfect blocking at the point of attack, a perfect seal block on Matt Hazeltine on the corner, and I had a lot of great downfield blocking, all I could see was Colts jerseys.

Q: Is there anything else about the team you'd like to talk about?

Moore: Looking back, it's almost hard to believe how many great players we had. I'm not just talking about the Hall of Famers, but players like Milt Davis, Leo Sanford, Big Daddy Lipscomb, Art Spinney... great players.

Great players, indeed, but maybe none as great as Lenny Moore. It might sound silly or maybe melodramatic to talk about any Hall-of-Fame player as forgotten, but it doesn't seem that Moore resides in the collective football conscience, which is strange given what he accomplished. He was one of the most important players on one of the greatest teams of all time.

Ballhawking Colts

If you asked football coaches what was the key to winning games, many of them would say turnovers. Sometimes it almost seems that coaches are obsessed with turnovers as if nothing else really matters. I doubt that most coaches really believe that–I hope they don't–but the subject seems to come up quite a bit. A team's giveaway/takeaway ratio does correlate well with winning games although other numbers correlate better.

What am I getting at? With all of the attention paid to turnovers, it strikes me as a bit odd that no one mentions the amazing ability of the late 1950s Colts to "force" turnovers, more specifically, interceptions. In 24 regular season games in 1958–59, the Colts intercepted 75 passes! If you think that's not too impressive because of the era, take a look at this:

NFL Interceptions by Team: 1958–59	
Baltimore	75
Pittsburgh	46
Chicago Bears	44
New York	43
Detroit	36
Los Angeles	35
Philadelphia	35
Cleveland	34
Chicago Cardinals	30
San Francisco	30
Washington	29
Green Bay	27
Average (excluding Baltimore)	**35.4**

If you think the interception total has something to do with teams throwing a lot against the Colts, consider that in 1958 the Colts intercepted 9.6 percent of their opponents' passes; the next best mark was 7.3 percent, and the league average was 6.2. In 1959, the Colts intercepted 11.4 percent of their opponents' passes, with the next best team at 7.7 percent and the league average at 6.0.

Allow me a brief, but related, digression. Given that Johnny Unitas did not throw a lot of interceptions, the Colts interception advantage was mind-boggling. In the same two seasons, Colts' passers threw just 25 interceptions.

That means that the Colts had a +50 interception advantage in just 24 games. Only three teams since 1950 have averaged at least two more interceptions per game than their opponents and two of those are the 1958 and 1959 Colts. (The 1960 Browns are the other.) Only four other teams have even averaged 1.5 more interceptions per game than their opponents.

Baltimore played a lot of zone defense and their four-man pass rush got a lot of pressure on the passer so the Colts didn't need to blitz that much. (Those two facts are related, of course, as it's harder to play zone defense if you're blitzing than if you're playing man-to-man.) Combine a good pass rush with agile linebackers and defensive backs and you get a lot of interceptions. However, to get as many INTs as the 1958–59 Colts got must have required an extraordinary combination of players.

Who were some of those ballhawking Colts? In 1958, the Colts' leading interceptors were defensive backs Ray Brown (8 interceptions), Andy Nelson (8), and Carl Taseff (7). None of these players played in the Pro Bowl following the 1958 season, although (as has already been noted) Andy Nelson received considerable mention on All-Pro teams.

In 1959, five Colts defenders had at least 5 interceptions, which is a feat unmatched by any other NFL team since 1950. Cornerback Milt Davis and linebacker Don Shinnick tied for the league lead with 7 interceptions, the first time teammates had done that. Andy Nelson had 6 interceptions; Ray Brown and linebacker Dick Szymanski had 5 each. It was the second time in three seasons that Davis had tied for the league lead; only Everson Walls has ever led (or co-led) the league three times, and only seven other players, besides Davis, have led twice.

Giants Hall-of-Fame middle linebacker Sam Huff once said that he still hears "Unitas to Berry" in his head, but NFL quarterbacks of the late 1950s must have heard "intercepted" far more than they wanted to when they played the Colts. Baltimore's ability to intercept passes was a remarkable skill and played a large role in the team's success.

I Knew Big Daddy Was Fast, But...

Jack Patera, the first head coach of the Seattle Seahawks, was the Colts' starting middle linebacker in 1956 and 1957. (Sometimes they were still called middle guards in those days, a leftover from the days of the five-man defensive line.) Baltimore released Patera not long before the start of the 1958 season. Head coach Weeb Ewbank explained his reasoning this way, "He's [Patera] still a good middle guard... our best linebacking unit is Leo

Transcendental Graphics

Ray Berry looks up to catch a Johnny Unitas pass.

Sanford, [Don] Shinnick, and Bill Pellington. We also want to work Dick Szymanski into linebacking and *we always have Big Daddy Lipscomb to fall back on"* (emphasis mine).

At 6 feet 6 inches and 288 pounds, Lipscomb was one of the two or three biggest players in the NFL in the 1950s. Only Doug Atkins of the Bears was taller (6-foot-8) and only John Baker of the Rams had a higher listed weight (290 pounds). Somehow, I don't think Lipscomb was an alternative at linebacker no matter how quick he was for his size. Neither *Total Football* nor *The Sports Encyclopedia: Pro Football* lists linebacker as one of the positions that Lipscomb played during his career. I have no idea what Ewbank was talking about.

Actually, one of the reasons the Colts released Patera was so they could keep both of their centers, Szymanski and Buzz Nutter. In 1958, the roster limit was just 35 players, so a player like Patera who only played one position was often at a disadvantage. He played for the Chicago Cardinals in 1958 and 1959, and they left him exposed in the expansion draft in 1960. The Cowboys, then the Dallas Rangers, drafted Patera; he played for them in 1960 and 1961. He was an assistant coach for 13 years with the Rams, Giants, and Vikings before being named the first head coach of the Seahawks in 1976. He was fired during the players strike of 1982 and never coached again.

The World's Largest Outdoor Insane Asylum

Baltimore's Memorial Stadium did not get that nickname because of Orioles' fans. It was the rabid behavior of Colts' fans that generated the stadium's moniker. Johnny Unitas even referred to the stadium's nickname during his Hall of Fame induction ceremony. Before you think the pet name came from a Colts' official or Baltimore native, it was actually bestowed by Cooper Rollow, a sportswriter with the *Chicago Tribune.*

How fanatical were Colts' fans? Well, I can tell you that for the team's annual intrasquad game in 1956, 50,000 people came to Memorial Stadium—yes, 50,000 for an intrasquad game. I vividly remember the fan reaction when Toni Linhart kicked a field goal in overtime to give the Colts a 10–7 win over the Miami Dolphins in 1975, a victory that for all intents and purposes clinched the AFC East title for Baltimore. The roar sounded as if it had been generated by 600,000 people, not the 60,000 that were present. The stadium literally shook and the roar lasted for several minutes. Even though I attended hundreds of Orioles' games there and worked at Memorial Stadium for four years as a member of the Orioles' organization, that 1975 game is, without question, my fondest memory of the stadium and one of the happiest days of my life. (I did not attend the legendary "Unitas We Stand" game where he threw his last pass as a Colt.)

Interestingly, many Colts believe that Memorial Stadium was more than a venue for sporting events. They believe that it was an important instrument for social harmony. Lenny Moore said, "Memorial Stadium was a catalyst for bringing people together." Joe Ehrmann, starting defensive tackle on the Colts' 1975–77 AFC East champions, went further when he said, "This stadium, this field, really represents the soul of the city of Baltimore. It created a venue for civic pride, for rich and poor, for CEOs and cabbies, for black and white."

Built as a no-frills facility in early 1950s for $5 million on the site of old Municipal Stadium, the presence of Memorial Stadium helped Baltimore land major league baseball and NFL football teams for Baltimore. In the Colts' "first" season of 1953, construction continued during the season and the seating capacity increased every week. (I put quotes around the word "first" because I am not counting the AAFC/NFL Colts of 1947–1950.)

To be as objective as I can be about a place that was in many ways my second home, Memorial Stadium was not a great place to watch a game. In order to save money, the upper deck was supported with columns instead of cantilevers. These columns created a large number of "obstructed-view" seats in the lower deck. While the horseshoe shape of the stadium may sound appropriate for a team named the Colts, in fact the shape meant that many seats near the middle of the football field were far away from the action. Also, the upper deck ended at the north 40-yard line, which meant that some potentially quality seats were missing. These flaws, however, were part of the stadium's "charm" in a way. I heard many fans joke about the obstructed-view seats even if they were sitting in them.

Memorial Stadium no longer stands on 33rd Street in Baltimore. Even the facade is gone. The facade was a memorial dedicated to those who lost their lives in World War I and World War II. The last line on the facade reads, "Time Will Not Dim the Glory of Their Deeds." While football and baseball are certainly not as important as wars to preserve freedom, that line seems appropriate in the context of the Colts and Orioles. Baltimoreans will not soon forget the Grand Old Lady of 33rd Street, the World's Largest Outdoor Insane Asylum.

The Coach: Weeb Ewbank

Coaching Record (with Colts Only)

	W	L	T	Pct	
1954	3	9	0	.250	
1955	5	6	1	.458	
1956	5	7	0	.417	
1957	7	5	0	.583	
1958	9	3	0	.750	NFL Western Conference title; NFL champs
1959	9	3	0	.750	NFL Western Conference title; NFL champs
1960	6	6	0	.500	
1961	8	6	0	.571	
1962	7	7	0	.500	
Total	**59**	**52**	**1**	**.531**	

I'm not the first person to comment on the irony in Weeb Ewbank's coaching career. Ewbank coached the Baltimore Colts in the game that made them, and supposedly pro football, famous–the 1958 NFL Championship Game. Of course, Ewbank also coached against Baltimore in the game where the Colts were made "infamous" by suffering one of pro football's all-time upsets, the Super Bowl III loss to the Jets.

Ewbank was the backfield coach at Brown University in 1946 and 1947; Brown's quarterback was a guy named Joe Paterno. Paul Brown hired Ewbank in 1949 as tackle coach for Cleveland. When the Colts hired Ewbank as head coach after the 1953 season, evidently he was not their first choice. Colts owner Carroll Rosenbloom wanted to hire Blanton Collier, also a Browns assistant, but Collier decided to take the head coaching job at the Univeristy of Kentucky. (Collier later returned to Cleveland as head coach, succeeding Paul Brown, and his Browns beat Rosenbloom's Colts in the 1964 NFL title game.)

According to the late John Steadman in his book *From Colts to Ravens,* Paul Brown was not happy about Ewbank leaving Cleveland. Steadman wrote, "For Ewbank to leave the Browns' staff–at least to Brown–was tantamount to violating a sacred trust. He figured he gave assistant coaches a chance to be a part of a great organization and he didn't want them taking his system someplace else and making it work for a team the Browns were going to have to play." Today, raiding the coaching staffs of successful teams is an accepted practice in the NFL.

Ewbank, though, gives a different account in *Sundays at 2:00 with the Baltimore Colts,* "We were at the 1953 Senior Bowl in Miami when Colts general manager Don Kellett asked to interview me for the Colts job. I had to get Brown's okay. Paul said, 'You're not going to be satisfied unless I let you do it, so go ahead.' Kellett and I talked down there and they hired me."

Several players have said that Ewbank's forte was assessing talent. Art Donovan told me that Ewbank could watch 10 guys play ping pong and after 10 minutes be able to tell which ones could play football. Johnny Unitas said, "One of Ewbank's greatest assets was that he was a tremendous judge of talent. He could see what talent people had for which positions and move them around. Alex Sandusky was a receiver at Clarion [in college]; Weeb moved him to guard." Sandusky played guard in the NFL for 13 seasons.

Lenny Moore told me that Ewbank was great at preparing the team. He said that they were almost never surprised by anything their opponent did in a game. In doing research for this book, I found that to be a common theme among successful coaches. Hall-of-Fame receiver Raymond Berry once told Moore, "We didn't realize that Weeb was a genius." Berry also said, "Weeb Ewbank was responsible for my making the team because he saw something in me when I was very raw. His ability to spot potential was critical because it took me two years before I really began to play, and in many cases I would have been out of the game by then."

Ewbank is remembered today as the only coach to win championships in both the NFL and AFL. He's also recalled as the person who coached both Johnny Unitas and Joe Namath. He should also be remembered, however, as someone instrumental in building one of the best and most important teams in pro football history.

The Quarterback: Johnny Unitas

Year	Team	Att	Comp	Yds	TD	Int	YPA	Rating	Lg Avg	W	L	Pct
1956	BAL	198	110	1,498	9	10	7.57	74.0	59.6	4	4	.500
1957	BAL	301	172	2,550	24	17	8.47	88.0	63.2	7	5	.583
1958	BAL	263	136	2,007	19	7	7.63	90.0	65.3	8	2	.800
1959	BAL	367	193	2,899	32	14	7.90	92.0	66.9	9	3	.750
1960	BAL	378	190	3,099	25	24	8.20	73.7	64.2	6	6	.500
1961	BAL	420	229	2,990	16	24	7.12	66.1	68.5	8	6	.571
1962	BAL	389	222	2,967	23	23	7.63	76.5	72.6	7	7	.500
1963	BAL	410	237	3,481	20	12	8.49	89.7	71.7	8	6	.571
1964	BAL	305	158	2,824	19	6	9.26	96.4	71.7	12	2	.857
1965	BAL	282	164	2,530	23	12	8.97	97.4	73.5	8	2	.800
1966	BAL	348	195	2,748	22	24	7.90	74.0	67.4	9	4	.692
1967	BAL	436	255	3,428	20	16	7.86	83.6	66.6	11	1	.917
1968	BAL	32	11	139	2	4	4.34	30.1	68.7	0	0	—
1969	BAL	327	178	2,342	12	20	7.16	64.0	71.6	7	5	.583
1970	BAL	321	166	2,213	14	18	6.89	65.1	65.6	10	2	.833
1971	BAL	176	92	942	3	9	5.35	52.3	62.2	3	2	.600
1972	BAL	157	88	1,111	4	6	7.08	70.8	66.3	1	4	.200
1973	SD	76	34	471	3	7	6.20	40.0	64.9	1	3	.250
Totals		**5,186**	**2,830**	**40,239**	**290**	**253**	**7.76**	**78.2**	**67.2**	**119**	**64**	**.650**
1956–65		3,313	1,811	26,845	210	149	8.10	83.8	68.5	77	43	.642

YPA = Yards Per Pass Attempt
Rating = Passer Rating
Lg Avg = League Passer Rating in that season
W, L, Pct = Team's Record in his starts

- Ninth-round pick by Pittsburgh (101st overall) in 1955.
- Cut by Steelers without playing at all in 1955 exhibition season.
- Named to 10 Pro Bowl teams (following every season from 1957 through 1967 except 1965), more than any other quarterback in NFL history.
- Named as quarterback on the NFL 50th anniversary team in 1969.
- Named as one of the four quarterbacks on the NFL 75th anniversary team in 1994.
- Two-time NFL MVP (1964, 1967; based on Associated Press voting)

Actually, it's hard to say if Unitas was a two-time MVP or three-time MVP. Let me explain: unlike baseball, which has had an "official" MVP award for decades, the NFL has only done so recently. If one looks at recent editions of the *National Football League Record & Fact Book,* the MVP list is based on the Associated Press voting. When people in the media say that Brett Favre is a three-time MVP, it is this award they are referring to. However, this hasn't always been the case. For example, the 1986 *Record & Fact Book* has no listing anywhere for NFL Most Valuable Players.

The AP didn't even start selecting an NFL MVP until 1957. The league itself began MVP selection in 1938 but stopped with the 1946 season. UP/UPI began choosing an NFL MVP in 1951, but for some reason didn't pick one in 1952 and then resumed in 1953. The Newspaper Enterprise Association started its selections in 1955; those stopped in 1989. *The Sporting News* began selecting an MVP in 1954. If one looks at *Total Football,* many seasons are shown as having more than one MVP or Player of the Year since all of the organizations who voted seldom agreed on one player. Johnny Unitas is shown as AP MVP in 1964 and 1967, but in 1959 he was picked as MVP by UP, *The Sporting News,* and the Maxwell Club. (Charley Conerly was named 1959 MVP by Associated Press and Newspaper Enterprise Association.) At one point in the HBO documentary about Unitas, the narrator (Liev Schreiber) says that Unitas "was named league MVP three times."

The following table shows the touchdown/interception ratio in 1958–59 of the starting quarterbacks in the NFL:

Quarterback	Pass Attempts	TD	Int
Johnny Unitas, BAL	630	51	21
Ed Brown, CHB	465	23	27
Charley Conerley, NYG	378	24	13
King Hill, CHC*	190	7	13
Bobby Layne, PIT	591	34	33
Eddie LeBaron, WAS	318	19	21
Milt Plum, CLE	455	25	19
Tobin Rote, DET	419	19	29
Bart Starr, GB	291	9	19
Y. A. Tittle, SF	407	19	30
Norm Van Brocklin, PHI	714	31	34
Billy Wade, LA	602	30	39
Average (excluding Unitas)	**439**	**22**	**25**

* Hill played for the Cardinals in 1958–59 and started in '59. The Cards' starting QB's in 1958 were Lamar McHan and M. C. Reynolds; McHan played for Green Bay in 1959.

The difference between Unitas and the rest of the league's starting quarterbacks is kind of amazing, isn't it?

No doubt, many people will say that Johnny Unitas's place in football history can't be measured with number tables and a few bullet points. Hey, I grew up in Baltimore, and Unitas is my favorite football player of all time and he always will be. I am very aware of his special place in history. But his numbers and accomplishments, even listed in cold black and white, are quite impressive. For the 17 seasons that Unitas played for the Colts, they had the best record in the NFL. Unitas didn't have a losing record as a starting quarterback until his final season in Baltimore.

His passing statistics are remarkable. I realize that I am more familiar with the standards for passer rating than most people, but from 1956 through 1965, Unitas's passing rating was more than 20 percent better than the league average as well as more than one standard deviation above the league average (and yes, passer rating is a very meaningful number because it correlates very well with winning). How about comparing him with Joe Montana? Unitas's passer rating was 30+ percent better than the league average for more seasons than Montana's.

Many people forget that Unitas had a terrific arm, at least until his elbow snapped in 1968. It would have been impossible for Unitas to have accomplished what he did, given the rules of the day, without the gift of a great arm. Unitas was excellent at reading defenses, obviously, but he was also among the first to master the art of "looking off"—looking at one side of the field or even faking a throw to make the defense flinch and then suddenly throwing the ball elsewhere. His high levels of courage and confidence, even for a pro football player, are constantly brought up by his former teammates and peers.

One time when a reporter asked Unitas if he'd ever given any thought to his place in football history, Unitas answered that the only thing that mattered was family and that football and everything else is nothing. I think it's safe to say that Unitas really didn't think of football as nothing. For one thing, when he crossed the picket line at Chargers' camp in 1974 (he retired shortly thereafter), he explained it this way, "Football has given me every opportunity I've ever had. No one else I know, from a poor section of Pittsburgh, has been able to sit down for lunch with three or four presidents of the United States." Unitas had tremendous pride in his football accomplishments and few NFL players, if any, have had as much to be proud of.

1958 Baltimore Colts Statistics

Passing

	Att	Comp	Comp Pct	Yds	Yds Per	TD	Int	Rating
Unitas	263	136	51.7%	2,007	7.63	19	7	90.0
Shaw	89	41	46.1%	531	5.97	7	4	72.8
Brown	2	1	50.0%	-1	-0.50	0	0	6.3
Colts	**354**	**178**	**50.3%**	**2,537**	**7.17**	**26**	**11**	**85.4**
Opponents	363	168	46.3%	2,248	6.19	9	35	35.1
League Average			49.4%		7.16			65.3

Colts' passers were sacked 16 times for 125 yards in losses.
The Colts sacked their opponents 32 times for 255 yards in losses.

Although the current NFL system of rating passers wasn't used in 1958, Johnny Unitas easily led the league. Only one other qualifying passer, Eddie LeBaron of the Redskins, had a rating of 80.0 or better, and he threw barely half as many passes (145) as Unitas.

The 1958 Colts are one of only five NFL teams since 1950 whose passing rating was at least 50 points higher than their opponents' for a season. Getting even more off the wall, the Colts' ratio of offensive to defensive passing rating, 2.43/1 (85.4 divided by 35.1 is 2.43), is the best of any team since 1950.

Rushing

	Att	Yds	Avg	Net Yards	TD
Ameche	171	791	4.63	+68	8
Moore	82	598	7.29	+251	7
Dupre	95	390	4.11	−11	3
Call	37	154	4.16		0
Unitas	33	139	4.21		3
Lyles	22	41	1.86		1
Pricer	10	26	2.60		1
Shaw	5	−3	−0.60		1
Brown	1	−9	−9.00		0
Colts	**456**	**2,127**	**4.66**	**+196**	**24**
Opponents	331	1,291	3.90	−109	13
League Average			4.23		

Lenny Moore led the NFL in average yards per carry for the third consecutive season. Alan Ameche was second in yards gained, albeit a distant second to Jim Brown who rushed for 1,527 yards. In case you're curious, or even if you're not, Brown's 1958 net yards figure was +440.

Receiving

	Rec	Yds	Avg	TD
Berry	56	794	14.18	9
Moore	50	938	18.76	7
Mutscheller	28	504	18.00	7
Dupre	13	111	8.54	0
Ameche	13	81	6.23	1
Lyles	5	24	4.80	1
Rechichar	4	34	8.50	1
Call	4	28	7.00	0
Pricer	3	14	4.67	0
DeCarlo	1	10	10.00	0
Pellington	1	−1	−1.00	0
Colts	**178**	**2,537**	**14.25**	**26**
Opponents	168	2,248	13.38	9
League Average			14.49	

Raymond Berry tied for the league lead in both receptions and touchdowns. Lenny Moore was fourth in receptions and second in receiving yards.

Kickoff Returns

	Ret	Yds	Avg	TD
Lyles	11	398	36.18	2
Pricer	9	168	18.67	0
Moore	4	91	22.75	0
Simpson	3	59	19.67	0
Rechichar	3	50	16.67	0
Taseff	1	50	50.00	0
Call	2	48	24.00	0
DeCarlo	1	0	0.00	0
Colts	**34**	**864**	**25.41**	**2**
Opponents	43	1,241	28.86	1
League Average			22.32	

Lenny Lyles was 1 return short of qualifying in average per return. His average would have led the league and been the third highest in NFL history.

The Colts were last in the NFL in kickoff coverage in 1958.

Punt Returns

	Ret	Yds	Avg	TD
Taseff	29	196	6.76	0
Rechichar	7	29	4.14	0
Moore	5	11	5.50	0
Simpson	1	1	1.00	0
Colts	**39**	**237**	**6.08**	**0**
Opponents	40	176	4.40	0
League Average			5.62	

Only two NFL teams averaged more than 7 yards a punt return in 1958 and only one NFL player (Jon Arnett of the Rams) averaged more than 10 yards a return.

Interceptions

	Int	Yds	Avg	TD
Nelson	8	199	24.88	1
Brown	8	149	18.63	0
Taseff	7	52	7.43	0
Pellington	4	44	11.00	0
Davis	4	40	10.00	0
Shinnick	3	23	7.67	0
Sanford	1	7	7.00	0
Colts	**35**	**514**	**14.69**	**1**
Opponents	11	169	15.36	3

As mentioned earlier, the 1958–59 Colts intercepted a lot of passes. Not counting the Colts, the average NFL team intercepted 19 passes in 1958.

Turnovers

Turnovers Committed:	22
Turnovers Forced:	52
Turnover +/–:	+30

A +30 turnover advantage in 12 games is 2.50 per game, which is the second best figure for any NFL team since 1950.

Punting

	No	Avg
Brown	41	39.9
Horn	19	32.5
Stone	1	28.0
Dupre	1	0.0
Colts	**62**	**36.8**
Opponents	62	44.1
League Average		40.7

Kicking

	XP	XPA	XP Pct	FG	FGA	FG Pct
Myhra	48	51	94.1%	4	10	40.0%
Rechichar	0	0	—	1	4	25.0%
Shaw	0	1	0.0%	0	0	—
Colts	**48**	**52**	**92.3%**	**5**	**14**	**35.7%**
Opponents	23	26	88.5%	6	17	35.3%
League Average			95.6%			46.9%

Colts' kickers had the second-worst field-goal percentage in the league.
Leading Scorer: Lenny Moore, 84 points

1958 Baltimore Colts Roster

Head Coach	Weeb Ewbank
QB/P	Dick Horn
QB	George Shaw
QB	Johnny Unitas
RB	Alan Ameche
RB	Jack Call
RB	L. G. Dupre
RB/WR	Lenny Moore
RB/KR	Billy Pricer
RB	Avatus Stone
WR	Raymond Berry
OE	Jim Mutscheller
C	Buzz Nutter
OG	Alex Sandusky
OG	Art Spinney
OG	Fuzzy Thurston
OT	Jim Parker
OT	Sherman Plunkett
OT	George Preas
DE	Ordell Braase
DE	Don Joyce
DE	Gino Marchetti
DT	Art Donovan
DT	Gene "Big Daddy" Lipscomb
DT/DE	Ray Krouse
LB/OG/K	Steve Myhra
LB	Bill Pellington
LB/OE/K/PR	Bert Rechichar
LB	Leo Sanford
LB	Don Shinnick
LB/C	Dick Szymanski
DB/QB/P	Ray Brown
DB	Milt Davis
DB/OE	Art DeCarlo
DB/RB/KR	Lenny Lyles
DB	Andy Nelson
DB	Johnny Sample
DB	Jackie Simpson
DB/PR	Carl Taseff

Hall of Famers: Ewbank, Unitas, Moore, Berry, Parker, Marchetti, Donovan.

CHAPTER 3

1962 Green Bay Packers: The Best of the Best

This chapter title doesn't necessarily mean that I am picking the 1962 Packers as the greatest NFL team of all time. What I am referring to is the fact that I believe Vince Lombardi was the greatest coach in NFL history and the 1962 Packers were his best team.

STARTING LINEUP – 1962 PACKERS

Offense		Defense	
LE (SE)	Max McGee	LE	Willie Davis
LT	Norm Masters	LT	Dave Hanner
LG	Fred "Fuzzy" Thurston	RT	Henry Jordan
C	Jim Ringo	RE	Bill Quinlan
RG	Jerry Kramer	LLB	Dan Currie
RT	Forrest Gregg	MLB	Ray Nitschke
RE (TE)	Ron Kramer	RLB	Bill "Bubba" Forester
FL	Boyd Dowler	LCB	Herb Adderley
QB	Bart Starr	RCB	Jesse Whittington
RB	Paul Hornung/Tom Moore	LS	Hank Gremminger
RB	Jim Taylor	RS	Willie Wood

Let me see if I can phrase this in a way that makes sense. In 1958, the year before Lombardi became head coach, the Packers' record was 1–10–1. Counting the tie as a half-win/half-loss, like the NFL does now (the NFL ignored ties in figuring percentages until 1972), the '58 Pack had a .125 winning percentage. In 1962, the Packers' record was 13–1, a .929 winning percentage. That means the Packers improved by more than .800 from 1958 through 1962, the only NFL team since 1950 to have that large an improvement in their winning percentage in a span of four seasons. Obviously, only very bad teams have the opportunity to make such dramatic progress, but of all of the very bad teams in the NFL in the last 57 years, only the Lombardi Packers made such an improvement. (From 1950–2001, not including 1982, 86 teams won less than 20 percent of their games in a season.)

It's not just that the Packers improved immediately upon Lombardi's arrival, but that they kept improving for three more seasons. Not counting playoff games, the Packers' record in Lombardi's first four seasons (1959–1962) was 39–13. In the four seasons before he became head coach, their record was 14–33–1.

Green Bay not only dominated during the season, the Packers were even better in the postseason. If one counts the 1965 Western Conference playoff, Lombardi's Packers won nine straight playoff games from 1961 through 1967. In most instances, playoff teams are evenly matched so winning nine in a row is very impressive. If you flipped a coin nine times, the probability that it would come up either heads or tails nine times is .4 percent; that's four-tenths of one percent.

In 1962, the Packers were at their peak. Coming off two consecutive appearances in the NFL title game and the NFL championship in 1961, the only things the Packers were worried about were injuries and unrealistic expectations. As Green Bay All-Pro safety Willie Wood said years later, "We were a great, great team in 1962. We had talent everyplace. Every guy knew what he was supposed to be doing. We were veterans then and I thought we were awesome." Even with the injury that caused Paul Hornung to miss much of the 1962 season, Willie Wood was right: the 1962 Packers were awesome.

Team in a Box

Record: 13–1

The Packers began the 1962 season with 10 consecutive wins, most by lopsided scores. Eight of the wins were by 11 or more points and five were by 27 or more points. For the season, 10 of their 13 wins were by 10 or more points and six were by at least 27 points.

The Packers' 1962 record was the best posted by any NFL team since the Bears were 11–0 in 1942.

Against Teams Over .500: 3–1, 110 Points Scored, 40 Points Allowed

The Packers did not have a tough schedule in 1962. Their four games against teams with winning records were the games against Western Conference foes Detroit and Chicago.

Points Scored/Allowed: 415/148 (1962 NFL Average: 312)

To me, the Packers' point differential is the most impressive accomplishment on their resume. They outscored their opponents by an average of 19.1 points per game, the best per-game point differential of any NFL team since 1950.

Yards Gained/Allowed: 4,791/3,277 (1962 NFL Average: 4,476)

The Packers' per-game yardage differential (+108.1) ranks sixteenth among all teams since 1950.

Opponents' Record: 78–98–6, .445

(Not counting games against the Packers; ties counted as a half-win and a half-loss.)

Adjusted Power Index:

Offense: +2.73
Defense: +3.95
TOTAL: +6.67

The popular image of the Packers is that of a team that won primarily by running the ball and playing defense. Green Bay threw fewer passes than any other NFL team in 1962, but their passing attack was effective, finishing second in average yards per pass attempt and third in passer rating. Of course, many would argue that the success of the Packers' running game set up the success of their passing game.

In any event, the 1962 Packers' Offense Power Index ranks in the top 10 percent among all teams since 1950; their Defense Power Index ranks in the top 2 percent.

Innovations/What You Should Know:

Vince Lombardi and the Packers did not invent the power sweep, Green Bay's signature play. The sweep was really an old single-wing play, the single-wing was football's dominant offensive formation until the 1940s, in that it massed great power at the point of attack. Both guards pulled ahead of the ball carrier and the tight end and other running back had important blocking assignments in the area the offense was attacking.

The 1962 season was important for a reason that didn't have anything to do with power sweeps and blitzes. It marked the first year of the single-network television contract with the revenues being distributed equally among all NFL teams. Prior to 1962, each team made its own television deal and, therefore, television revenues were not the same for every team. Imagine Green Bay trying to compete today against the New York Giants without the equal distribution of television revenues. It is not an overstatement that this development is one of the reasons that pro football is king of the professional sports world today.

Homegrown First-Round Picks:

RB Paul Hornung (Bonus Choice), 1957; TE Ron Kramer, 1957; LB Dan Currie, 1958; RB Tom Moore, 1960; DB Herb Adderley, 1961; RB Earl Gros, 1962.

As I pointed out with the 1955 Browns, for teams prior to the beginning of the common NFL–AFL draft in 1967 this category can be a misleading. One reason is the vastly smaller number of teams. For example, Jim Taylor was the Packers' second-round pick in 1958, but he was the fourteenth overall selection. Since 1967, the fourteenth pick has occurred in the middle of the first round.

This is an impressive list of players, including two Hall of Famers (Hornung, Adderley) and three other players who played in at least one Pro Bowl (Kramer, Currie, Moore). It should be noted that Hornung, (Ron) Kramer, and Currie were drafted before Lombardi arrived.

Pro Bowl Players:

LB Bill "Bubba" Forester, OT Forrest Gregg, G Jerry Kramer, TE Ron Kramer, RB Tom Moore, C Jim Ringo, QB Bart Starr, RB Jim Taylor, DB Willie Wood.

An interesting fact is that seven of the nine Packers named to the Pro Bowl in 1962 were with the team *before* Lombardi arrived.

Defensive linemen Willie Davis and Henry Jordan as well as linebacker Dan Currie were named to the Associated Press All-Pro first team in addition to six of the Packers' Pro Bowl players (Forester, Gregg, both Kramers, Ringo, and Taylor).

Game-by-Game:

Sep. 16th PACKERS 34, MINNESOTA 7 AT GREEN BAY

The second-year Vikings were no match for Green Bay in the 1962 season opener. As Bud Lea of the *Milwaukee Sentinel* wrote, "They tossed a Golden Glover into the ring against the world champion."

Paul Hornung scored 28 points on 3 touchdown runs, 2 field goals, and 4 extra points. He also completed an option pass, one of Vince Lombardi's favorite plays, for 41 yards to set up one of his field goals.

The Packers intercepted five Fran Tarkenton passes and harassed him all day, holding him to just 100 yards passing on 23 attempts.

Sep. 23rd PACKERS 17, ST. LOUIS 0 AT MILWAUKEE

Green Bay held the Cardinals to just 16 yards rushing on 16 carries. Behind the running of Jim Taylor, who finished with 122 yards on 23 attempts, the Packers put away stubborn St. Louis in the second half.

Monkey see, monkey do . . . the success of the Packers led to other teams "borrowing" things from them. In this game, Cards' star running back John David Crow threw 3 passes and, incredibly, he attempted 20 passes during the 1962 season.

Sep. 30th PACKERS 49, CHICAGO 0 AT GREEN BAY

Vince Lombardi may have stated the obvious after the game when he said, "It was our best performance to date—we were sharper in everything we did." However, many thought that the game turned on one play early in the third quarter. Trailing 14–0 with fourth-and-1 at their own 44-yard line, the Bears decided to go for the first down. Ronnie Bull was tackled for a 1-yard loss and four plays later the Packers scored to go ahead 21–0.

Green Bay intercepted five more passes, including one that was returned 58 yards for a touchdown by Herb Adderley for the Packers' final score. The Packers ran for 244 yards, led by Jim Taylor's 126 yards on 17 carries. Taylor also scored 3 touchdowns.

This was the worst defeat in Bears' history up to that time. From 1933 through 1961, the Bears had lost a game by 30 or more points just five times.

Oct. 7th PACKERS 9, DETROIT 7 AT GREEN BAY

This is the game profiled in the classic book *Run to Daylight!* A Herb Adderley interception and 41-yard return with a minute and a half left set up the Packers' game-winning field goal. Many Lions' players were upset, to say the least, that Milt Plum attempted a pass in that situation, even though it was third-and-8 at their own 49-yard line.

In this game, the option pass didn't work so well for Green Bay. Both attempts, one by Hornung and one by Tom Moore, were intercepted in Lions' territory.

If you noticed that the Packers' first four games were at home, give yourself a pat on the back (just don't break your arm). Green Bay still played their home games both in Green Bay *and* Milwaukee (they played their last game in Milwaukee in 1994). The Packers' first four games were at home every year (except one) from 1953 through 1963 as a concession to the late-season Wisconsin weather.

Oct. 14th PACKERS 48, MINNESOTA 21 AT MINNESOTA

Even though the Vikings scored more points than the total the Packers had allowed in their first four games, Minnesota was buried under a Green Bay offensive avalanche. Bart Starr completed 20 of 29 passes for 297 yards and three touchdowns, and Jim Taylor ran for a season-high 164 yards on just 17 attempts. Green Bay gained 506 yards of offense.

The win was costly, though. Paul Hornung suffered a knee injury in the first quarter that, except for a few snaps against Philadelphia, would cause him to miss five games. Offensive tackle Bob Skoronski (knee) and defensive back Jesse Whittington (pulled calf muscle) were also hurt.

Oct. 21st PACKERS 31, SAN FRANCISCO 13 AT MILWAUKEE

The Packers scored the game's final 21 points to erase a 13–10 deficit. The 49ers had taken the lead early in the third quarter on an 85-yard TD punt return by Abe Woodson.

Although the Packers did not allow an offensive touchdown, San Francisco was able to move the ball in the first half. 49ers halfback J. D. Smith ran for 101 yards before halftime; he got only 18 yards in the second half.

Green Bay got its running game going in the second half, as Jim Taylor ran for 132 yards after halftime. Tom Moore, subbing for the injured Paul Hornung, had 84 yards rushing for the game on just 14 carries. In the first six games of the season, Taylor gained 742 yards rushing and averaged 6.7 yards per carry.

Oct. 28th PACKERS 17, BALTIMORE 6 AT BALTIMORE

Bud Lea characterized this game as a "knock 'em down, drag 'em out brawl" and the Packers prevailed. Jim Taylor's 36-yard touchdown run, with nine minutes left, put the game away. It was the Packers' first win in Baltimore since 1957.

While the Packers showed respect for the Colts in their postgame comments, Baltimore didn't return the favor. Colts safety Andy Nelson was prophetic when he said, "Detroit will beat them on Thanksgiving Day."

Nov. 4th PACKERS 38, CHICAGO 7 AT CHICAGO

Green Bay improved to 8–0 by breaking open a close game in the second half. Seven Bears' turnovers were critical, but none like the "fumble" that led to the Packers' second touchdown. Green Bay punter and wide receiver Boyd Dowler was limited to punting duties due to a knee injury suffered in Friday practice. Ahead just 10–7 five minutes into the third quarter, Dowler got off a very short punt that hit the Bears' Roosevelt Taylor in the back. The ball was recovered by the Packers' Jim Ringo at the Chicago 28-yard line. The Packers scored in two plays to stretch their lead to 17–7 and they never looked back.

Nov. 11th PACKERS 49, PHILADELPHIA 0 AT PHILADELPHIA

This game was not as close as the final score. The *NFL Record & Fact Book* doesn't list the record for the largest yardage difference in a single game, but this game has to be right up there. The Packers outgained the Eagles 628 yards to 54. Green Bay had 37 first downs, Philadelphia 3.

Eagles All-Pro and eventual Hall-of-Fame wide receiver Tommy McDonald said this about the Packers after the game, "They're so great I don't even think I could make their rinky-dink team. If I was on the squad, I'd probably be chasing punts and kickoffs." To be sure, the 1962 Eagles finished just 3–10–1, but they were outscored by only 74 points for the entire season.

Nov. 18th PACKERS 17, BALTIMORE 13 AT GREEN BAY

The Packers won this game by thwarting Baltimore on three possessions near the Green Bay goal line. On two of those drives, the Colts reached the Packers' 1-yard line, twice they went on fourth-and-goal, and twice the defense held. On another possession, they reached the Green Bay 2-yard line but lost the ball on a fumble.

On the other side of the ball, the Colts totally shut down the Packers' offense, limiting them to 116 total yards and 8 first downs, but a Herb Adderley 103-yard kickoff return and the three goal-line stands gave Green Bay the win. After the game Vince Lombardi said, "That was our toughest game by far. The Colts' aggressive defense was great and that Johnny Unitas was tremendous." If Lombardi thought this game was tough . . .

Nov. 22nd DETROIT 26, GREEN BAY 14 AT DETROIT

The Lions' defense turned in an outstanding effort to hand the Packers their only loss of the season. Detroit's front seven, especially defensive tackle Roger Brown and middle linebacker Joe Schmidt, constantly pressured Bart Starr and shut down the Packers' running game. Starr was sacked an incredible 11 times, including once by Brown for a safety. Detroit led 26–0 until Green Bay finally scored two fourth-quarter touchdowns.

After the game, Lombardi seemed relieved to some degree, "I think that we will be a better football team for having lost this one. That business about an undefeated season was a lot of bunk. Nobody in his right mind could have expected it. . . . Detroit's defensive line blitzed and criss-crossed so well and so quickly that they were continually getting the jump on us. . . . We couldn't find their defensive line long enough to block it. The ball was snapped and they were gone."

The Lombardi genius was never more apparent than in his reaction to this game. He knew his team was down enough after losing and he knew there was no need to beat them over the head with it. It seemed like he always knew the right time to ease up.

Dec. 2nd PACKERS 41, LOS ANGELES 10 AT MILWAUKEE

Paul Hornung returned to the starting lineup and, coincidentally or not, the Packers' offense came to life after back-to-back subpar efforts. Bart Starr had a very productive day throwing the ball as he completed 15 of 20 passes for 260 yards.

Rams head coach Harland Svare, who took over the team when Bob Waterfield resigned after eight games, called the Packers, "the most powerful team I've ever seen."

Dec. 9th PACKERS 31, SAN FRANCISCO 21 AT SAN FRANCISCO

The Packers scored 21 unanswered points in the second half to defeat the 49ers. Jim Taylor scored his eighteenth touchdown of the season, which broke Don Hutson's team record set in 1942 and tied the existing record for the NFL shared by Steve Van Buren and Jim Brown.

Dec. 16th PACKERS 20, LOS ANGELES 17 AT LOS ANGELES

Detroit's 3–0 loss to Chicago earlier in the day had given the Packers the Western Conference title, but Green Bay eked out a win over the hapless Rams, who finished the season 1–12–1. The eventual winning touchdown came on a fourth-quarter, 83-yard TD pass from Starr to Hornung, who scampered untouched all the way and gave the Packers a 20–10 lead.

NFL MVP Jim Taylor ended the season with a bang, running for 156 yards in 23 attempts and scoring his nineteenth touchdown to set an NFL record. The record stood until 1965 when Gale Sayers scored 22 touchdowns as a rookie. Taylor ended Jim Brown's five-year reign as NFL rushing champ, gaining 1,474 yards with an impressive 5.4 average.

NFL Championship:

Dec. 30th PACKERS 16, NEW YORK 7 AT NEW YORK

On a brutally cold and windy day at Yankee Stadium, the Packers' defense and the elements gave Green Bay its second consecutive NFL title. (In 1961, the Packers crushed the Giants 37–0 in the title game.) The game-time temperature was 20 degrees and the winds blew from 25 to 40 miles per hour. Nobody calculated wind chills in those days, but those numbers calculate to a wind chill of approximately zero degrees.

Vince Lombardi had actually considered surprising the Giants by throwing the ball more than usual, but the elements made him change his mind. The game was a contest of power running, short passes, and field position.

The Packers scored first on a Jerry Kramer 26-yard field goal about seven minutes into the game. (Kramer had assumed the kicking duties after Paul Hornung hurt his knee on October 14 against Minnesota.) On the following possession, the Giants drove 47 yards to the Green Bay 15, but Dan Currie intercepted a Y. A. Tittle pass that had been slightly deflected by Ray Nitschke.

The Packers' first touchdown came in the second quarter after Currie forced a Phil King fumble that the Packers recovered at the Giants' 28-yard line. Green Bay took only two plays to score, with the first being that Lombardi favorite, a 21-yard option pass from Hornung to Boyd Dowler.

Trailing 10–0, the Giants forced a break midway through the third quarter when Erich Barnes blocked Max McGee's punt and Jim Collier recovered it in the end zone. McGee was punting because Boyd Dowler was still bothered by a bad knee.

On Green Bay's next possession, they punted again but New York's Sam Horner fumbled. The Packers recovered at the Giants' 40-yard line, and Jerry Kramer kicked a field goal with four minutes left in the third quarter. The Packers' defense stymied the Giants the rest of the way.

Kramer had kicked well filling in for Hornung. Although he wouldn't get any style points for his form, Kramer was successful on 9 of 11 field-goal attempts during the regular season and 38 of 39 extra-point attempts. If that doesn't sound remarkable given today's kicking standards, keep in mind that in 1962 only 49.7 percent of field goal attempts were successful.

Despite playing with an as yet undiagnosed case of hepatitis, Jim Taylor gained 85 tough yards on the ground as he, Hornung, and Tom Moore made enough first downs for the Packers to control the game.

Elsewhere Around the NFL (and Elsewhere):

Sep. 23rd Hall-of-Fame back Bobby Mitchell, traded to Washington by Cleveland before the 1962 season, scored the winning touchdown on a 50-yard catch and run with two minutes left as the 17-point underdog Redskins shocked the Browns 17–16 at Cleveland.

Oct 14th–

Oct 28th The world came to the brink of nuclear holocaust during the Cuban Missile Crisis. (See "Apocalypse Almost.")

Dec. 2nd Pittsburgh's Lou Michaels, kicker and defensive end, kicks four field goals in the Steelers' 19–7 win against the Cardinals. Michaels set an NFL record with 26 field goals in 1962.

What Happened the Next Season:

Paul Hornung was suspended for the entire 1963 season for betting on NFL games, but it wasn't his absence that caused Green Bay to fall short of its third straight NFL title. Tom Moore filled in more than capably for Hornung. The Packers' defense also played well as Green Bay posted an 11–2–1 record. Unfortunately for them, both losses came to conference rival Chicago. The Bears rode a great defense to an 11–1–2 record and the NFL championship.

Apocalypse Almost

I am not a historian or a political analyst. However, I felt compelled to discuss the events of October 1962 known as the Cuban Missile Crisis. As much as I love sports, pro football in particular, I understand their relative insignificance in the world. If things had happened just a little differently in 1962, it's very possible that the world as we know it would not exist today.

In April 1962, Jupiter missiles installed by the United States in Turkey, not far from the then Soviet Union, became operational. Late that month, Soviet premier Nikita Khrushchev vacationed in the Crimea across the Black Sea from Turkey. According to many sources, the presence of the U.S. missiles in Turkey led Khrushchev to think of deploying similar weapons in Cuba.

At the end of May, Khrushchev decided that the Soviet Union would deploy nuclear missiles in Cuba. A Soviet delegation was sent to Cuba, under the guise of a mission to study irrigation problems, to discuss this plan with Cuban leader Fidel Castro. He agreed to allow the Soviets to install nuclear weapons in Cuba. Sometime in July, the Soviet Union began shipping missiles to Cuba.

In mid-August circumstantial evidence developed from new intelligence suggested that the Soviet Union might be placing nuclear missiles in Cuba. However, the Soviets denied they were doing so even after U.S. pronouncements about the consequences of such an action, and the U.S. had doubts about their own intelligence sources.

In early October, U.S. intelligence learned that medium-range ballistic missiles, missiles that could be used in an offensive first strike, were indeed being deployed in Cuba. This information was startling for many reasons, not the least of which was Khrushchev's apparent disregard for provoking a potentially dangerous reaction from the United States. This evidence is what began the episode that most people know as the Cuban Missile Crisis, the most dangerous standoff of the Cold War.

On October 22, 1962, President Kennedy addressed the nation and revealed that the United States had "unmistakable evidence" that the Soviet Union had installed nuclear ballistic missiles in Cuba as well as having delivered nuclear capable bombers. He announced a quarantine, or blockade, and stated that the U.S. would "regard any nuclear missile launched from Cuba against any nation in the Western Hemisphere as an attack by the Soviet Union on the United States, requiring a full retaliatory response against the Soviet Union."

In the end, Khrushchev simply couldn't risk a nuclear war with the United States. Even though one of the reasons he placed missiles in Cuba was to narrow the gap in the nuclear offensive power of the two countries, he probably knew that the Soviet Union was still at a disadvantage. On October 28, he told President Kennedy that work on the Cuban missile sites would stop and that the missiles already in Cuba would be returned to the Soviet Union. Kennedy agreed to a non-invasion pledge regarding Cuba and secretly promised to withdraw the missiles from Turkey, as long as that could be done some time after the "end" of the crisis.

A football angle to this . . . in *The Pro Football Chronicle,* Dan Daly and Bob O'Donnell wrote that the Cuban Missile Crisis thwarted a plan by John, Robert, and Ted Kennedy to buy the Philadelphia Eagles after the death of Eagles' owner Jim Clark. Daly and O'Donnell claimed that John had actually instructed Ted to go to Philadelphia and meet with Eagles' management, but the plan was put on hold, forever as it turned out, by the escalation of the crisis in mid-October.

"If You Can Remember the Sixties"

Among other things, actor Dennis Hopper is famous for saying, "If you can remember the sixties, then you weren't there." Of course, he wasn't talking about football.

Given that the 1962 Packers are the only team from that decade in the book, you may think I have forgotten about the 1960s. Actually, that decade could have had as many as four teams make the book except for one small problem: three of them were upset in the Super Bowl or in the NFL Championship Game.

Chronologically, the first of these playoff disappointments is the 1964 Baltimore Colts. This team is discussed in the article on Don Shula in the 1972 Dolphins chapter, but a little redundancy is OK. In Shula's second season as Baltimore's head coach, his team compiled a 12–2 record, scored the most points in the league, allowed the fewest, and gained the most yards. Led by the incomparable Johnny Unitas, Baltimore had an excellent passing attack as Unitas easily led the league in yards per attempt and had a 19-to-6 touchdown-to-interception ratio, impressive since the league ratio was basically even (278 touchdowns, 276 interceptions). Lenny Moore bounced back from two injury-riddled seasons to become the first NFL player to score 20 touchdowns in a season (despite averaging only 3.72 yards per carry). Defensively, the Colts weren't exceptional against the run, but they got after the passer, leading the league with 57 sacks.

The '64 Colts' +6.58 Adjusted Power Index (API) was the second highest of the 1960s (behind the '62 Packers) and is the thirteenth best among all teams since 1950. Eight of the 12 teams ahead of them won the Super Bowl or pre-1966 NFL title and are, consequently, in the book. Oh, those details. The Colts, heavy favorites, lost to Cleveland 27–0 in the NFL title game. Since the criteria I set for making the book include winning it all, the 1964 Colts didn't get in.

The next '60s disappointment is another team coached by Don Shula, the 1968 Colts. With Earl Morrall having a great year replacing the injured Unitas, and with the defense shutting down just about every opponent, the Colts rolled to a 13–1 record. (The remarkable seasons Morrall had with Shula are discussed in the 1972 Dolphins' chapter.)

The '68 Colts' point differential (402 points scored, 144 allowed) remains the second-best since 1950 on a per-game basis (again, trailing only the 1962 Packers). The team was well-balanced, but the Colts' defense was a little ahead of the offense. The team was stingy against the run and used a good pass rush with a lot of zone coverage to stymie opponents. They allowed the fewest yards per completion and per attempt of any team in the league. The 1968 Colts also passed the "magic" +6.00 mark in API at +6.12, making them one of only 22 teams to do that since 1950. After "revenging" their 1964 loss to the Browns with a 34–0 stomping in the 1968 NFL title game, the Colts were huge favorites against the New York Jets in the Super Bowl. Yeah, I know... 16–7.

The last of the three teams that could have made the book if they hadn't stumbled at the finish line is the 1969 Minnesota Vikings. The Purple People Eaters had great defensive numbers, allowing fewer than 10 points and 200 yards per game for their entire 12–2 season. Minnesota allowed only 4 rushing touchdowns all year, yielded just 3.23 yards per rush, limited opponents to under 10 yards a completion and an amazingly low 4.96 yards per pass attempt, and intercepted 30 passes. All of those marks led the league. Their +4.35 Defense Power Index (DPI) is the fifth-best since 1950. Their offense was only adequate; even though they led the NFL in points scored, they were actually below the league average in yards gained. One could say that the defense gave them a lot of short fields, so that they didn't have the opportunity to gain a lot of yardage, but I think that over the course of a season a good offensive team would be above the league average in yards gained. Minnesota's API was +5.98, just a hair below the +6.00 "standard."

Of course, their API didn't matter because the Vikings didn't win the Super Bowl. After a come-from-behind win over the Rams in the first round of the 1969 playoffs (the final score was 23–20 after Minnesota trailed 17–7 at halftime and 20–14 in the fourth quarter), the Vikings cruised past Cleveland 27–7 in the NFL championship on a very cold day in Minnesota. In the Super Bowl, though, they were easily defeated 23–7 by 14-point underdog Kansas City. In particular, the Chiefs' very large defensive line overwhelmed the smaller Vikings' offensive line all day.

If these three teams had avoided the stumble at the finish line, I might have put them all in the book. However, as much of a Baltimore boy as I am, I don't think even I would have liked having three Colts' teams from an 11-season span to get in. It would have meant a lot more work for me, but then no one could say that I had forgotten the '60s.

The Core of the Packers

The transformation of the Packers under Vince Lombardi was truly amazing. Even though his first NFL coaching job was running the offense of the New York Giants from 1954 through 1958, the perception of Lombardi as a head coach that exists today was that of someone who wanted his offense not to lose the game so that his defense could win the game. In the classic *Run to Daylight!*, when talking about the beginning of his tenure as head coach, Lombardi said, "Our primary need was for defensive help because there is nothing more demoralizing to a whole squad than to see the opposition run roughshod over you." As is true of many perceptions, however, this one is not completely consistent with the facts. From 1960 through 1964 the Packers were comfortably above the league average in yards gained each year.

It is true, however, that while Lombardi was head coach, their defense was the core of the Packers. He helped transform the Packers defense into one of the most consistently excellent units in NFL history. The Packers' Defense Power Index (DPI) was +2.00 or higher for seven consecutive seasons from 1961 through 1967. That is the longest such string in the NFL since 1950. Keep in mind that only 13.6 percent of all teams since 1950 have produced a DPI of +2.00 or higher. That means that, on average, a little less than one season out of seven will have a Defense Power Index at that level; the Packers had seven out of seven.

The following list shows all of the teams that have had a DPI of +2.00 or higher for a minimum of five consecutive seasons:

Years	Team	Consecutive Years with +2.00 DPI
1961–1967	Green Bay Packers	7
1973–1978	Los Angeles Rams	6
1972–1976	Pittsburgh Steelers	5

That's a short list, folks. The Bears might have made the list if 1987 hadn't been a strike year, but I didn't want to count a season where 20 percent of the games were played by replacement players. Chicago did have a DPI of +2.00 or higher in 1984, 1985, 1986, and 1988. (See "The 46 Defense" in the 1985 Bears' chapter.)

The Packers' defense of the 1960s had five eventual Hall of Famers: defensive linemen Willie Davis and Henry Jordan, linebacker Ray Nitschke, and defensive backs Herb Adderley and Willie Wood. While the 1970s Steelers' defense could conceivably end up with one or two more players in the Hall of Fame, right now they have "only" four: defensive lineman Joe Greene, linebackers Jack Ham and Jack Lambert, and defensive back Mel Blount. By this measure, at least, the Packers' defense under Lombardi is more celebrated than the famous Steel Curtain.

All of the Packer defenders in the Hall of Fame have an interesting story. Without turning this into *War and Peace*... Willie Davis was a fifteenth-round pick of the Browns in 1956 from Grambling, but Davis did not suit up until 1958 because he served two years in the Army. He then spent two years with the Browns, where he actually played a fair number of snaps

Transcendental Graphics

From left to right, Paul Hornung, Vince Lombardi, Bart Starr, and Jim Taylor

on the offensive line. In 1960, he was traded to Green Bay for receiver A. D. Williams. Williams caught 1 pass in his only year with the Browns and was out of the NFL by 1962.

Henry Jordan was also drafted by the Browns. He was taken in the fifth round of the 1957 draft with a pick that ironically first belonged to Green Bay. After playing in Cleveland for two seasons, he was traded to the Packers in 1959 for a fourth-round draft pick. He was a consensus All-Pro selection from 1960 through 1964 and played in four Pro Bowls. Jordan had more responsibility for rushing the passer than most defensive tackles of his day and he was very good at it. Unfortunately, his post-retirement life was short; Jordan died of a heart attack in 1977 at the age of 42.

Ray Nitschke was drafted by the Packers as a fullback from the University of Illinois in 1958, the year before Lombardi arrived. He switched to linebacker as a rookie, which made him very happy because it enabled him to hit people more. Not to sound melodramatic, but Nitschke had a tough childhood: "My father died when I was three and my mother when I was fourteen, so I took it out on all of the other kids in the neighborhood. That's what I like about this game—the contact, the man-to-man, and you get it out of your system."

Willie Wood wasn't even drafted. He had been USC's starting quarterback for two seasons, but he was passed over in the 1960 draft because he was considered a player without a position. Realizing that his future in pro football, if he was to have one at all, was at defensive back, Wood wrote letters to three teams offering his services at that position. The Packers were the only team to answer.

The Packers drafted Herb Adderley in the first round in 1961 from Michigan State. Lombardi initially played him at wide receiver with no results before discovering that Adderley wanted to be a defensive back. "It scares me to remember how I almost mishandled him," Lombardi said, "to make something of him that he did not want to be." Adderley was a fine kick returner and very dangerous after he intercepted a pass; he returned 7 of his 48 career interceptions for touchdowns.

Altogether, a dozen different Packer defensive players made a total of 32 Pro Bowl appearances during Lombardi's tenure as head coach. Maybe the *real* core of the Packers was Lombardi, but the playing core of the team was their defense.

The Coach: Vince Lombardi

Coaching Record (with Packers Only)

	W	L	T	Pct	
1959	7	5	0	.583	
1960	8	4	0	.667	NFL Western Conference title
1961	11	3	0	.786	NFL Western Conference title; NFL champs
1962	13	1	0	.929	NFL Western Conference title; NFL champs
1963	11	2	1	.821	
1964	8	5	1	.607	
1965	10	3	1	.750	NFL Western Conference title; NFL champs
1966	12	2	0	.857	NFL Western Conference title; NFL & Super Bowl champs
1967	9	4	1	.679	NFL Western Conference title; NFL & Super Bowl champs
Total	**89**	**29**	**4**	**.746**	

Forgive me for repeating some of the material from the introduction to this chapter, but I think it's worth reiterating. In 1958, Green Bay's record was 1–10–1, a .125 winning percentage if the tie is counted as a half-win/half-loss. In 1962, Green Bay was 13–1, a .929 winning percentage. They are the only team since 1950 whose winning percentage improved by .800 or more in a four-season span.

Many teams have dramatic one-year improvements, but often regress or stall in the following season. Since 1950, 71 teams have had a year-to-year improvement of .300 or more in their winning percentage; 50 of those teams had a worse record the year after they "improved."

The general tendency for teams to regress towards the mean makes Lombardi's achievements so amazing. The Packers were better immediately, and they kept getting better.

Simply put, Lombardi was a legend whose presence is still felt in NFL locker rooms, and, because of his powerful words and work ethic, is quoted in many board rooms as well. I can't add anything to the body of knowledge about Lombardi. I'll just make some observations.

The media often "over-distills" Lombardi into a one-dimensional image as a quasityrant. The remark of the late Henry Jordan, former Packers' defensive tackle, "Yeah, he's fair. He treats us all like dogs," is often repeated. Lombardi was driven, and demanded a lot from his players and staff. While Lombardi may have never said, "Winning isn't everything, it's the only thing," he was certainly obsessed with winning. (What Lombardi often did say was, "Winning isn't everything, but making the effort to win is.")

As David Maraniss so clearly explains in *When Pride Still Mattered,* Lombardi was far more complicated than the popular image of him. First, he often struggled making important personal decisions, which runs contrary to the Lombardi image. He even wavered after the Packers formally offered him the job as head coach. Maraniss wrote, "As usual, once he had made a tentative decision that would take his life in a new direction, Lombardi faltered, his normal air of certitude suddenly vanished, and he became a contradictory mess, torn between impulsiveness and introspection, hardheaded self-interest and sentimentality... he could see all sides of an argument but no right side."

Lombardi was tough, but he was not inflexible. In fact, his ability to adjust when necessary was a large factor in his success. His early relationship with Bart Starr is a good example. In 1960, Lombardi's second season, he exploded at Starr during a practice for throwing an interception. Starr confronted Lombardi in his office afterward saying, "You're asking me to be the leader of this team and I'm challenged by that and I want to be the best leader I can be. But I can't be if you're chewing my butt out in front of the team you want me to lead. I can take any ass-chewing you want to deliver, but please do it in the privacy of your office where you can make your apologies to me. I will be an even better leader for you if you do that." Lombardi simply replied, "I hear you," and never again criticized Starr in front of the team. Starr marks that moment as the beginning of his "unbelievable" relationship with Lombardi.

Lombardi did not lead by brute force. He was an excellent teacher because he explained plays and strategy in a way that every player in the room could understand. He also explained the reason, the logic for doing what he wanted the team to do. He never said, in the way that many autocrats do, "We're doing this because I say so."

Lombardi had been a high school teacher (as well as a coach) at St. Cecilia's High School in Englewood, New Jersey. As basketball coach at St. Cecilia's (one of Lombardi's many responsibilities) one of Lombardi's players was Mickey Corcoran. Corcoran would later become Bill Parcells's high school coach. About Lombardi, Corcoran said, "He understood human behavior better than any person I've ever met." That part of Lombardi's makeup is not as well known as some of the other elements. Jerry Kramer, star guard for Lombardi's Packers, said, "He wanted you emotionally involved. And he would tug and push and pull and pat and hug and caress and kiss–do whatever he had to do. And he seemed to have a great ability to reach inside you and turn your motor on."

I am not trying to ignore Lombardi's shortcomings. He had them, I have them, we all do. People are more complicated than sound bites or video clips. Some in the media dwell on faults and frailties. Lombardi was aware of his own. Lombardi's son, Vincent, explained it well, "He went to Mass to repent for his anger. He thought, 'I've got this temper. I fly off the handle and offend people. I apologize. But it's this temper that keeps me on edge and allows me to get things done and people to do things.' Life was a struggle for him. He knew he wasn't perfect. He had a lot of habits that were far from perfect. His strengths were his weaknesses and vice versa."

The reason I think Lombardi is the greatest coach in pro football history is not just his impeccable on-field record. I think he was the greatest coach because it seems to me that he left the most lasting impression on his players. Many of his ex-players still say that a day doesn't go by when they don't think about Lombardi. Most of them credit him for whatever success they've had after football. In trying to distinguish among the most successful coaches in NFL history, all of whom have excellent won-lost records, it seems that this extra dimension separates Lombardi from the rest.

The Quarterback: Bart Starr

Year	Team	Att	Comp	Yds	TD	Int	YPA	Rating	Lg Avg	W	L	Pct
1956	GB	44	24	325	2	3	7.39	65.1	59.6	0	1	.000
1957	GB	215	117	1,489	8	10	6.93	69.3	63.2	2	7	.222
1958	GB	157	78	875	3	12	5.57	41.2	65.3	0	4	.000
1959	GB	134	70	972	6	7	7.25	69.0	66.9	4	2	.667
1960	GB	172	98	1,358	4	8	4.90	70.8	64.2	4	3	.571
1961	GB	295	172	2,418	16	16	8.20	80.3	68.5	11	3	.786
1962	GB	285	178	2,438	12	9	8.55	90.7	72.6	13	1	.929
1963	GB	244	132	1,855	15	10	7.60	82.3	71.7	9	1	.900
1964	GB	272	163	2,144	15	4	7.88	97.1	71.7	8	5	.615
1965	GB	251	140	2,055	16	9	8.49	89.0	73.5	10	3	.769
1966	GB	251	156	2,257	14	3	8.99	105.0	67.4	11	2	.846
1967	GB	210	115	1,823	9	17	8.68	64.4	66.6	9	3	.750
1968	GB	171	109	1,617	15	8	9.46	104.3	68.7	4	7	.364

Year	Team	Att	Comp	Yds	TD	Int	YPA	Rating	Lg Avg	W	L	Pct
1969	GB	148	92	1,161	9	6	7.84	89.9	71.6	5	5	.500
1970	GB	255	140	1,645	8	13	6.45	63.9	65.6	5	5	.500
1971	GB	45	24	286	0	3	6.36	45.2	62.2	0	2	.000
Total		**3,149**	**1,808**	**24,718**	**152**	**138**	**7.85**	**80.5**	**67.6**	**95**	**54**	**.638**
1961–66		1,598	941	13,167	88	51	8.24	90.5	70.9	62	15	.805

YPA = Yards Per Pass Attempt
Rating = Passer Rating
Lg Avg = League Passer Rating in that season
W, L, PctT = Team's Record in his starts

- Seventeenth-round pick by Green Bay, 199th overall, in 1956.
- In my opinion, it's ridiculous that the NFL doesn't retroactively recognize the leader in passing rating, the current system, for all years since 1933. Anyway, the NFL recognizes Bart Starr as the league passing leader in 1962, 1964, and 1966 under the system then in use. By the current system, Starr led the league in 1964, 1966, and 1968, although under current rules, which set 14 pass attempts per scheduled game as the minimum for qualifying, he didn't throw enough passes to qualify in 1968.
- Named NFL MVP by the Associated Press in 1966.
- Named MVP of the first two Super Bowls.
- Earned four Pro Bowl berths: after the 1960, 1961, 1962, and 1966 seasons.

As you can tell from the number of decisions as a starter, Vince Lombardi didn't immediately make Starr the starting quarterback when he took over as head coach in 1959. In *Run to Daylight!* Lombardi revealed one reason why that was the case, "When I first met him [Starr] he struck me as so polite and so self-effacing that I wondered if maybe he wasn't too nice a boy to be the authoritarian leader that your quarterback must be." Lombardi also said, "After looking at the movies that first preseason I came to the conclusion that he did have the ability—the arm, the ball-handling techniques and the intelligence—but what he needed was confidence."

Late in the 1959 season, with Lamar McHan injured and Joe Francis ineffective, Lombardi made Starr the starting quarterback. The Packers won their last four games to finish with their first winning record since 1947, and the rest of the league played second fiddle to the Packers for much of the next decade.

Bart Starr never threw as many as 300 passes in a regular season in his career. Lombardi's offense was based on the run and had the reputation for being conservative. While granting that teams who are leading, like Lombardi's Packers usually were, run the ball to control the clock and manage the lead, I thought it would be instructive to see where Green Bay ranked in pass attempts during Lombardi's tenure. Here it is:

Year	Pass Attempts	Green Bay Rank
1959	268	11 (of 12)
1960	279	11 (of 13)
1961	306	14 (of 14)
1962	311	14 (of 14)
1963	345	13 (of 14)
1964	321	14 (of 14)
1965	306	14 (of 14)
1966	318	15 (of 15)
1967	331	15 (of 16)

No noise in that data. I think the Packers' success influenced generations of football coaches and still does to this day. When coaches talk about the key to winning being running the ball, controlling the clock, and playing great defense, they are really talking about the Lombardi Packers. However, throwing infrequently doesn't mean throwing without success. Here is how they ranked in yards per pass attempt:

Year	Yards per Pass Attempt	Rank
1959	7.32	7 (of 12)
1960	7.14	6 (of 13)
1961	8.18	4 (of 14)
1962	8.43	2 (of 14)
1963	7.86	5 (of 14)
1964	7.74	3 (of 14)
1965	8.20	3 (of 14)
1966	8.90	1 (of 15)
1967	8.33	1 (of 16)

Enough said, the Packers had an effective passing game under Lombardi and Starr. I also think it's interesting to note that in 1966 and 1967, when the Packers' running game was not as effective as it had been earlier in Lombardi's tenure, Green Bay led the league in yards per pass attempt. The "counterargument" is that the Packers were still committed to running the ball and that commitment set up the passing game. By the way, the aggregate record of the teams that led the league in yards per pass attempt from 1959–1967 was 86–34–2, with three NFL titles and six appearances in the NFL Championship Game.

1962 Green Bay Packers Statistics

Passing

	Att	Comp	Comp Pct	Yds	Yds Per	TD	Int	Rating
Starr	285	178	62.5%	2,438	8.55	12	9	90.7
Roach	12	3	25.0%	33	2.75	0	0	34.4
Hornung	6	4	66.7%	80	13.33	0	2	70.1
Moore	5	2	40.0%	70	14.00	2	1	87.5
Pitts	2	0	0.0%	0	0.00	0	0	39.6
McGee	1	0	0.0%	0	0.00	0	1	0.0
Packers	**311**	**187**	**60.1%**	**2,621**	**8.43**	**14**	**13**	**84.9**
Opponents	355	187	52.7%	2,084	5.87	10	31	43.4
League Average			53.2%		7.85			72.6

Packers' passers were sacked 36 times for 290 yards in losses.
The Packers sacked their opponents 42 times for 338 yards in losses.

Mixing measuring methods (I have to employ some alliteration in the book somewhere) makes Starr's season look even better. Using the current NFL passing rating system with the 1962 qualifying number of passes, Starr was second in the NFL in passing behind Eddie LeBaron of the Cowboys (95.4 rating); LeBaron shared time at quarterback with Don Meredith.

The last team to have a defensive INT/TD ratio of better than 3-to-1 was the 1988 Vikings. In today's NFL that just doesn't happen. The 1962 Packers were the eleventh team since 1950 to accomplish the feat.

Rushing

	Att	Yds	Avg	Net Yards	TD
Taylor	272	1,474	5.42	+367	19
Moore	112	377	3.37	−79	7
Hornung	57	219	3.84	−13	5
Gros	29	155	5.34		2
Pitts	22	110	5.00		2
Starr	21	72	3.43		1
McGee	3	52	17.33		0
Roach	1	5	5.00		0
R. Kramer	1	−4	−4.00		0
Packers	**518**	**2,460**	**4.75**	**+352**	**36**
Opponents	404	1,531	3.79	−113	4
League Average			4.07		

Those rushing touchdown numbers are not typos; the Packers had 36 rushing TDs—still the NFL record—and allowed just 4, the fewest allowed (along with the 1969 and 1970 Vikings) by an NFL team since 1950. The 2000 Ravens allowed 5 rushing touchdowns in 16 games.

This was Jim Taylor's best season; 1962 was also the only year that Jim Brown was in the league that he didn't lead in rushing yardage. Not that most of you have any frame of reference for this—and that is not a knock on you as much as it is on me for caring about this stuff—but a net yards figure of +300 or better is truly exceptional. The next season, 1963, was Jim Brown's best year, and his net rushing yards figure was +684. Barry Sanders was +720 in 1997, but he had two extra games. Brown's 1963 net yards per scheduled game is the best in NFL history, not counting Beattie Feathers's disputed rushing totals from 1934.

Receiving

	Rec	Yds	Avg	TD
McGee	49	820	16.73	3
Dowler	49	724	14.78	2
R. Kramer	37	555	15.00	7
Taylor	22	106	4.82	0
Moore	11	100	9.09	0
Hornung	9	168	18.67	2
Carpenter	7	104	14.86	0
Pitts	3	44	14.67	0
Packers	**187**	**2,621**	**14.02**	**14**
Opponents	187	2,084	11.14	10
League Average			14.75	

Given their relatively low number of pass attempts, it's not surprising that no Packers' receiver ranked in the top five in the league in either number of catches or yards receiving.

Paul Hornung scored 7 touchdowns on 66 "touches" (rushing attempts and receptions) in 1962, the only back that year to average at least 1 touchdown per 10 touches with a minimum of 60 touches. Of course, scoring 7 touchdowns on 66 attempts from scrimmage is not the same as scoring 19 touchdowns on 294 touches, which is what Jim Taylor did. I bring this up because Hornung had a reputation of being able to "smell" the end zone, of being very tough to stop near the goal line. Whether that's true or whether he scored a lot of touchdowns *because* he had that reputation and, therefore, got a lot of attempts in the red zone, I can't say.

It is true that Hornung scored a lot of touchdowns for the number of times he handled the ball. In 1960, when Hornung set the single-season scoring record with 176 points in 12 games, he scored 15 touchdowns on 188 touches. In 1961, he scored 10 touchdowns on 142 touches. So, for 1960–62 Hornung scored 32 touchdowns on just 396 combined rushes and receptions, a very high percentage (8.1 percent). In 2000, Marshall Faulk set the single-season record scoring 26 touchdowns. His touchdown "percentage" was 7.8 percent.

Kickoff Returns

	Ret	Yds	Avg	TD
Adderley	15	418	27.87	1
Moore	13	284	21.85	0
Gros	1	7	7.00	0
Nitschke	1	7	7.00	0
Packers	**30**	**716**	**23.87**	**1**
Opponents	76	1,524	20.05	0
League Average			23.70	

The Packers led the NFL in kickoff coverage in 1962. Herb Adderley finished third in the league in kickoff return average behind San Francisco's Abe Woodson and New York's Johnny Counts, both of whom averaged 30+ yards per return.

Punt Returns

	Ret	Yds	Avg	TD
Wood	23	273	11.87	0
Pitts	7	17	2.43	0
Kostelnik	1	0	0.00	0
Packers	**31**	**290**	**9.35**	**0**
Opponents	20	183	9.15	0
League Average			8.20	

Interceptions

	Int	Yds	Avg	TD
Wood	9	132	14.67	0
Adderley	7	132	18.86	1
Gremminger	5	88	17.60	0
Nitschke	4	56	14.00	0

(continued next page)

Interceptions *(continued)*

	Int	Yds	Avg	TD
Whittenton	3	40	13.33	0
Quinlan	1	4	4.00	0
Hanner	1	1	1.00	0
Jordan	1	0	0.00	0
Packers	**31**	**452**	**14.58**	**1**
Opponents	13	122	9.38	0

The Packers intercepted the most passes of any team in the NFL in 1962 and intercepted the highest percentage of their opponents' passes. Willie Wood's 9 interceptions also led the league.

Turnovers

Turnovers Committed:	28
Turnovers Forced:	50
Turnover +/–:	+22

At +22, Green Bay easily led the league in turnover margin. The next best team, Detroit, was +5.

Punting

	No	Avg
Dowler	36	43.1
McGee	14	35.4
Packers	**50**	**40.9**
Opponents	58	43.2
League Average		42.0

Kicking

	XP	XPA	XP Pct	FG	FGA	FG Pct
J. Kramer	38	39	97.4%	9	11	81.8%
Hornung	14	14	100.0%	6	10	60.0%
Packers	**52**	**53**	**98.1%**	**15**	**21**	**71.4%**
Opponents	17	17	100.0%	9	22	40.9%
League Average			95.4%			49.5%

Leading Scorer: Jim Taylor, 114 Points

The Packers led the NFL in percentage of field goals made and "allowed" the lowest. Maybe Vince Lombardi scared the opposing kickers. I'm being a little facetious: the NFL doesn't keep any official records for blocked kicks and the game accounts don't always report every field-goal try, but it is possible that the Packers blocked more than their share of their opponents' field-goal attempts.

1962 Green Bay Packers Roster

Head Coach	Vince Lombardi		
QB	John Roach	DE	Willie Davis
QB	Bart Starr	DE	Bill Quinlan
RB	Earl Gros	DT/DE	Ron Gassert
RB/K	Paul Hornung	DT	Dave Hanner
RB/KR	Tom Moore	DT	Henry Jordan
RB/PR	Elijah Pitts	DT	Ron Kostelnik
RB	Jim Taylor	LB	Dan Currie
WR	Gary Barnes	LB	Bill Forester
WR	Lew Carpenter	LB	Ray Nitschke
WR/P	Boyd Dowler	LB	Nelson Toburen
WR/P	Max McGee	DB/KR	Herb Adderley
TE	Gary Knafelc	DB	Hank Gremminger
TE	Ron Kramer	DB	John Symank
C	Ken Iman	DB	Jesse Whittington
C	Jim Ringo	DB	Howie Williams
OG	Ed Blaine	DB/PR	Willie Wood
OG/K	Jerry Kramer		
OG	Fred "Fuzzy" Thurston		
OT	Forrest Gregg		
OT	Norm Masters		
OT	Bob Skoronski		

Hall of Famers: Lombardi, Starr, Hornung, Taylor, Ringo, Gregg, Davis, Jordan, Nitschke, Adderley, Wood.

Not that this has anything to do with anything, but look at the last names of who were usually the first two players to touch the ball on a Packers' offensive play: (Jim) Ringo, (Bart) Starr. And 1962 was the year Ringo Starr joined the Beatles–remember the '60s, indeed.

CHAPTER 4

1971 Dallas Cowboys: From Next Year's Champions to America's Team

Many of you reading this are not old enough to know that before the Cowboys became "America's Team," there were a number of seasons where many people called them "Next Year's Champions." Yes, that nickname was a putdown. When the Cowboys first made the playoffs and then lost two epic NFL Championship Games to Vince Lombardi's Packers in 1966 and 1967, there were fans and media alike that thought Dallas couldn't win the "Big One." Still, that was not the majority opinion. I mean, hey, they lost to the Packers.

STARTING LINEUP – 1971 COWBOYS			
Offense		**Defense**	
SE	Bob Hayes	LE	Larry Cole
LT	Tony Liscio	LT	Jethro Pugh
LG	John Niland	RT	Bob Lilly
C	Dave Manders	RE	George Andrie
RG	Blaine Nye	LLB	Dave Edwards
RT	Rayfield Wright	MLB	Lee Roy Jordan
TE	Mike Ditka	RLB	Chuck Howley
FL	Lance Alworth	LCB	Herb Adderley
QB	Roger Staubach	RCB	Mel Renfro
RB	Calvin Hill/Walt Garrison	SS	Cornell Green
RB	Duane Thomas	FS	Cliff Harris

After upset first-round playoff losses to the Browns in 1968 and 1969 and a last-second loss to the Colts in Super Bowl V, the criticism grew. Tom Landry even thought that the team's postseason defeats had a cumulative effect, saying, "The most difficult championship to win is the first one. After a club knows it is capable of winning, it gains a great deal of confidence in important games. Success breed success . . . failure, like success, has a carryover effect . . . after the loss to Cleveland [in 1968] we continued to be at a big psychological disadvantage in the playoffs and lost again."

Coming into the 1971 season, at least one Cowboy sensed a change. Star running back Calvin Hill made note of the differences as Dallas finished its exhibition season, "This team has a different attitude. Instead of going into a game with a defensive attitude, we are now going with the attitude that we are going to win. It's fantastic and we are going to get better and better."

With their first Super Bowl win in the 1971 season, the Cowboys shook off the label as "chokers" and "Next Year's Champions." The midseason move to Texas Stadium also helped to change the national image of the team. While the Cowboys weren't "officially" dubbed America's Team until an NFL Films editor put that name on their 1977 highlight film, in many ways the 1971 season represented the start of the Dallas glory years that led to the nickname.

Team in a Box

Record: 11–3

The Cowboys won their last seven games after Tom Landry installed Roger Staubach as the starting quarterback, instead of alternating Staubach with Craig Morton.

The Cowboys' 1966–1971 record was 63–19–2. Their 63 wins was the most by any NFL team during this period; their winning percentage, if ties are counted as a half-win/half loss, equaled the Colts' as the best at .762.

Against Teams Over .500: 2–1, 57 Points Scored, 41 Points Allowed

The Cowboys did not have a particularly tough schedule in 1971. Their three games against teams with winning records were the two against the Redskins, which they split, and one with the Rams.

Points Scored/Allowed: 406/222 (1971 NFL Average: 271)

As you might have guessed, given the Cowboys' points scored total relative to the league, Dallas easily led the NFL in scoring in 1971. They scored 62 more points than the second best team, the Raiders, and 91 more than the fourth best team, their Super Bowl opponent, the Dolphins.

Yards Gained/Allowed: 5,035/3,468 (1971 NFL Average: 4,002)

Dallas was the only team with 5,000+ yards of total offense. Their +111.9 per-game yardage differential ranks thirteenth among all NFL teams since 1950.

Opponents' Record: 74–99–9, .431

(Not counting games against the Cowboys; ties counted as half-win/half loss.)

The Cowboys had the third easiest regular season schedule among the 12 teams in the book. It also ranks among the easiest 3 percent of all schedules since 1950.

Adjusted Power Index:

Offense: +4.71
Defense: +1.90
TOTAL: +6.61

The 1971 Cowboys are one of the great but underrated offensive teams in NFL history, at least as measured by Power Index. Their Offense Power Index (OPI) ranks ninth best among all teams since 1950.

Innovations/What You Should Know:

As pointed pointed out elsewhere in this book, head coach Tom Landry was an innovator. Landry developed the Umbrella defense, the beginning of the modern 4–3. He brought in multiple formations with motion so the offense could disguise its intentions. He brought back the Shotgun, which is used today by most NFL teams.

Yet, Landry's "innovation" for 1971 backfired. In their game against the Bears, Landry alternated quarterbacks Craig Morton and Roger Staubach on almost every play. The Cowboys lost, and Landry named Staubach as his "permanent" starting quarterback. My point? No one knows everything about anything.

Texas Stadium opened in the middle of the 1971 season. The facility, built for $35 million, was the first to have a considerable number of luxury suites—381, to be exact. This put the Cowboys ahead of other NFL teams at the time in generating revenue from premium seating, something that is now taken for granted in new stadiums. Texas Stadium, however, was built before club seats became popular, which helps explain the desire of current Cowboys' ownership to acquire a new stadium with luxury suites, club seats, and all of the amenities seen in newer venues.

Transcendental Graphics

Roger Staubach

Homegrown First-Round Picks:

DT Bob Lilly, 1961; LB Lee Roy Jordan, 1963; QB Craig Morton, 1965; OG John Niland, 1966; RB Calvin Hill, 1969; RB Duane Thomas, 1970; DE Tody Smith, 1971.

That's a damn good collection of players. Lilly was the Cowboys' first first-round draft choice ever (as the franchise joined the league too late to participate in the 1960 draft). He developed into one of the greatest defensive players in NFL history.

Lilly, Jordan, Niland, and Hill earned a total of 26 Pro Bowl berths.

Pro Bowl Players:

DB Cornell Green, LB Chuck Howley, DT Bob Lilly, OG John Niland, DB Mel Renfro, QB Roger Staubach, P Ron Widby.

Game-by-Game:

Sep. 19th COWBOYS 49, BUFFALO 37 AT BUFFALO

A September 19 headline in the *Dallas Morning News* read, "Cowboys Ready to Outscore Bills." That's exactly what they did as Dallas scored two fourth-quarter touchdowns to overcome Buffalo QB Dennis Shaw's 353 yards passing and 4 TDs. The Bills led 14–7 at the end of the first quarter, trailed only 28–24 at halftime and 35–30 at the end of three quarters.

The wild game belied the fact that it was played in a quagmire. The rain and mud might actually have helped both quarterbacks, as the weather seemed to neutralize both teams' pass rush. The game saw three pass plays of over 70 yards, two by Buffalo (both of which were made possible by collisions between two Dallas defenders).

What won the game was the Cowboys' offensive balance. Calvin Hill and Walt Garrison combined for 162 yards on 38 carries, with Hill tying the team record by scoring 4 touchdowns. Craig Morton was 10 of 14, for 221 yards, 2 touchdowns, and no interceptions. The Bills, on the other hand, could not run the ball. O. J. Simpson (who?) gained just 25 yards on 14 carries.

Sep. 26th COWBOYS 42, PHILADELPHIA 7 AT PHILADELPHIA

Dallas intercepted seven Philadelphia passes, holding the Eagles to just 32 yards on the ground and 170 overall in a rout. Herb Adderley had three picks.

Craig Morton had another effective day after replacing an injured Roger Staubach; Morton completed 15 of 22 passes for 188 yards and 2 touchdowns, although, he also threw 2 interceptions. Staubach missed the season opener due to a leg injury and missed most of this game with a concussion.

The Eagles didn't score until the final two minutes, when Al Nelson returned a missed field goal 101 yards for a touchdown. He was no stranger to this; Nelson ran back a missed field goal 100 yards for a touchdown in 1966.

Oct. 3rd WASHINGTON 20, COWBOYS 16 AT DALLAS (COTTON BOWL)

Playing in a downpour for the third straight week, Dallas's defensive front seven was dominated by the Redskins' offensive line as Washington ran for 200 yards to beat the Cowboys. Dallas head coach Tom Landry was succinct when he said, "Washington just blew our people out of there." Dallas All-Pro defensive tackle Bob Lilly said, "Well, that brought us back to reality."

Meanwhile, the Cowboys could not run the ball, managing just 82 yards on the ground and averaging less than 3 yards per rush. The loss left Dallas in the unfamiliar position of looking up at a team above them in the standings as the Redskins moved to 3–0.

Oct. 11th COWBOYS 20, NEW YORK GIANTS 13 AT DALLAS

In a sloppy performance that saw the return of Duane Thomas to the Cowboys' lineup (see "Calvin Hill"), a 48-yard touchdown pass from Craig Morton to Bob Hayes with 3:40 left in the third quarter proved to be the difference. Thomas played on special teams in the first half, but returned to the backfield in the second half after Calvin Hill suffered a knee injury early in the third quarter and did not return. Showing his natural talents, Thomas gained 60 yards rushing on 9 carries despite having practiced for less than two weeks after returning from his holdout.

Dallas won despite committing six turnovers, but the Giants were almost as bad, turning the ball over five times themselves. Roger Staubach was replaced in the second half. As he put it, "I wouldn't have exactly made the Pro Bowl in the first half."

Oct. 17th NEW ORLEANS 24, COWBOYS 14 AT NEW ORLEANS

Despite second-half heroics from Roger Staubach, who replaced an ineffective Craig Morton in the third quarter, Dallas could not overcome a 17–0 halftime deficit and was upset by the Saints. The second New Orleans touchdown was set up by Al Dodd's 77-yard return of a missed Cowboys' field goal. Remember Al Nelson?

Morton was just 10 of 24 for 113 yards and 2 interceptions; Staubach was 7 of 10 for 117 yards and 2 touchdowns. Even though he benched Morton, Tom Landry didn't put all of the blame on him, "I really don't think it was that much the quarterback's fault. Craig was under a lot of pressure and we didn't run well."

Despite their poor start, the Cowboys may have been able to pull the game out, but were hurt when Charley Waters fumbled a punt at midfield with 11 minutes left in the game after Dallas had cut the New Orleans lead to 17–14. To be fair to Waters, he fumbled only after teammate John Fitzgerald backed into him. The Saints recovered at their own 49.

The loss dropped the Cowboys two games behind the 5–0 Redskins.

Oct. 24th COWBOYS 44, NEW ENGLAND 21 AT DALLAS (TEXAS STADIUM)

The Cowboys opened their new stadium with an easy win over the Patriots. On the fourth play of the game, Blaine Nye and Rayfield Wright made great blocks that sprung Duane Thomas loose for a 56-yard touchdown run. Roger Staubach, starting this week in the "my turn–your turn" quarterback position, threw 2 TD passes to Bob Hayes in the second quarter as Dallas took a 34–7 halftime lead.

Commenting on his status as quarterback, Staubach said after the game, "I don't think I hurt myself, but I'm still leery. You can have a good day like today and be washed out if you don't play well the next week." Staubach completed 13 of 21 passes for 197 yards. Hayes commented, "I think this game is just what we needed. I think this game is the one for us, the one to get things off." Hayes's comments proved to be just a little premature.

Oct. 31st CHICAGO 23, COWBOYS 19 AT CHICAGO

With the exception of Dallas's two-minute drill at the end of the first half and the last half of the fourth quarter, Tom Landry alternated Craig Morton and Roger Staubach at quarterback on every play. So, even though the Cowboys outgained the Bears 481 yards to 194, maybe the football "karma" was so messed up that Dallas had to lose. Seven turnovers didn't help, either.

Landry defended the way he used his quarterbacks, saying that it seemed to work because his team moved the ball. Regardless, he was not happy at the outcome, "I am very disappointed. . . . There is such a fine line between winning and losing and this year we're on the wrong side. We'll just try to win our next seven games, one at a time." Little did he know . . .

Nov. 7th COWBOYS 16, ST. LOUIS 13 AT ST. LOUIS

Morton or Staubach? The Cowboys' players were divided. According to Bob St. John in his biography of Tom Landry, most of the offensive players wanted Morton because they felt he was steadier. The defensive players sided with Staubach because they felt he just had a knack for getting something done, whether or not it was by design. On the Tuesday before the Cardinals' game, Landry decided to go with Staubach as his unquestioned starter to remove the uncertainty that he thought might be hurting the team.

Although it wasn't pretty, the Cowboys beat St. Louis on a Toni Fritsch field goal with 1:53 left in the game. Staubach didn't have a spectacular day throwing the ball (20 of 31 for 199 yards), but he made enough plays with his arm and with his feet, rushing for 60 yards on 7 carries. Combined with Duane Thomas's 101 yards on the ground, the Cowboys played keep-away with the Cardinals. Lance Alworth had eight catches and Mike Ditka caught a 4-yard TD pass, after making a nice adjustment on his route, that gave Dallas a 13–10 lead in the fourth quarter. Alworth and Ditka were two of the four future Hall of Famers that Landry had brought to the Cowboys in the late 1960s and early 1970s.

Nov. 14th COWBOYS 20, PHILADELPHIA 7 AT DALLAS

"The last 20 minutes was the sorriest passing exhibition I've ever put on," Roger Staubach said of his of his second-half performance. He was a little hard on himself. Staubach had 90 yards rushing on 6 attempts, including an important 20-yard run on Dallas's only effective drive of the day, a 95-yard TD drive, which gave the Cowboys a 10–0 halftime lead.

Defensive tackles Bob Lilly and Jethro Pugh pressured Eagles' quarterbacks Rich Arrington and Pete Liske into several mistakes, including 2 interceptions. They also limited Philadelphia to 44 yards rushing on 18 attempts.

Nov. 21st COWBOYS 13, WASHINGTON 0 AT WASHINGTON

As Tom Landry had predicted beforehand, this game was a defensive struggle. On Dallas's first possession, they had moved 57 yards to the Washington 29, but faced a third-and-6. As Roger Staubach described the play later, "I was looking for Alworth, but I noticed the whole outside had been cleared out. Nobody was over there so I took off. I was lucky." Lucky or not, Staubach's 29-yard run was the only touchdown of the game and the Doomsday defense made it stand up. Landry said, "Roger's run was the key play to the whole game. It put us in front early and kept some of the pressure off the offense."

After allowing 200 rushing yards to Washington in the first game, Dallas limited the Redskins to just 65 yards on 21 carries, although the leg injury to Washington's star running back Larry Brown no doubt hampered his play. Speaking of injuries, the Cowboys' Calvin Hill returned after missing five games, but saw only limited action.

The win put Dallas back on top of the NFC East with a 7–3 record, a half-game ahead of the 6–3–1 Redskins.

Nov. 25th COWBOYS 28, LOS ANGELES 21 AT DALLAS

The Rams outplayed the Cowboys at the line of scrimmage, but three Rams' turnovers and Ike Thomas's 89-yard TD return of the opening kickoff helped Dallas to an important win in their annual Thanksgiving game.

Roger Staubach excelled despite a painful neck injury, running for 33 yards and completing 8 of 14 passes for 176 yards, 2 touchdowns, and no interceptions. Those numbers don't sound like much three decades later, but it was a good day for 1971 and it's always a good day when your quarterback averages over 12 yards per pass attempt. (As I've said before, yards per pass attempt is the most important passing statistic.)

Two of the Rams' turnovers happened in the first half with Los Angeles driving and in Dallas territory. The second turnover happened when Rams running back Larry Smith was hit hard by linebackers Chuck Howley and Lee Roy Jordan and fumbled after catching a pass from Roman Gabriel. The third Dallas linebacker, Dave Edwards, recovered at the Cowboys' 13-yard line.

Dec. 4th COWBOYS 52, NEW YORK JETS 10 AT DALLAS

For the second week in a row, Ike Thomas ran the opening kickoff back for a touchdown, this time for 101 yards. With Calvin Hill's return to full health, Tom Landry finally got to use his "dream" backfield of Hill and Duane Thomas. It's hard to say anything other than that it really worked. Thomas ran for 112 yards on 14 carries while Hill ran for 62 yards on 11 attempts and caught 4 passes for 80 yards and 2 TDs. The pair scored a total of 5 touchdowns. It might have been a dream for Landry, but Walt Garrison, the odd man out, felt a little differently: "Watching those two [Hill and Thomas] I felt like the bastard son at a family picnic."

Roger Staubach had another effective day, hitting 10 of 15 passes for 168 yards, 3 touchdowns, and no interceptions. In the five games since he was made "the" starting QB, Staubach had yet to throw an interception.

Dec. 12th COWBOYS 42, NEW YORK GIANTS 14 AT NEW YORK

Dallas rolled over its second New York team in two weeks and clinched a playoff berth. Roger Staubach threw 3 touchdown passes, including 46- and 85-yard scores to Bob Hayes. Calvin Hill and Duane Thomas rushed for 193 yards on just 29 carries.

Dec. 18th COWBOYS 31, ST. LOUIS 12 AT DALLAS

Roger Staubach finally threw an interception, but it didn't much matter. Duane Thomas had 144 total yards and 4 touchdowns and the defense kept St. Louis out of the end zone and gave up only 215 yards. Dallas won its seventh straight game to win the NFC East. This was the sixth consecutive season that Dallas finished first in its division or conference. (Prior to 1967 there were no divisions, just two NFL conferences.)

St. Louis's All-Pro safety Larry Wilson was very impressed by the Cowboys, "Dallas is the best team we've played all year. It's the best Dallas team I've played against. I think they've put it all together."

Divisional Playoff:

Dec. 25th COWBOYS 20, MINNESOTA 12 AT MINNESOTA

Despite their lowest offensive output of the season, 183 yards, the Cowboys beat the Vikings as the Dallas defense "collected" five Minnesota turnovers, converted them into 13 points, and kept Minnesota out of the red zone until the fourth quarter. Minnesota head coach Bud Grant took some criticism for starting third-year quarterback Bob Lee instead of the more experienced Gary Cuozzo (in his ninth season) or Norm Snead (in his eleventh). Cuozzo had seen most of the time at quarterback for the Vikings during the season and, taking over for Lee in the fourth quarter, he led Minnesota to its only touchdown of this game.

"Defense won the game," Staubach said. "On offense we did just enough, nothing more." The "just enough" included zero turnovers.

Dallas scored both of its touchdowns in the third quarter after leading 6–3 at the half. The first TD was set up by a Cliff Harris interception in Minnesota territory. The Cowboys caught the Vikings in a blitz and Duane Thomas found a running lane, going in virtually untouched from the 13-yard line. For most of the day, however, Minnesota stopped the Dallas running game; the Cowboys gained just 98 yards on 39 attempts. In the end, though, the plus-5 in the turnover department carried Dallas to the win.

NFC Championship:

Jan. 2nd COWBOYS 14, SAN FRANCISCO 3 AT DALLAS

Once again, the Dallas defense played a superb game, pushing the Cowboys to their second consecutive trip to the Super Bowl. The 49ers gained just 239 yards of offense and made only nine first downs, while Dallas picked off three John Brodie passes. The first interception, by Dallas defensive tackle George Andrie on a screen pass, set up the first score of the game after a scoreless first quarter. Unfortunately for San Francisco, Andrie intercepted the ball at the 49ers nine-yard line; he was tackled by Brodie at the 2. Andrie and fellow tackle Bob Lilly both read the screen and Lilly thought that he blocked Brodie's view enough so he didn't see Andrie near the intended receiver, Ken Willard. On second and goal, Calvin Hill went over from a yard out.

The two defenses controlled the game, but Dallas had an advantage: Staubach's ability to run. Although he was sacked six times, he was the Cowboys' leading rusher with 55 yards on eight tries. His running also started the Cowboys' lone TD drive of the day. Leading just 7–3 late in the third quarter with a third and seven on its own 23-yard line, the 49ers pass rush flushed Staubach out of the pocket. He scrambled, reversed field, and hit Dan Reeves for a 17-yard gain for the first down. As Reeves explained, "Dave Wilcox [49ers linebacker] was on me. When Roger started running back toward us, Wilcox didn't know what to do. He goes up to tackle Staubach and Roger could throw to me for a first down. He stays on me and Roger could run for a first down. He went up and couldn't get back when Roger threw me the ball." Ultimately, Dallas went 80 yards in 14 plays and scored on a Duane Thomas TD run with a little over nine minutes left in the game. The Cowboys' defense took it from there.

Super Bowl VI:

Jan. 16th COWBOYS 24, MIAMI 3 AT NEW ORLEANS

With their offensive line controlling the line of scrimmage and with their defense shutting down the vaunted Miami running attack, the Cowboys shook off five years of playoff frustrations with an easy win in Super Bowl VI. Through 2002, this was the only Super Bowl in which one of the teams was held to no touchdowns.

Mixing cutback running by the backs with a couple of reverses to slow Miami's pursuit, the Cowboys ran for 252 yards and averaged over 5 yards a carry. Duane Thomas and Walt Garrison, starting in place of Calvin Hill, who had re-injured his knee against San Francisco, combined for 169 yards on 33 attempts. Meanwhile, the Dolphins were held to just 80 yards on the ground. Of course, once Miami got behind it had to pass on those rare occasions when it got the ball. Dallas had averaged 161 rushing yards per game during the regular season; Miami had averaged 174 and allowed 119. The Cowboys ran 69 plays to just 44 for the Dolphins.

After the game, Miami head coach Don Shula said, "We never got untracked. The Dallas defense completely controlled our offense.... I was worried all along about stopping the Dallas running game. At times, there were some gaping holes in our defense, but it was the cutbacks that killed us."

Before the game, much talk had centered on the matchup between Dallas All-Pro cornerback Mel Renfro and Miami All-Pro wide receiver Paul Warfield. Afterwards Renfro said, "I don't mind saying that I feel like I won that one. (Warfield had 4 catches for just 39 yards.) That's all I heard all week from the writers, 'Warfield, Warfield, Warfield.' That was supposed to be the key to the whole game, whether I could cover him or not. Honestly, I got sick and tired of being asked about it." Part of the obsession with Warfield was President Nixon's suggestion to Don Shula that the "down-and-in" pass to Warfield would work.

Tom Landry talked about the meaning of the win, "It's a rewarding thing for the players. I'm more satisfied with having won for the benefit of the Howleys and the Lillys. I never had a chance to play on a championship team and I was afraid that maybe some of these guys would miss it, too. That's my greatest satisfaction." For better or for worse, this Super Bowl win was the beginning of the ascension of Dallas to the title of "America's Team."

Elsewhere Around the NFL:

Sep. 26th Chicago backup quarterback Kent Nix, replacing injured starter Jack Concannon, threw a 26-yard touchdown pass to All-Pro wide receiver Dick Gordon with 1:42 left to cap a 17-point fourth quarter rally as the Bears upset the defending NFC Central champion Vikings 20–17 at Minnesota. Chicago surprised observers and delighted their fans with a 5–2 start, but sagged to finish 6–8 and cost head coach Jim Dooley his job after four seasons.

Nov. 25th Thanksgiving, 1971. Even though it wasn't the NFL, I just didn't think I could write about the 1971 football season and not mention the Nebraska–Oklahoma game. In a classic matchup of unbeaten powerhouses that lived up to the pregame hype, the Cornhuskers beat the Sooners 35–31 at Norman in one of the greatest football games ever, college or pro.

Dec. 5th The Rams' Willie Ellison ran for an NFL record 247 yards as Los Angeles beat New Orleans 45–28 at the Coliseum. After seeing limited time in his first four NFL seasons, Ellison started in 1971, ran for exactly 1,000 yards, and made the Pro Bowl. He finished his career with 3,426 yards.

What Happened the Next Season:

In 1972, Dallas failed to win its division for the first time since 1965. George Allen's Over-the-Hill-Gang Redskins won the NFC East title. Dallas went 10–4 and made the playoffs, even with the shoulder injury that sidelined Roger Staubach for most of the season and despite the turmoil surrounding Duane Thomas, which led to his trade to the Chargers. In the playoffs, after an unbelievable comeback win over San Francisco orchestrated by Staubach, Dallas ran into an inspired Washington defense and lost the NFC Championship Game 26–3.

Bullet Bob

Some people know that Bob Hayes is the only person to win an Olympic gold medal and a Super Bowl ring. Others know that his Olympic medal earned him acclaim as the "World's Fastest Human." I don't think too many people, at least not those outside of Dallas, know much more about him. I just wanted to recap, very briefly, what he did on the field, especially during the prime of his career.

Hayes was not just a track star in a football uniform, he made a lot of game-breaking plays for the Cowboys. He caught 45 touchdown passes in his first four NFL seasons (1965–68); no other NFL receiver was within 10 TD receptions of him in the same time period.

His average per catch and touchdown per reception rate were outstanding. I know comparing his average to the overall average is a bit misleading because Hayes, a wide receiver, is being compared to running backs and tight ends. Still, look at the differences during his prime:

Year	Rec	Yds	Avg	LG Avg	TD	TD Pct	LG Pct
1965	46	1,003	21.80	14.55	12	26.1%	11.1%
1966	64	1,232	19.25	13.41	13	20.3%	8.9%
1967	49	998	20.37	13.61	10	20.4%	9.8%
1968	53	909	17.15	13.61	10	18.9%	10.5%
1969	40	746	18.65	13.27	4	10.0%	9.7%
1970	34	889	26.15	13.16	10	29.4%	8.5%
1971	35	840	24.00	13.21	8	22.9%	6.0%

Hayes led the league twice each in touchdown receptions and average per catch. In 1968, he led the league in punt return average–20.80, the last qualifying player to average 20+ yards per return–and touchdowns.

His post-football life has not been a smooth ride. Hayes is a recovering alcoholic and admitted former drug user who spent 10 months in prison in 1980 on a drug conviction that was later overturned. He has had serious medical problems–including prostate cancer–that almost killed him. All of those circumstances are fact, but so is what Hayes did on the football field.

Calvin Hill

It has been my great privilege to be Calvin Hill's friend since the late 1980s, when we both worked for the Baltimore Orioles. He is a person of integrity and intelligence, a combination of traits that often seems to be in short supply.

Calvin was born and raised in Baltimore, received a scholarship to the prestigious Riverdale Country Day School (high school) in the Bronx, then went on to star at Yale despite interest from more well-known football schools like UCLA and Michigan. The Cowboys surprised everybody (including Calvin, but more on that later) by taking him in the first round of the 1969 NFL draft.

As a rookie, he led the league in rushing up until the last week of the season when he had to miss the season finale with an injury. Nevertheless, he was NFL Rookie of the Year, a Pro Bowl selection, and a consensus All-Pro. He surpassed the 1,000-yard mark twice (1972 and 1973), making him the first Cowboy to reach that plateau.

After playing professional football for 13 seasons (including one year in the World Football League), Calvin has been involved in numerous endeavors, serving on the President's Council on Physical Fitness and as an assistant to the director of the Peace Corps. He has also been an executive and consultant for a number of major international corporations, banks and national organizations, including the NCAA Foundation, the Duke University Divinity School, the International Special Olympics, and the Dallas Cowboys.

Among the many awards he has received are the NCAA Silver Anniversary Award in 1994—the award recognizes six distinguished former student-athletes on their 25th anniversary as college graduates—as well as induction into the Maryland and Connecticut sports halls of fame. Calvin and Janet Hill are the parents of NBA superstar Grant Hill.

Calvin and I sat down in 2001 to talk about his career, the 1971 Cowboys, and other assorted topics.

Q: Did you expect to be drafted in the first round out of college?

Calvin: My hope was—I was planning on going to divinity school—I could sign with the Colts, my hometown team, as a free agent and possibly make $4,000 or $5,000, which back then was a lot of money, as a bonus in lieu of a summer job.

The draft wasn't televised in those days and it received very little coverage. That void let me play a joke on one of my Yale teammates, Bruce Weinstein, who was drafted by Miami that year. I called him pretending to be from the New York Giants and told him that he had been drafted in the second round. He bought it until I started laughing and then he was really pissed.

I got a call from Gil Brandt telling me that Dallas had picked me in the first round, but until Tom Landry got on the phone—he had an unmistakable voice—I wasn't sure that someone wasn't playing a joke on me. After talking to Landry, I was almost in shock.

Q: How do you remember the 1971 season?

Calvin: In some ways, it was a bittersweet year. The Duane Thomas situation was a major distraction. He wanted to renegotiate his contract, in part because he found out that a couple of players the Cowboys had drafted after him were making more money, so he held out of training camp. When he returned after the Cowboys refused to renegotiate, he didn't talk to anyone while at practice or during the games. I think he realized that he had some power by not saying anything, but after awhile it's sort of like having an argument with your wife, it gets silly and you try to figure a way out, but you still want to save face. He never could figure out how to get out of it.

Duane's absence from training camp gave me a chance to reestablish myself after a disappointing 1970 season, and I played well in the preseason and at the start of the regular season, but in the fourth game of the year I hurt my knee—Spider Lockhart of the Giants hit me low—and missed six games. I played well after I came back late in the year, but I hurt the knee again against San Francisco in the playoffs.

On the other hand, we won the Super Bowl. The feeling of elation that comes over you while the clock is counting the final seconds, the feeling of satisfaction of having achieved a goal that the whole team has worked so hard for, those feelings are hard to describe. It's just a great feeling the moment the gun sounds and you know you're on top.

Q: For many years, Dallas seemed to have a pipeline to great players. Who deserves the credit?

Calvin: I think it was two things. First, it was Gil Brandt. Gil went outside of the box. I like to say that back then most teams picked players based on *Street and Smith's* [magazine], but Gil was willing to quantify things and come up with a program to not exclude anyone just because they didn't go to a big school. The Cowboys also spent more money in scouting than just about every other team.

The other thing is that Tom [Landry] did a pretty good job of developing talent. Guys learned how to play because he was a great teacher.

Calvin talked for quite some time, but something he said about successful coaches and teams, something that I think is lost on many who follow sports, is worth quoting.

Calvin: Great coaches not only understand the game, but they can impart their understanding to others. A coach can motivate emotionally for awhile, but at some point there has to be some substance. If there's no substance, players are not totally stupid and eventually they realize it's all BS and they stop believing in the coach and that's when you're in real trouble. . . . I believe the best teams are the smart teams.

When was the last time you heard a sportscaster talk about how a smart play or strategy won a game for the team? The talk is almost always about how a great player made an athletic play or about how this team was fired up. Just as in virtually every human enterprise, brains have a lot to do with success in sports. That fact helps explain why Calvin Hill was a great football player and why he has been a success well beyond the football field.

The Coach: Tom Landry

Coaching Record

	W	L	T	Pct	
1960	0	11	1	.042	
1961	4	9	1	.321	
1962	5	8	1	.393	
1963	4	10	0	.286	
1964	5	8	1	.393	
1965	7	7	0	.500	
1966	10	3	1	.750	NFL Eastern Conference title
1967	9	5	0	.643	NFL Capitol Division & Eastern Conference titles
1968	12	2	0	.857	NFL Capitol Division title
1969	11	2	1	.821	NFL Capitol Division title
1970	10	4	0	.714	NFC Eastern Division title; NFC champs
1971	11	3	0	.786	NFC Eastern Division title; NFC champs; Super Bowl champs
1972	10	4	0	.714	NFC Wild Card
1973	10	4	0	.714	NFC Eastern Division title
1974	8	6	0	.571	
1975	10	4	0	.714	NFC Wild Card; NFC champs
1976	11	3	0	.786	NFC Eastern Division title
1977	12	2	0	.857	NFC Eastern Division title; NFC champs; Super Bowl champs
1978	12	4	0	.750	NFC Eastern Division title; NFC champs
1979	11	5	0	.688	NFC Eastern Division title
1980	12	4	0	.750	NFC Wild Card
1981	12	4	0	.750	NFC Eastern Division title
1982	6	3	0	.667	NFC Playoffs
1983	12	4	0	.750	NFC Wild Card
1984	9	7	0	.563	
1985	10	6	0	.625	NFC Eastern Division title
1986	7	9	0	.438	
1987	7	8	0	.467	
1988	3	13	0	.188	
Total	**250**	**162**	**6**	**.605**	

In today's NFL, it's not likely that Tom Landry would have been allowed to reach legend status, at least not with the Cowboys. Take a look at the beginning of his tenure with Dallas. The Cowboys had five straight losing seasons to start their existence and didn't have a winning season until year seven. Yet, Landry remained as head coach. In fact, the Cowboys gave him a 10-year contract extension after the 1963 season that would begin when Landry's original contract expired in 1965.

Landry, as quoted in *Landry: The Legend and the Legacy* by Bob St. John, commented about the extension, "That was one of the most significant things that ever happened to me. I'm sure it shocked a lot of reporters. Everybody thought they were going to make a change. From then on, I decided to dedicate myself even more to being a good coach. Clint [Murchison, Cowboys' owner] was always so important. He never pressured any of us and was always so positive when we'd have a losing streak. We'd be in a slump and he'd write us some clever note. Today, everybody panics after a few bad years."

I thought it would be instructive to look at other expansion teams, how long it took for them to have a winning season, and how long their first head coach lasted. I realize that not all expansion teams are created equal. The Cowboys, for example, started with a significant disadvantage in that they were formed too late to participate in the 1960 college draft. Anyway, starting with Atlanta in 1966, the year of the AFL/NFL merger, here are the expansion teams:

Team	First Year with Winning Record	First Head Coach	His Record	Length of Tenure
Atlanta (1966)	1971, 6th season	Norb Hecker	4-26-1	2 seasons[1]
Miami (1966)	1970, 5th season	George Wilson	15-39-2	4 seasons
New Orleans (1967)	1987, 21st season	Tom Fears	13-34-2	3 seasons[2]
Cincinnati (1968)	1970, 3rd season	Paul Brown	55-56-1	8 seasons
Seattle (1976)	1978, 3rd season	Jack Patera	35-59-0	6 seasons[3]
Tampa Bay (1976)	1979, 4th season	John McKay	44-88-1	9 seasons
Carolina (1995)	1996, 2nd season	Dom Capers	30-34-0	4 seasons
Jacksonville (1995)	1996, 2nd season	Tom Coughlin	62-50-0	6 seasons[4]
Cleveland (1999)	N/A	Chris Palmer	5-27-0	2 seasons

1. Fired after three games of his 3rd season
2. Fired after seven games of his 4th season
3. Fired after two games of his 7th season
4. Through the 2001 season

Only the Saints took longer to have their first winning season than the Cowboys, but Landry was allowed to stay and eventually coached Dallas to an NFL record 20 consecutive winning seasons. (The Saints, conversely, were on their tenth coach before they surpassed .500.)

In his day, Landry was considered an innovator. Former Dallas running back Calvin Hill said, "I think that as a coach—both offensively and defensively—he was an incredible innovator. He was ahead of the learning curve on both sides of the ball." Steelers coach Chuck Noll said, "You always had to spend a lot of extra time preparing to play Tom Landry's teams." Landry was the first coach to hire a quality control specialist, someone whose only responsibility is to analyze game films and chart the tendencies of the opposition. Now, every NFL team has at least one quality control coach.

Landry invented the Flex defense, in reality because at the time he didn't have a lot of good players on the defensive side of the ball, but the Flex turned out to be a successful scheme. In the Flex, two defensive lineman, usually the right tackle and left end, lined up a few feet back of scrimmage, which afforded them better pursuit lanes laterally.

In the mid-1970s, he brought back and refined the Shotgun formation where the quarterback takes the snap from center five to seven yards deep. The Shotgun often gave the quarterback more time to see the field because he was already standing in his passing position as soon as the ball was snapped. Many NFL teams began using this formation after the Cowboys.

As in all fields of history, revisionism has crept into Tom Landry's image. Some now assert that Landry was overrated as a coach, that Gil Brandt and the Dallas computer brought in such good talent that Landry had to win. I'll let Calvin Hill tackle that one (pun intended), "The thing you have to look at is that there are some coaches who, when they leave, they leave something behind. Landry developed the Umbrella defense, the beginning of the modern 4–3. He brought in multiple formations with motion to disguise your intentions. He brought back the Shotgun, which many teams are still using today. He had a distinct impact on what a lot of people are doing now. Great coaches don't just emulate others, they bring something unique to the game."

In the end, the bottom line is that the coach gets the blame (and often gets the ax) when a team plays poorly. The fact that Landry was the coach while the Cowboys had 20 straight winning seasons can't be a coincidence.

The Quarterback: Roger Staubach

Year	Team	Att	Comp	Yds	TD	Int	YPA	Rating	Lg Avg	W	L	Pct
1969	DAL	47	23	421	1	2	8.96	69.5	71.6	1	0	1.000
1970	DAL	82	44	542	2	8	6.61	42.9	65.6	2	0	1.000
1971	DAL	211	126	1,882	15	4	8.92	104.8	62.2	9	0	1.000
1972	DAL	20	9	98	0	2	4.90	20.4	66.3	0	0	—
1973	DAL	286	179	2,428	23	15	8.49	94.6	64.9	10	4	.714
1974	DAL	360	190	2,552	11	15	7.09	68.4	64.2	8	6	.571
1975	DAL	348	198	2,666	17	16	7.66	78.5	65.8	9	4	.692
1976	DAL	369	208	2,715	14	11	7.36	79.9	67.0	11	3	.786
1977	DAL	361	210	2,620	18	9	7.26	87.0	61.2	12	2	.857
1978	DAL	413	231	3,190	25	16	7.72	84.9	65.0	11	4	.733
1979	DAL	461	267	3,586	27	11	7.78	92.3	70.4	11	5	.688
Total		**2,958**	**1,685**	**22,700**	**153**	**109**	**7.67**	**83.4**	**65.9**	**84**	**28**	**.750**

YPA = Yards Per Pass Attempt
Rating = Passer Rating
Lg Avg = League Passer Rating in that season
W, L, Pct = Team's Record in his starts

Roger Staubach was drafted in the tenth round in 1964 as a future draft. (See 1955 Cleveland Browns, "Homegrown First-Round Picks.") Many media reports make it sound like Staubach was the only future draft pick ever and that Dallas was so far ahead of everyone else. By my count, there were 80 players drafted as future picks in the 1964 NFL draft. In fact, the Cowboys also took Bob Hayes as a future draft that year. Dallas was not the only team to select players who wouldn't play for them immediately, they just picked the best ones.

Because of his Navy service commitment, Staubach didn't play in an NFL game until he was 27 and didn't become a regular until he was 29. In that context, what he achieved borders on unbelievable. Trust me when I tell you that I am no Cowboys fan; however, and this may sound really strange, but I think Staubach is actually underrated, at least outside of Dallas. He is remembered as "Captain Comeback," remembered for the Hail Mary pass to Drew Pearson in the playoff game against the Vikings in 1975, for the comeback against the Redskins in the last game of the 1979 season. You know, Dallas didn't win every game coming from behind in the fourth quarter. For example, when the Cowboys won Super Bowl XII at the end of the 1977 season, seven of their regular season wins were actually by more than a touchdown. They won their postseason games by 30, 17, and 17 points. I don't smell any fourth-quarter heroics in there.

My point (yeah, get to your point) is that his one-dimensional image as the comeback king has taken away from the multidimensional nature of his accomplishments. Staubach led the NFL in passing (passer rating) four times in only eight seasons as a starter: his first two seasons as a regular (1971, 1973) and his last two seasons. He won passing titles before the 1978 rules changes to liberate the passing game, and he won them after the rules took effect. (He nearly won five passing titles, but was edged out by Bob Griese, 87.8 to 87.0, in 1977.)

Dallas went to the playoffs in seven of his eight seasons as the starter, to the Super Bowl four times, and won it all twice. It goes without saying that a quarterback doesn't win or lose a game by himself, at least not usually, but the Cowboys' record with Staubach as the starter was sensational and he deserves much credit, and not just for the games that Dallas won in the fourth quarter.

As Calvin Hill explained:

> He [Staubach] was a playmaker. Tom [Landry] felt comfortable with Roger. Roger was the kind of guy you knew was going to be watching film at night. Obviously, he was very athletic which helped him make plays that most quarterbacks couldn't make. Roger was very, very competitive. I once told Craig Morton that I didn't know how he could sleep at night because he should know that Roger was up studying so he can take his job.
>
> He could make all the throws; he had a wonderful arm and he could make the right throw for the situation. He worked very hard and had an incredible will to win, but he also had the will to prepare. Many athletes compete hard on game day, but not as many have the will to do the work before the game or the understanding of the importance of preparation.

Calvin told me that among current NFL quarterbacks, Brett Favre is the one who most reminds him of Staubach. He said that Favre has the ability to scramble to buy time (like Staubach), the ability to make whatever throw he has to make, and an intense will to win. The biggest difference between Favre and Staubach is that Favre is still willing to take chances that Staubach wouldn't take late in his career.

Tom Landry once said, "Roger Staubach might be the best combination of a passer, an athlete, and a leader ever to play in the NFL." I think many of Staubach's teammates and opponents share a similar view. To me, Staubach is clearly one of the top four or five quarterbacks in NFL history.

1971 Dallas Cowboys Statistics

Passing

	Att	Comp	Comp Pct	Yds	Yds Per	TD	Int	Rating
Staubach	211	126	59.7%	1,882	8.92	15	4	104.8
Morton	143	76	53.1%	1,131	7.91	7	8	72.3
Reeves	5	2	40.0%	24	4.80	0	1	15.8
Hill	1	0	0.0%	0	0.00	0	1	0.0
D. Thomas	1	0	0.0%	0	0.00	0	0	39.6
Cowboys	**361**	**206**	**57.1%**	**3,037**	**8.41**	**22**	**14**	**88.8**
Opponents	421	209	49.6%	2,660	6.32	15	26	55.9
League Average			50.9%		6.72			62.2

Cowboys' passers were sacked 32 times for 251 yards in losses.
The Cowboys sacked their opponents 43 times for 336 yards in losses.

Hindsight is 20-20, of course, but one can easily wonder why Staubach didn't become "the" starting quarterback earlier than the eighth game of the season. His passing rating was 69 percent better than the league average, a ratio matched by precious few quarterbacks in NFL history, and the team was 9–0 (12–0 if you count the postseason) in the games he started in 1971.

Rushing

	Att	Yds	Avg	Net Yards	TD
D. Thomas	175	793	4.53	+89	11
Hill	106	468	4.42	+42	8
Garrison	127	429	3.38	–82	1
Staubach	41	343	8.37		2
Reeves	17	79	4.65		0
Williams	21	67	3.19		1
Welch	14	51	3.64		1
Hayes	3	18	6.00		0
Morton	4	9	2.25		1
Ditka	2	2	1.00		0
Alworth	2	–10	–5.00		0
Cowboys	**512**	**2,249**	**4.39**	**+190**	**25**
Opponents	353	1,144	3.24	–276	8
League Average			4.02		

Duane Thomas was nineteenth in the NFL in rushing attempts in 1971, but he led the league in rushing touchdowns. Calvin Hill missed six games with a knee injury, but his rushing touchdowns total was surpassed by only four backs in the NFL including Thomas. Many associated with the Cowboys' organization dreamt about what kind of backfield Hill and Thomas would have made, but Thomas's problems made those dreams moot.

The Cowboys' average per carry allowed ranks among the top 20 since the merger in 1970 although they didn't lead the league in 1971.

Receiving

	Rec	Yds	Avg	TD
Garrison	40	396	9.90	1
Hayes	35	840	24.00	8
Alworth	34	487	13.16	2
Ditka	30	360	12.00	1
Hill	19	244	12.84	3
Truax	15	232	15.47	1
D. Thomas	13	153	11.77	2
Richardson	8	170	21.25	3
Adkins	4	53	13.25	0
Williams	3	59	19.67	0
Reeves	3	25	8.33	0
Rucker	1	19	19.00	1
Welch	1	−1	−1.00	0
Cowboys	**206**	**3,037**	**14.74**	**22**
Opponents	209	2,660	12.73	15
League Average			13.21	

Bob Hayes led the NFC (and was fourth in the NFL) in TD catches and he led the NFL in average yards per reception. (See "Bullet Bob.")

Duane Thomas led the NFL in touchdowns; among 54 NFL backs with 100+ touches (rushes and receptions) in 1971, Calvin Hill led in touchdown percentage. (See "Calvin Hill.")

Kickoff Returns

	Ret	Yds	Avg	TD
Harris	29	823	28.38	0
I. Thomas	7	295	42.14	2
Welch	4	105	26.25	0
Ditka	3	30	10.00	0
D. Thomas	2	64	32.00	0
Waters	1	18	18.00	0

(continued next page)

Kickoff Returns *(continued)*

	Ret	Yds	Avg	TD
Lewis	1	15	15.00	0
Hayes	1	14	14.00	0
Williams	1	12	12.00	0
Green	1	0	0.00	0
Cowboys	**50**	**1,376**	**27.52**	**2**
Opponents	70	1,681	24.01	0
League Average			22.99	

Dallas led the NFL in average yards per kickoff return in 1971 helped tremendously by Ike Thomas's performance. He was Dallas' second-round pick in 1971, but that was the only year he played for the Cowboys as he was traded to Green Bay before the 1972 season.

Punt Returns

	Ret	Yds	Avg	TD
Harris	17	129	7.59	0
Waters	9	109	12.11	0
Adkins	4	5	1.25	0
Hayes	1	5	5.00	0
Cowboys	**31**	**248**	**8.00**	**0**
Opponents	26	231	8.88	0
League Average			7.02	

Interceptions

	Int	Yds	Avg	TD
Adderley	6	182	30.33	0
Howley	5	122	24.40	0
Renfro	4	11	2.75	0
Waters	2	37	18.50	0
Jordan	2	34	17.00	0
Green	2	16	8.00	0
Edwards	2	0	0.00	0
Harris	2	0	0.00	0
Lewis	1	0	0.00	0
Cowboys	**26**	**402**	**15.46**	**0**
Opponents	14	304	21.71	1

The 182 yards returning interceptions was a career high for Hall-of-Famer Herb Adderley, even though he led the league twice with lower figures. The 1971 season was a great year for returning interceptions (just not in Dallas). Hall-of-Famer Ken Houston, who played for Houston from 1967–72, set an NFL record returning 4 interceptions for touchdowns. That record has been tied by Jim Kearney and Eric Allen. Bill Bradley, not the basketball player/senator, intercepted 11 passes for Philadelphia and returned them for a total of 248 yards.

Turnovers

Turnovers Committed:	35
Turnovers Forced:	51
Turnover +/–	+16

The Cowboys forced the most turnovers in the NFL in 1971 and were tied for second in turnover margin.

Punting

	No	Avg
Widby	56	41.6
Opponents	65	41.5
League Average		40.8

Kicking

	XP	XPA	XP Pct	FG	FGA	FG Pct
Clark	47	47	100.0%	13	25	52.0%
Fritsch	2	2	100.0%	5	8	62.5%
Reeves	1	1	100.0%	0	0	—
Cowboys	**50**	**50**	**100.0%**	**18**	**33**	**54.5%**
Opponents	24	25	96.0%	16	25	64.0%
League Average			97.5%			58.7%

Leading Scorer:	Mike Clark, 86 Points
Leading Scorer, Non-Kicker:	Duane Thomas, 78 Points

1971 Dallas Cowboys Roster

Head Coach	Tom Landry
QB	Craig Morton
QB	Roger Staubach
RB	Walt Garrison
RB	Calvin Hill
RB	Dan Reeves
RB	Duane Thomas
RB/KR	Claxton Welch
RB	Joe Williams
WR/PR	Margene Adkins
WR	Lance Alworth
WR	Bob Hayes
WR	Gloster Richardson
TE	Mike Ditka
TE	Billy Truax
C	John Fitzgerald
C	Dave Manders
OG	John Niland
OG	Blaine Nye
OG/OT	Rodney Wallace
OT	Forrest Gregg
OT/OG	Tony Liscio
OT	Ralph Neely
OT	Don Talbert
OT	Rayfield Wright
K	Mike Clark
K	Toni Fritsch
P	Ron Widby

DE	George Andrie
DE/DT	Larry Cole
DE	Tody Smith
DE	Pat Toomey
DT/DE	Bill Gregory
DT	Bob Lilly
DT	Jethro Pugh
LB	Lee Roy Caffey
LB	Dave Edwards
LB	Chuck Howley
LB	Lee Roy Jordan
LB	D. D. Lewis
LB	Tom Stincic
DB	Herb Adderley
DB	Cornell Green
DB/KR/PR	Cliff Harris
DB	Mel Renfro
DB/KR	Ike Thomas
DB	Mark Washington
DB/PR	Charlie Waters

Hall of Famers: Landry, Staubach, Alworth, Ditka, Gregg, Lilly, Adderley, Renfro.

Chapter 5

1972 Miami Dolphins: Undefeated and Disrespected

The 1972 Dolphins are probably more respected now than they were in 1972. They suited up for Super Bowl VII as underdogs despite an undefeated record and the fact that they were playing a Washington franchise that had just completed its first double-digit win total in 30 years. To top it off, the Dolphins had reached the Super Bowl by winning the AFC Championship Game on the road. (Home field advantage was determined by division instead of record until 1975.) Critics downplayed the Dolphins' performance because of their schedule, which to be fair, was very easy.

STARTING LINEUP – 1972 DOLPHINS

Offense		Defense	
SE	Paul Warfield	LE	Vern Den Herder
LT	Wayne Moore	LT	Manny Fernandez
LG	Bob Kuechenberg	RT	Bob Heinz
C	Jim Langer	RE	Bill Stanfill
RG	Larry Little	LLB	Doug Swift
RT	Norm Evans	MLB	Nick Buoniconti
TE	Marv Fleming	RLB	Mike Kolen
FL	Howard Twilley	LCB	Tim Foley/Lloyd Mumphord
QB	Bob Griese/Earl Morrall	RCB	Curtis Johnson
RB	Eugene "Mercury" Morris	SS	Jake Scott
RB	Larry Csonka	FS	Dick Anderson

This lack of respect still bothers members of the team. Hall of Fame linebacker Nick Buoniconti said, "You know what kills me? We were unbeaten going into the Super Bowl, and we were still two-point underdogs to the Skins. Just no respect." Hall of Fame guard Larry Little seemed less agitated, but still disrespected, when he said, "When people talk about the great teams in NFL history, you hear about the Packers or the Steelers or the 49ers. You never hear much about the Dolphins and the teams that we had. If you look at what we accomplished, especially in 1972 and 1973, then we deserve to be mentioned with those teams. In fact, I really think that the 1972 team may have been the best team in league history."

The 1972 Dolphins deserve much more respect because what they did is unique in NFL history. In fact, some of you are probably saying, "Hey, the 1972 Dolphins have to be the greatest team of all time. They went undefeated and won the Super Bowl. What else is there?" That type of respect is more than they got in 1972.

Lurking in the background as the 1972 season began was the criticism by some that Don Shula's teams couldn't win the "big one." Shula's teams were 0–2 in Super Bowls, plus his Baltimore Colts were upset losers in the 1964 NFL Championship Game.

The Super Bowl loss to Dallas seemed to strengthen the resolve of the Dolphins' players to show how good they really were. As All-Pro wide receiver Paul Warfield put it, "Having come out of that game [Super Bowl VI] as a loser... there was a need to prove that we were better than the team that was humiliated by Dallas in that first Super Bowl appearance. At the beginning of training camp, Don talked about how we have to get back to the Super Bowl to prove that we were better. We were very unified under that goal, to get back to that one game and to prove that we could become champions."

Team in a Box

Record: 14–0

In case you don't know, no other NFL team has had an unblemished season and won the league championship. The Chicago Bears were undefeated and untied in 1934 and 1942, but lost the NFL title game in both seasons. In 1948, the Cleveland Browns were undefeated, untied, and won their league championship, but that was in the All-America Football Conference (AAFC).

Against Teams Over .500: 2–0, 43 Points Scored, 23 Points Allowed

The most significant criticism of the '72 Dolphins is the strength of their schedule, or lack thereof. (See "Opponents' Record.")

Points Scored/Allowed: 385/171 (1972 NFL Average: 284)

Miami led the league in both points scored and fewest points allowed. No team did that again until the 1996 Green Bay Packers.

Yards Gained/Allowed: 5,036/3,297 (1972 NFL Average: 4,080)

The Dolphins also gained the most yards in the league and allowed the fewest. Their per-game yardage differential (+124.2) ranks seventh among all NFL teams since 1950. No other NFL team since 1950 has led the league in all four basic team categories: points scored, fewest points allowed, yards gained, and fewest yards allowed.

Opponents' Record: 70–108–4, .396

(Not counting games against the Dolphins; ties counted as half-win/half loss.)

The 1972 Dolphins had the seventh easiest season schedule of all NFL teams since 1950, at least as measured by the aggregate record of their opponents.

Adjusted Power Index:

Offense: +3.40
Defense: +3.23
TOTAL: +6.63

This team is one of only six since 1950 with both an Offense Power Index (OPI) and a Defense Power Index (DPI) of +3.00 or better.

Innovations/What You Should Know:

What do Mack Lamb, Kim Hammond, and John Bramlett have in common? Forget about what they have in common! Who are they? They were players traded by the Dolphins to acquire future Hall-of-Famers Larry Little and Nick Buoniconti in 1969. Lamb was traded even up to San Diego for Little; Hammond, Bramlett, and a 1970 fifth-round pick were sent to the Boston Patriots for Buoniconti. The Patriots used the pick on Bob Olson, a linebacker from Notre Dame. Of course, Buoniconti was a linebacker from Notre Dame.

No offense to any of the players the Chargers and Patriots acquired, but there's no denying that the Dolphins made out like bandits. Lamb never played in the NFL after he was traded. Kim Hammond played one year in New England before exiting pro football for good. Bramlett played two years with the Patriots and one with the Falcons before his career ended. Bob Olson never played in the NFL.

Little and Buoniconti earned eight Pro Bowl berths with Miami and, of course, both players were later enshrined in the Pro Football Hall of Fame. What may be even more interesting than the lopsided nature of the trades is that they both occurred before Don Shula became head coach in 1970.

The 53 defense was designed by Miami in 1972, but it was not done to be innovative; it was developed out of necessity. Miami suffered a rash of injuries to their defensive line during preseason, which left them short at defensive end. Defensive coordinator Bill Arnsparger decided to use linebacker Bob Matheson, recently acquired from Cleveland, at defensive end since he played there a little with the Browns. Lining up at an end position, but standing like a linebacker, Matheson could either rush the passer or drop into coverage. He had 2 sacks in his first game at his new position and the 53 defense, named that because Matheson wore number 53, was born. It was really the birth of the modern 3–4 defense.

Homegrown First-Round Picks:

QB Bob Griese, 1967; RB Larry Csonka, 1968; OT Doug Crusan, 1968; DE Bill Stanfill, 1969.

Don't let the fact that there were only four homegrown first-round picks lead you to think Miami didn't draft well. The Dolphins' first year was 1966. Still, a lot of their key players were not Miami draft picks.

Eugene "Mercury" Morris, the Dolphins' "other" 1,000-yard rusher in 1972, was picked in the third round in 1969. Jim Kiick, Csonka's partner in crime, was a fifth-round pick in 1968. However, Jim Langer, one of two offensive linemen from this team who have been elected to the Hall of Fame, was signed as an undrafted free agent in 1970. Larry Little, the other Hall-of-Fame lineman, was acquired in a trade with San Diego in 1969. Hall-of-Fame linebacker Nick Buoniconti came in a one-sided trade with the Patriots in 1969.

Transcendental Graphics

Larry Csonka

Pro Bowl Players:

DB Dick Anderson, LB Nick Buoniconti, RB Larry Csonka, OT Norm Evans, OG Larry Little, RB Mercury Morris, DB Jake Scott, DE Bill Stanfill, WR Paul Warfield.

Having nine players selected to the Pro Bowl is not consistent with the notion that this team did not get the respect it "deserved."

Game-by-Game:

Sep. 17th DOLPHINS 20, KANSAS CITY 10 AT KANSAS CITY

Miami and Kansas City played a classic game in the previous year's playoffs, won 27–24 by the Dolphins in double overtime. That was the last football game played at Municipal Stadium; this was the first game played at Arrowhead Stadium.

Although it was hardly a dominating effort, Miami won in large part because the Chiefs committed 4 turnovers and had 9 penalties. Fullback Larry Csonka was Miami's main offensive weapon, gaining 118 yards rushing on 21 carries, but he gave the credit to others: "Besides our great defense, the difference was simple: [Bob] Griese. Griese called a fantastic game. He hit them with the right plays when they were in the wrong defenses."

Chiefs head coach Hank Stram had another explanation, "Turnovers and penalties are what killed us. It's our own fault, of course. We can't blame anybody but ourselves."

For all intents and purposes, the Dolphins put the game out of reach with a scoring burst at the end of the first half. Leading 7–0, Garo Yepremian kicked a field goal with a minute left in the half. On Kansas City's subsequent possession, Miami safety Jake Scott intercepted a Len Dawson pass at the Chiefs' 40-yard line. Miami took three plays to score on a Larry Csonka 1-yard run with 22 seconds left. Miami's first touchdown was also set up by a turnover as safety Dick Anderson recovered an Ed Podolak fumble; Miami then went 57 yards in seven plays to score on a Griese to Marlin Briscoe pass.

Sep. 24th DOLPHINS 34, HOUSTON 13 AT MIAMI

Miami overwhelmed the hapless Oilers, running for 274 yards and outgaining them 435 yards to 167. They also had an incredible 30–7 superiority in first downs. Houston went 4–9–1 in 1971 and would finish 1–13 in 1972.

The story of this game was the new turf at the Orange Bowl making its debut. A long rain caused the surface to get very slippery. The ever quotable Larry Csonka said, "If this was back in my home town, my buddies would go out and burn up that field for me.... It's not just the players that are hurt. It detracts from the game for the spectators because it makes things so much slower, so much sloppie."

Oct. 1st DOLPHINS 16, MINNESOTA 14 AT MINNESOTA

Miami's undefeated season almost ended here. The Vikings' defense shut down Miami's attack, but the Dolphins' defense kept the score close. The Dolphins trailed 14–6 with a little more than four minutes left. After another Miami drive stalled, head coach Don Shula sent Garo Yepremian in to try a 51-yard field goal even though he had never kicked one longer than 48 yards. He made the kick to cut the lead to 14–9 and on the subsequent possession, the Dolphins forced Minnesota to punt and gained possession on the Miami 40 with 2:29 left.

Aided by a roughing-the-passer penalty on Minnesota defensive lineman Bob Lurtsema, Miami moved down to the Minnesota 3-yard line in the final two minutes. (Two key completions from Bob Griese to Howard Twilley helped keep the drive going.) Then, as Miami tight end Jim Mandich explained, "Bob Griese called a Csonka off tackle play-action pass; naturally, everybody on Minnesota thought Csonka had the ball and I was wide open in the end zone and Griese got me the ball and won the game."

The Dolphins intercepted 3 Fran Tarkenton passes and sacked him five times. The teams combined for fewer than 500 yards of total offense.

Oct. 8th DOLPHINS 27, NEW YORK JETS 17 AT NEW YORK

The Dolphins were worried about Joe Namath's passing, so Miami defensive coordinator Bill Arnsparger came up with a couple of wrinkles. The result? Namath had a mediocre day, completing 12 of 25 passes for 156 yards, no touchdowns, and 1 interception. Arnsparger deployed five defensive backs on occasion, which was unusual for 1972, and even more unusual because he sometimes used five DBs in "non-passing" situations. Arnsparger also played his 53 defense often. The 53 defense was really just a 3-4 where Bob Matheson was a combination defensive end/linebacker with the option to rush the passer or drop into coverage. Matheson was Cleveland's first-round pick in 1967 and was traded to Miami for a second-round pick in 1971.

In retrospect, and even though Matheson's position was "ahead" of its time, I find it hard to believe that he was never named to an All-Pro or Pro Bowl team. The famous 53 defense was named after him and yet it didn't really get him recognition. Matheson played with Miami until 1979. He died in 1994 at the age of 49.

Oct. 15th DOLPHINS 24, SAN DIEGO 10 AT MIAMI

Although Miami won the game, it looked as if their season was in trouble when starting quarterback Bob Griese suffered a broken bone and dislocated ankle. The Dolphins turned to Earl Morrall, the 17-year veteran who had stepped in for an injured Johnny Unitas in 1968 and took the Baltimore Colts to Super Bowl III only to suffer through a terrible game in the Colts' upset loss to the Jets. Miami claimed Morrall on waivers in April 1972 from the Colts.

Morrall stuck with the game plan, passing sparingly, but completed 8 of 10 passes for 86 yards and 2 touchdowns. Many years later, Morrall recalled the moment when Griese was injured, "At that time, I didn't know what had happened, but then they called for the stretcher, then I knew I was it. I think having been around for a number of years certainly helped. At the time, you're thinking of the game plan, thinking of what we did all week . . . I went back to the things that had been successful in order to get some continuity going, get a little drive going, which we did. We went down the field and scored and that gave everybody a lift."

Oct. 22nd DOLPHINS 24, BUFFALO 23 AT MIAMI

"Fernandez stole the ball. Fernandez stole the ball." I'm sure a few New Englanders will probably think I'm committing heresy by changing the famous "Havlicek stole the ball" line from Celtics' lore. Anyway, with Miami struggling at home against the mediocre Bills in the fourth quarter, Dolphins defensive tackle Manny Fernandez made a play that proved vital in Miami's narrow win. He "stole" a handoff from Buffalo QB Dennis Shaw to fullback Jim Braxton to give Miami the ball deep in Buffalo territory, setting up the touchdown that provided the margin of victory.

Fernandez felt that the play was largely luck: "It was supposed to be a delayed trap to our defensive right side. I was anticipating a pass since it was second and long so I was really hyped up and coming. The center missed [the block] and it happened to be a delay which gave me time to get all the way in the action of the play. Had I been playing run I still would have been on the line of scrimmage, probably getting blocked by the center."

Buffalo gained only 177 yards against Miami's defense, while the Dolphins gained 221 yards just on the ground led by Larry Csonka (rushed for 107). Miami committed 4 turnovers, which kept the game close.

Oct. 29th DOLPHINS 23, BALTIMORE 0 AT BALTIMORE

This game was notable only because it marked Earl Morrall's return to Baltimore, where he had played for four seasons. He received a big ovation when he ran onto the field for Miami's first possession and was given the game ball.

As if the Colts didn't have enough problems playing the Dolphins, Baltimore's special teams also played very poorly. Curtis Johnson blocked a Baltimore punt in the second quarter to set up Miami's second touchdown and Hubert Ginn's recovery of a fumbled punt at the Baltimore 18 in the third quarter led to Miami's final touchdown.

Typical of Miami and the NFL in the early 1970s, the Dolphins ran the ball 52 times and attempted 17 passes. The Dolphins outgained the Colts 375–192.

Nov. 5th DOLPHINS 30, BUFFALO 16 AT BUFFALO

Mercury Morris gained 106 yards rushing on just 11 carries as the Dolphins moved to 8–0 despite gaining fewer than 100 yards passing for the fourth straight game.

Again, Buffalo gave the Dolphins all they could handle. In their first game, the Bills led 13–7 at halftime before losing 24–23. In this game, they trailed just 16–13 at the half and 23–16 at the end of three quarters.

Every account of this game tells the Marv Fleming story, so I will. He caught a 7-yard touchdown pass from Earl Morrall in the third quarter and found a $10 bill in the end zone. Apparently, Fleming was very excited about finding the money as punter Larry Seiple explained, "He was happier about that than the TD, which makes sense if you know Marv." It's hard to imagine a player today getting excited about finding a $10 bill anywhere.

Nov. 12th DOLPHINS 52, NEW ENGLAND 0 AT MIAMI

Don Shula's 100th career win as a head coach made him the first to accomplish the feat in 10 seasons. The Dolphins outgained New England 482 yards to 169, the fourth consecutive game Miami held its opponent to under 200 yards of offense. After not producing much in the air for four games, the Dolphins threw for over 300 yards, which was not common in 1972. Much of that yardage came while the backups for both teams were in the game; Miami backup QB Jim Del Gaizo completed 4 of 6 passes for 145 yards, including a 39-yard TD pass to Jim Mandich with the score 45–0 in the fourth quarter. Mandich later said, "I ran a post pattern against some stumbling linebacker. They were god-awful. Rub it in? Who cared?" So much for winning with class.

Nov. 19th DOLPHINS 28, NEW YORK JETS 24 AT MIAMI

Although it was not an easy win, the talk of an undefeated season grew after Miami moved to 10–0 and clinched the AFC East title. (Seeding for home-field advantage was not yet in place in 1972.)

The Jets led 17–14 at halftime and 24–21 at the end of three quarters, but Miami went ahead for good on Mercury Morris's second touchdown of the game, a 14-yard run with 11:11 left. Morris gained 107 yards rushing on 23 carries. Earl Morrall also scored a touchdown on a 31-yard run; believe it or not, on a team that wound up setting the NFL team rushing record, that was the longest touchdown run of the regular season for Miami.

Jets head coach Weeb Ewbank had high praise for the Dolphins, "Miami's the best team in the league. I think they'll go undefeated. Who can beat them?"

Nov. 27th DOLPHINS 31, ST. LOUIS 10 AT MIAMI

It wouldn't be the Cardinals. Little used second-year wide receiver Otto Stowe, replacing the injured Paul Warfield, had 6 catches for 140 yards and his first 2 NFL touchdowns as Miami cruised on a Monday night. Larry Csonka gained 114 yards rushing on 16 carries.

The game was a mismatch; St. Louis came in with a 2–7–1 record. Miami outgained the Cardinals 426 yards to 224 and had 24 first downs compared to 12 for St. Louis, which also committed 6 turnovers.

Dec. 3rd DOLPHINS 37, NEW ENGLAND 21 AT NEW ENGLAND

Behind Mercury Morris's 113 yards and Larry Csonka's 91, which put him over 1,000 for the second straight year, Miami literally ran over the Patriots as they gained 304 yards on the ground and 501 overall. If it weren't for 11 Miami penalties and 3 turnovers, the score would have resembled the first game between these teams (52–0).

Which leads me to a Shula story as told by Earl Morrall, "The night before the game, Shula let us go into Boston for a meal. A bunch of us took a bus in and we had dinner on the wharf. All the New England fans kept sending wine to our table, hoping we would imbibe heavily and we were only too glad to oblige. Next day at his pregame meeting, Shula jumped on us, 'You guys are losing your focus.' "

Csonka downplayed getting to 1,000 yards, "A lot of guys are getting 1,000 yards now. I think pretty soon there'll be a new figure to shoot at." After a total of seven 1,000-yard runners in 1970–71, 10 players reached that mark in 1972. In the last six years of the 14-game schedule (1972–77), 49 runners did it. Yet everyone still talks about the "1,000-yard runner." It's no longer a really big deal. In 2000, 23 players surpassed 1,000 yards rushing.

Dec. 10th DOLPHINS 23, NEW YORK GIANTS 13 AT NEW YORK

Although yards from scrimmage were close (367–343 in favor of Miami), 6 New York turnovers made the Giants victim number 13. Starting his first game since spraining his ankle on November 12, Paul Warfield had a big day with 4 catches for 132 yards and a touchdown.

After the game, someone suggested to Larry Csonka that Miami might be better off in the playoffs if it didn't go undefeated. Csonka's response, "I don't believe in that stuff. Winning breeds winning and the only thing that can beat us is a swelled head."

Dec. 16th DOLPHINS 16, BALTIMORE 0 AT MIAMI

This game was significant for two reasons: it gave the Dolphins a perfect regular season and it was Johnny Unitas's last game as a Colt.

The Dolphins ran Mercury Morris frequently in their attempt to become the first team to have two 1,000-yard rushers in the same season. He had 85 yards on 26 carries and, when the game ended, everyone thought he had finished the season with 991 rushing yards. (More on that in "Nothin' Up My Sleeve, Presto.")

Bob Griese played for the first time since his foot/ankle injury in Week 5 against San Diego. Head coach Don Shula was pleased, but his emotions were in check. "We're very happy to gain number 14 and go undefeated," he said. "It was a 40-man effort... I'm proud of the rushing record, breaking one that had held so many years. The offensive line came through consistently."

Divisional Playoff:

Dec. 24th DOLPHINS 20, CLEVELAND 14 AT MIAMI

In response to a suggestion that Miami had the easiest first-round playoff game, head coach Don Shula replied, "I could care less what people are saying. There are eight teams left competing for the world championship. All have to be solid football teams or they wouldn't be there." His words were almost too prophetic. The Browns stayed with the Dolphins all day, despite QB Mike Phipps's 5 interceptions.

Trailing 14–13 in the fourth quarter, Miami put together its only good drive of the day, moving 80 yards in six plays and scoring on Jim Kiick's 8-yard run with 4:54 left. Paul Warfield, who had starred with the Browns for six years before being traded to Miami in 1970, played a large role in the winning drive. He caught 2 passes for 50 yards and drew a pass-interference penalty that gave the Dolphins first-and-goal at the Cleveland 8-yard line; Kiick scored on the next play.

Miami gave up a first-round pick for Warfield; Cleveland used that pick to select Mike Phipps. Gracious as always, Warfield talked about the pressure on Phipps because of the trade, "Phipps has had a cloud hanging over him ever since he came to Cleveland. Every time I do something in Miami, it seems to reflect directly on him. A young quarterback shouldn't have to start out in pro football under that kind of pressure. The whole thing is unfair." Unfair or not, Phipps wound up as a disappointment in the NFL. He was his team's starting quarterback in just 5 of his 12 NFL seasons; in three of his years as a starter his passing rating was below 50.0.

Miami's other touchdown came in the first quarter when rookie Charlie Babb blocked Don Cockroft's punt at the 17, fell on the ball at the 6 untouched, then got up and ran the ball into the end zone. Miami led 10–0 at halftime, but Cleveland took its 14–13 lead on a fourth-quarter 27-yard TD pass from Phipps to Fair Hooker (if only I were a real comedian).

AFC Championship:

Dec. 31st DOLPHINS 21, PITTSBURGH 17 AT PITTSBURGH

The Steelers got to the AFC Championship Game on the strength of the "Immaculate Reception." (See "Elsewhere Around The NFL.") In the first quarter, they still seemed to be living the charmed life when Terry Bradshaw fumbled at the Miami 3-yard line and tackle Gerry Mullins fell on the ball in the end zone for a touchdown. On that play, however, Dolphins safety Jake Scott delivered a hit on Bradshaw that, in the quarterback's own words, "knocked me looney," and kept him out of the game until the middle of the fourth quarter. This was a very physical game, with players on both teams getting more than the usual amount of bumps and bruises.

Most people who remember this game know about punter Larry Seiple's 37-yard run (from punt formation) to set up Miami's first touchdown. Three other fourth-down plays were also important. Down 10–7 with fourth-and-1 at the Pittsburgh 4 in the third quarter, Miami went for it and Jim Kiick gained the first down. He scored two plays later.

The winning touchdown drive was set up by Maulty Moore's block of a Roy Gerela field-goal attempt; the ball was recovered by Miami's Curtis Johnson at the Pittsburgh 49. Then, in a very similar situation to the third-quarter drive, Miami, still ahead 14–10, eschewed the field goal attempt on fourth-and-1 at the Steelers' 4; Csonka got the yard and Kiick scored two plays later.

Bradshaw led Pittsburgh to a touchdown on his first series after returning to the game, but threw interceptions on each of the Steelers' last two possessions. Miami had earned a place in the Super Bowl for the second consecutive season.

Don Shula put Bob Griese in the game at the start of the second half, which was his first real playing time since his injury in October. Shula explained the move, "I went to Griese because we were not untracked [*sic*] offensively and he deserved a chance to move our football team."

Although they didn't have an overwhelming offensive performance, Miami ran well enough to control the clock and the tempo of the game. Pittsburgh All-Pro defensive tackle Mean Joe Greene praised Miami's offensive line, particularly center Jim Langer, "They won up front... [Larry] Little and Langer. That Jim Langer's a pretty damn good center. A center's kind of an odd man and you tend to take them for granted. Let me tell you, you have to pay close attention to him. He's a tough, strong dude."

Super Bowl VII:

Jan. 14th DOLPHINS 14, WASHINGTON 7 AT LOS ANGELES

First, no Garo Yepremian jokes... I'm sure others have pointed out the irony that the "perfect" team's Super Bowl win was marred by one of the most imperfect plays in football history.

The Miami defense, led by tackle Manny Fernandez, shut down Washington's offense, while the Dolphins' offense made enough plays to give them the Super Bowl championship and a perfect 17–0 season.

The game started slowly. The Redskins were unable to move the ball and the Dolphins didn't do much either until late in the first quarter. Miami advanced 63 yards in six plays and scored on third-and-4 from the Washington 28, Dolphins wide receiver Howard Twilley beat Redskins cornerback Pat Fischer to the outside, caught Bob Griese's pass at the 5 and dragged Fischer into the end zone with one second left in the quarter.

The game's next score came near the end of the first half. Miami's Nick Buoniconti intercepted a Billy Kilmer pass and returned it 32 yards to the Washington 27 with 1:51 remaining. On third-and-4, tight end Jim Mandich made a nice catch at the Redskins' 2. Two plays later, Jim Kiick went in from a yard out and Miami led 14–0 at halftime.

Miami played keep away for most of the second half, running the ball just well enough and neutralizing

Redskins running back Larry Brown. Quarterback Billy Kilmer was not up to the task of carrying the Washington offense on this day. He threw 3 interceptions and gained only 104 yards passing on 28 attempts.

Yepremian's feeble attempt at a pass after a blocked field-goal attempt with two minutes left literally gave away a touchdown, but Miami held on to win.

After the game, Griese felt the team had nothing left to prove, "What more is there we can show? People have knocked our schedule all year, but all I know is that other teams in other years haven't gone undefeated." Washington head coach George Allen said, "We thought we could run on Miami, but we couldn't. . . . I can't get out of here [Los Angeles] fast enough."

Elsewhere Around the NFL:

Oct. 2nd In a wild, wild game, New England upset the Redskins 24–23. Washington led 14–0 in the second quarter, but New England took the lead 17–14 in the third quarter. In the final quarter, the Redskins took the lead again at 21–17, but the Patriots scored to go ahead 24–21 with four minutes left, when Jim Plunkett's amazing throw on the run connected with running back Josh Ashton for a 24-yard TD. The Redskins then drove down the field, but Curt Knight missed a 27-yard field goal with a minute and a half left.

Washington held New England and then blocked a punt out of the end zone for a safety with less than a minute left to narrow the lead to 24–23. The Redskins returned the free kick to the New England 48, but Knight missed a 50-yard field goal.

The Patriots had won 21–20 the week before when Atlanta missed a *10-yard* field goal attempt (the goal posts were still on the goal line in 1972) in the game's last minute. Were the wins a sign of good things ahead? Not exactly. New England finished the year 3–11 and had to borrow Phil Bengston from the Chargers to coach the team when John Mazur resigned after nine games.

Dec. 23rd Is the "Immaculate Reception" the most famous play in NFL history? After a scoreless first half, the Steelers got 2 Roy Gerela field goals to hold a 6–0 lead over the Raiders late in the fourth quarter. After the second field goal, Oakland put together their best drive of the day and scored when Ken Stabler improvised and ran 30 yards to paydirt with 1:12 left.

You may have heard what happened next: With 22 seconds left and fourth-and-10 from his own 40, Pittsburgh's Terry Bradshaw was flushed out of the pocket and threw the ball to running back John "Frenchy" Fuqua, the quarterback's second option on the play. The ball and Oakland safety Jack Tatum arrived simultaneously; Fuqua was knocked down while the ball flew backwards. Franco Harris caught the ball out of the air and ran in for the touchdown to give Pittsburgh a 13–7 win. The play was controversial because: 1) it wasn't clear that Tatum had touched the ball and the rules at the time made it illegal for two offensive players to touch a pass consecutively and 2) there was no clear touchdown signal from any of the officials. Because Pittsburgh won so many Super Bowls in the 1970s, some people assume they won it the year of the "Immaculate Reception." Miami had something else to prove.

What Happened the Next Season:

The Dolphins' winning streak ended at 18 with a 12–7 loss to Oakland in the second game of the 1973 season, but Miami finished with a 12–2 record, another AFC East title, another AFC championship, and its second consecutive Super Bowl crown by way of an easy 24–7 win over the Vikings. Miami's wins were much more convincing in the '73 playoffs than they had been in '72; they outscored their opponents 85–33 compared to 55–38 in 1972. Taking ball control to an extreme, the Dolphins attempted just 15 passes combined in the AFC Championship Game and Super Bowl in 1973 while running the ball 106 times.

Nothin' Up My Sleeve, Presto!

The 1972 Dolphins' pursuit of being the first team with two 1,000-yard runners was not a small story. The *Miami Herald* had numerous features and updates about how many more yards Larry Csonka and/or Mercury Morris needed to reach 1,000. In the now defunct *Sports Encyclopedia: Pro Football,* the last sentence in the recap of the Dolphins' season is about Csonka and Morris becoming the first teammates to gain 1,000 yards apiece in one season.

What people may not remember is that when the season actually ended, everyone thought Morris had finished with 991 yards. On Thursday, December 21—five days after the Dolphins' last regular season game—the NFL announced that a review of game films had uncovered a play in which Morris was incorrectly given a loss of 9 yards rushing; therefore, his corrected rushing total for the year was 1,000 yards exactly.

I don't buy it for a second. You mean to tell me that NFL officials reviewed game films—in the pre-digital video age—to see if statistics were correctly recorded and that, miraculously, they found a 9-yard mistake for Mercury Morris less than a week after the season ended? The play in question—a disputed lateral/fumble against Buffalo on October 22—gained some notoriety because Miami fans booed loudly when the play was ruled a fumble and a recovery by Buffalo. Yet that turn of events still smells fishy, even 30 years later. Why haven't we heard any more stories about statistics being corrected? Even if officials reviewed the films at the request of the Dolphins, that is not right.

In the San Francisco 49ers' clubhouse on the day after the NFL announced the Morris "ruling," someone wrote this on a blackboard, "NFL search of 1969 stats finds [Doug] Cunningham [a 49ers running back] with 460 extra yards and he finished the season with 1,001 yards." I'm not the only one who is (or was) skeptical.

Why would the league go to such trouble to bestow the honor of being the first team with two 1,000-yard rushers on the Dolphins? Although he wasn't yet on the NFL Competition Committee (he would serve on that committee for 20 years), Miami head coach Don Shula was a powerful man in the league. Maybe the higher-ups in the NFL thought it would be "neat" if the perfect team also was the first with two 1,000-yard runners. Whatever the case, to me the whole thing stinks like a dead dolphin.

The Coach: Don Shula

Coaching Record (with Dolphins Only)

	W	L	T	Pct	
1970	10	4	0	.714	AFC Wild Card
1971	10	3	1	.750	AFC Eastern Division title; AFC champs
1972	14	0	0	1.000	AFC Eastern Division title; AFC champs; Super Bowl champs
1973	12	2	0	.857	AFC Eastern Division title; AFC champs; Super Bowl champs
1974	11	3	0	.786	AFC Eastern Division title
1975	10	4	0	.714	
1976	6	8	0	.429	
1977	10	4	0	.714	
1978	11	5	0	.688	AFC Wild Card
1979	10	6	0	.625	AFC Eastern Division title
1980	8	8	0	.500	
1981	11	4	1	.719	AFC Eastern Division title
1982	7	2	0	.778	AFC Playoffs; AFC champs
1983	12	4	0	.750	AFC Eastern Division title
1984	14	2	0	.875	AFC Eastern Division title; AFC champs
1985	12	4	0	.750	AFC Eastern Division title
1986	8	8	0	.500	
1987	8	7	0	.533	
1988	6	10	0	.375	
1989	8	8	0	.500	
1990	12	4	0	.750	AFC Wild Card
1991	8	8	0	.500	
1992	11	5	0	.688	AFC Eastern Division title
1993	9	7	0	.563	
1994	10	6	0	.625	AFC Eastern Division title
1995	9	7	0	.563	AFC Wild Card
Total	**257**	**133**	**2**	**.658**	

Reputations can be fleeting, and can often seem strange when viewed in retrospect. Don Shula is now universally acclaimed as a coaching legend, as someone who had the utmost respect from his players and his opponents. One of my all-time favorite football quotes is Bum Phillips speaking in praise of Shula, "He can take his'n and beat your'n, then he can take your'n and beat his'n." Of course, some of that stems from Shula breaking George Halas's career record for wins by a head coach. Some of that respect comes from the undefeated season.

Much in the same way that the Dallas Cowboys were once known as "Next Year's Champions" because of an alleged inability to win the "big one," Don

Shula was once known as the coach who couldn't win the "big one." That reputation started while Shula was coaching the Baltimore Colts.

In 1964, Shula's second season as Colts' head coach, Baltimore easily won the NFL Western Conference title with a 12–2 record. The team led the league in both points scored and fewest points allowed. The 1964 Colts are one of only 13 teams since 1950 with an Adjusted Power Index (API) of +6.50 or higher.

As one might expect, despite the fact that the NFL Championship Game was at Cleveland, the Eastern Conference winner, the Colts were a heavy favorite. After a scoreless first half, however, the Browns won easily, 27–0.

In 1967, the Colts were undefeated in their first 13 games (11–0–2), but had to beat the 10–1–2 Rams in Los Angeles in the last game of the regular season in order to win the Coastal Division title and advance to the playoffs. The Colts and Rams had tied earlier in the season and with this being the first year of an extra playoff round, divisional ties would no longer be played off but instead be decided by tie-breaker. Los Angeles won comfortably, 34-10.

Of course, 1968 brought Shula's most difficult defeat. Despite an injury to Johnny Unitas, Baltimore cruised en route to a 13–1 regular season record. The Colts outscored their opponents 402–144, the second best per-game point differential of any team since 1950. After a somewhat difficult win against the Vikings in the first playoff round, Baltimore routed the Browns in Cleveland 34–0 to win the NFL championship and earn a berth in the Super Bowl against the New York Jets. In case you don't know, the Jets, 17- to 18-point underdogs, beat the Colts 16–7 in what is widely regarded as the biggest upset in pro football history.

Shula became coach of the Dolphins in 1970 (in a bitter dispute, Miami had to give Baltimore its 1971 first-round draft pick as compensation), and the following year he led Miami to the Super Bowl against Dallas. Once again, Shula's troops were no match for their opponent as Dallas won 24–3, the only Super Bowl (so far) where one of the teams was held without a touchdown.

Let's stop here for a moment. In what can reasonably be argued to be the first extremely important games of his coaching career where the teams were at even strength (I left out the loss to Green Bay in the 1965 Western Conference playoff because the Colts had to play running back Tom Matte at quarterback due to injuries to Johnny Unitas and Gary Cuozzo), Shula's teams were 0–4 and were outscored 101–20. In two of those four games, his team was a prohibitive favorite.

My intention is not to criticize Shula. Far from it. The respect the football world has for Shula is genuine. When I hosted a sports talk show on a small radio station in Westminster, Maryland, in the mid-1980s, I was once fortunate enough to have former Colts Art Donovan and Jim Mutscheller as in-studio guests. At one point, I asked them who was the best coach in the NFL. Almost before I could finish the question, both of them answered, "Shula."

The point is that many fans and much of the media love to put labels on people. I guess it's an attempt to simplify a complex world, but it's a dangerous exercise. Don Shula's career, where he scaled great heights of achievement after some early disappointments, is a powerful reminder that labels are often totally inappropriate.

The Quarterback: Earl Morrall

Year	Team	Att	Comp	Yds	TD	Int	YPA	Rating	Lg Avg	W	L	Pct
1956	SF	78	38	621	1	6	7.96	48.1	59.6	1	3	.250
1957	PIT	289	139	1,900	11	12	6.57	64.9	63.2	6	6	.500
1958	PIT-DET	78	25	463	5	9	5.94	35.3	65.3	0	2	.000
1959	DET	137	65	1,102	5	6	8.04	69.1	66.9	0	0	—
1960	DET	49	32	423	4	3	8.63	94.2	64.2	2	0	1.000
1961	DET	150	69	909	7	9	6.06	56.2	68.5	2	2	.500
1962	DET	52	32	449	4	4	8.63	82.9	72.6	0	0	—
1963	DET	328	174	2,621	24	14	7.99	86.2	71.7	3	5	.375
1964	DET	91	50	588	4	3	6.46	75.7	71.7	3	0	1.000
1965	NYG	302	155	2,446	22	12	8.10	86.3	73.5	7	7	.500
1966	NYG	151	71	1,105	7	12	7.32	54.1	67.4	1	6	.143
1967	NYG	24	13	181	3	1	7.54	100.9	66.6	0	0	—
1968	BAL	317	182	2,909	26	17	9.18	93.2	68.7	13	1	.929
1969	BAL	99	46	755	5	7	7.63	60.0	71.6	1	0	1.000
1970	BAL	93	51	792	9	4	8.52	97.6	65.6	1	0	1.000
1971	BAL	167	84	1,210	7	12	7.25	58.2	62.2	7	2	.778
1972	MIA	150	83	1,360	11	7	9.07	91.0	66.3	9	0	1.000
1973	MIA	38	17	253	0	4	6.66	27.5	64.9	0	1	.000
1974	MIA	27	17	301	2	3	11.15	86.1	64.2	1	0	1.000
1975	MIA	43	26	273	3	2	6.35	82.8	65.8	1	0	1.000
1976	MIA	26	10	148	1	1	5.69	54.6	67.0	0	0	—
Total		**2,689**	**1,379**	**20,809**	**161**	**148**	**7.74**	**74.1**	**66.9**	**58**	**35**	**0.624**

YPA = Yards Per Pass Attempt
Rating = Passer Rating
Lg Avg = League Passer Rating in that season
W, L, Pct = Team's Record in his starts

Technically, Earl Morrall was the first pick (from Michigan State) in the 1956 NFL draft. Actually, he was second, as the bonus pick was still in effect in 1956. (See "1958 Baltimore Colts: Homegrown First-Round Picks.") Wait, I'll let Morrall tell the beginning of the story. This is Morrall as quoted in *Sundays at 2:00 with the Baltimore Colts* by Vince Bagli and Norman Macht: "Detroit and San Francisco had tied for last place in the NFL [in 1955], so they flipped a coin for the first draft pick. The 49ers won and selected me. San Francisco had Y. A. Tittle and the next year they drafted John Brodie, so they had three quarterbacks. Then they found out they needed a line-backer, so they traded me to Pittsburgh. Buddy Parker was the coach there. He had been at Detroit when they wanted to draft me. My second year there [1958], they traded me to Detroit for Bobby Layne."

Lions head coach George Wilson didn't have faith in Morrall, which made the quarterback's stay there very difficult; he started only 17 games in his six full seasons in Detroit. Wilson and Morrall both left the Lions after the 1964 season. In an ironic twist, Morrall went to the Giants to replace Y. A. Tittle. The silver lining in the cloud of Morrall's stint with the Lions was that Don Shula was a Detroit assistant coach from 1960 to 1962. As a head coach, Shula acquired Morrall twice. The first time was from the Giants in 1968 when Shula was in Baltimore, in a trade for tight end George "Butch" Wilson (more irony and a little weird). The second time was in Miami in 1972 when Shula claimed Morrall off of waivers from the Colts. Both times he played far more than expected in his first season with his new team due to an injury to the team's Hall-of-Fame quarterback, and both times he played well and the team had a very successful season, even though Morrall played poorly in Baltimore's upset loss to the Jets in the Super Bowl.

Granted, he played for some very good teams, but look at Morrall's record as a starter from 1968 until the end of his career; more specifically, from 1968 through 1972. In those five seasons, Morrall's team's went 31–3 with him as the starting QB. The record of those same teams when Morrall didn't start was 25–9–2. In any event, 31–3 is a remarkable record in the NFL.

Still, Morrall was relieved by Shula in two of the biggest games of his career. Johnny Unitas replaced him in Super Bowl III, and Bob Griese took over at halftime of the 1972 AFC Championship Game. How did he feel the second time? "Of course, I was surprised and hurt, but there was no debate about it with Shula," Morrall explained. "He said Griese had the job when he got hurt and now he's ready to play, so that was it." That did not affect Morrall's feelings about Shula as a coach. He also felt that Shula was the greatest coach in NFL history and added, "There's something about that man that is always so right."

Earl Morrall had a rare ride through pro football, both in terms of longevity and circumstances. He should also be remembered as the quarterback who started the majority of games for the only undefeated champion in NFL history.

The Quarterback: Bob Griese

Year	Team	Att	Comp	Yds	TD	Int	YPA	Rating	Lg Avg	W	L	Pct
1967	MIA	331	166	2,005	15	18	6.06	61.6	61.6	3	8	.273
1968	MIA	355	186	2,473	21	16	6.97	75.7	62.6	5	7	.417
1969	MIA	252	121	1,695	10	16	6.73	56.9	64.5	2	6	.250
1970	MIA	245	142	2,019	12	17	8.24	72.1	65.6	10	4	.714
1971	MIA	263	145	2,089	19	9	7.94	90.9	62.2	9	3	.750
1972	MIA	97	53	638	4	4	6.58	71.6	66.3	5	0	1.000
1973	MIA	218	116	1,422	17	8	6.52	84.3	64.9	12	1	.923
1974	MIA	253	152	1,968	16	15	7.78	80.9	64.2	10	3	.769
1975	MIA	191	118	1,693	14	13	8.86	86.6	65.8	7	3	.700
1976	MIA	272	162	2,097	11	12	7.71	78.9	67.0	5	8	.385
1977	MIA	307	180	2,252	22	13	7.34	87.8	61.2	10	4	.714
1978	MIA	235	148	1,791	11	11	7.62	82.4	65.0	6	3	.667
1979	MIA	310	176	2,160	14	16	6.97	72.0	70.4	7	5	.583
1980	MIA	100	61	790	6	4	7.90	89.2	73.7	2	2	.500
Total		**3,429**	**1,926**	**25,092**	**192**	**172**	**7.32**	**77.1**	**66.0**	**93**	**57**	**.620**

YPA = Yards Per Pass Attempt
Rating = Passer Rating
Lg Avg = League Passer Rating in that season
W, L, Pct = Team's Record in his starts

- Selected in the first round (fourth overall) of the 1967 AFL/NFL draft.
- Believed to be the first quarterback to wear glasses while playing.
- Inducted into the Hall of Fame in 1990, his fifth year of eligibility.
- Led the league once in passer rating (1977) and once in average yards per pass attempt (1975).

Bob Griese was not physically imposing. Between his eyeglasses and his listed 6-foot-1, 190-pound frame (which is at least a slight exaggeration), he wouldn't remind anyone of Terry Bradshaw. And Griese was not exceptionally durable. To be fair, few quarterbacks, if any, avoid injuries enough to play in every game. Nevertheless, Griese played in all of his team's games just three times in 14 seasons.

While he may not have had the "ideal" physical characteristics, Griese may have had the perfect mental attributes to play for Don Shula in the 1970s. Shula said, "He's probably the most unselfish guy I've ever been around. He got as much of a thrill calling the right running play for a touchdown as he did connecting on a bomb. That's just his makeup." Shula also thought that Griese may have been the smartest player he ever coached.

Even for the run-happy '70s, the Dolphins did not throw the ball much. Griese had been a star in college at Purdue (a two-time All American) and a first-round draft pick. He had thrown the ball with some frequency in his first three years in Miami. Some quarterbacks would have been unhappy and shown their displeasure with a new offensive scheme that de-emphasized the pass. If Griese was angry about throwing less, it never came out in public.

More on Griese's draft . . . 1967 was the first common AFL/NFL draft. Tolerate me for a bit as I look at the first round of that draft.

	Player	Position	College	Pro Team
1.	Bubba Smith	DL	Michigan State	Baltimore (from New Orleans*)
2.	Clint Jones	RB	Michigan State	Minnesota (from New York Giants)
3.	Steve Spurrier	QB	Florida	San Francisco (from Atlanta)
4.	Bob Griese	QB	Purdue	Miami
5.	George Webster	LB	Michigan State	Houston
6.	Floyd Little	RB	Syracuse	Denver
7.	Mel Farr	RB	UCLA	Detroit
8.	Gene Washington	WR	Michigan State	Minnesota
9.	Bob Hyland	OL	Boston College	Green Bay
10.	Loyd Phillips	DL	Arkansas	Chicago
11.	Cas Banaszek	OL	Northwestern	San Francisco
12.	Paul Seiler	OL	Notre Dame	New York Jets
13.	Ray McDonald	RB	Idaho	Washington
14.	Ron Billingsley	DL	Wyoming	San Diego
15.	Alan Page	DL	Notre Dame	Minnesota (from Los Angeles)
16.	Dave Williams	WR	Washington	St. Louis
17.	Gene Upshaw	OL	Texas A&I	Oakland
18.	Bob Matheson	LB	Duke	Cleveland
19.	Harry Jones	RB	Arkansas	Philadelphia
20.	Jim Detwiler	RB	Michigan	Baltimore
21.	John Charles	DB	Purdue	Boston Patriots
22.	John Pitts	DB	Arizona State	Buffalo
23.	Tom Regner	OL	Notre Dame	Houston (from Dallas)
24.	Gene Trosch	DL	Miami (FL)	Kansas City
25.	Don Horn	QB	San Diego State	Green Bay
26.	Les Kelley	RB	Alabama	New Orleans

* "From" refers to the team that originally had the pick. New Orleans had the first and last picks because it was an expansion team.

This is a book about pro football, but allow me a brief aside about the '67 college season. You'll notice that Michigan State dominated the draft list. The first two selections and four of the first eight came from MSU. In 1966, the Spartans were 9–0 going into their "Game of the Century" showdown with 8–0 Notre Dame. The Fighting Irish had three players taken in the first round of the 1967 draft. Although Bubba Smith knocked both Notre Dame starting quarterback Terry Hanratty and All-American starting center George Goeddeke out of the game, the Fighting Irish rallied from a 10–0 deficit to tie the contest early in the fourth quarter. Notre Dame had the ball on its own 30-yard line with 1:30 left, but head coach Ara Parseghian elected to settle for the tie and sat on the ball. As Dan Jenkins of *Sports Illustrated* put it, "Notre Dame tied one for the Gipper."

At the time, Michigan State couldn't go to the Rose Bowl because the Big Ten had a no-repeater rule, and the Spartans had gone in 1965. Meanwhile, Notre Dame routed USC 51–0 the next week to win the mythical, and I mean mythical, national championship. (You knew you'd get my opinion on this somewhere in this book: it is absolutely ridiculous that there is no playoff for the I-A football championship! To me, BCS stands for Bullshit Concoction System. I feel better now.)

Anyway, 28 players from the 1966 Michigan State–Notre Dame game went on to play in the NFL.

The 1967 draft was significant as the first under the AFL–NFL merger, but in terms of generating talent, it was nothing special. Like almost all first rounds, this draft had a mix of great players, credible players, and total busts. Alan Page and Gene Upshaw were among the best to ever play their position, Griese and Floyd Little were very good players, players like Bob Hyland and Cas Banaszek had good but unspectacular careers, but the first round also included Loyd Phillips, Paul Seiler, Ray McDonald, and Harry Jones. All things considered, Miami did pretty well by picking Bob Griese.

1972 Miami Dolphins Statistics

Passing

	Att	Comp	Comp Pct	Yds	Yds Per	TD	Int	Rating
Morrall	150	83	55.3%	1,360	9.07	11	7	91.0
Griese	97	53	54.6%	638	6.58	4	4	71.6
Del Gaizo	9	5	55.6%	165	18.33	2	1	100.5
Briscoe	3	3	100.0%	72	24.00	0	0	118.8
Dolphins	**259**	**144**	**55.6%**	**2,235**	**8.63**	**17**	**12**	**86.9**
Opponents	348	178	51.1%	2,029	5.83	10	26	47.4
League Average			51.7%		6.82			66.3

Dolphins' passers were sacked 21 times for 159 yards in losses.
The Dolphins sacked their opponents 33 times for 280 yards in losses.

Not to take any pot shots at Bob Griese (or at Don Shula for putting Griese back at the helm during the playoffs), but I am fascinated by the fact that Earl Morrall was so much more productive throwing the football than Griese was in the same offense. Morrall led the league in both passing rating and average yards per attempt. (Yes, 150 pass attempts were enough to qualify in 1972.)

Like the 1962 Packers, the Dolphins didn't throw the ball very much (Miami was twenty-fourth of twenty-six teams in passes attempted), but their passing game was effective.

Rushing

	Att	Yds	Avg	Net Yards	TD
Csonka	213	1,117	5.24	+235	6
Morris	190	1,000	5.26	+214	12
Kiick	137	521	3.80	−46	5
Ginn	27	142	5.26		1
Leigh	21	79	3.76		0
Morrall	17	67	3.94		1
Warfield	4	23	5.75		0
Griese	3	11	3.67		1
Del Gaizo	1	0	0.00		0
Dolphins	**613**	**2,960**	**4.83**	**+423**	**26**
Opponents	389	1,548	3.98	−62	8
League Average			4.14		

The Dolphins were the first team in NFL history to have two backs each with a thousand yards rushing. I remain skeptical that it really happened. (See "Nothin' Up My Sleeve, Presto!") Miami also set the NFL record for most yards rushing by one team in a season. The record lasted all of one year; in 1973 Buffalo, led by O. J. Simpson's 2,003 yards, became the first team to gain more than 3,000 rushing yards in one season. The 1978 Patriots now hold that record (3,165), which was accomplished in the first 16-game schedule; their record is likely to stand for quite some time, unless the current rules that favor the passing game are changed.

Although Jim Kiick still played a lot, Don Shula's decision to make Mercury Morris the number two back behind Csonka helped make the Dolphins' running game even more effective. (Morris had only 57 carries in 1971; Kiick had 162.) Whether or not he really gained 1,000 yards, Morris's speed forced defenses to defend the flanks, which opened up the area between the tackles for Csonka.

Receiving

	Rec	Yds	Avg	TD
Warfield	29	606	20.90	3
Kiick	21	147	7.00	1
Twilley	20	364	18.20	3
Briscoe	16	279	17.44	4
Morris	15	168	11.20	0
Stowe	13	276	21.23	2
Fleming	13	156	12.00	1
Mandich	11	168	15.27	3
Csonka	5	48	9.60	0
Ginn	1	23	23.00	0
Dolphins	**144**	**2,235**	**15.52**	**17**
Opponents	178	2,029	11.40	10
League Average			13.18	

Marlin Briscoe is the answer to a great trivia question, if I could only figure out how to phrase it. Anyway, no one would know that he led a Super Bowl champion team in touchdown receptions and managed to do it while catching just 16 passes. Heck, Jim Mandich was tied for second in TD receptions, and he only caught 11 balls all year.

Paul Warfield tied for fifty-second in the NFL in receptions in 1972. The Dolphins were second in the NFL in lowest opponents yards per catch; the Vikings allowed just 10.60 yards per reception.

Kickoff Returns

	Ret	Yds	Avg	TD
Morris	14	334	23.86	0
Leigh	6	153	25.50	0
Matheson	2	34	17.00	0
Ginn	1	25	25.00	0
Briscoe	1	0	0.00	0
Dolphins	**24**	**546**	**22.75**	**0**
Opponents	56	1,283	22.91	0
League Average			22.88	

Punt Returns

	Ret	Yds	Avg	TD
Leigh	22	210	9.55	0
Scott	13	100	7.69	0
Anderson	5	19	3.80	0
Dolphins	**40**	**329**	**8.23**	**0**
Opponents	17	67	3.94	0
League Average			7.14	

Miami's punt coverage was very good in 1972. Opponents returned only 17 of the Dolphins' 44 punts, and for miniscule yardage. Their opponent in the Super Bowl, Washington, led the league in punt coverage allowing only 2.05 yards per return on just 19 returns.

Interceptions

	Int	Yds	Avg	TD
Scott	5	73	14.60	0
Mumphord	4	50	12.50	1
Anderson	3	34	11.33	0
Foley	3	25	8.33	0
Johnson	3	20	6.67	0
Swift	3	5	1.67	0
Buoniconti	2	17	8.50	0
Babb	1	24	24.00	0
Den Herder	1	24	24.00	0
Kolen	1	14	14.00	0
Dolphins	**26**	**286**	**11.00**	**1**
Opponents	12	249	20.75	2

Miami tied for second in the league (with Minnesota) with 26 interceptions. Pittsburgh led with 28.

Turnovers

Turnovers Committed:	28
Turnovers Forced:	46
Turnover +/–:	+18

The Dolphins were second in the league in both turnovers forced and turnover plus/minus.

Punting

	No	Avg
Seiple	36	39.9
Lothridge	4	37.5
Anderson	4	36.8
Dolphins	**44**	**39.4**
Opponents	68	41.1
League Average		40.9

Kicking

	XP	XPA	XP Pct	FG	FGA	FG Pct
Yepremian	43	45	95.6%	24	37	64.9%
Opponents	18	21	85.7%	9	19	47.4%
League Average			96.5%			61.1%

Leading Scorer:	Garo Yepremian, 115 Points
Leading Scorer, Non-Kicker:	Eugene "Mercury" Morris, 72 Points

1972 Miami Dolphins Roster

Head Coach	Don Shula
QB	Jim Del Gaizo
QB	Bob Griese
QB	Earl Morrall
RB	Larry Csonka
RB	Hubert Ginn
RB	Ed Jenkins
RB	Jim Kiick
RB/PR/KR	Charlie Leigh
RB/KR	Eugene "Mercury" Morris
WR	Marlin Briscoe
WR	Otto Stowe
WR	Howard Twilley
WR	Paul Warfield
TE	Marv Fleming
TE	Jim Mandich
TE/P	Larry Seiple
C	Jim Langer
OG/OT	Al Jenkins
OG	Bob Kuechenberg
OG	Larry Little
OT	Doug Crusan
OT	Norm Evans
OT/C	Howard Kindig
OT	Wayne Moore
K	Garo Yepremian
P	Bill Lothridge
DE	Vern Den Herder
DE/DT	Bob Heinz
DE	Bill Stanfill
DT	Jim Dunaway
DT	Manny Fernandez
DT	Maulty Moore
LB	Larry Ball
LB	Nick Buoniconti
LB	Mike Kolen
LB/DE	Bob Matheson
LB	Jesse Powell
LB	Doug Swift
DB	Dick Anderson
DB	Charlie Babb
DB	Tim Foley
DB	Curtis Johnson
DB	Lloyd Mumphord
DB/PR	Jake Scott

Hall of Famers: Shula, Griese, Csonka, Warfield, Langer, Little, Buoniconti.

CHAPTER 6

1979 Pittsburgh Steelers: The Amazing Run of the Steel Curtain

STARTING LINEUP – 1979 STEELERS			
Offense		**Defense**	
SE	John Stallworth	LE	L. C. Greenwood
LT	Jon Kolb	LT	Joe Greene
LG	Sam Davis	RT	Gary Dunn
C	Mike Webster	RE	John Banaszak
RG	Gerry Mullins/Steve Courson	LLB	Jack Ham
RT	Larry Brown	MLB	Jack Lambert
TE	Bennie Cunningham	RLB	Robin Cole
FL	Lynn Swann	LCB	Ron Johnson
QB	Terry Bradshaw	RCB	Mel Blount
RB	Sidney Thornton/Rocky Bleier	SS	Donnie Shell
RB	Franco Harris	RS	J. T. Thomas

Although the Packers won five NFL titles in seven seasons from 1961–1967, it certainly can be argued that the Steelers' run of four Super Bowl titles in six seasons from 1974 through 1979 is at least as impressive. The Packers had to win nine postseason games in order to win their five titles, including the first two Super Bowls and a conference playoff to break a tie. The Steelers had to win 12 postseason games to win those four Super Bowls.

During those six seasons, Pittsburgh had a remarkable 67–20–1 regular-season record, including an otherworldly 38–6 record at home. The Steelers nearly doubled the point total of their opposition, outscoring them 2,075–1,189. Think about that: over a *six-year* period Pittsburgh outscored their opponents by almost a 2–to–1 margin. Only 27 teams since 1950, and only 16 since 1970, have outscored their opponents by a 2–to–1 margin or better for just one season.

In this period, 16 different Steelers earned a total of 50 Pro Bowl berths. Doing the math, that means the Steelers averaged more than eight players a year, for six years, on the Pro Bowl team.

Nine Pittsburgh players from the Steel Curtain era are in the Hall of Fame. That doesn't include head coach Chuck Noll, who was inducted in 1993, or L. C. Greenwood, who may also make it to Canton some day.

"Amazing" is really not a strong enough word to describe the Steel Curtain era. The Steelers owned the NFL during their run. It's almost as if the Steelers' long period of mediocrity was an investment and the championships were the payoff.

As defending Super Bowl champions, and with three Super Bowl titles in five years, the age of some key players was about the only thing to worry the Steelers coming into the 1979 season. Ten of their 22 starters were 30 or older that year, including players like Terry Bradshaw, Jack Ham, Mel Blount, and Joe Greene. As it turned out, father time waited another year before collecting his toll from the Steelers.

Team in a Box

Record: 12–4

The Steelers won the AFC Central title for the sixth consecutive season and seventh time in eight years.

Against Teams Over .500: 7–3, 270 Points Scored, 174 Points Allowed

As you can see, the Steelers played 10 of their 16 regular-season games against teams with winning records. That is the highest number, and highest proportion, of any team in the book.

As you can also see, Pittsburgh performed very well in these games. All games count, but if one excludes the eight-turnover debacle against the Chargers, then the Steelers outscored winning teams 263–139 in nine games.

Points Scored/Allowed: 416/262 (1979 NFL Average: 321)

The Steelers led the NFL in points scored. So what? That was a far more amazing accomplishment than it seems at first glance. (See "What's a Turnover?") The Steelers also knew how to squeeze an opponent late in the game: Pittsburgh outscored its opponents 145–48 in the fourth quarter.

Yards Gained/Allowed: 6,258/4,270 (1979 NFL Average: 5,055)

Pittsburgh's per-game yardage differential (+124.3) was the sixth-best of any team since 1950 and the best of any team in this book. None of the other Steelers' teams during their period of excellence had a differential of better than +93.9.

Opponents' Record: 131–109, .546

(Not counting games against the Steelers.)

Given the number of games they played against teams with winning records, it should come as no surprise that the 1979 Steelers had the most difficult regular-season schedule of any team in the book.

Adjusted Power Index:

Offense: +3.96
Defense: +2.72
TOTAL: +6.69

The '79 Steelers' Offense Power Index (OPI) was better than their Defense Power Index (DPI). This was the only one of the great Pittsburgh teams in which that was the case. That's not to say that the '79 Steelers' defense was not as dominant as its predecessors. Their average DPI from 1972–78 was +2.65.

The '79 Steelers' DPI ranks in the top 7 percent of all teams since 1950. Their OPI ranks in the top 3 percent. *That's* a great team.

Innovations/What You Should Know:

Opponents used to say this about the Steelers in the 1970s, "They start trapping you when you get off the team bus." A Trap play works just like it sounds: a defender is "allowed" to make some penetration across the line of scrimmage, only to be knocked down by a blocker coming from another angle. The Steelers' potent running game of the 1970s was very dependant on trap plays. Their offensive linemen needed to be quick, so they couldn't be too large, but they needed strength as well.

That last point is another trademark of the Steelers teams of the 1970s. Opposing players and coaches used to remark that it looked like the Steelers' offensive linemen had legs growing out of their shoulders instead of arms. Pittsburgh's Larry Brown entered the NFL in 1971 as a 240-pound tight end. By 1977, he was a 280-pound offensive tackle.

How the linemen got so strong became an issue due to the allegations of former offensive lineman Steve Courson, who played for Pittsburgh from 1978 to 1983. Courson, who developed a serious heart condition that he alleged came from excessive steroid use, claimed that the Steelers and the NFL condoned the use of steroids. Courson's allegations came to light in a lawsuit he filed in an attempt to obtain full disability benefits due to his heart condition. Courson lost his lawsuit in 1999 and his appeal was denied in 2000.

Homegrown First-Round Picks:

DT Joe Greene, 1969; QB Terry Bradshaw, 1970; RB Franco Harris, 1972; DB J. T. Thomas, 1973; WR Lynn Swann, 1974; TE Bennie Cunningham, 1976; LB Robin Cole, 1977; DB Ron Johnson, 1978; RB Greg Hawthorne, 1979.

Of course, the Steelers are famous for having built their powerhouse through the draft. This list is very impressive. The first three—Greene, Bradshaw, Harris—are all in the Hall of Fame and earned a total of 22 Pro Bowl selections.

Lynn Swann was inducted into the Hall of Fame in 2001. He was part of the Steelers' amazing 1974 draft. (See "The Year Pittsburgh Hit the Jackpot.")

Pro Bowl Players:

DB Mel Blount, QB Terry Bradshaw, DT Joe Greene, DE L. C. Greenwood, LB Jack Ham, RB Franco Harris, LB Jack Lambert, DB Donnie Shell, WR John Stallworth, C Mike Webster.

Ten Pro Bowl players is a lot for any team, even for the 1970s Steelers.

Game-by-Game:

Sep. 3rd STEELERS 16, NEW ENGLAND 13 (OT) AT NEW ENGLAND

Opening on Monday night, the banged up Steelers beat the Patriots in overtime after tying the game with just 4:09 left in regulation. Joe Greene missed the game after spraining his knee in warm-ups, Dwight White missed the game due to an ankle injury, and L. C. Greenwood left the game in the third quarter after spraining his knee. Veteran offensive linemen Gerry Mullins and Larry Brown also missed the game with injuries. Terry Bradshaw played well: 15 of 26, 221 yards, 1 TD, 0 INT.

Sep. 9th STEELERS 38, HOUSTON 7 AT PITTSBURGH

In the first rematch of the 1978 AFC Championship Game, won by Pittsburgh 34–5 in an icy drizzle, the Steelers once again dominated the Oilers. Houston quarterback Dan Pastorini was hounded by the Steel Curtain for 5 sacks and 3 interceptions until he was knocked out of the game in the third quarter trying to tackle Steelers' defensive tackle John Banaszak, who had intercepted a pass.

The Oilers were limited to 22 net yards passing and Earl Campbell gained just 38 yards on 16 carries. Pittsburgh's offense wasn't that productive (256 yards), but it didn't have to be. Oilers head coach Bum Phillips was succinct after the game, "They kicked us." Longtime Oilers' defensive end Elvin Bethea said, "They are the best team I've ever played."

Sep. 16th STEELERS 24, ST. LOUIS 21 AT ST. LOUIS

Perhaps a bit flat after their big win against Houston, the Steelers came back to beat St. Louis after trailing 21–7 at the end of three quarters. Matt Bahr kicked the winning field goal with just 13 seconds left in regulation. Terry Bradshaw gave the Cardinals credit, "They were geared up, fired up, raring to go and blowing fire."

Four Steelers' turnovers kept the Cardinals in the game. Pittsburgh had a 25–12 advantage in first downs and a 398–212 advantage in total yards.

Sep. 23rd STEELERS 17, BALTIMORE 13 AT PITTSBURGH

Starters Franco Harris, L. C. Greenwood, Dwight White, and Ron Johnson missed the game due to injuries. Thirteen Steelers had injuries that caused them to miss the game or restrict their playing time. Still, Pittsburgh had enough to beat the Colts. The winning score came on a fourth-quarter, 28-yard screen pass from Bradshaw to tight end Bennie Cunningham, a play that the Steelers hadn't used in two years.

Running back Sidney Thornton, starting in place of Harris, ran for 129 yards on 13 carries, including a 75-yard run. Bradshaw was 19 of 29 for 249 yards and 2 touchdowns, but he also threw 2 interceptions.

Sep. 30th PHILADELPHIA 17, STEELERS 14 AT PHILADELPHIA

The Steelers turned the ball over on their first four possessions of the second half and saw their two-season winning streak end at 12 games. Steelers head coach Chuck Noll praised the opponent, "I've got nothing but a great deal of admiration for the Eagles. They had a great effort. There were many 'ifs', but they didn't happen. The reality is that they did a job."

The Eagles' offensive line did a great job protecting quarterback Ron Jaworski, who was only sacked once. They also created enough running room for running back Wilbert Montgomery who gained 98 yards on 28 carries. Sidney Thornton had another productive day for Pittsburgh with 88 yards on 16 carries.

Oct. 7th STEELERS 51, CLEVELAND 35 AT CLEVELAND

For the first time all season, the Steelers' offensive line was healthy. The result was a team record 361 yards rushing and a Pittsburgh win over stubborn Cleveland. The Steelers led 21–0 at the end of the first quarter and 44–21 early in the fourth quarter, but the Browns cut the lead to 44–35 with nine minutes left. A 15-play, 94-yard, eight-minute Steelers' TD drive finally put the game away.

The teams combined for 980 yards of offense, 522 for Pittsburgh. Franco Harris rushed for 153 yards, the fourth-highest single game total of his career, on just 19 carries. Sidney Thornton had his third consecutive solid game with 98 yards on 18 rushes. Rocky Bleier had 81 yards on just 4 carries, including a 70-yard run on the second play of the fourth quarter.

Cleveland defensive back Thom Darden came away impressed by the Steelers, "It's going to be pretty hard for someone to keep them out of the big one [the Super Bowl]."

Oct. 14th CINCINNATI 34, STEELERS 10 AT CINCINNATI

The Steelers turned the ball over nine times, seven on fumbles, and suffered an embarrassing loss to the Bengals, who were 0–6 coming into the game (they eventually finished the year at 4–12). Cincinnati returned 2 fumbles for touchdowns in the second quarter to take a 27–3 halftime lead.

Terry Bradshaw fumbled three snaps from center—in the third quarter.

Joe Greene summed it up, "It was just a complete lack of concentration."

Oct. 22nd STEELERS 42, DENVER 7 AT PITTSBURGH

The Steelers rebounded to stomp the Broncos on a Monday night. Denver was hardly a pushover in 1979; they finished 10–6 and made the playoffs. The Steelers scored 21 second-quarter points to take a 28–7 halftime lead.

Terry Bradshaw completed 18 of 24 passes for 267 yards with 2 touchdowns. Franco Harris ran for 121 yards on 17 carries. Bradshaw accounted for his successful night this way, "Denver plays all those zones. I had time to throw the ball . . . their zones aren't that hard to read. It was just a case of them not being able to get to me." Neither Bradshaw nor backup QB Mike Kruczek were sacked.

Pittsburgh's defense scuttled the Denver ground game: the Broncos gained just 53 yards on 17 attempts, and suffered 4 sacks and 2 interceptions.

Oct. 28th STEELERS 14, DALLAS 3 AT PITTSBURGH

In a highly anticipated rematch of the previous Super Bowl, Pittsburgh powered its way to a convincing, if not overwhelming, win against the Cowboys. The Steelers' defense held Dallas to 2 yards or less on 41 of their 68 offensive plays, while the Steelers' ground game made good yardage and chewed up the clock. Franco Harris had another 100-yard day, 102 yards on 18 carries, and Sidney Thornton added 68 more on 14 attempts.

This was the fourth straight time that Pittsburgh had beaten Dallas, and Steelers' defensive end Dwight White couldn't resist a few digs at the Cowboys after the game, "If I was them, I'd really start to respect the Pittsburgh Steelers. . . . It was convincing. I'd say that if any group needed to be convinced about the Pittsburgh Steelers, it was the Dallas Cowboys. And being the intelligent people I know them to be, I know the Cowboys will admit it."

Joe Greene voiced his belief about the Cowboys' offensive system, which relied on multiple formations, backfield shifts, and men-in-motion. "Nobody will beat us like that," he said. "To beat us, you've got to run the ball down our throats. Very few teams will ever beat us doing what they do."

Dallas wide receiver Drew Pearson knew he had been in a tough game, saying, "I feel like I was in the ring with Joe Frazier. If you're not ready to play a physical game, then you better not step on the field with Pittsburgh."

Nov. 4th STEELERS 38, WASHINGTON 7 AT PITTSBURGH

The Redskins had allowed the fewest points in the league coming into this game, but were burned by Pittsburgh's passing game when they decided to play their free safety up to stop the run and left their cornerbacks man-to-man with the Steelers' John Stallworth and Lynn Swann. The two wide receivers combined for 11 catches and 232 yards, with each gaining at least 100 yards. Redskins All-Pro safety Ken Houston said, "Stallworth's their best receiver and he might be the best in the league."

Nov. 11th STEELERS 30, KANSAS CITY 3 AT KANSAS CITY

After a game that saw his Chiefs outgained 355 yards to 127, head coach Marv Levy said this about the Steelers, "They're the best for two reasons. Offense and defense. There is no weakness on that club. No weakness. None. Their offense is balanced. We did a good job on the run, they threw. They have a great, pressure defense."

Nov. 18th SAN DIEGO 35, STEELERS 7 AT SAN DIEGO

After four straight easy wins by a combined score of 124–20, turnovers and the Chargers' defense led to a San Diego rout. The Steelers turned the ball over eight times and were limited to 191 yards of offense. Led by Fred Dean, the Chargers' defensive line harassed Bradshaw into throwing 5 interceptions in addition to shutting down the Steelers' running game. Pittsburgh gained just 66 yards rushing on 29 carries. San Diego took away Stallworth and Swann by doubling both of them, as well as dropping their linebackers deep to give Bradshaw no room to throw downfield. The Chargers' defensive line took care of the rest.

The loss dropped the Steelers' record to 9–3, the same as San Diego and Houston. Pittsburgh would end up "leading" the league with 52 turnovers committed. They turned the ball over 17 times, or roughly one-third of their season total, in just two games: the first Cincinnati game and the San Diego debacle.

Nov. 25th STEELERS 33, CLEVELAND 30 (OT) AT PITTSBURGH

For the second time in 1979, the Steelers and Browns played a wild game, and for the second time, Pittsburgh won. Matt Bahr's field goal six minutes into overtime ended this thriller. The Steelers had tied the game on a field goal with just 24 seconds left in regulation.

The Browns mimicked what the Chargers had done the week before, double-covering both Stallworth and Swann. Bradshaw adjusted and was far more productive in the short to medium passing game. He finished 30 of 44 for 364 yards, his career high for yardage in a game. Franco Harris, Rocky Bleier, and Bennie Cunningham combined for 20 catches for 194 yards.

The Steelers also ran for 255 yards, 151 of those by Harris. Pittsburgh gained 606 yards of offense, giving them a total of 1,128 yards in the two games against Cleveland. It was the fourth time in 1979 that the Steelers had gained at least 500 yards on offense.

Terry Bradshaw said after the game, "This was more satisfying than blowing them out. It has to be the most gratifying win of the year."

Dec. 2nd STEELERS 37, CINCINNATI 17 AT PITTSBURGH

The Steelers easily atoned for their prior loss to the Bengals, as Terry Bradshaw threw for 339 yards. Lynn Swann caught 5 passes for 192 yards, including 2 long touchdowns.

Dec. 10th HOUSTON 20, STEELERS 17 AT HOUSTON

On a Monday night, the Oilers outslugged the Steelers and moved into a first-place tie with Pittsburgh at 11–4. Pittsburgh had beaten Houston in each of their last three meetings by a combined score of 85–15. The loss was especially costly, as perennial All-Pro linebacker Jack Ham suffered an ankle injury that would require surgery and sideline him for the rest of the season, including the playoffs.

Earl Campbell became the first back to rush for 100 yards against the Steelers in 1979. He had 109 yards on 33 carries for the game after gaining just 36 yards on 16 carries in the first half. He also made the big runs on a 69-yard touchdown drive that gave Houston a 20–10 lead with 2:10 left.

Pittsburgh then moved swiftly down the field, 71 yards on three plays, to cut the lead to 20–17. On the ensuing

Transcendental Graphics

Franco Harris, *center*, runs after the hand-off from Terry Bradshaw, *left*.

onside kick, it appeared that the Steelers' Larry Anderson had legally recovered, but the officials ruled that he had touched the ball before it went the required 10 yards.

Chuck Noll complemented the Oilers after the game, "I think the Houston Oilers played the best I have ever seen them play, with a great effort."

Even though the two teams were tied for first, Pittsburgh held the relevant tiebreaker, best net points in division games, so they would win the division if they beat Buffalo in the last game of the season.

Dec. 16th STEELERS 28, BUFFALO 0 AT PITTSBURGH

The Bills didn't have a chance. Pittsburgh would clinch the AFC Central title with a win (because Houston had lost to Philadelphia), and the Steelers were at Three Rivers Stadium, where they had won 33 of their last 37 regular season games.

Pittsburgh outgained Buffalo 415 yards to 156 and finished with a 24–8 advantage in first downs. The Steelers surpassed 200 yards rushing, led by Franco Harris's 100. Pittsburgh was also bolstered by the return of a healthy Sidney Thornton, who had been hampered for over a month with an ankle injury.

Buffalo rookie linebacker Jim Haslett, a Pittsburgh native and now head coach of the Saints, was ejected from the game in the second quarter after a fight on the sidelines.

Divisional Playoff:

Dec. 30th STEELERS 34, MIAMI 14 AT PITTSBURGH

The Steelers scored 3 touchdowns in the first quarter on drives of 62, 62, and 56 yards. The game was over right then.

Despite missing starters Jon Kolb and Gerry Mullins, Pittsburgh's offensive line played a dominant game. Joe Greene thought that second-year guard Steve Courson particularly shone, "It goes back to our offensive line. Did you see number seventy-seven? [Courson's number] He was awesome, that's the word for it."

Terry Bradshaw also had praise, "The offensive line did a tremendous job and made everything possible. They manhandled Miami's defensive line."

Miami head coach Don Shula was disappointed after the game, "You can't be proud of the fact that we didn't even challenge in a game that was so important." He spoke very highly of the Steelers: "Sure they remind me of our great Miami teams. They don't have any weaknesses. They have a great offense, great defense, and an outstanding kicking game."

AFC Championship:

Jan. 6th STEELERS 27, HOUSTON 13 AT PITTSBURGH

This game will always be best known for The Catch That Wasn't. Trailing 17–10 near the end of the third quarter and with first-and-goal from the Pittsburgh 6-yard line, Oilers quarterback Dan Pastorini threw a pass to wide receiver Mike Renfro in the right corner of the end zone. Renfro made a nice catch over Steelers cornerback Ron Johnson and appeared to come down with the ball and with both feet inbounds. However, side judge Don Orr ruled that Renfro did not have possession when he came down with the ball. Orr did not make a definitive signal, and the officials huddled for a couple of minutes before ruling the play was not a touchdown. The Oilers ended up "settling" for a field goal on that drive.

What gets lost in the discussion over the Renfro play is that the Steelers clearly outplayed the Oilers. While Houston had some success throwing the ball, Pittsburgh completely shut down NFL rushing leader Earl Campbell, limiting him to just 15 yards on 17 carries. The Oilers did not score an offensive touchdown; their lone TD was a 75-yard interception return by Vernon Perry in the first quarter. Offensively, the Steelers had a balanced attack gaining 161 yards rushing and 197 passing.

Sometimes, the team that plays better doesn't win. Nobody should mistake me for a Steelers fan, either. Still, there really is no question as to which team played better on this day.

Before the game, many observers had dubbed this game the "real" Super Bowl. Houston head coach Bum Phillips, in his down-home yet eloquent way, took both sides of the argument: "No, that wasn't the Super Bowl. That was just us and Pittsburgh. . . . I don't think anybody can beat Pittsburgh except Houston, and we didn't."

Super Bowl XIV:

Jan. 20th STEELERS 31, LOS ANGELES 19 AT PASADENA

For most of the two weeks before the Super Bowl, Chuck Noll dodged questions comparing his Steelers to other great teams of the past and questions comparing the 1979 team to other Steelers' teams. At the last press conference, two days before the game, Noll finally gave in. When asked once again to compare the 1979 Steelers to his other teams he said, "This team, right now, is the best."

After watching Steelers' game film, Rams backup QB Bob Lee said, "It's hard to believe they lost four games." Despite what Lee thought, the Rams—11-point underdogs—gave the Steelers all they could handle.

Los Angeles shut down Pittsburgh's running game (Harris and Bleier gained just 71 yards on 30 carries). The Rams built leads of 13–10 at halftime, and 19–17 at the end of three quarters. The Rams' offensive line played well, giving third-year quarterback Vince Ferragamo time to throw. Ferragamo had become the starter after Pat Haden broke his finger late in the season. The Rams won three of Ferragamo's four regular season starts, then won playoff games at Dallas and at Tampa Bay to get into the Super Bowl. In Super Bowl XIV, Ferragamo completed 15 of 25 passes for 212 yards.

The Steelers won the game in the fourth quarter by making big plays in the passing game. About three minutes into the quarter on third-and-8 from their own 27-yard line, Pittsburgh ran "60 Prevent Slot Hook and Go," where John Stallworth, lined up as a slot receiver, faked a hook route and then took off down the field. The play went for a 73-yard touchdown. The Steelers had run the play several times in practices before the game, and it had never worked.

After a Jack Lambert interception, a 45-yard pass from Bradshaw to Stallworth helped set up Franco Harris's 1-yard TD run with less than two minutes left. Although Bradshaw threw 3 interceptions, ultimately it was his productive passing that won the game. He completed 14 of 21 passes for 309 yards and 2 touchdowns. His 14.71 yards per pass attempt is still the Super Bowl record.

Stallworth summed things up when he said, "This was a typical game for us. We've had a lot of turnovers all year, but we have the type of people who come back." Bradshaw saluted the Rams, "I wasn't surprised at the way the Rams played. They believed they could win. That's what makes great teams."

Rams defensive end Fred Dryer spoke about what separated Pittsburgh from the rest of the league, "What probably makes the Steelers different from Dallas, LA, or any of the good teams in the NFL is the long pass. They do it so well."

For a number of reasons, Pittsburgh had its fourth Super Bowl title in six seasons.

Elsewhere Around the NFL:

Oct. 14th In his second career start, rookie quarterback Phil Simms threw for 300 yards and 2 touchdowns to lead the Giants to their second win of the season, 32–16 over winless San Francisco. The 49ers head coach was also a rookie: Bill Walsh. The two would meet many more times, with much more on the line.

Nov. 4th In his team's tenth game, St. Louis running back Ottis Anderson led the Cardinals to a 37–7 win over Minnesota, gaining 164 yards on 25 carries, becoming the first Cards' rookie to rush for 1,000 yards in a season. Anderson finished third in the NFL in rushing in 1979 with 1,605 yards behind two moderately famous guys: Earl Campbell and Walter Payton.

Dec. 16th With the Bears' 42–6 win over St. Louis earlier in the day, Washington needed to beat arch-rival Dallas at Texas Stadium to make the playoffs. That all but seemed assured, as the Redskins led the Cowboys 34-21 with seven minutes left. Dallas QB Roger Staubach, playing in his last regular-season game, had other ideas. He threw 2 TD passes in the final minutes, including one to Tony Hill with 39 seconds left, to lead the Cowboys to a 35–34 win, which knocked the Redskins out of the playoffs.

What Happened the Next Season:

The run of the Steel Curtain came to an end in 1980. The Steelers had a lot of injuries: John Stallworth played only three games, offensive lineman Sam Davis missed the entire season, while fellow linemen Steve Courson and Jon Kolb missed a total of 17 games between them, and Franco Harris and Lynn Swann each missed three games. The truth, though, was the team was getting old. Pittsburgh finished third in the AFC Central at 9–7, and out of the playoffs. The 1980s would be much different than the '70s in Pittsburgh.

What's a Turnover?

The Steelers led the NFL in 1979 with 416 points scored. OK, what's so great about that? Is it that it's the only time in their history that Pittsburgh has led the entire NFL in points scored? Well, that's true, but that's not what makes their accomplishment so amazing. (The Steelers have had some woefully inept offensive teams in their history. In 1940, they scored 60 points in the entire 11-game season.)

What makes their league-leading point total so remarkable is that they *committed the most turnovers in the league!* Pittsburgh's 52 turnovers was the worst figure in the NFL in 1979. The 1979 Steelers are one of only two teams since 1950 (the 2001 St. Louis Rams are the other) to lead the league in points scored while committing the most turnovers. In that period, about one-third of all teams that cough up the ball the most times have finished last or next-to-last in the league in points scored. Here are the teams with the most turnovers in a season since the merger in 1970 (except the strike seasons of 1982 and 1987), where they ranked in points scored, and their record:

Year	Team	Points Scored Rank	Overall Record
1970	Buffalo	23 (of 26)	3–10–1
1971	Houston	16 (of 26)	4–9–1
1972	San Diego	18 (of 26)	4–9–1
1973	Houston	23 (of 26)	1–13
1974	Atlanta	26 (of 26)	3–11
1975	New England	14 (of 26)	3–11
1976	New York Jets	26 (of 28)	3–11
1977	Cleveland	12 (of 28)	6–8
1978	San Francisco	28 (of 28)	2–14
1979	Pittsburgh	1st (of 28)	12–4
1980	San Diego	4 (of 28)	11–5
1981	Cleveland	24 (of 28)	5–11
1983	New York Giants	25 (of 28)	3–12–1
1984	LA Raiders	9 (of 28)	11–5
1985	Buffalo	28 (of 28)	2–14
1986	LA Raiders	16 (of 28)	8–8
	San Diego	15 (of 28)	4–12

Year	Team	Points Scored Rank	Overall Record
1988	Tampa Bay	22 (of 28)	5–11
1989	Detroit	19 (of 28)	7–9
1990	Cleveland	27 (of 28)	3–13
1991	Tampa Bay	26 (of 28)	3–13
1992	New England	27 (of 28)	2–14
1993	Houston	4 (of 28)	12–4
1994	Houston	28 (of 28)	2–14
1995	Arizona	28 (of 30)	4–12
1996	New York Jets	27 (of 30)	1–15
1997	New Orleans	30 (of 30)	6–10
1998	San Diego	29 (of 30	5–11
1999	Arizona	29 (of 31)	6–10
	Minnesota	4 (of 31)	10–6
2000	San Diego	26 (of 31)	1–15
2001	St. Louis	1 (of 31)	14–2

For the most part, "leading" the league in turnovers is not the way to have a good season. Granting that the size of the league has changed since 1970, on average the team that has committed the most turnovers has ranked twentieth in points scored. Eight of these 31 teams finished last or next-to-last in the league in points scored. The combined record of these teams is 164–328–4.

So you can see why leading the league in points scored—not to mention going 12–4 and winning the Super Bowl—was an extraordinary feat for the 1979 Steelers. NFL coaches won't believe this, but a team's turnover margin is in no small way due to luck. How do I know this? Forty percent of the time a team's turnover margin flip-flops from one season to the next; that is, if they were positive one season they're negative the next season or vice versa. That's kind of a high percentage if turnover ratio is primarily a team skill. The correlation between turnover margins in successive seasons is rather small, not zero, but small enough to strongly suggest that luck plays a large role in turnovers. But leading the league in points and turnovers in the same year? That fact makes 1979 Steelers' achievements even more remarkable and suggests that the true quality of the team was even better than its numbers.

The Year Pittsburgh Hit the Jackpot

Lynn Swann, Jack Lambert, John Stallworth, Mike Webster. What do they have in common besides being important members of the Steelers' Super Bowl champion teams? As some of you probably know, they were all taken in the 1974 draft. Swann, Lambert, Stallworth, and Webster earned a total of 25 Pro Bowl berths, not to mention four inductions to the Pro Football Hall of Fame. How does that number compare to other NFL teams in the same time period, say the 1970s?

As it turned out, those 25 Pro Bowl berths for one draft was pretty good. I analyzed player drafts from 1970–1979 and the team, the position, the round, the overall pick, and how many NFL seasons/games/Pro Bowls for each—more than 4,000 draft picks. Take a look at the top five 1970s drafts as measured by the number of Pro Bowl berths:

Year	Team	Total Pro Bowl Berths from Draft
1974	Pittsburgh Steelers	25
1975	Dallas Cowboys	20
1971	Pittsburgh Steelers	14
1971	Los Angeles Rams	13
1975	Los Angeles Rams	13

Total Pro Bowl Berths includes those earned by players no longer playing for the team that drafted them. In this case, all 25 of those Pro Bowl berths were earned while playing for Pittsburgh.

For the entire decade, the average NFL team's drafts (not including Seattle or Tampa Bay, which entered the league in 1976) produced 27 Pro Bowl berths. That means the Steelers got just about as much "star power" in one draft as the average team got in 10 drafts. Pittsburgh's 1971 draft (Jack Ham/Mike Wagner) was very productive as well.

The teams that made up the top five individual drafts also dominated the decade. The Rams led with 70 Pro Bowl berths for the decade. Pittsburgh had 60 and Dallas had 51. Nine teams had fewer than 20. LA, Pittsburgh, and Dallas all had pretty successful decades, although the Rams failed to win the Super Bowl. As a group, draft success, even measured as simply as the number of Pro Bowl berths, correlated to on-field success in the 1970s.

Yes, I know that drafts at the end of the decade would show up on the field in the following decade. Yes, there is a Pro Bowl selection bias in favor of players on good teams. However, it is also true that teams that win have more Pro Bowl caliber players and/or players having Pro Bowl caliber seasons.

Here is a chart showing the 1970s won–lost record for the top five drafting teams (as measured by Pro Bowl berths) and the bottom six (including a tie among the bottom feeders).

	Avg PBB	Avg W	Avg L	AGG Pct	Avg WS
Top Five	51.8	93.6	48.2	.658	8.2
Bottom Six	11.8	62.7	78.8	.444	3.7

PBB = Pro Bowl berths
AGG Pct = Aggregate (group) winning percentage
Avg WS = Average number of winning seasons from 1970–79

One could make the argument that the organizations that draft well are also the ones that do other things well, which is why they win. While that is probably true, drafting the "raw material" is usually a key part of a winning football team.

Empirically as well as subjectively, the Steelers' 1974 draft was one for the ages. Winning by building through the draft, as Pittsburgh did under Chuck Noll, only works if you draft the right players. The Steelers usually drafted the right players.

The Coach: Chuck Noll

Coaching Record

	W	L	T	Pct	
1969	1	13	0	.071	
1970	5	9	0	.357	
1971	6	8	0	.429	
1972	11	3	0	.786	AFC Central Division title
1973	10	4	0	.714	AFC Wild Card
1974	10	3	1	.750	AFC Central Division title; AFC champs; Super Bowl champs
1975	12	2	0	.857	AFC Central Division title; AFC champs; Super Bowl champs
1976	10	4	0	.714	AFC Central Division title
1977	9	5	0	.643	AFC Central Division title
1978	14	2	0	.875	AFC Central Division title; AFC champs; Super Bowl champs
1979	12	4	0	.750	AFC Central Division title; AFC champs; Super Bowl champs
1980	9	7	0	.563	
1981	8	8	0	.500	
1982	6	3	0	.667	AFC Playoffs

(continued next page)

Coaching Record *(continued)*

	W	L	T	Pct	
1983	10	6	0	.625	AFC Central Division title
1984	9	7	0	.563	AFC Central Division title
1985	7	9	0	.438	
1986	6	10	0	.375	
1987	8	7	0	.533	
1988	5	11	0	.313	
1989	9	7	0	.563	AFC Wild Card
1990	9	7	0	.563	
1991	7	9	0	.438	
Total	**193**	**148**	**1**	**.566**	

Like many successful NFL head coaches, Chuck Noll has what thoroughbred racing people would call a great pedigree. A Cleveland native, Noll played seven years for the Browns under Paul Brown. When he was inexplicably passed over for the head coaching position at his alma mater, the University of Dayton, Noll joined the staff of legendary coach Sid Gillman with the AFL Chargers in 1960. In 1966, he joined almost-teammate Don Shula's staff in Baltimore. (Shula had played for the Browns in 1951–52; Noll's first year with Cleveland was 1953.)

"You learn something from everyone," Knoll once said. "Sid was one of the game's prime researchers and offensive specialists. In six years with him, I had more exposure to football than I normally would have received in twelve years. From Don, I learned the importance of organization and the proper attitudes. I also learned from Paul Brown, but in a different way because I played for him."

Noll was probably not Pittsburgh's first choice to replace Bill Austin as head coach in 1969. The Steelers were interested in Penn State's Joe Paterno, but Dan Rooney, entrusted by his father with the responsibility of picking the new head coach, enjoyed an almost instant rapport with Noll. As Rooney later recalled, "From the very beginning he impressed me. To be honest, we hit it off very well. I remember his knowledge of the game was the thing that impressed me the most, and not just his knowing formations and so forth. He had a very good understanding of our players and our situation, which I thought was remarkable for another team's assistant coach. I knew from the beginning that Chuck was a guy we had to give a lot of consideration to."

Throughout Noll's stay as Steelers' head coach, Rooney and he remained close. Theirs was a relationship unique among owner and head coach in the NFL. That bond and the faith that the Rooneys had in Noll is what kept them from even thinking about making a change during Noll's first seasons in Pittsburgh. Art Rooney, Jr. expressed his family's feelings about Noll this way, "Chuck Noll is the best thing to happen to the Rooneys since they got on the boat in Ireland."

Noll believed in building through the draft. Free agency for NFL players didn't exist during Noll's tenure, and he avoided trades because he didn't want "someone else's problems." He said, "You build with draft choices. You find people with talents adaptable to your plans, and then you teach them to do things the way we do them."

The general perception of Noll during his days with Pittsburgh was that he was cold and unemotional. He certainly was no Bum Phillips, his unconstrained division rival with Houston.

Noll and Terry Bradshaw never had a good relationship, according to Bradshaw. In his book *It's Only a Game,* Bradshaw commented, "Chuck Noll took to me like a duck takes to an oil spill. When I did something wrong, as I came off the field he would be right there in my face. I wasn't used to that type of treatment; the coaches I had played for had always been extremely supportive. But not Chuck Noll. He and I would enjoy as much success together as any coach and quarterback in pro football history, but the scars he inflicted those first few seasons never went away."

Other players, however, claimed that Noll was not as cold as his reputation. Star linebacker Jack Ham said, "In reality, he cared immensely about his players." Ham also said, "I think of all the people who were involved in the Steelers organization during our Super Bowl years, Chuck Noll is by far the most deserving to be inducted into the Pro Football Hall of Fame."

During the Steelers' glory years, the NFL was dominated by a select few franchises. Here are the top five teams in winning percentage from 1972–79:

1972–79	W	L	T	Pct	Division Titles	Super Bowl Titles
Pittsburgh Steelers	88	27	1	.763	7	4
Oakland Raiders	84	30	2	.733	5	1
Dallas Cowboys	84	32	0	.724	5	1
Miami Dolphins	84	32	0	.724	4	2
Los Angeles Rams	81	33	2	.707	7	0

In retrospect, one can understand the frustration of Rams' fans during this period. They won as many division titles as Pittsburgh, yet appeared in just one Super Bowl—and lost to the Steelers. This chart also shows just how successful the Steelers were under Noll during this time.

The Quarterback: Terry Bradshaw

Year	Team	Att	Comp	Yds	TD	Int	YPA	Rating	Lg Avg	W	L	Pct
1970	PIT	218	83	1,410	6	24	6.47	30.4	65.6	3	5	.375
1971	PIT	373	203	2,259	13	22	6.06	59.7	62.2	5	8	.385
1972	PIT	308	147	1,887	12	12	6.13	64.1	66.3	11	3	.786
1973	PIT	180	89	1,183	10	15	6.57	54.5	64.9	8	1	.889
1974	PIT	148	67	785	7	8	5.30	55.2	64.2	5	2	.714
1975	PIT	286	165	2,055	18	9	7.19	88.0	65.8	12	2	.857
1976	PIT	192	92	1,177	10	9	6.13	65.4	67.0	4	4	.500
1977	PIT	314	162	2,523	17	19	8.04	71.4	61.2	9	5	.643
1978	PIT	368	207	2,915	28	20	7.92	84.7	65.0	14	2	.875
1979	PIT	472	259	3,724	26	25	7.89	77.0	70.4	12	4	.750
1980	PIT	424	218	3,339	24	22	7.88	75.0	73.7	9	6	.600
1981	PIT	370	201	2,887	22	14	7.80	83.9	72.9	8	6	.571
1982	PIT	240	127	1,768	17	11	7.37	81.4	73.4	6	3	.667
1983	PIT	8	5	77	2	0	9.63	133.9	75.9	0	0	—
Total		**3,901**	**2,025**	**27,989**	**212**	**210**	**7.17**	**70.9**	**67.8**	**106**	**51**	**.675**
1975–79		1,632	885	12,394	99	82	7.59	78.2	66.0	51	17	.750

YPA = Yards Per Pass Attempt
Rating = Passer Rating
Lg Avg = League Passer Rating in that season
W, L, Pct = Team's Record in his starts

Bradshaw was the first pick in the 1970 draft. By the flip of a coin, that pick belonged to Pittsburgh. The Steelers and Bears had both finished 1–13 in 1969, and not long before the draft a coin toss decided which team picked first. Chicago called heads and, obviously, the coin came up tails. Who did the Bears end up picking? They didn't take anybody; they traded the pick to their arch-rival, the Packers, in exchange for running back Elijah Pitts, offensive lineman Bob Hyland, and linebacker Lee Roy Caffey. The three players Chicago received played a *combined* two seasons with the Bears. Green Bay picked defensive lineman Mike McCoy, who played 11 years in the NFL—seven with Green Bay—and enjoyed a solid career, but he was not a major star.

As usually happens with first overall pick, Pittsburgh received numerous trade proposals. Steelers owner Art Rooney, intervening in draft matters for probably the only time, did not let Pittsburgh trade the pick. As he said later, "I was tired of giving away great players and suffering through fifteen years of them coming back to town with other teams." Quarterbacks that the Steelers had drafted or acquired only to be released or traded included Johnny Unitas, Len Dawson, and Earl Morrall.

Although Pittsburgh ended nearly four decades of mediocrity by making the playoffs in 1972 and winning the Super Bowl in 1974, Bradshaw struggled during his first five seasons. At times, because of his arm and his strength, he made plays that few other quarterbacks could make. At other times, he made poor decisions and threw interceptions hand over fist. As Bradshaw later related, "There was a lot of pain in those growing stages. I wouldn't want to go through it again, but I wouldn't change it. It had to happen."

Bradshaw had his first genuinely productive season in Pittsburgh's second Super Bowl title year, 1975. By the end of the 1970s, the Steelers' passing game was a major factor in their second pair of Super Bowl championships.

I'm kind of a chart freak (if you hadn't noticed), but I am fascinated by the clear demarcation of Bradshaw's career, before and after he became an effective passer.

Bradshaw	Pass Att	Comp Pct	YPA	TD	Int	Passer Rating
1970–1974	1,227	48.0%	6.13	48	81	53.2
1975–1983	2,674	53.7%	7.65	164	129	79.1

It is unusual for a top-flight quarterback to take that long to develop his passing skills. In another situation on another team with another owner, Bradshaw may not have been given that much time. Success is almost always a combination of talent, effort, and luck/circumstance.

So, where do I think Bradshaw rates among the all-time great quarterbacks? First, one has to define what makes a great quarterback. For me, it is a player who can throw the ball very effectively and who consistently plays on winning teams. I think playing on winners is a proxy for that elusive quality called leadership. A championship here and there certainly doesn't hurt. While there's no doubt that Bradshaw had great physical talent, that his passing was a key component to at least the 1978 and 1979 Super Bowl titles, and that his toughness was an important part of the Steelers' playing psyche, I can't rate Bradshaw among the upper echelon of quarterbacks, even with four Super Bowl titles. His record as a passer is just not strong enough for me to compare him to Johnny Unitas or Joe Montana.

Different offensive systems shape passing statistics differently. The type of passing attack that the Steelers used, particularly in the late 1970s, was not conducive to very high completion percentages and low interception rates.

However, I think almost everyone would concede that the individual player has something to do with the numbers he compiles, that it's not solely a function of his teammates' ability and the offensive system. Bradshaw had only two seasons, 1975 and 1978, where his passing rating was substantially better than the league average. His interception rate was usually the biggest reason why his rating wasn't higher. In his book *It's Only a Game* Bradshaw talked about his interceptions, "I had a strong arm. I was a gambler. Most of the interceptions I threw were caused by my own ego. I can throw that ball past the defender. Man, I had confidence. I also had a lot of interceptions."

I am not taking that one remark and concluding that all of Bradshaw's "bad" passes were his fault. I don't hold Bradshaw's "low" completion percentage against him because yards per pass attempt is much more important. Regardless, the elite passers in history have been able to compile much better numbers than Bradshaw, and not all of them played in low-risk passing schemes. The way I define a great quarterback, his passing performance has to be more distinguishable from the norm than Bradshaw's. For that reason, I don't consider him to be among the upper echelon of NFL quarterbacks.

1979 Pittsburgh Steelers Statistics

Passing

	Att	Comp	Comp Pct	Yds	Yds Per	TD	Int	Rating
Bradshaw	472	259	54.9%	3,724	7.89	26	25	77.0
Kruczek	20	13	65.0%	153	7.65	0	1	67.3
Steelers	**492**	**272**	**55.3%**	**3,877**	**7.88**	**26**	**26**	**76.6**
Opponents	480	226	47.1%	2,912	6.07	19	27	56.4
League Average			54.1%		6.87			70.4

Steelers' passers were sacked 27 times for 222 yards in losses.
The Steelers sacked their opponents 49 times for 351 yards in losses.

Bradshaw's passing rating wasn't great, but his average gain per pass attempt was a yard better than the league average, and that usually correlates well with team success. The Steelers ran a high-risk, high-reward passing game. Only three teams threw more interceptions, but Pittsburgh led the NFL in yards per pass attempt.

Rushing

	Att	Yds	Avg	Net Yards	TD
Harris	267	1,186	4.44	+118	11
Thornton	118	585	4.96	+113	6
Bleier	92	434	4.72	+66	4
Hawthorne	28	123	4.39		1
A. Anderson	18	118	6.56		1
Bradshaw	21	83	3.95		0
Moser	11	33	3.00		1
Kruczek	4	20	5.00		0
Smith	1	12	12.00		0
Swann	1	9	9.00		0
Steelers	**561**	**2,603**	**4.64**	**+359**	**25**
Opponents	506	1,709	3.38	−315	9
League Average			4.00		

The Steelers were second in the NFL in rushing yards and first in yards per carry. Sidney Thornton led the AFC and was second overall in the NFL in yards per carry.

Receiving

	Rec	Yds	Avg	TD
Stallworth	70	1,183	16.90	8
Swann	41	808	19.71	5
Cunningham	36	512	14.22	4
Harris	36	291	8.08	1
Bleier	31	277	8.94	0
Smith	17	243	14.29	2
Thornton	16	231	14.44	4
Grossman	12	217	18.08	1
Hawthorne	8	47	5.88	0
Bell	3	61	20.33	0
Moser	1	6	6.00	0
Brown	1	1	1.00	1
Steelers	**272**	**3,877**	**14.25**	**27**
Opponents	226	2,912	12.88	19
League Average			12.70	

John Stallworth was fourth in the NFL among wide receivers in receptions and second in yardage. Among the 66 backs with at least 100 touches (rushes and receptions) in 1979, Sidney Thornton ranked first in both average per touch and touchdown percentage. He was the Steelers' second-round pick in 1977 from Northwestern State in Louisiana and this was his best season, by far, of the six he played.

Kickoff Returns

	Ret	Yds	Avg	TD
L. Anderson	34	732	21.53	0
A. Anderson	13	200	15.38	0
Hawthorne	2	46	23.00	0
Moser	1	6	6.00	0
Cole	1	3	3.00	0
Steelers	**51**	**987**	**19.35**	**0**
Opponents	81	1,668	20.59	0
League Average			20.28	

Punt Returns

	Ret	Yds	Avg	TD
Smith	16	146	9.13	0
Bell	45	378	8.40	0
Dornbrook	1	0	0.00	0
Swann	1	−1	−1.00	0
Steelers	**63**	**523**	**8.30**	**0**
Opponents	31	276	8.90	0
League Average			7.66	

Interceptions

	Int	Yds	Avg	TD
Lambert	6	29	4.83	0
Shell	5	10	2.00	0
Wagner	4	31	7.75	0
Winston	3	48	16.00	1
Blount	3	1	0.33	0
Ham	2	8	4.00	0
Woodruff	1	31	31.00	0
Johnson	1	20	20.00	0
L. Anderson	1	19	19.00	0
Banaszak	1	3	3.00	0
Steelers	**27**	**200**	**7.41**	**1**
Opponents	26	401	15.42	1

The Steelers were fourth in the NFL in interceptions in 1979.

Turnovers

Turnovers Committed:	52
Turnovers Forced:	42
Turnover +/−:	−10

As pointed out in "What's a Turnover?," Pittsburgh committed the most turnovers of any team in the league in 1979. In case you're interested, their 42 forced turnovers ranked eighth in the league and their turnover plus/minus ranked twenty-fourth.

Punting

	No	Avg
Colquitt	68	40.2
Opponents	100	40.0
League Average		39.3

There must have been some kind of special teams' disease in the NFL in 1979. Look at the league averages for kickoff returns, punt returns, and punting and compare them to, let's say, 1999 and 2000:

Year	Kickoff Returns	Punt Returns	Punting
1979	20.28	7.66	39.3
1999	21.23	9.35	41.7
2000	21.93	9.98	41.7

The poor kick and punt return averages can at least be partially explained because 1979 was the first year of new rules limiting how players on receiving teams could block, and it probably took players and officials some time to get used to the new rules. I can't explain why punting was so mediocre that year.

Kicking

	XP	XPA	XP Pct	FG	FGA	FG Pct
Bahr	50	52	96.2%	18	30	60.0%
Opponents	28	31	90.3%	16	26	61.5%
League Average			90.3% (!)			63.1%

Leading Scorer: Matt Bahr, 104 Points

Leading Scorer, Non-Kicker: Franco Harris, 72 Points

1979 Pittsburgh Steelers Roster

Head Coach	Chuck Noll
QB	Terry Bradshaw
QB	Mike Kruczek
QB	Cliff Stoudt
RB/KR	Anthony Anderson
RB	Rocky Bleier
RB	Franco Harris
RB	Greg Hawthorne
RB	Rick Moser
RB	Sidney Thornton
WR/PR	Theo Bell
WR/PR	Jim Smith
WR	John Stallworth
WR	Lynn Swann
TE	Bennie Cunningham
TE	Randy Grossman
C/OG	Thom Dornbrook
C	Mike Webster
OG	Steve Courson
OG	Sam Davis
OG/OT	Gerry Mullins
OT	Larry Brown
OT	Jon Kolb
OT/C	Ted Peterson
K	Matt Bahr
P	Craig Colquitt
DE/DT	John Banaszak
DE	L. C. Greenwood
DE	Dwight White
DT	Tom Beasley
DT/DE	Gary Dunn
DT/DE	Steve Furness
DT	Joe Greene
LB	Robin Cole
LB	Tom Graves
LB	Jack Ham
LB	Jack Lambert
LB	Loren Toews
LB	Zack Valentine
LB	Dennis Winston
DB/KR	Larry Anderson
DB	Mel Blount
DB	Ron Johnson
DB	Donnie Shell
DB	J. T. Thomas
DB	Mike Wagner
DB	Dwayne Woodruff

Hall of Famers: Noll, Bradshaw, Harris, Stallworth, Swann, Webster, Greene, Ham, Lambert, Blount.

CHAPTER 7

Football Hodgepodge

Sounds like a *Jeopardy* category, doesn't it? "I'll take Football Hodgepodge for $400, Alex." This chapter will contain things that don't quite belong in any team chapter, such as the piece about the teams that just missed the cut, and other assorted odds and ends. Let's start with . . .

They Just Missed the Cut

Not that Jimmy Johnson or Jerry Jones could give a shit, but the Mike Jones tackle that kept Kevin Dyson out of the end zone at the end of the Rams–Titans Super Bowl also kept the **1992 Dallas Cowboys** out of the book. Well, at least it kept them from having their own chapter.

The 1992 Cowboys were a superbly balanced team with an unadjusted Power Index over +6.00. Because of a soft schedule, though, their Adjusted Power Index (API) was +5.90. The 1992 Cowboys are one of only nine teams since 1950 with an Offense and Defense Power Index each at +2.90 or better. Five of the other eight teams are in the book. If the 1999 Rams had lost the Super Bowl, the Cowboys would have "made" the book as the twelfth team. I guess I could have put them in anyway, but I didn't like the idea of 13 teams and all of the teams that are in made the "magic" +6.00 cutoff. If the '92 Cowboys had compiled an API just .10 higher, I would have included them.

If one uses the difference between Offense and Defense Power Index as a measure of balance—the smaller the difference, the more balanced the team—then the 1992 Cowboys are the fourth most-balanced team of the nearly 1,100 team seasons since 1950. Of all teams with an overall Power Index of +4.00 or better—and only about 9 percent of teams have reached ever that level—the 1992 Cowboys are the most balanced.

The most amazing thing about the Cowboys' return to glory is how quickly it happened. In 1988, Tom Landry's last year as head coach, the Cowboys were 3–13. In Jimmy Johnson's first year as head coach, 1989, they were 1–15. That's four wins in two seasons. In 1991–92, the Cowboys won 24 games and a Super Bowl title.

Emmitt Smith had a great season in 1992, rushing for 1,713 yards with a 4.6 yards per carry average, and 18 touchdowns. Michael Irvin had a very good season (79 receptions for 1,396 yards and 7 touchdowns). Troy Aikman had an excellent year, hitting almost 64 percent of his passes and throwing a career-high 23 TDs. The Cowboys' defense allowed the fewest yards in the league, despite having no Pro Bowl players.

Of course, 1992 marked the first of Dallas's three Super Bowl wins in four seasons. Maybe some of you think that feat should have gotten the team its own chapter. If this book had been like *Baseball Dynasties,* where teams *had* to be very good or great for at least three consecutive seasons to be included, then the early 1990s Cowboys would have been represented. Since the focus here is single-season greatness, the 1992 Cowboys missed by the barest of margins.

I really don't want to discuss teams that are close in time to others of the same franchise, but the **1984 San Francisco 49ers** won the Super Bowl, had a 15–1 regular-season record, and a great +5.56 Adjusted Power Index (API). The 1984 team, even though it was prior to Jerry Rice's arrival, was the first great San Francisco team. I think that even Bill Walsh would admit that the 1981 team, the first 49ers Super Bowl champion, was not a "great" team, at least not on the historic sense of the word.

To me, one of the most amazing things about the '84 team was that the *entire* starting secondary went to the Pro Bowl: Ronnie Lott, Eric Wright, Carlton Williamson, and Dwight Hicks. It was the unexpected great play of their secondary in 1981, with three rookie starters (Lott, Wright, and Williamson), that played a major role in San Francisco's Super Bowl win that year.

In 1984, Joe Montana had the first of his three seasons with a passer rating of better than 100. Counting the postseason, Montana threw at least 1 touchdown pass in 16 of the 18 games he played in. Wendell Tyler (remember him?) ran for 1,262 yards and an excellent 5.1 average. Tyler was known as a fumbler (two years earlier he suffered an NFL-worst 10 fumbles in a nine-game season), but he was a productive back.

Once again ignoring the "rule" about not discussing teams that are close in time to others of the same franchise, the **1977 Dallas Cowboys** won the Super Bowl and had an outstanding +5.58 API. The Cowboys' running game returned to prominence with the addition of rookie Tony Dorsett; he surpassed 1,000 yards even though he was brought along slowly with just 21 carries in his first three games. Roger Staubach had one of his better seasons: a passing rating of 87.0 (1977 NFL rating was just 61.2) and a TD–INT ratio of 18–9. The Cowboys' defense was stingy against the run, allowing the fewest rushing yards in the NFC and just a 3.6 average yards per carry. They were tough against the pass, too, allowing just a 48.2 passing rating while leading the conference with 53 sacks. The Cowboys were excellent in the postseason, outscoring three opponents 87–23 and outgaining them 1,020 yards to 594.

Breaking the rule again—maybe it shouldn't be a rule—both the **1974 and 1975 Pittsburgh Steelers** won the Super Bowl and had APIs of greater than +5.00 (1974: +5.08, 1975: +5.16). The 1974 team was a "surprise" Super Bowl winner since most people expected the Oakland Raiders to win it all after they had defeated two-time defending champion Miami 28–26 in a thrilling playoff game. The Steelers, however, had the best API in the league in 1974. (Oakland was sixth and Miami was seventh.) The 1975 Steelers were expected to win and did. That year was Terry Bradshaw's first productive season throwing the football. He had an 88.0 passing rating, competing almost 58 percent of his passes with a TD–INT ratio of 18–9. In his five NFL seasons prior to 1975, Bradshaw had a 53.2 passing rating, completing 48 percent of his passes and a TD–INT ratio of 48–81.

Instead of listing the API for every other Super Bowl or pre-1966 NFL champion, I will discuss the best championship team, as determined by API, for those franchises that had more than one team win it all. Chronologically, the first of these teams is the **1952 Detroit Lions.** The Lions won the NFL championship in 1952 and 1953; the 1953 team was, thankfully, the last all-white NFL champion. The '52 Lions (+4.25 API) started the season slowly, with two losses in their first three games. They lost just once the rest of the way; the Lions lost to the Bears 24–23 in week 9. The Lions scored more than 40 points five times in their last nine games. They wound up tied with the Rams for the National Conference title (the Conferences were named American and National in 1950–52) and in those days the only tiebreaker was a conference playoff. Detroit earned its way to the championship game by beating Los Angeles, 31–21. In the NFL title game against Cleveland, the Lions rode 3 turnovers and three missed field goals by Lou Groza, who was playing with cracked ribs, to a 17–7 win.

Detroit's Cloyce Box caught 15 touchdown passes during the regular season; Bobby Layne kept the offense going through the air since the running game was hampered by Doak Walker's injury. Layne also led all NFL quarterbacks in rushing and was second on the Lions, with 411 yards. The Lions' defense was tough to run on and forced 57 turnovers, the most per-game of any NFL team since 1950, keeping in mind that is somewhat misleading, as the rate of turnovers has declined over time.

Lon Babby would never forgive me if I didn't discuss the **New York Giants from the mid-1950s to the early 1960s.** The Giants played in six NFL title games in eight seasons from 1956 to 1963. The 1959 team that lost to Baltimore in the NFL title game had the best API of these teams (+5.35), while the only one to win the NFL title, 1956, had just a fair API of +2.34. The 1961–63 team that lost three straight championship games had good APIs between +3.41 and +4.57. The team that was successful in the '50s won on defense, while the early '60s team won more with offense.

The **1983 Los Angeles Raiders** had the best API (+3.64) of the three Raiders' teams that won the Super Bowl: 1976, 1980, 1983. (The 1973 club had the best API [+4.57] of any Raiders' team since the merger in 1970.) The 1983 season was the Raiders' first AFC West title since 1976, but was the franchise's seventh since 1970. Quarterback Jim Plunkett, who had led the Raiders to their Super Bowl win in 1980, when they were still in Oakland, was benched during 1983. Plunkett, however, returned and played well when his substitute, Marc Wilson, suffered a shoulder injury. Even with the quarterback carousel, the Raiders led the AFC with 442 points scored. Tight end Todd Christensen caught 92 passes and 12 touchdowns. Marcus Allen ran for 1,014 yards and fullback Frank Hawkins chipped in with 526 and a fine 4.8 average. The Raiders played exceptionally well in the postseason, winning three games by a combined score of 106–33, including their 38–9 shellacking of the Redskins in the Super Bowl. Washington had set a then-NFL record scoring 541 points during the regular season, but the Raiders shut down the Redskins' running game and tormented QB Joe Theismann, sacking him six times.

Bill Parcells would probably say that someone like me, who has never played and/or coached organized football, has no business writing a football book. That belief would no doubt be reinforced by the fact that neither of his Super Bowl champion Giants teams got their own chapter. The **1986 New York Giants** had a slightly higher API than the 1990 squad (+3.57 to +3.26). Actually, the 1985 Giants had a better API (+4.59) than either Super Bowl winner, but they ran into a rather large obstacle in the NFC Championship Game that year. The '86 Giants were led on defense by "LT," Lawrence Taylor, who was named league MVP and led the league with 20 1/2 sacks. Little Joe Morris (I bet he hates being called that) had a great year, rushing for 1,516 yards and 14 touchdowns. Not to sound condescending, Coach Parcells, but a tree has no idea how big the forest is.

The Long and Short of Schedules

I am fascinated by the fact that both the easiest and most difficult opponents' schedules in the last half-century happened in 1975. The Cleveland Browns, playing in a division where the other three teams had records of 10–4 or better, had the toughest schedule. Not counting games against the Browns, their opponents had a 116–66 record, which is a .637 winning percentage. (It should be no surprise that Cleveland finished 3–11.)

Three other teams have had a schedule with an opponents' collective winning percentage of .600 or higher: the 1973 San Francisco 49ers (.621), the 1951 Chicago Cardinals (.606), and the 1970 Green Bay Packers (.604). All three of these teams had losing records: '73 San Francisco, 5–9; '51 Chicago Cards, 3–9; '70 Green Bay, 6–8.

The 1975 Minnesota Vikings' opponents had an aggregate winning percentage of .346, which is the easiest schedule since 1950 by a relatively wide margin. The 1999 Rams had the second easiest schedule at .375. One might think that an easy schedule would be a detriment in the postseason because a team with such a schedule wouldn't be used to tough competition. Well, of the teams with the 10 easiest schedules, three won the Super Bowl: the '99 Rams, the 1972 Dolphins, and the 1970 Colts. Nine teams have won either the Super Bowl or pre-1966 NFL title with an opponents' aggregate winning percentage of .450 or lower.

Home–Road Records

I felt compelled to show the home and road records of the 12 teams profiled in the book.

	Home			Road		
	W	L	T	W	L	T
1955 Cleveland Browns	5	1	0	4	1	1
1958 Baltimore Colts	6	0	0	3	3	0
1962 Green Bay Packers	7	0	0	6	1	0
1971 Dallas Cowboys	6	1	0	5	2	0
1972 Miami Dolphins	7	0	0	7	0	0
1979 Pittsburgh Steelers	8	0	0	4	4	0
1985 Chicago Bears	8	0	0	7	1	0
1989 San Francisco 49ers	6	2	0	8	0	0
1991 Washington Redskins	7	1	0	7	1	0
1994 San Francisco 49ers	7	1	0	6	2	0
1996 Green Bay Packers	8	0	0	5	3	0
1999 St. Louis Rams	8	0	0	5	3	0
Totals	**83**	**6**	**0**	**67**	**21**	**1**

That's not a bad home record, huh? By the way, 83–6 is a .933 winning percentage.

In the above comparison, the 1972 Dolphins and 1989 49ers stand out because they went undefeated on the road. Counting those two, only seven teams in a full season since 1950 have gone undefeated and untied in road games. Three of the other five were teams whose seasons ended in disappointment: the 1968 Colts, the 1968 Cowboys, and the 2001 Rams. The other two? The 1984 49ers and the 1990 49ers. Only seven teams since 1950 have had perfect road records, and San Francisco did it three times in seven seasons. It's no surprise that San Francisco holds the NFL record for most consecutive road wins with 18 straight road games from 1988 through 1990. The next highest figure is 11.

These Teams Weren't So Good

The 1976 Buccaneers . . . I expect that's what immediately comes to mind when most fans think of really bad teams. Yeah, the Bucs went 0–14 in their first season and were really bad, but there have been other awful teams, including some that I think are even worse. The 1976 Bucs didn't even have the worst Adjusted Power Index (API) in Tampa Bay history; that "honor" goes to the 1986 crew, but then what would you expect from an organization that wanted Vinny Testaverde instead of Steve Young? (Tampa Bay traded Young to San Francisco in 1987 to make room for number one draft pick Testaverde.) Here are the 10 worst single-season API's since 1950 (it pains me to remember number one):

Team	API
1981 Baltimore Colts	−8.34
1986 Tampa Bay Buccaneers	−8.03
1970 Boston Patriots	−7.63
1999 Cleveland Browns	−7.47
1952 Dallas Texans	−7.42
1967 Atlanta Falcons	−7.36
1972 New England Patriots	−7.30
1990 New England Patriots	−7.23
1978 Baltimore Colts	−7.20
1976 Tampa Bay Buccaneers	−7.16

Surprisingly, there are no Saints teams here. The worst API for a New Orleans team was −6.21 in 1970.

Here are the records of these stellar teams:

Team	Record	
1981 Baltimore Colts	2–14	the wins were by a total of three points; the only team they beat was also 2–14
1986 Tampa Bay Buccaneers	2–14	both wins were by less than a touchdown against teams with a combined 9–23 record
1970 Boston Patriots	2–12	
1999 Cleveland Browns	2–14	the wins were by a total of six points
1952 Dallas Texans	1–11	one four-point win
1967 Atlanta Falcons	1–12–1	a one-point win over a 3-8-3 team
1972 New England Patriots	3–11	two one-point wins
1990 New England Patriots	1–15	a two-point win
1978 Baltimore Colts	5–11	
1976 Tampa Bay Buccaneers	0–14	

Only the 1978 Colts' record seems out of place, but that's why I called them the worst 5–11 team in history in "The Dam Burst" in the 1999 Rams chapter. The reason I showed so many of the narrow wins is that more than one of these teams could have also been winless with just a little less luck.

To show the weaknesses of some of these teams, here are the five worst Offense and Defense Power Indexes:

Worst OPIs		Worst DPIs	
1970 Boston Patriots	−5.08	1981 Baltimore Colts	−6.28
1988 Detroit Lions	−4.88	1972 New England Patriots	−5.01
1974 Atlanta Falcons	−4.86	1986 Tampa Bay Buccaneers	−5.01
1977 Tampa Bay Buccaneers	−4.75	1978 Baltimore Colts	−4.84
1992 Seattle Seahawks	−4.71	1980 New Orleans Saints	−4.73

Any of those numbers jump out at you? The difference between the 1981 Colts and the second worst team is almost twice as large as the difference between the 1972 Patriots and the tenth-worst DPI, the 1961 Minnesota Vikings at −4.31. By itself, the 1981 Colts' Defense Power Index would be the nineteenth worst *overall* Adjusted Power Index since 1950.

At least the Saints snuck on to one of these lists. The Patriots managed to make each of the lists, as did the Bucs. Throughout Tampa Bay's history, the club has struggled on the offensive side of the ball. Not counting the strike seasons of 1982 and 1987, how many Buccaneers' teams have had positive OPI's through the 2001 season? Uno, un, one. Only the 2000 team finished with a plus OPI, all of +0.11. Even that is "tainted" because the team was below the league average in yards gained, but finished above average in points scored with the help of a defense that scored 6 touchdowns and forced 41 turnovers. Tampa Bay's 2000 ratio of yards gained to points scored (11.98–1) was easily the lowest in the NFL, far lower than the league average of 15.45–1 and far lower than the Buccaneers' historical average from 1976 through 1999 of 17.60–1. In fact, their 2000 ratio is the fifth-lowest since 1978, but only one of the four teams with a lower ratio was also below the league average in yards gained like the 2000 Bucs.

As for the brutal '81 Colts, I mercifully witnessed just three or four Colts' games that year. My two best friends (Brad Adler and Gary Lazarus), both of whom I have known since elementary school, saw them all.

It's Time to Go to the Weekly Massacre

Brad Adler and *Gary Lazarus*

Brad: The 1981 Baltimore Colts were a sorry bunch indeed. As a die-hard Colts' fanatic, the season was very difficult to accept. To say that the Colts were poor defensively would be like saying that Custer ran into a few Indians at Little Big Horn. As you sat in the Memorial Stadium seats that year and witnessed the worst defense the NFL had ever served up, you couldn't help but wonder if there were really 11 men on the defensive side of the ball. "Yeah! That's what the problem is—it must be."

It became so horrendous, and to be honest, comical, that Gary made a remark that will "live in infamy." (OK, so it wasn't Pearl Harbor.) Every week, as we prepared to go to the game, Gary and I would become more and more hysterical and boisterous about the merits of our home town team. After the first six games that year, we knew it was going to be a long season (the Colts were 1–5 and had already surrendered 186 points), and Gary said, "Well, it's time to go to the weekly massacre." To this day, some 20 years later, we still laugh when we repeat that comment. Of course, Gary was no doubt influenced by the fact that the game we were about to attend pitted our pitiful Colts against the "Air Coryell" Chargers. Just how prophetic was Gary, you ask? Final score: Chargers 43, Colts 14. The Colts had a moral victory that day, though; they held Dan Fouts to under 300 yards passing. He only threw for 298.

Gary: A horrendous defense it was. When you remember names like Mike Fultz, Hosea Taylor, Anthony (don't call me Bubba) Green, Joe Federspiel (whom Colts Hall-of-Famer Art Donovan referred to as "Glockenspiel"), and Ricky Jones, was it any surprise? With regard to this, let me discuss two points:

1. The terrible performance of the Colts of the late '70s and early '80s was largely a result of their horrendous drafts in the 1970s. Taken as a whole, the Colts' drafts in the '70s were among the worst of any team for any decade in NFL history. During the 1970s, when the Colts selected such stalwarts as Len Dunlap and Randy Burke in the first round, only John Dutton, Roger Carr, and Bert Jones could be considered successful first-round

picks. Ironically, both Jones and Dutton were later traded for draft picks, which the Colts then proceeded to waste.

2. Since the 1981 Colts got blown out almost every week, you would predict the talent on offense was also terrible. However, the offense—with players such as Bert Jones, Roger Carr, Ray Butler, Curtis Dickey, and Randy McMillian—was considered above average by most NFL observers. They still managed to produce an NFL-low 259 points in 1981, ranking eleventh in the AFC in both rushing and passing yards. Why did this potentially good unit underachieve? Some of the blame has to go to the defense, which was so bad it kept the offense from getting onto the field. Also, the Colts were constantly playing catch up, which usually made the game plan obsolete by the end of the first quarter. Frustration certainly set in as the year progressed. It got so bad that when Jones criticized Dickey for missing a block in a late-season game, Dickey refused to speak to his quarterback for the rest of the season.

Having lived through the debacle that some people referred to as Baltimore Colts football from 1978–1983, we can only think of one way to conclude this article. Thank you, Ravens!

CHAPTER 8

1985 Chicago Bears: The New Monsters of the Midway

STARTING LINEUP – 1985 BEARS			
Offense		**Defense**	
SE	Willie Gault	LE	Mike Hartenstine
LT	Jim Covert	LT	Steve McMichael
LG	Mark Bortz	RT	Dan Hampton
C	Jay Hilgenberg	RE	Richard Dent
RG	Tom Thayer	LLB	Otis Wilson
RT	Keith Van Horne	MLB	Mike Singletary
TE	Emery Moorehead	RLB	Wilber Marshall
FL	Dennis McKinnon	LCB	Mike Richardson
QB	Jim McMahon	RCB	Leslie Frazier
RB	Walter Payton	SS	Dave Duerson
RB	Matt Suhey	FS	Gary Fencik

The 1985 Chicago Bears' combination of winning and charisma made them a phenomenon outside of Chicago. Their Monday night game against the Dolphins is still the highest-rated Monday night game ever. Terry O'Neil, executive producer of NFL football on CBS in 1985, said that he received numerous letters from Virginia, Washington Redskins' territory, begging him to show the Bears instead of the Redskins as the "local" team. CBS received protests from California to Wisconsin after most of the country was switched from the Bears–Falcons blowout to the Redskins–Steelers game, even though the latter was a much closer game. Half of the U.S. population watched at least some part of the Super Bowl against the Patriots, making it, at the time, the most watched TV program in history.

This team would have represented the good and the bad to Papa Bear George Halas. It is highly doubtful that he would have approved of the hype surrounding Refrigerator Perry and Jim McMahon's headbands, and it's *truly* doubtful he would have enjoyed the "Super Bowl Shuffle." In general, the cult of personality that the Bears generated would not have been something that Halas would have liked. Noted writer William Barry Furlong once penned this about Halas, the Bears' founder, owner, and coach, "He has all the warmth of breaking bones, a personality as daring as twin beds."

It's just as clear, however, that Halas would have loved the Bears when they were on the field. Their domination of their opponents, as well as their physical and intimidating style of play would have reminded him of his best teams, the teams that earned the Bears the nickname "The Monsters of the Midway." While Jim McMahon was no Sid Luckman, the 1985 Bears made a lot of big plays through the air, similar to the Luckman-led Bears. Although the modern-day running game uses significantly fewer backs than the teams of the '40s, '50s, or '60s, both the 1985 Bears and Halas's best teams had very effective running attacks. Halas's best teams played ferocious defense that often stymied opposing offenses, and the 1985 Bears played the same way. The Bears under Halas almost always played hard for 60 minutes, and so did the 1985 Bears. All things considered, I guess Papa Bear wouldn't mind if we called the 1985 Bears "The New Monsters of the Midway." He'd just have to acknowledge that they were popular all over the country.

Much in the same way that the Dolphins' loss to the Cowboys in Super Bowl VI was a motivating factor for them in the following season, the Bears' 23–0 loss to the 49ers in the 1984 NFC Championship Game was an inspiration to Chicago for the 1985 season. Or as Mike Ditka put it at the start of 1985 training camp, "You're only as good as your last game, and our last game wasn't very good."

A big issue that the Bears had to deal with in 1985 was players holding out because they were either unsigned or unhappy with their contracts. Pro Bowl defensive end Richard Dent returned to camp in early August, All-World linebacker Mike Singletary rejoined the team in mid-August after his contract was restructured, but 1984 All-Pro safety Todd Bell and linebacker Al Harris held out *all season.* While it's hard to say that the Bears' defense missed them, the holdouts certainly were a distraction.

Team in a Box

Record: 15–1

The Bears began the 1985 season with 12 straight wins, which fueled comparisons to the undefeated 1972 Dolphins. On Monday Night Football, December 2, the Bears and Miami met in a showdown of sorts. Obviously, the angle of the Dolphins "protecting" their legacy has been discussed to no end and, indeed, the Dolphins kept the Bears from an undefeated season by winning 38–24. A forgotten aspect of that game is that it came in the middle of an impressive run by Miami, the defending AFC champion, which reeled off seven straight wins to end the season (the Chicago game was number four in the streak). The Dolphins wound up winning the AFC East with a 12–4 mark. The Miami game was the only time in their last 16 games, including the postseason, that the Bears allowed 20 or more points.

Of the Bears' first 12 wins, only three were by fewer than 10 points.

Against Teams Over .500: 5–1, 178 Points Scored, 71 Points Allowed

This is one of the most impressive accomplishments among the many achieved by the Bears in 1985. Given Chicago's dominance of the NFL's top teams, perhaps the Bears' playoff run should have been no surprise at all. More than half of the points the Bears surrendered to teams with winning records came in just one game, the loss to Miami.

Points Scored/Allowed: 456/198 (1985 NFL Average: 345)

Since the adoption of the 16-game schedule in 1978, the 1985 Chicago Bears are the only team to score 400 or more points while allowing fewer than 200 in a season. They are one of only five teams since 1950 to outscore its opponents by 250 or more points.

The Bears just missed being the first team since the 1972 Dolphins to lead the league in points scored and fewest points allowed. The San Diego Chargers scored 11 more points than the Bears.

Yards Gained/Allowed: 5,837/4,135 (1985 NFL Average: 5,271)

The Bears' per-game yardage differential (+106.4) ranks twentieth among all NFL teams since 1950. For the entire season, the Bears had only 83 fewer yards of total offense than the 49ers, who were rightfully known for their very productive attack. The Bears' offense also led the conference in average yards per completion and average yards per pass attempt, including sacks.

While the Bears' defense was outstanding, of course, it's somewhat surprising that their yards allowed figure is "only" the seventeenth best since 1978.

Opponents' Record: 120–120, .500

(Not counting games against the Bears.)

Adjusted Power Index:

Offense: +2.90
Defense: +4.35
TOTAL: +7.25

The 1985 Bears are one of only four teams since 1950 with an adjusted Power Index of +7.00 or higher.

The Bears' defense was outstanding, their +4.35 Defense Power Index is the fifth-best since 1950, but their offense was very good as well. Only 6 percent of all teams since 1950 have had an Offense Power Index of +2.90 or higher. It's somewhat bewildering how little notoriety the offense received for its performance, as opposed to the notoriety received for its personalities such as Jim McMahon. It is true, of course, that the Chicago defense set up many scores for the offense; the Bears forced 54 turnovers, the fifth-best total since 1978.

Innovations/What You Should Know:

The 46 Defense is discussed elsewhere in this chapter, but perhaps the "real" reason for the Bears' success in 1985 was good karma brought on by the return of former All-Universe linebacker Dick Butkus to the Bears' family. That year, Butkus was hired as a color man on the team's radio broadcasts, a role he would fill for 10 seasons.

Butkus retired after the 1973 season because of a debilitating knee injury. In 1974, he sued the Bears, charging them with improper handling of the injury. Before the two parties settled out of court (Butkus received a reported $600,000), a lot of bad blood was stirred up. For example, the Bears refused to retire Butkus's uniform number 51 and other players were issued the number. (The Bears retired Butkus's number in 1994.)

On the air, Butkus was what one would expect. He was demonstrative, to say the least, and very emotional. Current Bears' radio analyst Hub Arkush said that WGN, then the team's flagship station, encouraged Butkus's groaning and grunting in the booth.

Butkus's radio career with the Bears ended after the 1994 season. A 1997 operation, in which Butkus was given an artificial knee, significantly diminished the pain.

Homegrown First-Round Picks:

RB Walter Payton, 1975; DT Dan Hampton, 1979; LB Otis Wilson, 1980; OT Keith Van Horne, 1981; QB Jim McMahon, 1982; OT Jimbo Covert, 1983; WR Willie Gault, 1983; LB Wilber Marshall, 1984; DT William Perry, 1985.

A very impressive first-round history. Look at the list: in every year from 1979 through 1985, the Bears drafted a player (two in 1983) who started in the Super Bowl. Five of these nine players were selected for the Pro Bowl after the 1985 season.

Jerry Vainisi, Bears' GM from 1983 to 1987, believes that the first-round picks in 1982, 1983, and 1984 were among the most important transactions in turning the Bears into a Super Bowl contender. (See "The Vainisi Connection.")

Mike Singletary, a 10-time Pro Bowler including this season, was a second-round Bears pick in 1981. As an aside, would history have been different if the Chargers had drafted Singletary in the first round that year as many predicted they would?

Pro Bowl Players:

OT Jimbo Covert, DE Richard Dent, S Dave Duerson, DT Dan Hampton, QB Jim McMahon, RB Walter Payton, LB Mike Singletary, LB Otis Wilson.

Richard Dent was the team's only Pro Bowl player who had not been a relatively high Bears' draft choice. Dent was picked by Chicago in the eighth round in 1983; the Bears drafted Dave Duerson in the third round that same year.

Game-by-Game:

Sep. 8th BEARS 38, TAMPA BAY 28 AT CHICAGO

Playing on a day when the field temperature reached 133 degrees on the AstroTurf, the Bears stormed back from a 28–17 halftime deficit to beat the Buccaneers. Two plays into the third quarter, Chicago's Richard Dent made a great play to tip a Steve DeBerg pass that wound up in the hands of cornerback Leslie Frazier, who ran it back 29 yards for a touchdown. Frazier said, "I was thinking interception because they ran the play in the first half and he threw behind the receiver. If he had thrown to the receiver, I felt I could have intercepted it."

Most Bears' defensive players were not happy with the effort. Mike Singletary simply called it, "Embarrassing."

Sep. 15th BEARS 20, NEW ENGLAND 7 AT CHICAGO

No one knew it at the time, of course, but this was a Super Bowl preview (see "The Postseason Monster Shuffle"). Except for a fourth quarter 90-yard touchdown pass from Tony Eason to Craig James, the Bears' defense shut down the Patriots, just like what would happen about 4 months later. Chicago forced four New England turnovers, recorded 6 sacks, and held the Patriots to just 27 yards rushing.

Walter Payton missed much of the game with bruised ribs, but Jim McMahon picked up the slack, hitting 13 of 21 passes for 232 yards and a touchdown. McMahon missed most of the fourth quarter with a stiff neck, but by that time Chicago was in control of the game with a 20–0 lead.

Sep. 19th BEARS 33, MINNESOTA 24 AT MINNESOTA

This may be the game that really started the Jim McMahon legend. He talked his way into the game in the third quarter, after he hadn't started because of a "mysterious" back injury that had kept him out of practice before this Thursday night game. McMahon threw 3 touchdown passes in 6:40, turning a 17–9 deficit into a 30–17 lead. In less than two quarters, McMahon threw for 236 yards on 8-of-15 passing as the Bears gained a season high 480 yards of offense.

Sep. 29th BEARS 45, WASHINGTON 10 AT CHICAGO

The Redskins led 10–0, but Willie Gault's 99-yard kickoff return sparked the Bears to a 31-point second quarter and an easy win. On the play, Redskins' punter and kickoff specialist Jeff Hayes suffered a thigh injury chasing Gault. On Washington's next possession, Redskins quarterback Joe Theismann made his only NFL punt; the ball went off the side of his foot for a 1-yard punt. Chicago got the ball at the Washington 14-yard line, and on the first play Jim McMahon threw a touchdown pass to Dennis McKinnon. The Bears never looked back.

Oct. 6th BEARS 27, TAMPA BAY 19 AT TAMPA BAY

In another relatively uninspired effort against the Buccaneers, the Bears trailed 12–3 at the half before taking control of the game. Walter Payton scored twice in the second half to become the sixth player in NFL history to reach 100 touchdowns. Jim McMahon threw for 292 yards on 22-of-34 passing; tight end Emery Moorehead had 8 catches for 118 yards. This was the only game of the season in which the Bears failed to sack the opposing quarterback.

Oct. 13th BEARS 26, SAN FRANCISCO 10 AT SAN FRANCISCO

Chicago moved to 6–0 for the first time since 1942 with a very impressive road win, as they totally dominated the defending Super Bowl champions. The Bears' offense showed great balance, gaining 189 yards rushing and 183 yards passing. Chicago's defense shut down Joe Montana and the much-heralded 49ers' offense, yielding just 11 first downs and 183 total yards while sacking Montana seven times. San Francisco's only score came on a 43-yard interception return by Carlton Williamson.

Mike Ditka was very proud of his team's performance: "Today was our day, a great win for us. We beat a heckuva football team. We challenged them with our offensive and defensive lines. That's as good as we can play."

Walter Payton felt the Bears had a score to settle after losing 23–0 to the 49ers in the 1984 NFC Championship Game. Payton said, "Unfortunately, when the 49ers beat us last year they didn't show much courtesy or dignity. They said negative things about our offense after shutting us out.

We thought about that all during the offseason. A team of All-Pros couldn't have stopped us."

Oct. 21st BEARS 23, GREEN BAY 7 AT CHICAGO

I don't want to comment on the Refrigerator Perry "phenomenon" because I think it's much ado about nothing. Suffice to say that he scored his first NFL touchdown on a 1-yard run in this Monday night game.

The Bears lost 4 fumbles, but Green Bay trumped that with 4 interceptions plus 1 lost fumble.

Oct. 27th BEARS 27, MINNESOTA 9 AT CHICAGO

Chicago had another good offensive game against the Vikings, gaining 413 yards, but it was a defensive play that tilted the game in the Bears' favor. Leading just 13–7 at halftime, Bears linebacker Otis Wilson picked off a Tommy Kramer pass and ran it back 23 yards for a touchdown. Minnesota was never in the game after that, gaining just 236 yards on offense and throwing 5 interceptions.

Nov. 3rd BEARS 16, GREEN BAY 10 AT GREEN BAY

Walter Payton rushed for a season high 192 yards on 28 attempts. It was the third-highest single game total of Payton's career. It's a good thing that Payton had a great day because Chicago gained just 58 yards in the air.

The defense surrendered a long touchdown pass to a running back, 55 yards from Jim Zorn to Jessie Clark, and the Bears trailed 10–7 after three quarters. The defense got some of it back in the fourth quarter when Steve McMichael sacked Zorn in the end zone for a safety. Payton's 27-yard touchdown run provided the winning margin.

Nov. 10th BEARS 24, DETROIT 3 AT CHICAGO

The Lions were held to just 106 yards of offense, including only 38 net passing yards, and the Bears had a 41:02 to 18:58 advantage in time of possession. With Jim McMahon out with an injury, Chicago's running game picked up the slack. The Bears ran for a season-high 250 yards: both Walter Payton and Matt Suhey surpassed 100 yards. Suhey gained 102 yards on just 16 carries.

Nov. 17th BEARS 44, DALLAS 0 AT DALLAS

This game was significant for many reasons. Mike Ditka played for Tom Landry and Landry had given Ditka his first job as a coach. The two teams played during the regular season in 1984, with the Cowboys winning in Chicago, 23–14. The Bears hadn't defeated Dallas in six games going back to 1971. (Ironically, Ditka played for the Cowboys in that game.) The teams played a preseason game in 1985, and Dallas won 15–13. The game was notable for the numerous fights that occurred, including one where Dallas defensive tackle Randy White hit Chicago's Mark Bortz in the helmet with Keith Van Horne's helmet; White was ejected from the game.

The most important aspect of this game, however, is that it matched the reigning "America's Team" against the up-and-coming NFL power and media darling. The lopsided nature of the game, at the time the worst defeat in the history of the Cowboys and the first time they had been shut out in 219 regular-season games, really stamped the Bears as an NFL force.

Ditka called the win "no big deal," but his players didn't agree. Safety Dave Duerson said, "He downplayed it, but it was written on his face."

Cowboys general manager Tex Schramm simply said, "Embarrassing, just embarrassing." Tony Dorsett added, "It felt like a nightmare, except I was awake all the way through it. Never in my career as a football player has something like this happened. I don't know how to describe this shellacking except to say it was a royal beating."

Nov. 24th BEARS 36, ATLANTA 0 AT CHICAGO

This game concluded a three-game stretch where the Bears outscored their opposition 104–3 and outgained them 1,117–396. In those three games the Bears allowed a total of 135 passing yards. The Falcons had *minus* 22 yards passing. Henry Waechter had 2 sacks and a safety; he would finish the season with 2 1/2 sacks.

Dec. 2nd MIAMI 38, BEARS 24 AT MIAMI

Although this game was discussed earlier, it's certainly worth noting Dan Marino's stats: he completed 14 of 27 passes for 270 yards and 3 touchdowns to lead Miami to victory. Two of the touchdown passes were over 30 yards; giving up the occasional long pass was the one "weakness" of the Bears' defense.

Walter Payton set a new NFL record with his eighth consecutive 100-yard rushing game. The record is now 14 straight games set by Barry Sanders in 1997.

Dec. 8th BEARS 17, INDIANAPOLIS 10 AT CHICAGO

Walter Payton rushed for 100 yards for the ninth consecutive game, gaining 111 yards on 26 carries. In the nine games, Payton rushed for 1,127 yards on 213 carries, a 5.3 average, and 7 touchdowns.

The game was tied 3–3 at halftime; the Bears went on a 63-yard scoring drive capped by Payton's 16-yard touchdown run late in the third quarter. A fourth-quarter Calvin Thomas TD run made the game 17–3, but the Colts scored on a 61-yard touchdown pass from Mike Pagel to Wayne Capers to make it 17–10.

Dec. 14th BEARS 19, NEW YORK JETS 6 AT NEW YORK

After the game, Jets star offensive tackle Marvin Powell said, "The Monsters of the Midway live. I heard all about the Monsters from my father. Well, today I found out that they're for real. They're Monsters. All of them."

The Bears held the Jets to just 159 yards of total offense, the fifth time they held an opponent to fewer than 200 yards during the regular season.

Dec. 22nd BEARS 37, DETROIT 17 AT DETROIT

Despite the score, Bears coach Mike Ditka was unhappy about his team's performance in the regular-season finale. "Say I'm concerned. Say I'm terrified. Anything you want," said Ditka. "We couldn't beat a playoff team today. We would have been eliminated." The Bears led just 6–3 at halftime, but Dennis Gentry's 94-yard TD return of the second-half kickoff opened the floodgates.

Chicago got 6 sacks, the eleventh time they recorded four or more in a game. They also forced 7 turnovers, the eleventh time they forced three or more.

Divisional Playoff:

Jan. 5th BEARS 21, NEW YORK GIANTS 0 AT CHICAGO

NFC Championship:

Jan. 12th BEARS 24, LOS ANGELES 0 AT CHICAGO

Super Bowl XX:

Jan. 26th BEARS 46, NEW ENGLAND 10 AT NEW ORLEANS
(See "The Postseason Monster Shuffle.")

Elsewhere Around the NFL:

Nov. 17th The Buccaneers are demolished 62–28 by the Jets. Tampa Bay head coach Leeman Bennett switches quarterbacks and, the following week, gives a USFL refugee his first NFL start. That quarterback was Steve Young. Tampa Bay beat Detroit in overtime 19–16.

Nov. 18th On a Monday night, much of America saw the end of Joe Theismann's career as his right leg was severely broken while being sacked by Lawrence Taylor. Not many people remember that the Redskins won the game 23–21 behind Jay Schroeder.

Nov. 25th Twelve games into the season, Bum Phillips resigned as head coach of the New Orleans Saints, ending a colorful and successful career. He was succeeded by his son Wade, who had been the Saints' defensive coordinator, and who later was head coach with Denver and Buffalo.

What Happened the Next Season:

The Bears' defense remained dominant, setting a record for the fewest points allowed in a 16-game season with 187 (a record that was broken by the 2000 Baltimore Ravens), and led Chicago to a 14–2 regular season record. Jim McMahon went in and out of the lineup with a shoulder injury, so the Bears used four quarterbacks during the season. One of those quarterbacks was Doug Flutie.

In the playoffs, the Bears were held to just 220 yards of offense, and were upset by Washington 27–13 in Chicago; the Bears were outscored 20–0 in the second half. Walter Payton gained just 38 yards on 14 carries and Doug Flutie completed just 11 of 31 passes for 134 yards, 50 of those on a touchdown pass to Willie Gault. Washington had made the playoffs as a Wild-Card team and had to beat the Rams the week before to advance.

The Vainisi Connection

For me, the world is filled with just enough eerie coincidences to make me wonder about forces that exist in dimensions beyond those that we can see. The Vainisi connection is one of those coincidences. Jerry Vainisi, the Bears' general manager in 1985, is the brother of Jack Vainisi. Before David Maraniss's outstanding biography of Vince Lombardi, *When Pride Still Mattered,* few people knew who Jack Vainisi was. In case you still don't know, Jack Vainisi was the personnel manager of the Green Bay Packers. He played a much larger role in their success of the 1960s than he has ever been credited with, especially outside the midwest. Not only did he scout and recommend the nucleus of the Packers' dynasty, a nucleus that included seven eventual Hall of Famers, but Jack Vainisi was the person most responsible for bringing Vince Lombardi in as head coach.

In the same relentless way that he scouted players, Vainisi had done a lot of homework about Lombardi and was the first person to call him about the possibility of his becoming head coach, even though Vainisi didn't have the authority to make the call. Vainisi then successfully convinced the Packers' executive board to pursue Lombardi.

The Vainisi family hailed from the North Side of Chicago and grew up as Bears' fans. Jack Vainisi went to grammar school with George Halas, Jr. After playing a year at Notre Dame, Jack Vainisi was drafted into the Army and contracted rheumatic fever, which permanently damaged his heart and ended his playing days. Vainisi, however, was able to find a job scouting for the Packers in 1950 and worked his way up in the organization. Unfortunately, Jack Vainisi never lived to see the Packers rule the NFL. His heart condition and workload proved to be too much, and he died on the Sunday after Thanksgiving in 1960 at the age of 33.

Having played on Thanksgiving, the Packers' next game wasn't until the Sunday after he died, ironically against the Bears. The Packers dedicated the game to Vainisi and routed the Bears 41–13.

As Jack Vainisi grew up in the shadow of the Bears and wound up playing a large role in the success of their arch-rival, the Packers, younger brother Jerry Vainisi "cut his football teeth" with the Packers and wound up playing a large role in the success of the Bears. As a kid, Jerry Vainisi worked part time as the Packers' ballboy. He realized that he did not have the talent to be a professional athlete, but was inspired by his brother to get into the administrative end of a football organization:

> The idea of becoming a general manager appealed to me. That was my goal and it struck me that the best way to pursue it was to have a background in business and law. The game was becoming more and more complex. So that's what I pointed toward at Georgetown ... that's what I've always trained myself for. Jack started me thinking, no question about it.

Jerry Vainisi worked as a tax accountant at Arthur Anderson in Chicago, but a letter of recommendation written and circulated around the NFL by Vince Lombardi changed Vainisi's career path. In 1972, George Halas, Jr., the school classmate of older brother Jack, hired Jerry to work for the Bears. Jerry Vainisi became Bears' general manager in August of 1983.

As general manager, Vainisi was the top of the football pyramid for the Bears, although he didn't operate in a vacuum. As he described it to me, football operations was a "four-headed monster" meaning Bears president/CEO Mike McCaskey, Mike Ditka, Bears director of personnel Bill Tobin, and Vainisi. Whereas Vainisi was responsible for contract negotiations and trades, draft picks were made through a consensus of the four of them.

Vainisi had a very good relationship with Ditka. When talking about his hiring as Bears' head coach, Ditka once said, "I didn't have anybody in my corner except Jerry Vainisi." Ditka was hired as head coach by George Halas, Sr.; he was not the choice of then-Bears general manager Jim Finks. Finks's resignation and the appointment of Vainisi to the position facilitated the decision-making process. Vainisi attributed his relationship with Ditka as being the result of their both being "Halas's guys" and both really wanting only what was best for the Bears.

As pointed out in the Bears' "Team in a Box," Vainisi credits Chicago's first-round picks in 1982, 1983, and 1984 as being among the most important transactions in turning them around. The selection of Jim McMahon in 1982 was the first time the Bears had chosen a quarterback in the first round since the forgettable Bob Williams was picked in 1951 and, more importantly, represented an acknowledgment by the organization of the importance of the passing game. (See "The Quarterback: Jim McMahon.") The selections of Covert and Gault in 1983 gave the Bears a quality offensive lineman to help protect the quarterback and a receiver with the speed to stretch the defense. Marshall, drafted in 1984, was a play-making linebacker who some felt was the Bears' best defensive player in 1985.

Vainisi later worked for the Detroit Lions and for what was then the World League of American Football, now known as NFL Europe. He is currently a partner at the Chicago law firm of Hinshaw and Culbertson.

In the same way that older brother Jack's contribution to a successful NFL team was "obscured" by a dynamic and successful head coach, Jerry's contribution to the Bears' success of the 1980s has been lost in the shadow of Mike Ditka, among other big shadows cast by famous Bears. Maybe some of you see the Vainisi story as simply a likely outcome of proximity, family, and the old boy network, but it strikes me as more than that.

Number 34

I am not ashamed to admit that I cried the day Walter Payton died. Of course, I was aware that he had been ill, but his death was still a shock. I had always felt a bond with Payton from the first time I read about him in *The Sporting News* while he was still at Jackson State, although I don't exactly know why I felt that way. Perhaps it came from the belief I had at that time that *The Sporting News* was the sports bible, and that if they wrote a favorable article about someone, especially someone from a small school, then the subject of the article had to be worthy. My then-hometown team, the Colts, had a chance to draft Payton even after they traded away the first pick in the 1975 NFL draft. By virtue of their 1974 record (2–12), the Colts had the first pick in the next draft, but traded it to Atlanta for All-Pro offensive tackle George Kunz and Atlanta's first-round pick, which was the third pick overall. With the top pick, Atlanta took quarterback Steve Bartkowski; the second pick was defensive lineman Randy White by Dallas. With Walter Payton still on the board at number 3, the Colts instead selected North Carolina guard Ken Huff; then-Colts GM Joe Thomas had made rebuilding the offensive line his top priority. Huff had a decent, but undistinguished 11-year career. The Bears took Payton with the fourth pick. Ironically (for me), Payton's first regular season NFL game was against the Colts, who held him to no yards in 8 carries.

Mike Ditka was an assistant coach with the Cowboys when they took Randy White instead of Payton; that's not a knock because White turned out to be one of the greatest defensive linemen in history. Still, it adds another twist to the Payton story. Ditka recounted the draft discussions shortly after Payton's death, "I remember discussing whether we'd draft Walter or Randy White," Ditka said. "I remember we always had a staff meeting about those things and coach [Tom Landry] always took a vote and all the offensive coaches for sure voted for Walter. Of course, the defensive coaches voted for Randy, who was quite a college player also and a great Hall of Famer. And

Allsport

Walter Payton, *number 34,* carries
the ball in Super Bowl XX.

Tom was really a defensive coach, so we ended up taking Randy. I think things happen because they're supposed to happen and Walter was supposed to be a Chicago Bear."

On November 20, 1977, I was watching the Bears–Vikings game and late in the first quarter I decided to keep track of how many yards Walter Payton had. When I was 11 or 12 years old, I often kept stats for football games that I watched on TV, but had long since stopped. For some reason, however, I had the urge that day to keep track of what Payton was doing. That was the day he set the NFL single-game rushing record, which stood until Corey Dillon broke it in 2000. Naturally, I wish I still had that sheet of paper.

If it weren't for the players strike in 1982, Payton could very well have had 11 consecutive 1,000-yard seasons; he rushed for 1,000 or more yards in every other year from 1976 through 1986. He rushed for at least 1,300 yards and averaged at least 4.2 yards per carry nine times, which is remarkable when one considers that Payton was the Bears' biggest offensive threat and the focus of opposing defenses, for almost his entire career. Payton, of course, was a major contributor to Chicago's success in 1985, although his contribution has been overshadowed by the cult of personality the Bears generated. That was his eleventh NFL season, and he had one of his finest years, rushing for 1,551 yards and a 4.8 average per carry, the second best average of his career. He is the Bears' all-time leading *receiver* with 492 catches. I wonder how many people know that Payton led the NFL in kickoff return average as a rookie; that's not a significant part of his career résumé, but it's an example of how good Payton was at anything he did on the football field.

Of course, Payton brought more to the Bears than his immense on-field talent and production. He was the true leader of the team, an inspiration to many of his teammates. If Payton wanted to play somewhere else during that long part of his career when the Bears struggled, he never said it publicly. Although he didn't give every interview he was asked for, when he spoke he always talked about team goals; he was definitely not a player who sought controversy. Payton also kept the team loose as its prankster, a role that he continued almost until the day he died. The week before his death, Payton purposely sent former Bears running back Matt Suhey to wrong addresses on a trip to Mike Singletary's house, and then had him hide a hamburger and a malt in Singletary's garage.

Despite his accomplishments and fame, both in Chicago and around the world of sports, Payton felt unappreciated as he expressed in a *Chicago Tribune* article in December 1985:

> I'm just here. I'm overlooked. . . . All the emphasis is put on the spectaculars. People that are in there day in and day out working and sacrificing and trying to build a positive attitude and image, that doesn't sell papers. . . . I guess I'm dull and that's the way they try to keep it.

One would be surprised at how many great athletes have a sense of being slighted or overlooked and use that as motivation. His teammates and coaches, of course, appreciated Payton. In that same article, Bears offensive tackle Jimbo Covert called Payton "the glue who holds this team together." Mike Ditka said that Payton was, "the very best player I've ever seen, period—at any position." Dan Hampton called Payton, "Easily the best football player of our time. Bar none."

Whether he was the best football player of our time or not, there can be no denying that few athletes had more impact on their community and on their sport than Walter Payton.

The 46 Defense

Three of the top six Defense Power Index (DPI) marks of all time were compiled by the 1984, 1985, and 1986 Bears. The 46 defense earned its name because free safety Doug Plank, who wore number 46 until his retirement in 1982, played in a middle linebacker position. The 46 defense was just one scheme in the Bears' defensive arsenal, but it received most of the attention and credit for the team's success.

Bears defensive coordinator Buddy Ryan was the primary architect of the 46 defense, and you could write a book just about Ryan, his relationship (or lack thereof) with Mike Ditka, his move to the Eagles, etc. The scheme basically put eight men in the box and lined up three defensive linemen (usually Steve McMichael, Dan Hampton, and Richard Dent) head-up on the center and two guards, making it impossible to double-team the man on the center. The two "outside" linebackers, Otis Wilson and Wilber Marshall, would both play on the strongside, one across from the tight end and the other just outside of him.

Although the 46 defense generated tremendous pass pressure because of the sheer number of rushers (usually at least five players) as well as the fact that any combination of eight players could rush the passer, it was also effective against the run, partly because of so many players close to the line of scrimmage, and partly because of the talents of left defensive end Mike Hartenstine and middle linebacker Mike Singletary. The 1984–86 Bears recorded 198 sacks, the most in any three-year period since 1978. They got at least 60 sacks in all three seasons; only 20 times since 1978 has a defense recorded 60 or more.

The weakness of the 46 was that the corners had to play tight man-to-man coverage. Ryan didn't play zone coverage with the 46. "If you drop back in zone," he said, "they can unload the ball before you get there."

With Ryan's departure after the 1985 season to become head coach of the Eagles, the Bears used the 46 less often. Other teams began to copy the Bears, at least in terms of more aggressively attacking the line of scrimmage and the backfield. To counter these blitzes, teams began to run timing routes on pass plays and spread the field with their formations so that the defense couldn't play so many people in the box. As is always the case in sports, it's not just the strategy that makes a successful approach, the players have to execute that strategy. The Bears of the mid-1980s had an outstanding collection of players who made their defense, including the 46 scheme, probably the greatest defense ever assembled. I offer apologies to my hometown Ravens, but they have to keep up their 2000 pace for another couple of seasons to truly be in this class.

The top ten DPI marks since 1950:

Team	ADI
1970 Minnesota Vikings	+5.44
1971 Baltimore Colts	+4.79
1986 Chicago Bears	+4.59
1984 Chicago Bears	+4.46
1969 Minnesota Vikings	+4.35
1985 Chicago Bears	+4.35
1988 Minnesota Vikings	+4.25
2000 Tennessee Titans	+4.25
2000 Baltimore Ravens	+4.22
1964 Green Bay Packers	+4.21

The 1984–86 Bears have the best three-year DPI (+13.41) since 1950. If the strike year of 1987 is "exempted" from these calculations, then the Bears have three of the eight seasons of a +10.00 or better DPI over three years (1983–85, 1984–86, 1985–86, and 1988).

1985 Bears: The Postseason Monster Shuffle

I'm not the first person to suggest that the Bears' performance in the playoffs in 1985 is the best by any team in history. They came into the playoffs as the favorites to win the Super Bowl and were, up to that time, probably the most celebrated team in NFL history. They still probably hold that distinction. Just about everything the Bears did that year was news, and the way they dominated their opponents in the postseason was more newsworthy because of their immense and rapidly growing fame.

The Bears' first playoff test came against the New York Giants, who were coached by Bill Parcells. They were quarterbacked by Phil Simms who led the NFC with 3,829 yards passing. Joe Morris had an excellent year in his first year as their feature back, rushing for 1,336 yards, a 4.5 average per carry, and 21 touchdowns. The Giants' offense finished second in the conference in yards gained and third in points scored. Defensively, the Giants led the NFL in 1985 with 68 sacks; Lawrence Taylor contributed 13 of those. New York's defense held opponents to just 3.5 yards per rush, the best mark in the league.

The game was no contest. Although the final score was only 21–0, the Bears totally dominated the Giants. Three missed field goals by Kevin Butler on a cold and windy day kept the score closer than the game actually was.

The wind played a factor in the Bears' first score, a very weird play indeed. In the first quarter, facing fourth-and-long from their own 12, the Giants naturally sent in punter Sean Landeta and the rest of the punt team. For some reason—Landeta blamed the wind—the ball and Landeta's foot barely touched one another and Chicago's Shaun Gayle picked the ball up at the New York 5 and went in for the touchdown. Officially, it was a minus-7 yard punt and a 5-yard punt return.

The one Giants' threat in the first half ended with a missed 19-yard field goal by Eric Schubert, one of three kickers New York used that year. The kick, right at the end of the first half, hit the left upright and bounced back and kept the score at 7–0 Bears. Although the Giants made a few big plays throwing the football (the one "weakness" of the 46 defense), on 9 of their first 11 possessions they went three and out. The Bears held Joe Morris to 32 yards on 12 carries and sacked Phil Simms six times; Richard Dent had 3 1/2 sacks. Chicago outgained New York from scrimmage 363 yards to 181. The Bears' underrated passing attack also made some big plays, including a 46-yard completion from Jim McMahon to tight end Tim Wrightman to set up Chicago's last touchdown. McMahon threw for 216 yards and 2 touchdowns on just 21 attempts. (Remember, the Bears led the NFC in yards per completion and net yards per passing attempt in 1985.) The team that had led the NFL in sacks failed to register even a single sack against the Bears.

Next came the Los Angeles Rams. The Rams won the NFC West with an 11–5 record and shut out Dallas 20–0 in their first playoff game to reach the NFC Championship Game. During the regular season, Eric Dickerson rushed for 1,234 yards and 12 touchdowns, despite holding out until the third game of the year.

The Bears had less success moving the ball against the Rams than they had against the Giants, but the Rams had no success whatsoever. The Rams managed only 130 yards of offense for the entire game, and Eric Dickerson was limited to just 46 yards on 17 carries. The Bears moved the ball enough in the first quarter to take a 10–0 lead, and LA was never in the game.

Fittingly, the Bears' defense scored the final touchdown of the game as Wilbur Marshall returned a Dieter Brock fumble 52 yards to make the final score 24–0. No team had ever posted consecutive playoff shutouts in the same year. The Philadelphia Eagles posted back-to-back playoff shutouts in the NFL championships games in 1948 and 1949, both played in extreme weather conditions.

The Super Bowl was a rematch of the second-week game, in which the Bears defeated the New England Patriots 20–7 in Chicago. In that regular season meeting, the Bears had almost completely shut down the Patriots offense; New England's only score came on a 90-yard pass from Eason to running back Craig James in the fourth quarter. The Patriots began the season 2–3, but survived an injury to starting quarterback Tony Eason to win 9 of their last 11 games and earn a wild-card berth. Veteran Steve Grogan played well until Eason was able to return to the lineup.

After two road playoff wins, New England advanced to the Super Bowl by beating the Dolphins in Miami in the AFC championship after 18 consecutive losses at the Orange Bowl. The Patriots had a good running game, led by Craig James's 1,227 yards and 4.7 average per carry, and a pair of big-play wide receivers in Stanley Morgan and Irving Fryar, the first pick in the 1984 draft. Combined, Morgan and Fryar averaged over 18 yards per catch and caught 12 touchdowns on just 78 receptions. Defensively, the Patriots were tough to run against, allowing just 3.6 yards per rush, and had two ball-hawks in the secondary—Pro Bowl cornerback Raymond Clayborn and Pro Bowl safety Fred Marion.

Publicly, both teams maintained they had improved since their first meeting, and that the first game had little relevance on what would happen in the Super Bowl. "What happened in September has no bearing at all on what's going to happen out there Sunday," Mike Ditka said. "They were a young football team. We caught them unaware a little. They didn't realize we could play as good as we could on defense that early." Patriots All-Pro guard John Hannah, who missed the regular season game against the Bears, believed that the Patriots had become more comfortable with head coach Raymond Berry's offense as the season had progressed, saying, "We were all trying to find our niche in the offensive scheme. Now we know where Craig James is going to run. We know where Tony Eason is sitting in the pocket. We know how long it will take for him to get his pass off."

Most, but not all, football observers thought the Bears would win, but few seemed to think the game would be a blowout. Both franchises were making first-ever Super Bowl appearances, and there was much to get acclimated to during the two weeks leading up to the game. Some people used that time to rationalize that the Patriots could win. Here are a few predictions by some of the country's prominent sports writers:

Howard Balzer, *The Sporting News,* Bears 13–0
Jim Dent, *Dallas Times Herald,* Bears 41–7
Gordon Forbes, *USA Today,* Bears 24–7
Will McDonough, *Boston Globe,* Patriots 13–10

Hubert Mizell, *St. Petersburg Times,* Patriots 17–13
Art Spander, *San Francisco Examiner,* Bears 13–3
Paul Zimmerman, *Sports Illustrated,* Bears 17–10

What happened, of course, was one of the most lopsided games in NFL playoff history, as the Bears won easily by the score of 46–10. Although New England scored first, kicking a field goal after recovering a Bears' fumble, they were dominated from the very beginning. How dominated? New England made positive yardage on just one of their first 16 plays. By half-time, with the Bears leading 23–3, the Patriots had been outgained 236 yards to −14. In keying on Walter Payton, the Patriots were able to control him (he gained just 61 yards on 22 carries), but Matt Suhey was effective (52 yards on 11 carries) and the Bears' underrated passing game made big plays. Jim McMahon completed 12 of 20 passes for 256 yards; his 12.80 average gain per attempt is the second-best in Super Bowl history. In holding the Patriots to just 123 yards of total offense, the second-lowest total ever in a Super Bowl, the Bears sacked New England quarterbacks seven times, and the Patriots were just 1-for-10 on third down conversions. (It wasn't exactly the Bears' 73–0 win over Washington in the 1940 NFL Championship Game, but it was in the same neighborhood.)

The Bears held each of their three 1985 playoff opponents to fewer than 200 yards of offense; Chicago outgained them 1,003 yards to 434. In the NFC championship and Super Bowl, the Rams and Patriots combined to average just 2.2 yards per play. The Bears' running game was effective enough, but the passing game made most of the big offensive plays. Jim McMahon had an outstanding postseason performance, completing 39 of 66 passes for 636 yards (an excellent 9.64 yards per attempt, especially given the competition), 3 touchdowns, no interceptions, and a 106.6 passing rating. All things considered, the team's total domination of their playoff opponents may be its most impressive achievement.

The Coach: Mike Ditka

Coaching Record (with Bears Only)

	W	L	Pct	
1982	3	6	.333	
1983	8	8	.500	
1984	10	6	.625	NFC Central Division title
1985	15	1	.938	NFC Central Division title; NFC champs; Super Bowl champs
1986	14	2	.875	NFC Central Division title
1987	11	4	.733	NFC Central Division title
1988	12	4	.750	NFC Central Division title
1989	6	10	.375	
1990	11	5	.688	NFC Central Division title
1991	11	5	.688	NFC Wild Card
1992	5	11	.313	
Total	**106**	**62**	**.631**	

- Ditka is one of just two people (Tom Flores is the other) to have played for a Super Bowl champion, been an assistant coach for a Super Bowl champion, and been the head coach of a Super Bowl champion. He also played for the 1963 NFL champion Bears.
- During the Bears' run of five straight NFC Central Division titles, 1984 through 1988, their regular season record of 62–17 was the best in the NFL. San Francisco had the next-best record at 58–20–1.
- Chicago's 29 wins in 1985–86 is an NFL record for two seasons.

Say what you want about his personality or the fact that the Bears won "only" one Super Bowl during his tenure, but there can be no doubt that Mike Ditka was a successful head coach with Chicago. He coached the Bears for 11 years to a 106–62 regular season record; in the 11 years before he became head coach their record was 67–94–1. The Bears won the NFC Central in Ditka's third year; Chicago had never won that division prior to his arrival.

In the last important move he made before he died, George Halas, Sr. hired Mike Ditka as head coach on January 20, 1982. Of course, Halas had drafted Ditka in the first round back in 1961. Ditka was an outstanding tight end until foot and knee injuries diminished his production: he was inducted to the Hall of Fame in 1988. Ditka always felt an enormous sense of gratitude to Halas, who may have been the only man to think of Ditka as a head coach. He was not exactly the first choice of Jim Finks, Chicago's GM when Ditka was hired. They observed an uneasy truce until Finks resigned in 1983. When asked what the Bears' success meant to him, Ditka replied, "It means one thing: I've repaid a confidence." In fact, a letter written to

Halas when Ditka was still with the Cowboys as an assistant coach may have played a large role in the hiring. While being very careful not to imply that he was after the job of then-Bears head coach Neill Armstrong, Ditka expressed the desire to help return the team to its glory days as head coach, if and when the opportunity became available.

Ditka's intensity and his fierce will to win came early. In a November 1985 *Chicago Tribune* article, Ditka was quoted as saying, "I hate to lose. When I was a kid playing Little League baseball, boy I hated to lose. I cried. It just hurt my feelings to lose. I don't like to lose. I'm not proud of that, but I just don't like to lose." Richie Petitbon, former Bears safety and Ditka's teammate from 1961 to 1966 said, "I have never met a player with more desire."

Ditka is a man who leaves few people unaffected, you either love him or hate him, but his desire to win is genuine. Although Ditka's volatility was undeniable, Jerry Vainisi said that Ditka would often admit he was wrong after he'd had a chance to cool down. Former Dallas general manager Tex Schramm said, "When you get down to it, Mike is smart. A lot of people want to picture him as the tough bully. But Mike has a lot of sensitivity and compassion. You know he's competitive, but he also has good sense when he lets himself have good sense."

Ditka once said that it was simply meant to be that Walter Payton was a Chicago Bear. Actually, I think that applies more to Ditka than it does to Payton or anyone else in football.

The Quarterback: Jim McMahon

Year	Team	Att	Comp	Yds	TD	Int	YPA	Rating	Lg Avg	W	L	Pct
1982	CHI	210	120	1,501	9	7	7.15	79.9	73.4	3	4	.429
1983	CHI	295	175	2,184	12	13	7.40	77.6	75.9	7	6	.538
1984	CHI	143	85	1,146	8	2	8.01	97.8	76.1	7	2	.778
1985	CHI	313	178	2,392	15	11	7.64	82.6	73.5	11	0	1.000
1986	CHI	150	77	995	5	8	6.63	61.4	74.1	6	0	1.000
1987	CHI	210	125	1,639	12	8	7.80	87.4	75.2	5	1	.833
1988	CHI	192	114	1,346	6	7	7.01	76.0	72.9	7	2	.778
1989	SD	318	176	2,132	10	10	6.70	73.5	75.6	4	7	.364
1990	PHI	9	6	63	0	0	7.00	86.8	77.3	0	0	—
1991	PHI	311	187	2,239	12	11	7.20	80.3	76.2	8	3	.727
1992	PHI	43	22	279	1	2	6.49	60.1	75.3	1	0	1.000
1993	MIN	331	200	1,968	9	8	5.95	76.2	76.7	8	4	.667
1994	ARI	43	23	219	1	3	5.09	46.6	78.4	0	1	.000
1995	GB	1	1	6	0	0	6.00	91.7	79.2	0	0	—
1996	GB	4	3	39	0	0	9.75	105.2	76.9	0	0	—
Total		**2,573**	**1,492**	**18,148**	**100**	**90**	**7.05**	**78.2**	**75.9**	**67**	**30**	**.691**
1984–88		1,008	579	7,518	46	36	7.46	81.4	74.4	36	5	.878

YPA = Yards Per Pass Attempt
Rating = Passer Rating
Lg Avg = League Passer Rating in that season
W, L, Pct = Team's Record in his starts

- First-round pick (fifth overall) by Chicago in 1982.
- Selected to one Pro Bowl (after the 1985 season).
- Rushed for 987 yards on 163 carries, a 6.1 average, and 8 touchdowns from 1983 through 1986.
- Never played in all of his team's games in a season and played in 10 games or more only five times in his 15 NFL seasons.
- From 1984 through 1988, the Bears were 26–12 in games *not* started by McMahon.

McMahon is best remembered for the sunglasses, the headbands, the feuds with Mike Ditka, and all sorts of off-field things. Maybe McMahon is a symbol of the "new era" of sports and sports journalism, where the game matters only as much, or maybe even less, than the stuff outside the game. All of the "extra-curricular" attention has led many to forget that McMahon was, for most of his career, a good quarterback. For example, it's rare that a rookie quarterback can compile a passing rating better than the league average. Although McMahon did not possess phenomenal arm strength or athletic ability, he had a good arm, was fairly mobile, and had an uncanny ability to make quick reads of the defense.

Some of his teammates thought that McMahon's "antics" were at least partly an act. Bears center Jay Hilgenberg said, "Football is such a mind game and Jim plays it to the hilt. Nobody knows what he's thinking, where he's coming from, or what he's going to do next. When he's in there, that gives us a big edge."

McMahon admits that he doesn't think football is sacred or as difficult to understand as some in the game think. "I've never pretended to take football seriously," he said. "I don't think the game is that hard. It's like chess. You're trying to outmaneuver the other team, expose the weaknesses you see. I've had some great coaching over the years. I've tried to pick people's brains and find things out, but to me, it's not that hard."

Did all of his off-field endeavors interfere with his devotion to football and, directly or indirectly, his ability to stay healthy? At times, some of his teammates and coaches thought so. In 1986, these sentiments became more prevalent in the Bears' organization. McMahon ended up having shoulder surgery in November of that year after being the victim of a cheap shot by Packers defensive end Charles Martin. Upon examination, doctors discovered that McMahon had been playing with a partially torn rotator cuff. Most of McMahon's teammates loved his reckless playing style; Jerry Vainisi, Chicago GM from 1983 to 1987, thinks the Bears could have won the Super Bowl in 1984 and 1986 if McMahon had been healthy.

Without knowing Jim McMahon, it's hard for me to say whether he could have played more than he did, even with his injuries. He played hurt—even playing with a broken hand for part of 1985—and he certainly was not always careful with his body on the football field. As for his off-field conditioning regimen, only Jim McMahon can address that topic. It is certain that McMahon's fame exceeded his on-field accomplishments. It also seems to me that when one strips away the hype, Jim McMahon was a very capable NFL quarterback in large part because he understood the game so well.

1985 Chicago Bears Statistics

Passing

	ATT	COMP	COMP PCT	YDS	YDS PER	TD	INT	RATING
McMahon	313	178	56.9%	2,392	7.64	15	11	82.6
Fuller	107	53	49.5%	777	7.26	1	5	57.3
Tomczak	6	2	33.3%	33	5.50	0	0	52.8
Payton	5	3	60.0%	96	19.20	1	0	143.8
Buford	1	1	100.0%	5	5.00	0	0	87.5
Bears	**432**	**237**	**54.9%**	**3,303**	**7.65**	**17**	**16**	**77.3**
Opponents	522	249	47.7%	3,299	6.32	16	34	51.2
League Average			54.8%		7.04			73.5

Bears' passers were sacked 43 times for 227 yards in losses.
The Bears sacked their opponents 64 times for 483 yards in losses.

Not counting sacks, the Bears were second in the NFC and fourth in the NFL in average yards per pass attempt. Counting sacks, they were first in the NFC and fourth in the NFL. They didn't throw a lot of passes–the Bears were twenty-sixth in passes attempted including sacks–but they got big plays from their passing game.

The Bears' 51.2 opponents' passing rating is the fifth lowest (or best) for all NFL teams since 1978.

Rushing

	Att	Yds	Avg	Net Yards	TD
Payton	324	1,551	4.79	+224	9
Suhey	115	471	4.10	−1	1
McMahon	47	252	5.36		3
Gentry	30	160	5.33		2
Thomas	31	125	4.03		4
Sanders	25	104	4.16		1
Fuller	24	77	3.21		5
Gault	5	18	3.60		0
Perry	5	7	1.40		2
Tomczak	2	3	1.50		0
McKinnon	1	0	0.00		0
Margerum	1	−7	−7.00		0
Bears	**610**	**2,761**	**4.53**	**+257**	**27**
Opponents	359	1,319	3.67	−155	6
League Average			4.10		

This was Payton's fourth and last 1,500-yard rushing season, and the ninth of his 10 1,000-yard seasons. He finished third in the league in yardage behind Marcus Allen of the Raiders (1,759 yards) and Gerald Riggs of the Falcons (1,719 yards). For what it's worth, Payton led the league in net yards rushing.

The 1985 Bears are one of only eight teams since 1950, and one of only two since 1978, to outrush their opponents by at least 90 yards per game. They are the only team since 1978 to rush for at least 20 more touchdowns than their opposition.

How often does the team's backup QB finish second on the squad in rushing touchdowns as Steve Fuller did?

Receiving

	Rec	Yds	Avg	TD
Payton	49	483	9.86	2
Moorehead	35	481	13.74	1
Gault	33	704	21.33	1
Suhey	33	295	8.94	1
McKinnon	31	555	17.90	7
Wrightman	24	407	16.96	1
Margerum	17	190	11.18	2
Gentry	5	77	15.40	0
Thomas	5	45	9.00	0
Maness	1	34	34.00	0
McMahon	1	13	13.00	1
Sanders	1	9	9.00	0
Anderson	1	6	6.00	0
Perry	1	4	4.00	1
Bears	**237**	**3,303**	**13.94**	**17**
Opponents	249	3,299	13.25	16
League Average			12.83	

A weakness of the 46 defense, in 1985 the only weakness, was that it could be beaten occasionally for long passes. The Bears allowed more yards per reception than the league average and one of only three 90+ yard touchdown passes in the NFL that year.

Kickoff Returns

	Ret	Yds	Avg	TD
Gault	22	577	26.23	1
Gentry	18	466	25.89	1
Taylor	1	18	18.00	0

(continued next page)

Kickoff Returns *(continued)*

	Ret	Yds	Avg	TD
McKinnon	1	16	16.00	0
Sanders	1	10	10.00	0
Marshall	0	2	—	0
Bears	**43**	**1,089**	**25.33**	**2**
Opponents	85	2,115	23.42	0
League Average			20.99	

Willie Gault was second in the league in kickoff return average because Ron Brown of the Raiders averaged an excellent 32.79 yards to lead the league. Dennis Gentry was 2 returns short of qualifying; his average would have placed him third in the NFL.

Punt Returns

	Ret	Yds	Avg	TD
Taylor	25	198	7.92	0
Ortego	17	158	9.29	0
Duerson	6	47	7.83	0
McKinnon	4	44	11.00	0
Maness	2	9	4.50	0
Gentry	0	47	—	0
Bears	**54**	**503**	**9.31**	**0**
Opponents	23	203	8.83	0
League Average			9.28	

Interceptions

	Int	Yds	Avg	TD
Frazier	6	119	19.83	1
Duerson	5	53	10.60	0
Fencik	5	43	8.60	0
Richardson	4	174	43.50	1
Marshall	4	23	5.75	0
Wilson	3	35	11.67	1
Taylor	3	28	9.33	0
Dent	2	10	5.00	1
Singletary	1	23	23.00	0
Rivera	1	4	4.00	0
Bears	**34**	**512**	**15.06**	**4**
Opponents	16	99	6.19	1

Chicago's 34 interceptions led the NFL in 1985. The league average, excluding the Bears, was 21. Their 4 touchdown returns tied for the league lead with Dallas and the Rams.

Sack Leaders

(Sacks have been an official statistic for individual players only since 1982.)

Dent	17.0
Wilson	10.5
Hampton	6.5

Dent led the NFL in sacks in 1985.

Turnovers

Turnovers Committed:	31
Turnovers Forced:	54
Turnover +/–:	+23

The Bears' led the league with 54 forced turnovers. Teams must be taking better care of the ball, because no defense has forced as many as 50 turnovers in a season since 1989.

Punting

	No	Avg
Buford	68	42.2
Opponents	90	40.4
League Average		41.4

Kicking

	XP	XPA	XP Pct	FG	FGA	FG Pct
Butler	51	51	100.0%	31	37	83.8%
Opponents	22	23	95.7%	12	19	63.2%
League Average			95.7%			72.2%

Leading Scorer: Kevin Butler, 144 Points
Leading Scorer, Non-Kicker: Walter Payton, 66 Points

1985 Chicago Bears Roster

Head Coach	Mike Ditka		
QB	Steve Fuller	DE	Richard Dent
QB	Jim McMahon	DE	Mike Hartenstine
QB	Mike Tomczak	DE	Tyrone Keys
RB	Dennis Gentry	DT	Dan Hampton
RB	Walter Payton	DT	Steve McMichael
RB	Thomas Sanders	DT/FB	William Perry
RB	Matt Suhey	DT/DE	Henry Waechter
RB	Calvin Thomas	LB	Brian Cabral
WR	Brad Anderson	LB	Wilber Marshall
WR	Willie Gault	LB	Jim Morrissey
WR	James Maness	LB	Ron Rivera
WR	Ken Margerum	LB	Mike Singletary
WR	Dennis McKinnon	LB	Cliff Thrift
WR	Keith Ortego	LB	Otis Wilson
TE	Emery Moorehead	DB	Dave Duerson
TE	Tim Wrightman	DB	Gary Fencik
C	Tom Andrews	DB	Leslie Frazier
C	Jay Hilgenberg	DB	Shaun Gayle
OG	Kurt Becker	DB	Reggie Phillips
OG	Mark Bortz	DB	Mike Richardson
OG	Stefan Humphries	DB	Ken Taylor
OG/C	Tom Thayer		
OT	Jimbo Covert		
OT	Andy Frederick		
OT	Keith Van Horne		
K	Kevin Butler		
P	Maury Buford		

Hall of Famers: Ditka (as a player), Payton, Hampton, Singletary.

Among the 748 articles about the Bears in the *Chicago Tribune* in 1985 (yes, 748, although that number is dwarfed by the 1,626 Bears articles the *Tribune* printed in 1986) was one in late December about the only three Bears' players who, at the time, had earned no off-the-field income in 1985. They were linebacker Jim Morrissey, punt returner Keith Ortego, and defensive lineman Henry Waechter.

CHAPTER 9

1989 San Francisco 49ers: Didn't Miss a Beat

STARTING LINEUP – 1989 49ERS

Offense		Defense	
SE	John Taylor	LE/LT	Pierce Holt
LT	Bubba Paris	NT/RT	Michael Carter
LG	Guy McIntyre	RE/LE	Kevin Fagan
C	Jesse Sapolu	LOLB/RE	Charles Haley
RG	Bruce Collie	LILB	Matt Millen
RT	Harris Barton	RILB	Michael Walter
TE	Brent Jones	ROLB	Keena Turner
FL	Jerry Rice	LCB	Darryl Pollard
QB	Joe Montana	RCB	Don Griffin
RB	Roger Craig	SS	Chet Brooks
RB	Tom Rathman	FS	Ronnie Lott

It had to be tougher than it looked for George Seifert to take over as 49ers head coach from Bill Walsh. After all, Walsh was the primary architect in San Francisco's rise to NFL king of the hill. San Francisco won three Super Bowls in Walsh's last eight seasons as head coach, including his last season in 1988.

It must have been difficult for Seifert, but it sure didn't look like it. Like all teams, the 49ers won some close games, but their two losses in 1989 were by a total of five points. Like all NFL teams San Francisco suffered injuries, but that didn't stop them from easily compiling the best record in the league.

Brent Jones, the starting tight end for the 49ers from 1989 to 1997, told me, "I think that George just picked up where Bill left off. . . . The natural inclination for a new coach is to be over-involved on both sides of the ball . . . so I think the hands-off approach and more of a leader/manager position as a head coach really served him well." What Brent meant is that Seifert continued running the defense as he had under Walsh and, at least early on, left the offense to the offensive coordinator (at the time, Mike Holmgren). No doubt, that coaching continuity helped keep the 49ers successful.

San Francisco's record in its last three seasons under Bill Walsh was 33–13–1, with one Super Bowl title; in their first three seasons under Seifert their record was 38–10, with one Super Bowl title. The hits just kept on coming.

Obviously, the football world watched the 49ers in 1989 to see of the departure of Bill Walsh from the sidelines would affect the team on the field. As Glenn Dickey wrote in *49ers: The Rise, Fall, and Rebirth of the NFL's Greatest Dynasty,* "Seifert faced an impossible task. No coach could have replaced Walsh in the eyes of 49ers fans because Walsh had assumed mythic status by the time he left. Seifert would never be a legendary figure." Legendary or not, Seifert's calm demeanor helped the team deal with the pressure of losing Walsh as well as the incredibly high expectation level created by many years of success.

Team in a Box

Record: 14–2

Although the 49ers won their share of close games (three of their wins were by six points or less), both of their losses were close. They lost by one point in their first game against the Rams, and by four points to the Packers. With a bit of luck, San Francisco could have been undefeated.

Against Teams Over .500: 6–2, 207 Points Scored, 156 Points Allowed

Their performance against winning teams is one of the most impressive parts of the 1989 49ers "résumé." The way San Francisco played in the 1989 postseason is really impressive.

Points Scored/Allowed: 442/253 (1989 NFL Average: 330)

San Francisco led the NFL in points scored in 1989 and was third in fewest points allowed.

Yards Gained/Allowed: 6,268/4,618 (1989 NFL Average: 5,219)

The 49ers led the league in yards gained and were fourth in fewest yards allowed. Of all of the teams during the 49ers' run, the 1989 team had the fourth-highest yards gained total, behind the teams in 1998, 1993, and 1984.

Opponents' Record: 115–125, .479

(Not counting games against the 49ers.)

The aggregate record of the 49ers' opponents underestimates the overall strength of their schedule. They played half of their regular season games against teams with winning records, but they also played 1–15 Dallas and 3–13 Atlanta (twice).

Adjusted Power Index:

Offense: +3.79
Defense: +2.50
TOTAL: +6.29

Only 16 teams since 1950 have had an Offense Power Index (OPI) and a Defense Power Index (DPI) of at least +2.50. Their OPI ranks in the top 3 percent of all teams since 1950.

Innovations/What You Should Know:

According to Glenn Dickey, a sports columnist for the *San Francisco Chronicle* during the 49ers' dynasty, the San Francisco players had a mission in 1989. They wanted to prove that the 49ers could win without Bill Walsh.

That sentiment came as a surprise to Walsh, who at the time didn't realize that many of his players feared him and, in a few extreme cases, hated him. All-Pro safety Ronnie Lott pledged that 1989 would be the "we'll show Walsh" year. Apparently, Lott was angry at Walsh for not telling the players that he was retiring. As it turned out, the players succeeded in their mission.

Homegrown First-Round Picks:

DB Ronnie Lott, 1981; WR Jerry Rice, 1985; OT Harris Barton, 1987; RB Terrence Flagler, 1987; LB Keith DeLong, 1989.

Those first two guys were pretty good.

Roger Craig was the first player San Francisco drafted in 1983, but he was picked in the second round.

Pro Bowl Players:

RB Roger Craig, DB Ronnie Lott, OG Guy McIntyre, QB Joe Montana, WR Jerry Rice, WR John Taylor.

Craig, Montana, and Taylor were named to the Pro Bowl team, but were either replaced or didn't play due to injury.

The third round of the draft was very good to the 49ers. McIntyre was picked by the 49ers in the third round in 1984. Montana was a third-round pick in 1979. (See "The Quarterback: Joe Montana.") Completing the trifecta, John Taylor was a third-round pick in 1986.

Game-by-Game:

Sep. 10th 49ERS 30, INDIANAPOLIS 24 AT INDIANAPOLIS

The Colts weren't happy about the way San Francisco played (more on that later) but with the 49ers' Roger Craig running for 131 yards on 24 attempts and Joe Montana and Jerry Rice hooking up on a 58-yard touchdown pass with 5:21 left, the 49ers gave new head coach George Seifert a win in his first regular-season game. The Montana–Rice TD came against an all-out blitz by Indianapolis. As Colts head coach Ron Meyer noted, "We had seven people coming at Montana. We just didn't get there on time."

The Colts' players, specifically their defensive linemen, felt that the 49ers used "questionable" techniques. Colts' defensive end Donnell Thompson said, "They take more cheap shots than any offensive line I've seen in my nine years in the league." He was referring to the 49ers' frequent use of chop blocks, which are legal as long as they are thrown from a head-on direction and the defensive player is not otherwise engaged. San Francisco center Jesse Sapolu said that he was kicked twice by Thompson out of frustration.

Indianapolis's Eric Dickerson ran for 106 yards to become the seventh player in NFL history to reach 10,000 yards rushing. He was also the fastest to reach that mark, doing it in his first 91 games.

Sep. 17th 49ERS 20, TAMPA BAY 16 AT TAMPA BAY

Trailing 16–13 with just over three minutes to play, Joe Montana led the 49ers on a 10-play, 70-yard drive, culminated by his 4-yard TD run with 40 seconds left. Through three quarters, all of the scoring came on field goals as Tampa Bay led 9–6. San Francisco scored the first touchdown of the game after a 68-yard drive that ended with a two-yard pass from Montana to Rice. The 49ers held Tampa Bay and got the ball back, but Joe Montana threw an interception with six minutes left and the Buccaneers then moved 60 yards in seven plays to take the 16–13 lead.

Commenting on San Francisco's winning drive, Tampa Bay quarterback Vinny Testaverde said, "They are a team that has done it so many times, but it was a sick feeling watching them do it live."

Sep. 24th 49ERS 38, PHILADELPHIA 28 AT PHILADELPHIA

Down 18–10 after three quarters, Joe Montana threw 4 touchdown passes in the fourth quarter to stun the hometown Eagles. Philadelphia head coach Buddy Ryan said, "I guess they showed us why they are the world champions. Defensively, we played great football for three quarters, but in the fourth quarter, which we say is our quarter, we gave up 28 points."

The Eagles hounded Montana all day, sacking him eight times. San Francisco also committed 3 turnovers and could only gain 46 yards rushing on 19 carries. Head coach George Seifert said, "I can't imagine a team putting itself in the hole more often than we did in this game. I think overcoming all of that speaks for the poise of these players."

By game's end, Montana had completed 25 of 34 passes for 428 yards and 5 touchdowns. Jerry Rice and John Taylor combined for 12 receptions for 300 yards and 3 touchdowns.

Oct. 1st LA RAMS 13, 49ERS 12 AT SAN FRANCISCO

Los Angeles drove 72 yards in eight plays after recovering a Tom Rathman fumble to set up Mike Lansford's 26-yard field goal with two seconds left. The win kept the Rams undefeated at 4–0, and put them a game ahead of San Francisco.

San Francisco's defense played well, allowing just 37 rushing yards and controlling Jim Everett and LA's passing game, up until the Rams' last possession. Everett completed four passes for 72 yards on the drive that led to the game winning kick.

Oct. 8th 49ERS 24, NEW ORLEANS 20 AT NEW ORLEANS

Two disputable touchdown catches, one each by Jerry Rice and John Taylor, helped San Francisco beat NFC West rival New Orleans.

On Rice's third-quarter 60-yard TD catch, replay official Gaylor Bryan said that he would have ruled that Rice dropped the ball just before he crossed the goal line, but he never had the chance because the San Francisco completed its extra point attempt before he could finish his review.

On Taylor's 32-yard touchdown with eight minutes left in the game, Saints cornerback Toi Cook seemed to knock the ball loose before Taylor had possession in the end zone. This play was reviewed and the replay official upheld the call on the field.

Montana completed 21 of 29 passes for 291 yards, 3 touchdowns and no interceptions. Rice had seven catches for 149 yards.

Before the game, the 49ers suspended starting cornerback Tim McKyer for insubordination. Although he was reinstated later in the season, this effectively ended his career in San Francisco. He was traded to Miami after the season.

Oct. 15th 49ERS 31, DALLAS 14 AT DALLAS

Although quarterback Steve Young started and played well in place of injured Joe Montana, San Francisco "let" hapless Dallas stay in the game until the fourth quarter when the 49ers scored 17 points to break a 14–14 tie. San Francisco tight end Brent Jones offered his explanation, "I don't think we were flat. We just had some unfortunate penalties and missed some assignments. Then everyone got frustrated and we had to correct that at halftime."

The 49ers got a big play from their special teams in the third quarter when Steve Wallace blocked a field goal attempt by Dallas's Roger Ruzek, and San Francisco's Johnny Jackson returned the ball 75 yards for a touchdown.

Oct. 22nd 49ERS 37, NEW ENGLAND 20 AT PALO ALTO

In the aftermath of the October 17 earthquake that struck the Bay Area—causing the World Series to be postponed for 10 days in the process—the 49ers–Patriots game was moved to Stanford Stadium.

The 49ers paid a price for the win. Safety Jeff Fuller's NFL career ended when he broke three transverse processes, bones in the spinal column. Backup fullback Harry Sydney's season came to an end with a broken arm. Joe Montana sprained his left knee just before halftime; he had to leave the game for good in the third quarter.

Steve Young's numbers after replacing Montana were sensational: 11 of 12 for 188 yards and 3 touchdowns, including TD passes of 50 yards to Jerry Rice and 43 yards to John Taylor.

Oct. 29th 49ERS 23, NEW YORK JETS 10 AT NEW YORK

Ronnie Lott and Joe Montana were out with injuries. Steve Young, linebacker Keena Turner, defensive tackle Michael Carter, and cornerback Darryl Pollard left the game due to injuries. Still, San Francisco thrived in the Meadowlands. The 49ers' defense registering 9 sacks, including 3 by Charles Haley. Third-string quarterback Steve Bono connecting on 4 of 5 passes, including a 45-yard touchdown pass to Jerry Rice.

Turner talked about the 49ers attitude, "What you've got to realize is you've got a team whose expectations from itself are very high. This team isn't just happy being 7–1. This team is complaining about it. We're one of the unhappiest 7–1 teams in the league. We're not complacent."

Nov. 6th 49ERS 31, NEW ORLEANS 13 AT SAN FRANCISCO

Not to pick on George Seifert, but his reaction to Joe Montana's play after his return from injury might be the understatement of all time, "Joe is an extremely poised and experienced quarterback. He can come in after being out and play the way he did."

Montana hit 22 of 31 passes for 302 yards, 3 touchdowns and no interceptions. Two of the touchdowns were to Jerry Rice, who broke the team record for career touchdown receptions with 60. He would catch just a few more touchdowns.

New Orleans head coach Jim Mora was succinct, "That was a real butt kicking tonight." The Monday night win coupled with the Rams' overtime loss to Minnesota the day before pushed San Francisco's lead over Los Angeles to three games.

Nov. 12th 49ERS 45, ATLANTA 3 AT SAN FRANCISCO

Falcons head coach Marion Campbell was asked what the turning point of this game was. His answer, "It's been such a long day. We don't want to live through any more of these." Campbell retired two weeks later.

Although the 49ers started a bit slowly and led only 7–3 early in the second quarter, they made up for lost time.

For the game, San Francisco had 30 first downs to 11 for Atlanta and outgained the Falcons 515 yards to 192. The 12 teams in the book played a total of 178 regular season games. This was one of only five where the yardage differential was more than 300 yards.

Roger Craig had his second 100-yard rushing day of the season, gaining 109 yards on 17 carries. Joe Montana had a nice, efficient day: 16 of 19 for 270 yards, 3 TDs and no interceptions.

One interesting tidbit is that Atlanta's only score came on a 23-yard field goal by quarterback Chris Miller. Falcons kicker Paul McFadden suffered a thigh injury in pregame warmups. As it turned out, the injury was pretty inconsequential.

Nov. 19th GREEN BAY 21, 49ERS 17 AT SAN FRANCISCO

Penalties hurt San Francisco, as their winning streak ended at six games. Not only did penalties account for 35 of the 73 yards the Packers moved to score the winning touchdown in the fourth quarter, but a penalty also wiped out an apparent 49ers' touchdown on the same drive. San Francisco's Chet Brooks intercepted a Don Majkowski pass and returned it 94 yards, but 49ers defensive end Daniel Stubbs was flagged for lining up in the neutral zone.

San Francisco outgained Green Bay 360 yards to 248, but they couldn't overcome the penalties (10 in all) and 4 turnovers, including Joe Montana's first interception in six games.

Head coach George Seifert said after the game, "We've got some difficult games in front of us and now they're even more difficult. I'm sure a lot of people penciled this in as a game we should win." (Truth be told, the Packers wound up with their first 10-win season since 1972. Lindy Infante earned coach of the year honors, and Majikowski led the NFL with 4,318 passing yards.)

Nov. 27th 49ERS 34, NEW YORK GIANTS 24 AT SAN FRANCISCO

After the 49ers' 38–16 loss to the Rams in the last regular season game of 1988, Giants QB Phil Simms allegedly said this about San Francisco, "They lay down like dogs." The loss kept the Giants out of the playoffs as the Rams got the last NFC playoff berth.

The 49ers' defense remembered that line in this highly anticipated Monday night game, as they racked up 6 sacks on Simms. San Francisco defensive end Pierce Holt, who had 4 sacks, remarked after the game, "It [Simms's comment] wasn't part of the motivation going into the game, but it was worth a little bit of satisfaction afterward. I had a pretty good feeling thinking about what he said as we walked off the field."

The Giants fought hard, tying the game at 24–24 midway through the fourth quarter after trailing 24–10 at the half. The 49ers, who gained 226 yards in the first half, struggled to move the ball in the second half. After going back in the lead 27–24, San Francisco's third interception of Simms led to a Tom Rathman TD with 1:08 left to ice the game.

Dec. 3rd 49ERS 23, ATLANTA 10 AT ATLANTA

Trailing 10–6 at halftime, the 49ers rallied in the second half behind Steve Young, who replaced an injured Joe Montana (bruised ribs). San Francisco offensive tackle Bubba Paris summed up the game, "They [Atlanta] were like desperados. They came out and played what most people would consider undisciplined football. Whenever you find a team that says, 'we have nothing to lose,' they always have the potential of surprising you–and they did. But a good team will look at what they do and make the proper adjustments."

The Falcons really keyed on Jerry Rice and limited him to 3 short catches, but John Taylor had 5 receptions for 162 yards, including a 38-yard touchdown from Young in the third quarter.

Dec. 11th 49ERS 30, LA RAMS 27 AT LOS ANGELES

San Francisco trailed the Rams 17–0 at the end of the first quarter, but Joe Montana and John Taylor led the 49ers back to win the Monday night game and clinch the NFC West title and homefield advantage throughout the NFC playoffs. Taylor became the first player in NFL history to have 2 TDs of at least 90 yards in the same game. He turned a 10-yard pass into a 92-yard touchdown in the second quarter and turned another short pass into a 96-yard TD in the fourth quarter. In all, Taylor caught 11 passes for a team-record 286 yards. With a big assist from Taylor, Montana threw for a team-record 458 yards.

Taylor's heroics aside, 49ers defensive end Pierce Holt thought the ejection of fellow lineman Charles Haley late in the third quarter was a big factor in the comeback, "I think that pumped us up. We had lost one of our best players and we knew we had to play better." Haley was ejected for "vehemently" protesting a roughing the quarterback penalty.

Dec. 17th 49ERS 21, BUFFALO 10 AT SAN FRANCISCO

Roger Craig ran for 105 yards to surpass the 1,000-yard mark for the third time in his career, and the 49ers scored all of their points in the second half to defeat the eventual AFC East champions.

Dec. 24th 49ERS 26, CHICAGO 0 AT SAN FRANCISCO

With substitutes getting much of the playing time, San Francisco easily defeated the Bears to end Chicago's disappointing season with a thud. Chicago started the season 4–0, but finished 6–10.

Although he didn't have a great day passing in less than a full day, Joe Montana finished the year with a record passing rating of 112.4. As it turned out, that record wouldn't last too long.

Divisional Playoff:

Jan. 6th 49ERS 41, MINNESOTA 13 AT SAN FRANCISCO

San Francisco and Minnesota met in the playoffs for the third straight year. Continuing their payback for Minnesota's 36–24 upset win in 1987, the 49ers moved the ball at will against a defense that had allowed the fewest yards in the league while also recording the most sacks. Even though San Francisco had already won three Super Bowls before this season, this was their largest margin of victory ever in a playoff game. Of course, that would change real soon.

The 49ers completely dominated the first half, outgaining Minnesota 320 yards to 120 to take a 27–3 halftime lead. Unlike Minnesota, whose offense hadn't changed in two years according to one 49ers' defender, San Francisco tried new formations copied from other Vikings' opponents. For example, the 49ers occasionally lined up wide receiver John Taylor at tight end to create coverage problems. Offensive line coach Bobb McKittrick was honest about his strategy, "I'm a plagiarist. If I see something that does good, I'll use it."

Tackles Bubba Paris and Steve Wallace did a great job neutralizing Minnesota's Chris Doleman who had led the NFL with 21 sacks in 1989. Double-teaming took care of his linemate Keith Millard, third in the league with 18 sacks and named NFL defensive player of the year by the Associated Press and *Pro Football Weekly.* Paris said of Doleman, "He's a great player and I respect him, but he did a lot of talking before the game. During the game, he didn't have much to say."

The Vikings had 71 sacks during the regular season; they had none in this game. With time to throw, Joe Montana completed 17 of 24 passes for 241 yards, 4 touchdowns (all in the first half) and no interceptions. Roger Craig ran for 125 yards on 18 carries. As was often the case, a great run after a catch was a big play for San Francisco. Their first touchdown came after Jerry Rice caught a short pass from Montana at the 49ers' 36-yard line and turned it into a long touchdown with some great moves and broken tackles.

NFC Championship:

Jan. 14th 49ERS 30, LA RAMS 3 AT SAN FRANCISCO

After two close regular season games between the two teams, San Francisco completely shut down the Rams' offense, despite lingering injuries to many 49ers' defensive players, and won easily. Los Angeles gained just 156 yards of offense and made only 9 first downs. The Rams were fourth in the NFL in 1989 averaging 378 yards gained per game. San Francisco frustrated Rams wide receivers Willie Anderson and Henry Ellard by being more physical. San Francisco cornerback Eric Wright said, "In every defense we had, those guys were getting bumped." Ronnie Lott added, "We rolled the dice and said if they could beat us with little swing passes to [Greg] Bell, they would deserve to win."

Meanwhile, the 49ers once again moved the ball with ease. Led by Joe Montana's performance (26 for 30, 262 yards, 2 touchdowns, no interceptions), San Francisco gained 442 yards and had 29 first downs. Montana's second touchdown pass gave him 31 career TDs in the playoffs, breaking Terry Bradshaw's record. The win put San Francisco in its second straight Super Bowl and fourth in nine seasons.

Super Bowl XXIV:

Jan. 28th 49ERS 55, DENVER 10 AT NEW ORLEANS

This was Denver's third Super Bowl appearance in four seasons, but they had lost the previous two by a total of 51 points. San Francisco was a 12-point favorite, although Terry Bradshaw didn't think that was a big enough spread. Now a TV commentator, Bradshaw predicted right before the game that San Francisco would win 55–0. Although that prediction was no doubt influenced by his semi-feud with Denver quarterback John Elway, it turned out that Bradshaw was almost right on the money.

It was the most one-sided Super Bowl ever—and for Super Bowls, that's saying a lot. It's hard to describe or chronicle the performance in cold black-and-white text, but I'll try. Denver had allowed 20 or more points just four times during the regular season; San Francisco had 27 points at halftime. The Broncos had 136 receiving yards. Jerry Rice had 148 yards receiving. At one point, Joe Montana completed 13 consecutive passes; the Broncos completed 11 passes all day. Montana's passing rating for the game was 147.6, John Elway's was 19.4.

Some people think the game turned when Denver's Bobby Humphrey fumbled near midfield midway through the first quarter, with Denver trailing 7–3. That can't possibly explain what happened. San Francisco was a superior team playing a great game.

San Francisco safety Chet Brooks explained how his team shut down Elway, "He's not a quarterback who reads zones. We played 90 percent zones and 10 percent man-to-man." Cornerback Eric Wright thought that Elway "was totally in shock."

Denver head coach Dan Reeves had no illusions as to why the game evolved as it did, "The 49ers are playing at a level right now that not many people in the National Football League can match. I can't say enough good things about them. We're a long way from that level."

The 49ers outscored their three playoff opponents 126–26 and outgained them 1,306–708. They had earned their fourth Super Bowl title, and second in a row, with a postseason performance unmatched by almost any other team in NFL history.

Elsewhere Around the NFL:

Sep. 17th — Dan Marino threw 3 touchdown passes to reach the 200 career mark, as Miami beat New England 24–10. It took Marino just 89 games to get to 200; the quickest before Marino was Johnny Unitas's 121.

Oct. 13th — In one of the biggest and most significant trades in NFL history, Dallas traded Herschel Walker to Minnesota for five players, six conditional draft picks, and a first-round pick in 1992. Jimmy Johnson used some of those extra picks in trades; he traded for Pittsburgh's 1990 first-round pick and drafted Emmitt Smith. Other trades using those draft picks brought him other picks that let him draft Russell Maryland and Darren Woodson.

Just to make sure he was happy, Walker got $2 million to agree to the trade, even though he didn't have a no-trade clause in his contract. Walker never made the impact that Minnesota had hoped for, and losing all of those draft picks made it difficult for the Vikings to find the final pieces to turn a good team into a Super Bowl team.

Nov. 23rd The Eagles and Cowboys met in what would later be called "The Bounty Bowl." Philadelphia's 27–0 win was marred by many fights, and after the game, Dallas head coach Jimmy Johnson accused Philadelphia head coach Buddy Ryan of putting out a bounty on Dallas kicker, and ex-Eagles kicker, Luis Zendejas. After an investigation, the NFL said that it found no evidence that rewards had been offered for knocking any players out of the game. Seventeen players were fined by the league for fighting in that game.

What Happened the Next Season:

San Francisco posted a 14–2 record in 1990 and advanced to the NFC Championship Game against the Giants. Although New York's defense defused the 49ers offense, San Francisco had the ball and a 13–12 lead late in the game. With 2:36 left, Roger Craig fumbled, Lawrence Taylor recovered and the Giants moved into position for a 42-yard game-winning field goal by Matt Bahr. Craig was not back with San Francisco in 1991, signing with the Raiders as a Plan B free agent.

Year after Year

If you've already read the 1962 Packers' chapter, then you know that the Lombardi Packers were the only team whose defense achieved a Defense Power Index (DPI) of +2.00 or better for seven consecutive seasons. You may also remember that only two other teams attained a DPI of +2.00 or better for as many as five straight years.

While there is an article about the greatest offensive teams of all time in the 1994 49ers' chapter, that article focuses on just one or two seasons. I also wanted to look at offensive excellence over a longer period of time.

The offensive dominance of the 49ers becomes starkly clear when looking at spans of more than just a couple of seasons. In fact, what they did is unbelievable.

Ignoring the strike season of 1987, the 49ers achieved an Offense Power Index (OPI) of +2.00 or better for *13* straight seasons starting in 1983. (One more time: I exclude 1982 because of the truncated and interrupted season and I exclude 1987 because one-fifth of the games that counted were played with replacement players.) Here are the best such streaks since 1950:

Team	Years with +2.00 OPI	Total
San Francisco 49ers	1983–1996 (excluding 1987)	13 seasons
San Diego Chargers	1978–1985 (excluding 1982)	7 seasons
Los Angeles Rams	1950–1954	5 seasons
Buffalo Bills	1989–1992	4 seasons
Cincinnati Bengals	1985–1989 (excluding 1987)	4 seasons
Dallas Cowboys	1977–1980	4 seasons
Dallas Cowboys	1992–1995	4 seasons
Denver Broncos	1995–1998	4 seasons
Houston Oilers	1990–1993	4 seasons
Oakland Raiders	1974–1977	4 seasons

Those 13 seasons represent about one-fifth of all the +2.00 or better OPI's in that period (63 in total), which is amazing in a 28–30 team league. (San Francisco also finished in the top five in the league in OPI in each of those seasons.) What makes the 49ers' streak even more remarkable is that it was not accomplished with the same nucleus of players, the time span was simply too long for that. Most, if not all, of the other teams on the list had a relatively stable core of offensive players for their period of offensive achievement. San Francisco kept its offensive productivity high despite changing its cast of characters.

Looking at this list, while the Air Coryell Chargers and the Van Brocklin–Waterfield Rams had offenses that excelled for a long time, any discussion of the greatest offenses of all time starts and ends with the 49ers.

Brent Jones

Brent Jones had a terrific 11-season career in the NFL with the 49ers (1987–97), which included playing on three Super Bowl champions and in four Pro Bowls. Jones was originally drafted by the Steelers in the fifth round in 1986, but fate intervened and not in a good way initially (more on that story later).

After retiring, Jones joined CBS Sports in 1998, first as a studio analyst and now as a game analyst. He graciously talked with me in the summer of 2001 about his days with the 49ers. He first talked about what happened at the beginning of his NFL career.

Jones: I was in a car accident about a week after the draft, a drunk driver coming down the wrong side of the street hit me and my wife, and I suffered a herniated disk in my neck. The initial prognosis was six months. The Steelers were patient at first, but then something happened and they decided they weren't going to be patient. The irony was that they really had no tight end and they originally told me that I was going to be their tight end of the future.

What was a frustrating situation at the time turned out to be the greatest break I could have ever gotten.

Q: Once you got to the 49ers, you never played on a team that won fewer than ten games. What was it like to play on such a great team?

Jones: The beauty of it was that every year that I went to training camp, we thought we could win the Super Bowl. That is so distinct and unlike any other organization. In fact, there wasn't a year that I wasn't disappointed if we didn't go to the Super Bowl. That made you work that much harder in the offseason.

Q: What exactly is the "West Coast offense?"

Jones: I'm going to go back to Bill Walsh; it's a controlled passing game. People make the mistake of thinking that in the West Coast offense teams don't throw the ball down the field. If you look at our offenses those years, we threw the ball very aggressively.

If you talk to Bill and to the 49ers' assistant offensive coaches during that period—people like Dennis Green, Mike Holmgren, and Mike Shanahan—they'll tell you that what really makes the West Coast offense "pop" is diversity. That means using every potential receiver as a target, including the running backs and the tight end. A team can design a defense to cover the wide receivers, but they can't take everybody out of the passing game. On the other hand, that means a team running this offense needs to have players at all those positions who are good receivers.

Q: Were there any major differences between Joe Montana and Steve Young?

Jones: They were both great leaders in the huddle, but Steve was more emotional and Joe was more cool and calm. Steve would sometimes get on guys during the course of a game; if Joe got on you, it was significant. He wouldn't grab you by the jersey or single you out unless it was something that absolutely needed to be said.

Joe was the master of what I call that Magic Johnson pass, the no-look pass. You had to always be ready because he could be looking at the other side of the field and all of a sudden the ball was coming your way. Guys would look silly sometimes because Joe would throw the ball and it would hit them in the head because they just weren't looking. Nobody had the vision that Joe had.

Q: Do you have any specific, unique thoughts about the 1989 and 1994 49ers' teams?

Jones: I remember the '89 team as just being flawless on both sides of the ball and I remember an unbelievable confidence on offense in both years where we had the feeling that we could score at any time. A big difference between the teams is that in '89 the club was almost completely homegrown whereas in '94 we had acquired some high-profile, high-priced free agents like Deion Sanders.

Another big difference between the two teams is that in '89 John Taylor was at the top of his game and he may have been the most underrated number two receiver in history. Of course, we ran a "righthanded" offense with Joe Montana in 1989 and more of a "lefthanded" offense with Steve Young in 1994.

Jones remembered something unusual that happened with offensive coordinator Mike Holmgren the week before the Super Bowl against the Broncos.

Jones: Kind of an interesting story that week. Mike Holmgren and the players would analyze defenses all week and he kept telling us how great the Denver defense was. Sometimes you just can't BS the players, and amongst the players we saw things on their defense that we absolutely knew we could exploit. After a meeting the Friday before the game, Holmgren asked me what I thought about the Bronco defense and I told him I thought we'd score 50 [points]. He looked at me and he kind of laughed and said, "Yeah, I've been having to put up a good front all week about how good they are, but I think we're going to kill these guys." Coaches almost never say things like that; I think he was just tired of having to put up a charade.

Of course, they were both right as San Francisco defeated Denver 55–10 in the most one-sided Super Bowl ever as the 49ers capped one of the most dominating postseason runs of all time.

The Coach: Bill Walsh

Coaching Record

	W	L	T	Pct	
1979	2	14	0	.125	
1980	6	10	0	.375	
1981	13	3	0	.813	NFC Western Division title; NFC champs; Super Bowl champs
1982	3	6	0	.333	
1983	10	6	0	.625	NFC Western Division title
1984	15	1	0	.938	NFC Western Division title; NFC champs; Super Bowl champs
1985	10	6	0	.625	NFC Wild Card
1986	10	5	1	.656	NFC Western Division title
1987	13	2	0	.867	NFC Western Division title
1988	10	6	0	.625	NFC Western Division title; NFC champs; Super Bowl champs
Total	**92**	**59**	**1**	**.609**	

Yes, I know Walsh didn't coach the 49ers in 1989. George Seifert is "profiled" in the 1994 49ers' chapter, and it seemed silly to write about a San Francisco team from the 1980s without writing about Bill Walsh.

The 49ers' two-year improvement from 1979 to 1981 is one of only eight times since 1950 that a team's winning percentage improved by .600 or more in two seasons. Since the adoption of the 16-game schedule in 1978, the 1981 49ers are the only team to win at least 13 games the season after finishing 6–10. Here's some less useful information: on average, a team that was 6–10 one season had a 7–9 record the next, which is consistent with the notion of teams drifting toward the center. Fifty-seven percent of 6–10 teams had a better record the next season whereas 30 percent had a worse record. That's enough about 6–10 seasons—the 49ers wouldn't finish with fewer than 10 wins, except for the nine-game 1982 season, for 18 seasons (1981–98).

Walsh coached under Marv Levy at the University of California in the early 1960s. He then coached three years at Stanford, the last of which (1965) he was on the same staff as Dick Vermeil. Al Davis gave Walsh his first pro coaching job in 1966. After two seasons in Oakland, Walsh coached under Paul Brown in Cincinnati. He was with the Bengals for eight seasons and left when he wasn't named as head coach to replace Brown. Walsh spent a year with the Chargers as offensive coordinator, where his quarterback was Dan Fouts, before returning to the college ranks as Stanford's head coach. It was after two seasons there that he was named 49ers' head coach and general manager.

What looked to the outside world as a hopeless situation in San Francisco—the 49ers were 2–14 the year before Walsh got there and had the same record his first season—was actually an opportunity to start from the ground up. Much of the foundation of what is now called the West Coast offense was actually developed by Walsh and Brown in Cincinnati, primarily to maximize the productivity of Bengals quarterback Virgil Carter, who was mobile and athletic but didn't have a great arm.

Walsh, of course, is acclaimed as an offensive genius or just plain genius. Michael Silver of *Sports Illustrated* thinks Walsh "has been the most important figure in pro football in the last twenty years, and possibly ever." San Diego GM John Butler said, "There's no question on the offensive side, Bill Walsh was it. So many people have taken his teachings and moved on with them." Steve Young on Walsh, "When I came to the team in 1987, Bill was probably twenty years ahead of his time. He changed the game. Watch all the people using his stuff now."

One would think that Walsh's talent and success made him the darling of ownership. According to Glenn Dickey in his book, *49ers: The Rise, Fall, and Rebirth of the NFL's Greatest Dynasty,* once the 49ers won their first Super Bowl, that was 180 degrees from reality. Dickey wrote, "For the rest of his coaching career with the 49ers [after the first Super Bowl title], Walsh had to live with the fact that Eddie [DeBartolo] would go into a rage at every loss, and Walsh would go to bed wondering if he'd have a job when he woke up."

Dickey also wrote that while Walsh and Joe Montana had a great in-game relationship, the extremely competitive nature of both made it impossible for them to share the spotlight. Dickey wrote, "Walsh wanted people to think the system had made Montana—who, in turn, wanted people to think that his play had made Walsh's system."

One area where Walsh may not receive quite enough credit is his ability to evaluate players. Consistent with his personality, Walsh was proactive in acquiring talent. In 13 years "in control" of the 49ers, 10 as coach/GM and three as GM, he made 52 trades involving draft picks. Former Packers GM Ron Wolf said, "It was with personnel that he absolutely made a splash. He created a dynasty through his personnel decisions."

Walsh was criticized for his 1985 draft-day trade with New England that enabled the 49ers to move up 12 spots in the first round. He traded San Francisco's first-, second-, and third-round choices for the Patriots' first and third. He used the first-round pick, number 16 overall, on a small college wide receiver with suspect speed. The player was Jerry Rice. As Walsh explained later, "The knock was he wasn't fast enough. All I ever saw on film was him running away from players." For someone with the reputation of being a football scientist, Walsh paid less attention to things like 40-yard dash time and vertical leap than he did to instinct and intuition.

Walsh drafted Joe Montana, Ronnie Lott, Roger Craig, Guy McIntyre, and Charles Haley. Those five players earned a total of 32 Pro Bowl berths. Rice earned 12 more. Just as impressively, only two of those six players (including Rice) were picked in the first round.

It's safe to say that very few people have had an impact on pro football like Bill Walsh. Some people like to say there's no substitute for hard work. I think Walsh is a great example that there's no substitute for innate ability.

The Quarterback: Joe Montana

Year	Team	Att	Comp	Yds	TD	Int	YPA	Rating	Lg Avg	W	L	Pct
1979	SF	23	13	96	1	0	4.17	81.1	70.4	0	1	.000
1980	SF	273	176	1,795	15	9	6.58	87.8	73.7	3	4	.429
1981	SF	488	311	3,565	19	12	7.31	88.4	72.9	13	3	.813
1982	SF	346	213	2,613	17	11	7.55	88.0	73.4	3	6	.333
1983	SF	515	332	3,910	26	12	7.59	94.6	75.9	10	6	.625
1984	SF	432	279	3,630	28	10	8.40	102.9	76.1	14	1	.933
1985	SF	494	303	3,653	27	13	7.39	91.3	73.5	9	6	.600
1986	SF	307	191	2,236	8	9	7.28	80.7	74.1	6	2	.750
1987	SF	398	266	3,054	31	13	7.67	102.1	75.2	10	1	.909
1988	SF	397	238	2,981	18	10	7.51	87.9	72.9	8	5	.615
1989	SF	386	271	3,521	26	8	9.12	112.4	75.6	11	2	.846
1990	SF	520	321	3,944	26	16	7.58	89.0	77.3	14	1	.933
1992	SF	21	15	126	2	0	6.00	118.4	75.3	0	0	—
1993	KC	298	181	2,144	13	7	7.19	87.4	76.7	8	3	.727
1994	KC	493	299	3,283	16	9	6.66	83.6	78.4	9	5	.643
Total		**5,391**	**3,409**	**40,551**	**273**	**139**	**7.52**	**92.3**	**74.8**	**118**	**46**	**.720**
1983–90		3,449	2,201	26,929	190	91	7.81	95.2	75.1	82	24	.774

YPA = Yards Per Pass Attempt
Rating = Passer Rating
Lg Avg = League Passer Rating in that season
W, L, Pct = Team's Record in his starts

I don't have anything to add to the legend of Joe Montana, so I'll go with the facts. The first thing I want to note is Montana's performance in the 1989 playoffs. As if his regular season weren't good enough, Montana's numbers jumped to an otherworldly level in the postseason. He completed 65 of 83 passes (78.3 percent) for 800 yards, 11 touchdowns, and no interceptions. That works out to a neat little rating of 146.4 against playoff-caliber teams. Completion percentage is overrated, but 78.3 percent is still remarkable, as is an 11–0 touchdown-to-interception ratio.

As I've stated before, Montana was selected by San Francisco as the last pick in the third round, the eighty-second overall selection, of the 1979 draft. In retrospect, that's kind of hard to believe, isn't it? Why did he last so long? It is not my intention to do a mini-biography of Montana here, but the reasons heard most often for his lasting that long in the draft were his indifferent attitude toward practice (implying a poor work ethic), inconsistent college performance, and some doubts about his arm strength.

What is interesting, I think, is to look at the 1979 draft and who went ahead of Montana as well as a history of quarterbacks drafted in the 1970s.

Transcendental Graphics

Joe Montana

Taken by Atlanta three picks ahead of Montana was running back William Andrews from Auburn. Andrews was a college backfield mate of Joe Cribbs (who played eight seasons in the NFL, one in the USFL, and earned three Pro Bowl berths). Andrews instantly became one of the very best players in the NFL, rushing for 288 yards in his first two games, and developing into an outstanding runner and receiver before a terrible knee injury short-circuited his career. In the last year before he got hurt (1983), Andrews ran for 1,567 yards, averaged 4.73 yards per carry, and caught 59 passes for 609 yards.

Who were the two players selected between Andrews and Montana? Would you believe Rick Berns (running back, Tampa Bay) and Mike Wellman (center, Los Angeles Rams)? Talk about the sublime and the ridiculous. Obviously, hindsight is 20-20, but still . . . Berns played four seasons in the NFL, gaining a total of 255 yards rushing; Wellman played in 1979 and 1980 with Green Bay, appearing in just 20 games. Of course, even the 49ers passed on Montana once before drafting him (they traded their 1979 first-round pick to Buffalo as part of the foolhardy package for O. J. Simpson in 1978). San Francisco picked running back–wide receiver James Owens from UCLA in round two. He played six years in the NFL, but only two for the 49ers. In fact, the pick used to select Montana wasn't even San Francisco's; it originally belonged to Dallas, which traded the pick to Seattle, which in turn, traded the pick to San Francisco as part of the package that allowed the Seahawks to move up in the third round in 1979 and take linebacker Michael Jackson. Jackson played eight years, all for Seattle.

Three quarterbacks were picked ahead of Montana in 1979: Jack Thompson (The Throwin' Samoan), selected by Cincinnati as the third overall pick; Phil Simms, picked by the Giants at number 7; and Steve Fuller, by Kansas City at number 23 overall. Only Simms lived up to his draft status.

By my count, there were 187 quarterbacks drafted by NFL teams in the 1970s; 43 of those were selected eighty-second overall (Montana's slot) or earlier. Here is a table showing some of the quarterbacks drafted eighty-second overall or earlier in the 1970s and what they did in the NFL:

Player (School)	Team	Year	Round	Pick	NFL Yrs	NFL Games
Leo Hart (Duke)	ATL	1971	3	59	2	3
Karl Douglas (Texas A&I)	BAL	1971	3	78	0	0
Gary Sheide (BYU)	CIN	1975	3	64	0	0
Mark Miller (Bowling Green)	CLE	1978	3	68	2	10

Player (School)	Team	Year	Round	Pick	NFL Yrs	NFL Games
David Jaynes (Kansas)	KC	1974	3	66	1	2
Bill Cappleman (Fla. St.)	MIN	1970	2	51	2	8
Mike Wells (Illinois)	MIN	1973	4	80	1	7
Carl Summerell (E. Carolina)	NYG	1974	4	80	2	10
Jeb Blount (Tulsa)	OAK	1976	2	50	1	5
Gary Keithley (UTEP)	STL	1973	2	45	1	14

OK, that was for shock value. Overall, 12 of the quarterbacks taken number 82 or higher made at least one Pro Bowl team in their career and seven made more than one. Yet those numbers are similar to the 10 "busts" shown in the chart above.

Montana and Dan Fouts were the most successful of the quarterbacks drafted in the 1970s although some people would rate Terry Bradshaw with those two. Guess what? Fouts was also picked in the third round (number 64 overall).

What about first-round quarterbacks? (Yes, we're straying far from the topic of Joe Montana.) Sixteen quarterbacks went in the first round, three (Bradshaw, Jim Plunkett, Steve Bartkowski) were chosen first overall, while five more went in the top five picks. Among all first-rounders, Jerry Tagge (Green Bay, 1972, number 11 overall) and Steve Pisarkiewicz (St. Louis Cardinals, 1977, number 19) were the two most obvious disappointments. Bradshaw played in more regular-season games (168) and earned more Pro Bowl berths (three) than any other first-round quarterback from the '70s.

I guess the point of all this is to show, in some small way, that drafting football players is an inexact science, despite the numerous workouts and computerized scouting reports. Many people feel that Joe Montana is the best quarterback in history, yet he was only the eighty-second player selected in the draft and was taken after such stalwarts as Reginald Lewis, Jeff Moore, James Ramey, and Mel Land (not to mention Rick Berns and Mike Wellman).

1989 San Francisco 49ers Statistics

Passing

	Att	Comp	Comp Pct	Yds	Yds Per	TD	Int	Rating
Montana	386	271	70.2%	3,521	9.12	26	8	112.4
Young	92	64	69.6%	1,001	10.88	8	3	120.8
Bono	5	4	80.0%	62	12.40	1	0	157.9
49ers	**483**	**339**	**70.2%**	**4,584**	**9.49**	**35**	**11**	**114.8**
Opponents	564	316	56.0%	3,568	6.33	15	21	68.5
League Average			55.8%		7.15			75.6

49ers' passers were sacked 45 times for 282 yards in losses.
The 49ers sacked their opponents 43 times for 333 yards in losses.

Not bad, huh? The 49ers team passing rating of 114.8 is the NFL record; they are one of only eight teams since 1950 to average 9 or more yards per pass attempt. They are the most recent of eight teams to average at least 3 more yards per pass attempt than their opponents. How about this for minutia: they are the only team in history with a TD/INT ratio of at least 3/1 and an average gain of over nine. Actually, that's a great way to show how well they could throw the ball.

As good as Joe Montana was during the regular season, he was even better in the playoffs. (See "The Quarterback: Joe Montana.")

Another tidbit: the 49ers were 11–2 with Montana as the starting QB, 3–0 with Steve Young.

Rushing

	Att	Yds	Avg	Net Yards	TD
Craig	271	1,054	3.89	−17	6
Rathman	79	305	3.86	−7	1
Montana	49	227	4.63		3
Flagler	33	129	3.91		1
Young	38	126	3.32		2
Sydney	9	56	6.22		0
Rice	5	33	6.60		0
Henderson	7	30	4.29		1
Taylor	1	6	6.00		0
Helton	1	0	0.00		0
49ers	**493**	**1,966**	**3.99**	**+18**	**14**
Opponents	372	1,383	3.72	−87	9
League Average			3.95		

San Francisco's running game was good enough in 1989. They were tenth in the NFL in rushing yards and thirteenth in average per rush.

Receiving

	Rec	Yds	Avg	TD
Rice	82	1,483	18.09	17
Rathman	73	616	8.44	1
Taylor	60	1,077	17.95	10
Craig	49	473	9.65	1
Jones	40	500	12.50	4
Wilson	9	103	11.44	1
Sydney	9	71	7.89	0
Flagler	6	51	8.50	0
Walls	4	16	4.00	1
Henderson	3	130	43.33	0
Williams	3	38	12.67	0
Greer	1	26	26.00	0
49ers	**339**	**4,584**	**13.52**	**35**
Opponents	316	3,568	11.29	15
League Average			12.81	

Jerry Rice led the NFL in receiving yards and TD catches while finishing fifth in receptions. John Taylor tied for fourth in the league in TD receptions.

As Brent Jones explained it to me (see "Brent Jones") this distribution of pass receptions helps show, at least in part, that the West Coast offense is an offense that uses all of its potential targets in the passing game. The two starting running backs caught 122 passes, about 60 each; the starting tight end and wide receivers combined for 182 catches, about 60 each.

Kickoff Returns

	Ret	Yds	Avg	TD
Flagler	32	643	20.09	0
Tillman	10	206	20.60	0
Sydney	3	16	5.33	0
Taylor	2	51	25.50	0
Henderson	2	21	10.50	0
Greer	1	17	17.00	0
Jackson	1	0	0.00	0
49ers	**51**	**954**	**18.71**	**0**
Opponents	76	1,435	18.88	0
League Average			19.40	

Punt Returns

	Ret	Yds	Avg	TD
Taylor	36	417	11.58	0
Griffin	1	9	9.00	0
Greer	1	3	3.00	0
Romanowski	1	0	0.00	0
49ers	**39**	**429**	**11.00**	**0**
Opponents	35	361	10.31	0
League Average			9.11	

Interceptions

	Int	Yds	Avg	TD
Lott	5	34	6.80	0
Brooks	3	31	10.33	0
Wright	2	37	18.50	0
Jackson	2	35	17.50	0
Griffin	2	6	3.00	0
Turner	1	42	42.00	0
Holmoe	1	23	23.00	0
McKyer	1	18	18.00	0
Romanowski	1	13	13.00	0
Pollard	1	12	12.00	0
Millen	1	10	10.00	0
DeLong	1	1	1.00	0
49ers	**21**	**262**	**12.48**	**0**
Opponents	11	140	12.73	0

The 49ers were tied for ninth in the league in interceptions.

Sack Leaders

(Sacks have been an official statistic for individual players only since 1982.)

Haley	10.5
Holt	10.5
Fagan	7.0

Haley and Holt tied for elevnth in the NFC in sacks.

Turnovers

Turnovers Committed:	25
Turnovers Forced:	37
Turnover +/−:	+12

San Francisco committed the second fewest turnovers in the league and ranked second in the league in turnover margin.

Punting

	No	Avg
Helton	55	40.5
Opponents	74	38.9
League Average		40.2

Kicking

	XP	XPA	XP Pct	FG	FGA	FG Pct
Cofer	49	51	96.1%	29	36	80.6%
Opponents	26	26	100.0%	23	31	74.2%
League Average			97.0%			72.5%

Leading Scorer: Mike Cofer, 136 Points
Leading Scorer, Non-Kicker: Jerry Rice, 102 Points

1989 San Francisco 49ers Roster

Head Coach	George Seifert		
QB	Steve Bono	DE	Kevin Fagan
QB	Joe Montana	DE/DT	Pierce Holt
QB	Steve Young	DE/DT	Pete Kugler
RB	Roger Craig	DE	Larry Roberts
RB	Terrence Flagler	DE	Danny Stubbs
RB	Keith Henderson	DT	Jim Burt
RB	Tom Rathman	DT	Michael Carter
RB	Harry Sydney	DT/DE	Kevin Lilly
RB	Spencer Tillman	DT	Rollin Putzier
WR	Mike Barber	LB	Keith DeLong
WR	Terry Greer	LB	Jim Fahnhorst
WR	Jerry Rice	LB	Antonio Goss
WR	John Taylor	LB/DE	Charles Haley
WR	Mike Wilson	LB	Steve Hendrickson
TE	Brent Jones	LB	Matt Millen
TE	Wesley Walls	LB	Bill Romanowski
TE	Jamie Williams	LB	Keena Turner
C	Jesse Sapolu	LB	Michael Walter
C/OG	Chuck Thomas	DB	Chet Brooks
OG	Jeff Bregel	DB	Jeff Fuller
OG/OT	Bruce Collie	DB	Don Griffin
OG	Guy McIntyre	DB	Tom Holmoe
OG	Terry Tausch	DB	Johnny Jackson
OT/OG	Harris Barton	DB	Ronnie Lott
OT	Dave Cullity	DB	Tim McKyer
OT	William "Bubba" Paris	DB	Darryl Pollard
OT	Steve Wallace	DB	Mike Richardson
K	Mike Cofer	DB	Eric Wright
P	Barry Helton		

Hall of Famers: Montana, Lott... so far. I think Jerry Rice will get in. Maybe Steve Young, too.

CHAPTER 10

1991 Washington Redskins: With Any Given Quarterback

I'm sure that most of you are aware of the saying, "On any given Sunday," which means, supposedly, that in the NFL any team can beat any other team. For Joe Gibbs, that saying could have been changed to "With any given quarterback," meaning that his team was capable of winning the Super Bowl almost regardless of who was playing quarterback.

STARTING LINEUP – 1991 REDSKINS

Offense		Defense	
SE	Gary Clark	LE	Charles Mann
LT	Jim Lachey	LT	Eric Williams
LG	Raleigh McKenzie	RT	Tim Johnson
C	Jeff Bostic	RE	Fred Stokes
RG	Mark Schlereth	LLB	Wilber Marshall
RT	Joe Jacoby	MLB	Matt Millen
TE	Ron Middleton	RLB	Andre Collins
FL	Art Monk	LCB	Martin Mayhew
QB	Mark Rypien	RCB	Darrell Green
RB	Earnest Byner	SS	Danny Copeland
H-B	Don Warren	FS	Brad Edwards

It's not mere trivia that his three Super Bowl champions had three different quarterbacks; it is a reflection of his greatness as a coach. Think about the teams that have repeated or had many championships in a relatively short period of time. Terry Bradshaw quarterbacked all four of the Steelers' Super Bowl championships. Joe Montana was the QB for the first four of the 49ers' titles. Troy Aikman was the QB for the three Super Bowls Dallas won in the '90s. Obviously, it is easier to win the Super Bowl with continuity at the game's most important position than without it, and it is easier to win with a consistently great quarterback than without one, all of which makes what Gibbs and his teams accomplished more remarkable.

Nobody should mistake me for a Redskins' fan, but I am very impressed by Joe Gibbs's accomplishments. The 1991 Redskins were the best of his many fine teams.

Amidst ever-increasing retirement rumors, Joe Gibbs started 1991 training camp hoping to find out what kind of team he really had and what kind of quarterback Mark Rypien really was. In 1990, Gibbs once complained that he was never sure which team would show up to play; as he put it, it was either "Elmer and the boys or a pretty good football team." From the beginning of the season, however, it was apparent that the 1991 Redskins were not Elmer and the boys.

Allsport

Joe Jacoby

Team in a Box

Record: 14–2

The Redskins won their first 11 games before losing 24–21 to arch-rival Dallas on November 24. Washington's two losses were by a total of five points.

The 1991 season was the eighth time in nine seasons that the Redskins won 10 or more games.

Against Teams Over .500: 6–2, 236 Points Scored, 116 Points Allowed

Of all the teams in the book, only the 1985 Bears did better against teams with winning records. The 1989 49ers were also 6–2, but their point differential was not as good: theirs was +51 in eight games, while the '91 Redskins were +120.

Points Scored/Allowed: 485/224 (1991 NFL Average: 304)

Washington's point differential was the second best of any NFL team since the adoption of the 16-game schedule in 1978. On a per-game basis, they had the sixth-best differential among all NFL teams since 1950.

Yards Gained/Allowed: 5,741/4,293 (1991 NFL Average: 4,909)

Opponents' Record: 127–113, .529

(Not counting games against the Redskins.)

Adjusted Power Index:

Offense: +3.96
Defense: +2.93
TOTAL: +6.89

Washington's Offense Power Index (OPI) ranks in the top three percent since 1950; their Defense Power Index (DPI) ranks in the top six percent.

Innovations/What You Should Know:

Joe Gibbs took the two-tight end, one-back offense he had run as offensive coordinator under Don Coryell in San Diego, and made it a running offense in Washington. He designed it, in large part, to deal with the Giants' amazing linebacker Lawrence Taylor. The Redskins would put the second tight end in Taylor's face, and in conjunction with the offensive tackle, Taylor would have two blockers to deal with on most plays.

Although teams today don't use the one-back offense as their primary offensive set, most teams do feature just one running back. The fullback has become a position where the emphasis is on blocking and catching the ball, like the second tight end (or H-back) in Gibbs's one-back offense.

Homegrown First-Round Picks:

WR Art Monk, 1980; DB Darrell Green, 1983; DT Bobby Wilson, 1991.

Washington had no first-round picks between 1984 and 1990. The players that the Redskins picked first in those years (whether that was in the second or third round) did not contribute much to this team, with the exception of kicker Chip Lohmiller.

Quarterback Mark Rypien was a sixth-round pick in 1986, and Pro Bowl offensive tackle Jim Lachey was acquired in a trade with the Raiders in 1988. The Redskins traded for two of their three primary running backs in the 1991 season, acquiring Earnest Byner (Cleveland) and Gerald Riggs (Atlanta) in 1989.

Pro Bowl Players:

RB Earnest Byner, WR Gary Clark, DB Darrell Green, OT Jim Lachey, K Chip Lohmiller, DE Charles Mann, QB Mark Rypien, OG Mark Schlereth.

Gary Clark was picked in the second round of the supplemental draft (the draft of USFL players) in 1984. In the college draft, Charles Mann was a third-round pick in 1983, and Mark Schlereth was a tenth-round pick in 1989.

Game-by-Game:

Sep. 1st REDSKINS 45, DETROIT 0 AT WASHINGTON

The 1991 season opener marked the fifteenth time that the Lions had played in Washington since the Boston Redskins moved to the nation's capital in 1937. It also marked the fifteenth time that the Redskins beat the Lions in Washington.

This was the most lopsided regular season win in Redskins' history. Head coach Joe Gibbs said, "This is about as good as we've ever played. Everything worked." Barry Sanders missed the game with a rib injury, not that it would have mattered. If any player can turn a 45–0 loss into a win, that's the story of the century.

Washington's defense held the Lions on the first possession of the game; the Redskins went 62 yards in 12 plays on their first possession to go up 7–0. Darrell Green intercepted Rodney Peete on Detroit's first play after the touchdown, and the Redskins went 20 yards to score and make it 14–0. On their next possession, the Lions had to punt and Brian Mitchell ran it back 69 yards for a TD. Game, set, match...

The Lions gained just 154 yards of offense and made only 9 first downs. Meanwhile, Mark Rypien completed 15 of 19 passes for 183 yards and 2 touchdowns.

Sep. 9th REDSKINS 33, DALLAS 31 AT DALLAS

The annual Redskins–Cowboys Monday night game was a wild one. Dallas took a 21–10 lead with about six minutes to go in the first half as Emmitt Smith caught his only touchdown pass of the season. Smith had scored the Cowboys' second TD on a 75-yard run, but he missed much of the second half with a stomach virus and dehydration. His absence and some Redskins' defensive adjustments slowed down Dallas' in the second half. Washington linebacker Matt Millen said, "We were a little too conscious of their cutbacks at first, but once we settled in we were okay."

Washington nudged ahead 23–21 in the third quarter, but Dallas led 24–23 at the end of three quarters. In essence, the Redskins won the game on the strength of an eight-minute, 14-play, 85-yard touchdown drive that ended with Gerald Riggs's 1-yard TD run with 12:48 left. The big play on the drive was a run from punt formation. The Redskins had a fourth-and-1 from their own 48. Seeing something in the Cowboys' alignment that they liked, center Raleigh McKenzie snapped the ball to upback Brian Mitchell, who ran 3 yards for the first down.

Chip Lohmiller tied the NFL record with 2 field goals of at least 50 yards in the same game, and kicked 4 field goals, all of at least 45 yards, in the game.

Sep. 15th REDSKINS 34, PHOENIX 0 AT WASHINGTON

Washington pummeled the Cardinals, who had won their first two games. The Redskins outgained Phoenix 350 yards to 165, sacked Tom Tupa four times, and intercepted three passes. Two were picked off by Wilber Marshall, and he ran one back 55 yards for a touchdown in the third quarter.

Sep. 22nd REDSKINS 34, CINCINNATI 27 AT CINCINNATI

The winless Bengals gave the undefeated Redskins all they could handle, coming back from a 27–10 third-quarter deficit to tie the score at 27 with about 10 minutes left in regulation. Cincinnati's defense was so aggressive in attacking the line of scrimmage that Washington QB Mark Rypien said, "They pressed us all day. Sometimes it looked like they had more guys coming than they actually had. When you see eight guys at the line of scrimmage, it looks like nine or ten are coming at you."

Like in the first Dallas game, the Redskins were able to put together a game-winning drive in the fourth quarter. The Redskins' defense forced Cincinnati to go three and out after the Bengals' Richard Fain had intercepted a Mark Rypien pass at Cincinnati's 2-yard line. After the punt, Washington had the ball on their own 47 with 5:17 left. In an effort to spread out Cincinnati's defense, Washington went to a four-wide receiver formation on this possession, but the game-winning drive was exclusively on the ground. Three carries each by Earnest Byner and Gerald Riggs were all the Redskins needed to score the winning touchdown in three minutes. On the ensuing possession, Boomer Esiason's fourth-down pass was broken up by linebacker Andre Collins, with 1:09 left to seal the game.

Sep. 30th REDSKINS 23, PHILADELPHIA 0 AT WASHINGTON

Three home games, three shutouts . . . the Redskins held the Eagles to staggering totals of 81 yards of offense and 4 first downs. The Eagles were already without quarterback Randall Cunningham, who was injured in the first game of the year and would miss the entire season. To make matters worse, they lost Jim McMahon at the end of the first quarter. Backup quarterback Pat Ryan was simply overmatched by Washington's defense; he completed 4 of 14 passes for 24 yards and 3 interceptions.

Despite the Eagles' injuries, the shutout was still impressive because Washington committed 4 turnovers, all by Mark Rypien, who threw 2 interceptions and lost 2 fumbles. However, Rypien was still productive in the air (15 of 23, 204 yards, 1 touchdown), the Redskins ran for 173 yards, 95 by Earnest Byner, and held the ball for nearly 39 minutes. The last time Washington posted three shutouts in a single season was 1945.

Oct. 6th REDSKINS 20, CHICAGO 7 AT CHICAGO

On a cold, windy day, the Redskins' defense made enough big plays to hold the Bears to seven points and help Washington to a 6–0 record. Joe Gibbs praised his defenders after the game, "Our defense is leading us. They're a tight-knit group and have a real good feeling about what they're doing. This is the best defense we've played here in a long time and I just hope we keep it going."

The Bears outgained the Redskins 319 yards to 243, but Washington intercepted three Jim Harbaugh passes and it took 42 Bears' pass attempts to net 199 yards passing. Mark Rypien was affected by the wind and the Bears held the Redskins to under 100 yards on the ground, but a 26-yard TD pass from Rypien to Art Monk late in the first half gave Washington a 10–0 lead.

As is the case with most successful head coaches, Joe Gibbs was always trying to find ways to motivate his team and keep them from being complacent. He said after the game, "We can't start thinking we're better than we are. We can beat any team in this league and we can be beaten by any team. We understand we're not a dominant team." Not a dominant team? In their first six games, Washington outscored its opponents 189–65. Oh, that Gibbs.

Oct. 13th REDSKINS 42, CLEVELAND 17 AT WASHINGTON

Ricky Ervins replaced an injured Earnest Byner in the third quarter, and ran for 133 yards and 2 touchdowns on 13 carries to help the Redskins turn a 21–17 game into a 42–17 blowout. Washington's Art Monk caught seven passes and moved past Charlie Joiner for second place in career receptions. The only other year that Washington had started 7–0 was 1940.

Oct. 27th REDSKINS 17, NEW YORK GIANTS 13 AT NEW YORK

It was a tale of two games. Perhaps a bit rusty after their bye, the Redskins were outgained 207 yards to 35 in the first half, and trailed 13–0. In the second half, however, Washington outgained New York 219 yards to 64 and scored 17 unanswered points to go to 8–0 for the first time in franchise history.

Although he didn't have a good day passing, Mark Rypien threw 2 touchdowns to Gary Clark, including a 54-yarder on third-and-12 with 12:50 left in the game that gave Washington the lead for good.

Clark said that the Redskins were "very upbeat when we got inside" at halftime because they were losing only 13–0 despite being totally dominated. The Giants were in the red zone three times in the first half, but got just one touchdown. On one drive Giants QB Jeff Hostetler overthrew Rodney Hampton at the goal line, and on another drive the Giants were hurt by an unnecessary roughness penalty on fullback Maurice Carthon.

The loss dropped the defending Super Bowl champion Giants to 4–4, and with resurgent Dallas at 5–3, the Redskins were in control of the NFC East. Talking about the Giants and the division race, Rypien said, "We knew it was a chance to pretty much eliminate them [New York] from the division title race. You'd have to say we're in the driver's seat right now."

Nov. 3rd REDSKINS 16, HOUSTON 13 AT WASHINGTON

The Redskins seemed certain to get their first loss of the season. The Oilers tied the game with 1:42 left on Lorenzo White's 1-yard run that capped a 10-play, 79-yard drive. On the kickoff, Washington's Brian Mitchell fumbled and Houston's Mike Dumas recovered at the Redskins 23-yard line. The Oilers ran three plays to get to the 16-yard line with just four seconds remaining. However, Houston's Ian Howfield missed a 33-yard field goal and the game went into overtime.

Washington won the overtime toss, but punted on its first possession. On Houston's second play, the Redskins' Darrell Green wrestled the ball away from the Oilers' Haywood Jeffires for an interception at the Houston 33-yard line. After three plays, Chip Lohmiller kicked the game-winning 41-yard field goal.

The Redskins did a good job containing the Houston run-and-shoot attack—the Oilers gained 242 net yards passing, but it took 42 pass plays—and totally stopped the Oilers on the ground. Lorenzo White gained just 14 yards on 11 carries. Even though the Redskins had success running the ball, led by Earnest Byner's 112 yards on 21 attempts, Washington's passing game was thwarted; Mark Rypien threw for just 195 yards on 34 attempts.

This was Houston head coach Jack Pardee's first game at RFK Stadium since he was fired as Redskins' head coach in 1981. Speaking of first games, and this has nothing to do with anything, but this was the first NFL game I had seen in person in 10 years.

Nov. 10th REDSKINS 56, ATLANTA 17 AT WASHINGTON

Atlanta blitzed all day and left their corners exposed. Washington protected Mark Rypien and he bombed the Falcons for 442 yards and 6 touchdowns as the Redskins won easily. Rypien completed "only" 16 of 31 passes, but like I keep saying, completion percentage is not anywhere near as important as yards per pass attempt. He almost broke Sammy Baugh's 48-year old team record for passing yards in a game (446), but declined to go back in even after he was informed how close he was. He tied Baugh's team record for TD passes in a game.

Gary Clark had "only" 4 catches, but for 203 yards and 3 touchdowns, including touchdowns of 61 and 82 yards. Despite playing without injured Pro Bowl tackle Jim Lachey, the Redskins repelled Atlanta's blitzes and did not allow a sack for the fifth straight game. Washington allowed just 4 sacks in their first 10 games.

Atlanta's "colorful" head coach Jerry Glanville said, "We just got our butts kicked. . . . They don't have any weaknesses. Hold it, maybe their punt protection is not so good." Washington center Jeff Bostic was amazed by the Falcons' strategy, "That's a dream come true, playing us like that. With our receivers, you want a team to blitz. We've been blitzed before, but I've never seen a team stay with it like that. Surprised? I was more than surprised. I was shocked."

Nov. 17th REDSKINS 41, PITTSBURGH 14 AT PITTSBURGH

Steelers head coach Chuck Noll was impressed, "They're the best team we've played by far. We didn't make first downs and we couldn't get them off the field. That was great execution on their part. When we backed off, they went in front of us. When we came up, they went over us."

In a game that was not even as close as the one-sided score, the Redskins became just the eighth NFL team to have an 11–0 record. Pittsburgh's defense played close to the line of scrimmage to stop the Redskins' running game. Mark Rypien burned them with long passes, completing 21 of 28 throws for 325 yards, and 2 touchdowns. Two long passes were key: a 63-yard completion to Art Monk on their third play from scrimmage to set up Washington's first touchdown and a 49-yard TD pass to Gary Clark in the fourth quarter.

The Redskins' defense held the Steelers to 41 yards rushing on 14 carries and sacked quarterback Neil O'Donnell five times.

Nov. 24th DALLAS 24, REDSKINS 21 AT WASHINGTON

The final score was close, but the Cowboys ended Washington's hopes of an unbeaten season by being aggressive and by outplaying the Redskins. Instead of avoiding Washington cornerback Darrell Green like all other opponents had done, Dallas threw at him using Michael Irvin, who caught nine passes for 130 yards. The Cowboys tied the game at 7–7 in the first quarter, converting on fourth-and-5 from the Redskins' 33. Dallas moved the ball in the air, even after Troy Aikman left the game with a knee injury in the third quarter, as backup QB Steve Beuerlein played well. In all, the Cowboys outgained the Redskins 399 yards to 262 and had a 23–14 advantage in first downs.

Jimmy Johnson explained Dallas's strategy, "If you have a big gorilla, you don't hit him lightly. We felt to have any chance, we'd have to play aggressive. We knew we weren't going to beat 'em unless we played that way."

Dec. 1st REDSKINS 27, LA RAMS 6 AT LOS ANGELES

Washington's first-half performance was so sluggish that head coach Joe Gibbs kicked a chair across the locker room at halftime. Whether that was the reason or not, the Redskins played much better in the second half, outscoring the Rams 20–0 to clinch the NFC East title.

On the third play of the third quarter, linebacker Wilber Marshall and defensive back Martin Mayhew stripped the ball from the Rams' Willie Anderson, with Marshall recovering. Mark Rypien then threw a 30-yard TD pass to Ricky Sanders. Rypien threw another touchdown in the quarter, 24 yards to Ricky Ervins, to end the competitive phase of the game.

Rypien had another very good day throwing the ball, hitting 15 of 24 passes for 269 yards and the 2 touchdowns.

Dec. 8th REDSKINS 20, PHOENIX 14 AT PHOENIX

New Orleans' loss to Dallas earlier in the day meant that the Redskins clinched home-field advantage throughout the NFC playoffs. For that or some other reason, Washington didn't play well in the first half and trailed 14–0 at halftime. In the third quarter, though, the Redskins scored on their first two possessions on drives of 80 and 71 yards, and the defense neutralized Phoenix's weak offense. For the quarter, Washington outgained Phoenix 155–0. Two fourth-quarter field goals by Chip Lohmiller provided the winning margin and boosted the Redskins to 13–1.

After not being as productive in recent weeks, Washington's running game was improved, led by Earnest Byner's 116 yards on 25 rushes.

Joe Gibbs was pleased at the turn of events, "We got everything we set out for. We've got all our goals.... We came roaring back the second half again. We've done that before and I'm proud I've got guys like this."

Dec. 15th REDSKINS 34, NEW YORK GIANTS 17 AT WASHINGTON

Mark Rypien threw two more long touchdowns to Gary Clark (65 and 50 yards) as Washington dropped the defending Super Bowl champions to 7–8. Earnest Byner gained 68 yards rushing to surpass 1,000 for the second straight year, and Ricky Ervins gained 85 yards on just 13 carries.

Dec. 22nd PHILADELPHIA 24, REDSKINS 22 AT PHILADELPHIA

Roger Ruzek's 38-yard field goal with 13 seconds left gave the Eagles the win. The Redskins led 13–7 at halftime and 16–7 after three quarters, but Philadelphia scored 17 fourth-quarter points, as quarterback Jeff Kemp led the comeback. The loss kept Washington from becoming the third NFL team to win 15 games in the regular season.

Divisional Playoff:

Jan. 4th REDSKINS 24, ATLANTA 7 AT WASHINGTON

The Falcons thought that the Redskins ran up the score in their regular season game, won by Washington 56–17. Falcons defensive end Tim Green said, "A guy would have to be a liar to say they didn't rub our noses in it."

Joe Gibbs, of course, had a different opinion, "Let's set the record straight. We threw the ball three times. Two of those were going to be possession-type passes. It so happened that they pressed us and we hit a fade for a touchdown. We were trying to run all the time in the fourth quarter. Anybody that saw that game wouldn't say we were throwing to run the score up."

On a windy, rainy day, the Redskins' defense limited the Falcons to 193 yards of offense, just 52 in the second half, and forced 6 turnovers to key the victory. Washington's running game was in high gear, as Ricky Ervins and Earnest Byner combined for 161 yards on 37 attempts. After a scoreless first quarter, the Redskins scored twice in three minutes in the second quarter, the second one on a short drive after an Atlanta fumble. The Falcons scored before halftime to make it 14–7, but simply could not move the ball in the second half.

The hard feelings still lingered after the game, at least for Falcons head coach Jerry Glanville, who ran off the field after the game without the traditional postgame handshake with the opposing coach.

NFC Championship:

Jan. 11th REDSKINS 41, DETROIT 10 AT WASHINGTON

Remember the first game of the regular season? The Redskins made it 16 wins in 16 games against the Lions in Washington and advanced to the Super Bowl.

On Detroit's second play from scrimmage, Redskins' defensive end Charles Mann ran over Lions rookie offensive tackle Scott Conover and sacked quarterback Erik Kramer, forcing a fumble that was recovered by Washington's Fred Stokes. Two plays later, Gerald Riggs went over from the 2-yard line.

The Lions didn't quit, though, and trailed (17–10) at the half. The second half was all Washington. The defense kept the pressure on Kramer and backup Andre Ware, recording 5 sacks, three by Wilber Marshall. The Redskins also limited Barry Sanders to 44 yards on 11 carries; Sanders had missed the season opener.

Mark Rypien threw two second-half touchdowns, including a 45-yarder to Gary Clark, and had another very efficient day throwing the ball: 12 of 17 for 228 yards and no interceptions. The Redskins got their running game going with 78 yards rushing in the second half.

Joe Gibbs talked about the feeling in the stadium, "The emotion of that stadium today is something I won't forget. That's why you fight so hard to get the home-field advantage." Mann thought Washington may have come out a little too ready, "We were so fired up in the first quarter that we were drained by the half." Drained or not, the Redskins had earned their fourth Super Bowl berth in 10 years under Joe Gibbs.

Super Bowl XXVI:

Jan. 26th REDSKINS 37, BUFFALO 24 AT MINNEAPOLIS

Washington took control of the game by scoring 17 points in a 5:45 span in the second quarter to win their third Super Bowl under Joe Gibbs. It was Buffalo's second Super Bowl loss in two seasons (the next two years had similar results).

The game was scoreless until Washington's outburst, although the Redskins put together an 87-yard drive in the first quarter, only to come up with nothing when Art Monk's apparent touchdown was overturned in instant replay. Holder Jeff Rutledge fumbled the snap on the subsequent field-goal attempt.

The Redskins' scoring spree started with a 34-yard Chip Lohmiller field goal. Buffalo could not move on the next possession, and Chris Mohr's punt went just 23 yards. The Redskins took just five plays to go 51 yards and take a 10–0 lead. On the following possession, Jim Kelly threw an interception to Darrell Green. Washington went 55 yards in five plays to lead 17–0; that was the halftime score.

The Redskins made it 24–0 when linebacker Kurt Gouveia intercepted another Kelly pass, the first play of the second half, and returned the pick 23 yards to the Buffalo 2. Gerald Riggs scored the touchdown.

Buffalo managed to cut the lead to 24–10, but as they had so often in 1991, Mark Rypien and Gary Clark hooked up for a touchdown (30 yards) to make it 31–10, basically ending the game.

Rypien was the Super Bowl Most Valuable Player with what was really a typical game for him that season: 18 of 33 for 292 yards and 2 touchdowns. Washington's defense made

Thurman Thomas disappear; the AFC's leading rusher during the regular season (1,407 yards) gained 13 yards on 10 carries. Jim Kelly had to throw on virtually every play in the second half, and wound up with a Super Bowl-record 58 pass attempts. He also ended up with a Super Bowl-record 4 interceptions; Washington piled 5 sacks on him.

Speaking of sacks, the Redskins did not allow one in the playoffs—they did not allow a sack in 13 of their 19 games.

Elsewhere Around the NFL:

Sep. 22nd Don Shula joined George Halas in the 300-win club for NFL head coaches when Miami beat Green Bay 16–13. The Dolphins' only touchdown was defensive tackle Chuck Klingbeil's recovery of a Don Majkowski fumble in the end zone.

Nov. 17th On the first play of the fourth quarter of the Lions–Rams game, Detroit guard Mike Utley suffered a career-ending spinal injury. Utley was blocking Los Angeles defensive tackle David Rocker, when Rocker leaped to block QB Erik Kramer's pass and came down on Utley's head and neck. After lying on the field for several minutes, Utley was secured to a stretcher. While being carried off the field, Utley, remarkably, gave the thumbs-up sign. The Lions, 6–4 entering this game, finished the season 12–4 and won the NFC Central title.

Today, Mike has voluntary movement of muscles in his lower body and participates in a "gaiting" program with the help of leg braces and crutches. He also established the Mike Utley Foundation in December of 1991. The organization is dedicated to helping people with spinal cord injuries.

Dec. 13th Former Redskins' star defensive end Dexter Manley announced his retirement after failing a league-mandated drug test. Manley, playing for Tampa Bay, had received an "indefinite" ban from the NFL in November of 1989 as a third-time drug offender, but was reinstated a year later.

What Happened the Next Season:

After the Super Bowl win over Buffalo, Joe Gibbs brushed aside retirement rumors. However, 1992 would turn out to be his last season as an NFL head coach. Mark Rypien staged a long holdout and finished last in passing rating in the NFC. Jim Lachey and Darrell Green also held out for much of training camp. Still, the Redskins finished 9–7, made the playoffs as a Wild Card, and won their first playoff game at Minnesota before losing at San Francisco. Two months after the season ended, Gibbs retired.

The Little Big Guy

Gary Clark is listed at 5 feet 9 inches, 175 pounds. Even for a wide receiver, that's not big. Small or not, Clark was an extremely productive player for the Redskins, but was seemingly overshadowed by other players.

Clark's NFL career started in 1985, the same year as Jerry Rice's. Clark first played professionally in the USFL with Jacksonville in 1984 and actually played both in the USFL and NFL in 1985. He played alongside Art Monk, who at one time held the NFL record for career receptions and most consecutive games catching a pass. Clark and Monk were definitely opposites in terms of personality. In researching the 1991 Redskins, a theme that consistently recurred was how emotional Clark was, and how different that made him from most of his teammates.

Monk, for example, was quiet and workmanlike. Clark himself noted that difference when talking about his relationship with head coach Joe Gibbs, "I'm sure he'd rather have me be more like Art. On the other hand, he probably knows I wouldn't compete the same way if I wasn't myself. My teammates know that when I'm unhappy I verbalize it. Not everyone on our team does that."

Clark's personality may have been one reason he left as a free agent after the 1992 season, as one of the first group of free agents. New head coach Richie Petitbon didn't care for Clark's disposition, and he no doubt persuaded Redskins GM Charley Casserly not to make a serious offer to Clark. In hindsight, his production diminished after he left Washington and he played just three more years in the league.

While he was with Washington, however, Clark made a lot of big plays. In his prime, from 1986 through 1991, only Jerry Rice had more receiving yards than Clark, and only Rice and Mark Clayton caught more touchdown passes. Rice, Al Toon, and Andre Reed were the only wide receivers with more receptions. Here is a chart showing the numbers for 10 prominent wide receivers from 1986 to 1991:

	Rec	Yds	Avg	TD
Jerry Rice, SF	477	8,145	17.08	90
Gary Clark, WAS	413	6,904	16.72	48
Henry Ellard, LA RAMS	381	6,388	16.77	32
Andre Reed, BUF	421	5,829	13.85	45
Ernest Givins, HOU	371	5,740	15.47	31
Mark Clayton, MIA	358	5,525	15.43	55
Art Monk, WAS	408	5,502	13.49	36
Anthony Carter, MIN	334	5,460	16.35	37
Eric Martin, NO	363	5,341	14.71	36
Al Toon, NYJ	440	4,573	10.39	26

There is only one Jerry Rice, but Clark's performance in this period compares more than favorably to any wide receiver except San Francisco's number 80. Clark was named to four Pro Bowls during this period; again, only Rice had more with six; Andre Reed also had four. It may only have been Clark who thought he was overshadowed. He once said, "They kept not wanting to give me respect, but I'm consistent and stubborn." He was also outstanding in his prime.

The Coach: Joe Gibbs

Coaching Record

	W	L	Pct	
1981	8	8	.500	
1982	8	1	.889	NFC Playoffs; NFC champs; Super Bowl champs
1983	14	2	.875	NFC Eastern Division title; NFC champs
1984	11	5	.938	NFC Eastern Division title
1985	10	6	.625	
1986	12	4	.750	NFC Wild Card
1987	11	4	.867	NFC Eastern Division title; NFC champs; Super Bowl champs
1988	7	9	.438	
1989	10	6	.625	
1990	10	6	.625	NFC Wild Card
1991	14	2	.875	NFC Eastern Division title; NFC champs; Super Bowl champs
1992	9	7	.563	NFC Wild Card
Total	**124**	**60**	**.674**	

In a series of articles I wrote for ESPN.com, I called Gibbs the second-best coach in NFL history behind Vince Lombardi. In particular, I was swayed by three of his teams winning the Super Bowl with three different quarterbacks. Absolutely meaning no disrespect to Gibbs, but after doing much more research, and particularly examining the records of Paul Brown and Bill Walsh, I can't say unequivocally that I would rank Gibbs at number two.

Nevertheless, there's no question that he is one of the few members of the upper echelon of pro football coaches. There's also no question that achieving coaching greatness took its toll on Gibbs. He resigned as Redskins' head coach in March 1993, at the age of 52.

Lon Babby, who represents pro athletes including Grant Hill and Tim Duncan, told me that, one May, he was speaking to Gibbs about some legal matters and asked him what he was doing. Gibbs replied that he was watching game film trying to figure out how to stop Lawrence Taylor–in May. Sometimes he would sleep in his office and not leave Redskin Park all week until Thursday afternoon, when he had to tape his weekly TV show.

In his *New Historical Baseball Abstract,* Bill James wrote about how most of the general public fails to realize how much hard work is involved with being a major league player. The same can be said for coaches, managers, and other executives. While innate ability is a prerequisite for success (you can't win the Kentucky Derby with a nag no matter how good the jockey or trainer is), so is genuine effort. While Gibbs is certainly not the only NFL head coach with a grueling schedule, his success shows that both hard work and ability are important.

Unlike some of his "brothers in arms" as Gibbs called his fellow coaches, no one seemed to ever have anything bad to say about Gibbs the person. Frank Broyles, who had Gibbs on his Arkansas coaching staff for two seasons, said, "He [Gibbs] is so likeable, so pleasant. Joe not only was a brilliant coach, but an outstanding person." Washington defensive tackle Eric Williams remarked, "In a game with a lot of liars and cheaters and crooks, he was different. Joe was a shining star. He was honest. He was tough, but honest. He was brilliant at what he did. You couldn't ask for more of a coach or a human being."

Gibbs played and/or worked for some of the most renowned coaches in the business before becoming a head coach. In addition to the aforementioned Broyles, Gibbs played for Don Coryell at San Diego State; later, Coryell hired him as offensive backfield coach for the Cardinals and as offensive coordinator for the Chargers. The Redskins hired Gibbs away from San Diego.

Gibbs also coached under John McKay at USC for two seasons. In talking about his stints as an assistant coach under such distinguished head coaches, he once remarked, "Every year was a learning experience for me. You watch those guys, you learn and you say 'that's what I want to be.' "

Gibbs had a reputation for being very intuitive, particularly about offensive strategy, but some of it was just common sense. In an internet column, Dick Vermeil related a story about Gibbs's preparation for the 1983 NFC Championship Game against San Francisco. Gibbs told Vermeil his coaches spent hours trying to figure out a game plan. He finally said, "Fellas, let's do a computer study of all our plays from the regular season. The most productive plays will go into the game plan." The Redskins won 24–21.

Soon after Gibbs's retirement, Vermeil acknowledged that, "no one would compare with him in the 1980s except Bill Walsh. They were the best of the NFL coaches in the '80s. His work ethic was beyond reproach. What other compliment can you pay him? He actually doesn't need anybody glorifying his credentials."

He also wasn't too stubborn to copy tactics from other teams. Late in 1991, Gibbs added the no-huddle offense to the Redskins' scheme. He admitted that he copied it from the Bills because they were so effective with it. When the Redskins and Bills met in the Super Bowl, Washington was well schooled in how to stop Buffalo.

Since his retirement from football Gibbs has translated his success to the auto racing world. Joe Gibbs Racing (JGR) was formed in 1991, and the next year his team won NASCAR's most important race, the Daytona 500. JGR cars have finished in the top five in one-third of their races.

In March 2002, Gibbs returned to the NFL as a minority owner of the Atlanta Falcons under new Falcons chairman, president, and CEO Arthur Blank.

As Joe Gibbs demonstrates, nice guys don't have to finish last. Anyone with talent and a real work ethic can finish at the top, nice guy or not.

The Quarterback: Mark Rypien

Year	Team	Att	Comp	Yds	TD	Int	YPA	Rating	Lg Avg	W	L	Pct
1988	WAS	208	114	1,730	18	13	8.32	85.2	72.9	3	3	.500
1989	WAS	476	280	3,768	22	13	7.92	88.1	75.6	9	5	.643
1990	WAS	304	166	2,070	16	11	6.81	78.4	77.3	7	3	.700
1991	WAS	421	249	3,564	28	11	8.47	97.9	76.2	14	2	.875
1992	WAS	479	269	3,282	13	17	6.85	71.7	75.3	9	7	.563
1993	WAS	319	166	1,514	4	10	4.75	56.3	76.7	3	7	.300
1994	CLE	128	59	694	4	3	5.42	63.7	78.4	2	1	.667
1995	STL	217	129	1,448	9	8	6.67	77.9	79.2	0	3	.000
1996	PHI	13	10	76	1	0	5.85	116.2	76.9	0	0	—
1997	STL	39	19	270	0	2	6.92	50.2	77.2	0	0	—
2001	IND	9	5	57	0	0	6.33	74.8	78.5	0	0	—
Total		**2,613**	**1,466**	**18,473**	**115**	**88**	**7.07**	**78.9**	**76.8**	**47**	**31**	**.603**
1988–91		1,409	809	11,132	84	48	7.90	88.5	75.5	33	13	.717

YPA = Yards Per Pass Attempt
Rating = Passer Rating
Lg Avg = League Passer Rating in that season
W, L, Pct = Team's Record in his starts

- Drafted by the Redskins in the sixth round (146th overall) in 1986 from Washington State.
- Spent all of 1986 season (knee injury) and most of 1987 season (back injury) on injured reserve.
- Two-time Pro Bowl selection (1989 and 1991 seasons).

Rypien was not a one-year wonder. He earned two Pro Bowl berths in his first four seasons and was Most Valuable Player of Super Bowl XXVI. After that, his life was never quite the same.

Rypien held out of training camp for about three weeks until mid-August 1992. (Pro Bowl players Darrell Green and Jim Lachey and first-round draft choice Desmond Howard also held out until late August.) Rypien eventually signed a three-year contract worth $9 million, making him the NFL's second-highest-paid player, plus incentives and with a team option for a fourth year. NFL free agency was a year away.

This was not Rypien's first contract hassle with the Redskins. In 1990, Rypien refused to sign a multiyear contract because he felt the amount wasn't close to what he was worth. Consequently, he played out his option that year and, as a result, was the lowest-paid quarterback in the NFL despite having made the Pro Bowl the year before. In 1991, Rypien and the Redskins could not agree on a multiyear contact so he signed a one-year deal after a 10-day holdout.

All of that seemed to work out well for Rypien. He couldn't have played much better in 1991 and, of course, the team won the Super Bowl, which should have given him some leverage in contract negotiations. Nevertheless, that turn of events didn't prevent more problems.

Publicly, Washington head coach Joe Gibbs wasn't concerned about Rypien's 1992 holdout, "It won't take Rip as long to get into the groove because he went to summer school." That's not how it worked out. Rypien suffered through two sub-par seasons with Washington, in part due to a shoulder injury, before becoming an NFL nomad.

As his career sputtered, Rypien faced even more difficulties off the field. Both his youngest son and his wife developed cancer. Andrew Rypien was diagnosed with brain cancer in July 1997 and, despite two operations, died a little more than a year later. In 1998, Annette Rypien was diagnosed with cervical cancer; she eventually recovered after surgery. (Mark and Annette Rypien recently divorced.)

Mark Rypien had signed with Atlanta as a free agent in April 1998, but given what was happening in his family he decided he would spend some time away from football and told the Falcons he would not play that year. They released him in July and "some time away" turned out to be three seasons. Rypien signed with Indianapolis as Peyton Manning's backup in August of 2001. He played sparingly, but he was back in the NFL.

There should be a little football in here ... Rypien was a classic long passer, and the great protection of the Redskins' offensive line helped him turn Washington into the NFL's top deep threat. To see if his numbers matched his reputation, I logged all touchdown passes of 25 or more yards in 1991. Which quarterback had the most? Take a guess...

1991 QB	Long TDs
Mark Rypien	14
Jim Kelly	11
Chris Miller	10
Steve Young	8
Five Tied With	6

Half of Rypien's touchdown passes were 25 yards or longer; the league average was 31 percent. Rypien threw 6 TD passes of 50+ yards; Steve Young, remarkably, had 7. Those two plus Jim Kelly were the only quarterbacks in the league with at least 5 touchdown passes of 50+ yards.

Here are the 1991 NFL leaders in yards per completion:

1991 QB	Yards per Completion
Mark Rypien	14.31
Chris Miller	14.10
Steve Young	13.98
Jay Schroeder	13.56
John Elway	13.44

The 1991 NFL average was 12.01 yards per completion.

1991 Washington Redskins Statistics

Passing

	Att	Comp	Comp Pct	Yds	Yds Per	TD	Int	Rating
Rypien	421	249	59.1%	3,564	8.47	28	11	97.9
Rutledge	22	11	50.0%	189	8.59	1	0	94.7
Byner	4	1	25.0%	18	4.50	1	0	85.4
Redskins	**447**	**261**	**58.4%**	**3,771**	**8.44**	**30**	**11**	**98.0**
Opponents	549	292	53.2%	3,292	6.00	13	27	58.8
League Average			57.4%		6.89			76.2

Redskins' passers were sacked nine times for 79 yards in losses.
The Redskins sacked their opponents 50 times for 345 yards in losses.

Those sack numbers are no misprint. The 1991 Redskins are one of only three teams since 1950 to record at least 40 more sacks in a season than their opponents. (The NFL kept track of sacks accumulated as a team many years before the stat became official for individual pass rushers in 1982.) Looking at a slightly larger group, the nine teams who were +35 in sacks or better had an aggregate record of 91–42–1. When a sack differential is that high, it's not just about being ahead and forcing the other team to throw a lot.

Adding sacks into the equation, the Redskins are one of only seven teams since 1950 to average at least three more yards per pass attempt than their opponents (8.10 to 4.92). They are one of only two teams to do this since the merger in 1970. (The 1984 Dolphins are the other.) The seven teams since 1950 have a combined record of 79–14–1. *Every* one of those seven played in the Super Bowl or a pre-1966 NFL Championship Game.

Maybe only I care about this, but if you'll indulge me, look at the passing ratings. Both players other than Rypien who attempted passes had a lower rating than he did, and yet the team rating was higher than Rypien's. How? The improvement in TD percentage and INT percentage more than offset the slight decline in completion percentage and yards per attempt.

Rushing

	Att	Yds	Avg	Net Yards	TD
Byner	274	1,048	3.82	−28	5
Ervins	145	680	4.69	+110	3
Riggs	78	248	3.18	−58	11
Sanders	7	47	6.71		1
Monk	9	19	2.11		0

	Att	Yds	Avg	Net Yards	TD
Mitchell	3	14	4.67		0
Rypien	15	6	0.40		1
Clark	1	0	0.00		0
Rutledge	8	−13	−1.63		0
Redskins	**540**	**2,049**	**3.79**	**−72**	**21**
Opponents	348	1,346	3.87	−21	11
League Average			3.93		

Armchair Harry speaking: "Average per carry is overrated. Look at Gerald Riggs. He scored 11 touchdowns and that's what counts: putting the ball in the end zone." Listen, nothing takes place in a vacuum. Events occur in context. Obviously, Gerald Riggs's average per carry "suffered" because he carried the ball a lot in short yardage situations. It should be just as obvious that a back can rush for a lot more touchdowns if he's the one usually carrying the ball near the goal line.

The Redskins' favorite running play and the play most closely associated with Joe Gibbs's offense was the counter-trey. Yet no Washington team under Gibbs ever led the NFL, or even the NFC, in rushing yardage or average per carry.

	Redskins League Ranking	
Year	Rushing Yards	Yards per Carry
1986	16	22
1987*	—	—
1988	25	26
1989	14	19
1990	6	14
1991	7	18

*1987 is omitted because it was a strike year when replacement games counted.

People can say that I'm missing the point, but the facts are the facts. Gibbs's first few teams did have more success running the ball, but teams adjust in the NFL.

Receiving

	Rec	Yds	Avg	TD
Monk	71	1,049	14.77	8
Clark	70	1,340	19.14	10
Sanders	45	580	12.89	5

(continued next page)

Receiving *(continued)*

	Rec	Yds	Avg	TD
Byner	34	308	9.06	0
Ervins	16	181	11.31	1
Orr	10	201	20.10	4
Warren	5	51	10.20	0
Middleton	3	25	8.33	0
Hobbs	3	24	8.00	0
Ji. Johnson	3	7	2.33	2
Riggs	1	5	5.00	0
Redskins	**261**	**3,771**	**14.45**	**30**
Opponents	292	3,292	11.27	13
League Average			12.01	

In 1991, his last great season, Gary Clark finished second in the NFL in receiving yardage. He was one of six players to catch at least ten touchdown passes that year. (See "The Little Big Guy.")

This was no West Coast offense. The object of the passing game was to throw the ball downfield to the wide receivers, not to get everyone into the passing game. The Redskins' three top pass catchers, all wide receivers, accounted for 71 percent of their pass completions in 1991. Only run-and-shoot teams like the Houston Oilers of the day placed more emphasis on getting the ball to their wide receivers; in the run-and-shoot, that is the passing game.

Kickoff Returns

	Ret	Yds	Avg	TD
Mitchell	29	583	20.10	0
Ervins	11	232	21.09	0
Jo. Johnson	5	83	16.60	0
Gouveia	3	12	4.00	0
Hobbs	1	16	16.00	0
Redskins	**49**	**926**	**18.90**	**0**
Opponents	66	1,153	17.47	0
League Average			18.89	

Punt Returns

	Ret	Yds	Avg	TD
Mitchell	45	600	13.33	2
Hobbs	1	10	10.00	0
Redskins	**46**	**610**	**13.26**	**2**
Opponents	31	190	6.13	0
League Average			8.74	

Brian Mitchell finished second in the NFL in punt return average behind Detroit's Mel Gray, who returned barely half as many punts (25). If one applied the same concept behind net rushing yards to punt returns, Mitchell had a better mark than Gray (+207 to +166) and led the league. Mitchell is the all-time NFL leader in career punt return yardage, is tied for second with 8 punt return TDs, and has a career average of nearly 11 yards per return.

Interceptions

	INT	YDS	AVG	TD
Marshall	5	75	15.00	1
Green	5	47	9.40	0
Edwards	4	52	13.00	0
Mayhew	3	31	10.33	1
Collins	2	33	16.50	1
S. Johnson	2	5	2.50	0
Gouveia	1	22	22.00	0
T. Johnson	1	14	14.00	0
Coleman	1	0	0.00	0
Copeland	1	0	0.00	0
Mays	1	0	0.00	0
Stokes	1	0	0.00	0
Redskins	**27**	**279**	**10.33**	**3**
Opponents	11	109	9.91	1

Former Bears' linebacker Wilber Marshall tied with Buffalo's Darryl Talley for the league lead in interceptions by a linebacker.

Washington's 27 interceptions was second best in the NFL behind New Orleans' 29.

Sack Leaders

(Sacks have been an official statistic for individual players only since 1982.)

Mann	11.5
Stokes	6.5
Marshall	5.5

Mann was tied for fifth in the NFC in sacks.

Turnovers

Turnovers Committed:	23
Turnovers Forced:	41
Turnover +/−:	+18

The Redskins and Saints tied for the league lead in turnover plus/minus.

Punting

	No	Avg
Goodburn	52	39.8
Opponents	85	37.6
League Average		41.4

Kicking

	XP	XPA	XP Pct	FG	FGA	FG Pct
Lohmiller	56	56	100.0%	31	43	72.1%
Opponents	26	26	100.0%	14	18	7.8%
League Average			97.2%			73.5%

Leading Scorer: Chip Lohmiller, 149 Points
Leading Scorer, Non-Kicker: Gerald Riggs, 66 Points

Lohmiller's 149-point season is the third-highest total in NFL history by a player without any touchdowns. His field-goal percentage was nothing special, but his attempts were longer than the average kicker: an average of 39.1 yards per attempt compared to the league average of 36.3. Only Phoenix's Greg Davis had a longer average field-goal attempt.

1991 Washington Redskins Roster

Head Coach	Joe Gibbs
QB	Stan Humphries
QB	Jeff Rutledge
QB	Mark Rypien
RB	Earnest Byner
RB/KR	Ricky Ervins
RB/KR/PR	Brian Mitchell
RB	Gerald Riggs
WR	Gary Clark
WR	Stephen Hobbs
WR	Joe Johnson
WR	Art Monk
WR	Ricky Sanders
TE	John Brandes
TE	James Jenkins
TE	Jimmie Johnson
TE	Ron Middleton
TE	Terry Orr
TE	Don Warren
C	Jeff Bostic
OG	Mark Adickes
OG	Russ Grimm
OG/C/OT	Raleigh McKenzie
OG	Mark Schlereth
OG	Ralph Tamm
OT/OG	Joe Jacoby
OT	Jim Lachey
OT	Ed Simmons
K	Chip Lohmiller
P	Kelly Goodburn
DE	Jason Buck
DE	Marcus Koch
DE	Charles Mann
DE	Fred Stokes
DT/DE	James "Jumpy" Geathers
DT	Tim Johnson
DT	Eric Williams
DT	Bobby Wilson
LB	Ravin Caldwell
LB	Monte Coleman
LB	Andre Collins
LB	Kurt Gouveia
LB	Wilber Marshall
LB	Matt Millen
DB	Danny Copeland
DB	Travis Curtis
DB	Brad Edwards
DB	Darrell Green
DB	Terry Hoage
DB	A. J. Johnson
DB	Sidney Johnson
DB	Martin Mayhew
DB	Alvoid Mays
DB	Clarence Vaughn
DB	Alvin Walton

Hall of Famers: Gibbs.

For such a successful team, I think surprisingly few players from Gibbs's Redskins will receive Hall of Fame consideration. Darrell Green is a "lock." After that, I'm not sure. Art Monk caught a lot of passes (at one time, he held the NFL career reception record), but he played in only three Pro Bowls and was a consensus All-Pro selection just once, in 1984. Is the Hall of Fame for durable Chevys or for Ferraris?

CHAPTER 11

1994 San Francisco 49ers: The Monkey off His Back

STARTING LINEUP – 1994 49ERS			
Offense		**Defense**	
SE	John Taylor	LE	Dennis Brown
LT	Steve Wallace	LT	Bryant Young
LG	Jesse Sapolu	RT	Dana Stubblefield
C	Bart Oates	RE	Rickey Jackson
RG	Derrick Deese	LLB	Lee Woodall
RT	Harris Barton	MLB	Gary Plummer
TE	Brent Jones	RLB	Ken Norton
FL	Jerry Rice	LCB	Eric Davis
QB	Steve Young	RCB	Deion Sanders
RB	Ricky Watters	SS	Tim McDonald
RB	William Floyd	FS	Merton Hanks

Don't think for a minute that Steve Young wasn't acutely aware of the expectations of following Joe Montana, of the whispers that he wasn't really a winner–not when compared to Montana's four Super Bowl wins. The whispers grew louder when Young took the 49ers to back-to-back conference championships, only to lose to Dallas each time. While on the sidelines during the waning minutes of their Super Bowl win over the Chargers, Young asked his teammates, only half-jokingly, to take the monkey off his back; the players obliged and pulled off the imaginary monkey. During one moment in the locker room after the game, Young emphatically stated that no one could ever take this championship away from him and the team.

Steve Young has a very competitive nature, so it only makes sense that he would feel enormous pressure to lead the 49ers to a Super Bowl title, especially given what they had accomplished with Joe Montana. When Montana's elbow injury in the early 1990s led to the transition to Young as the quarterback, he was aware that the fans still thought that the 49ers were Montana's team. "I could understand that because the fans had formed an emotional attachment when the team had won four Super Bowls with Joe as the quarterback," Young said. "They didn't want to see any change."

During the 1994 season, 49ers' fans came to appreciate Steve Young. After the season, Young didn't have to worry about the monkey on his back anymore.

In addition to dealing with the doubters who didn't think Steve Young could take the 49ers to a Super Bowl title, the 1994 club had to deal with integrating high-profile free agents into the team. After allowing 38 points to Dallas in the 1993 NFC Championship Game, 49ers management decided to beef up the defense via free agency, which was in its second year in the NFL.

San Francisco signed six key free agents, only one of whom (center Brad Oates) was an offensive player. Defensively, they brought in longtime Saints linebacker–defensive end Rickey Jackson, former Bears defensive end and Super Bowl XX MVP Richard Dent (who hurt his knee in the second game of the year and didn't play again that season), and celebrity cornerback Deion Sanders. Although the 49ers eventually had to pay the free agency bill, their aggressive efforts kept the team at or near the top of the heap until 1999.

Allsport

Steve Young

Team in a Box

Record: 13–3

In the context of their run as NFL kings of the hill, a 13–3 record was nothing extraordinary. The 49ers won 13 or more games in eight times between 1981 and 1998.

Against Teams Over .500: 4–2, 161 Points Scored, 109 Points Allowed

Points Scored/Allowed: 505/296 (1994 NFL Average: 324)

Only one other team (Dallas) even scored 400 points in 1994.

The 1994 49ers are one of 10 teams since 1978 to outscore their opponents by at least 200 points. Five of the other nine won the Super Bowl, and the only one to miss the Super Bowl was the 1998 Minnesota Vikings.

Yards Gained/Allowed: 6,060/4,839 (1994 NFL Average: 5,086)

Since 1978, 39 teams have gained 6,000 or more yards in a season. Nine of those are 49ers' teams between 1983 and 1998.

Opponents' Record: 116–124, .483
(Not counting games against the 49ers.)

Of the five 49ers' teams that won the Super Bowl, only one (1988) played a regular-season schedule in which their opponents had an aggregate winning record.

Adjusted Power Index:

Offense: +5.12
Defense: +1.15
TOTAL: +6.27

This team had the sixth highest Offense Power Index (OPI) of any team since 1950. The 1993 49ers are second. (See "The Greatest Offenses of All Time.")

Innovations/What You Should Know:

In 1987, the 49ers traded two draft picks (a second-round and a fourth-round) and a reported $1 million to Tampa Bay in exchange for Steve Young. The Buccaneers traded Young to make room for number one draft pick, quarterback Vinny

Testaverde. Out of curiosity, I compared their passing statistics and won–lost records of their teams during the period they were starters in the same league, 1991–98.

1991–98	Att	Comp	Yds	YPA	TD	Int	Rating	W	L
Young	3,240	2,162	26,783	8.27	195	76	102.4	95	33
Testaverde	3,122	1,805	22,207	7.11	149	109	81.3	53	74

Actually, Testaverde's passing statistics are better than I thought they'd be. Of course, he was only with Tampa Bay for the first two of those eight seasons and had his best seasons elsewhere. Still, Testaverde is no Steve Young.

Homegrown First-Round Picks:

WR Jerry Rice, 1985; OT Harris Barton, 1987; RB Dexter Carter, 1990; DB Dana Hall, 1992; DT Dana Stubblefield, 1993; DE Todd Kelly, 1993; DT Bryant Young, 1994; RB William Floyd, 1994.

Although much has been made of San Francisco's free agent signings and their contribution to the 1994 team, the 1993–94 first-round selections of Stubblefield, Young, and Floyd were very important additions.

Pro Bowl Players:

DB Merton Hanks, TE Brent Jones, DB Tim McDonald, C Bart Oates, DB Deion Sanders, OG Jesse Sapolu, DT Dana Stubblefield, RB Ricky Watters, QB Steve Young.

Jones, McDonald, Oates, and Sanders were all signed as free agents, although Jones was a "traditional" free agent in that he was signed after being released by Pittsburgh in 1987. (See "Brent Jones" in the 1989 49ers' chapter.) Young was obtained in a trade with Tampa Bay in 1987. Sapolu was an eleventh-round pick in 1983; Hanks was a fifth-round pick in 1991.

Game-by-Game:

SEP. 5TH 49ERS 44, LA RAIDERS 14 AT SAN FRANCISCO

On the first Monday night game of the season, Jerry Rice scored 3 touchdowns to set a new NFL career record as San

Francisco won in a rout. Rice scored his first touchdown of the season on the 49ers' fourth play from scrimmage on a 69-yard pass from Steve Young. Rice's second touchdown, which tied Jim Brown with 126 in his career, came on a 23-yard run in the fourth quarter. The record-breaker came with 4:05 left in the game on a nice catch on a 38-yarder.

Rice, as you can imagine, was thrilled, "I can't think of a better evening. Monday Night Football and you've got everybody in the world watching. Plus, I really wanted it to be at home. What a day." He finished with 7 catches for 169 yards. Steve Young threw for over 300 yards (308 on 19 of 32 passing), 4 touchdowns, and was the game's leading rusher with 51 yards on 5 carries.

The 49ers completely dominated the Raiders, outgaining them 448 yards to 181. San Francisco linebacker Gary Plummer made some less than flattering remarks about the Raiders before the game. When asked about those comments after the game, he said, "I didn't have any ulterior motives when I said what I said. I just always hated them. I hated their fans. Their mystique. The silver and black. Everything. Where I came from, you tell it like it is."

The happiness of the evening was tempered by injuries to three of San Francisco's starting offensive linemen. Pro Bowl tackle Harris Barton missed seven games, and the 49ers had to play with a banged up offensive line in his absence.

Sep. 11th KANSAS CITY 24, 49ERS 17 AT KANSAS CITY

Nine penalties and 4 turnovers doomed San Francisco in their first game against Joe Montana. Of course, the game was billed as Montana vs. Young, so when the Chiefs won, Montana got most of the credit. While Montana played well, the Chiefs' defense, plus the San Francisco turnovers and penalties, played a larger role in the outcome of the game. In general, the media oversimplifies cause and effect, especially when icons are involved.

San Francisco defensive back Merton Hanks said, "We shot ourselves in the foot. It was more what we did to ourselves than what we did. If you're going to lose, you want to get your butt kicked; you don't want to beat yourself and that's what we did."

Sep. 18th 49ERS 34, LA RAMS 19 AT LOS ANGELES

San Francisco overcame an incredible 177 yards on 14 penalties for their eighth straight win over the Rams. Between the penalties and the early success of Jerome Bettis, Los Angeles kept the game close in the first half. The key sequence was San Francisco moving 77 yards with 1:30 left in the first half and no timeouts to score on a Steve Young 1-yard sneak as time expired. That touchdown gave the 49ers a 17–10 halftime lead.

Young completed 31 of 39 passes for 355 yards and 2 touchdowns. He also ran for 2 touchdowns.

This game marked the San Francisco debut of Deion Sanders, who signed a one-year contract as a free agent on September 15.

Sep. 25th 49ERS 24, NEW ORLEANS 13 AT SAN FRANCISCO

Deion Sanders's 74-yard interception return for a touchdown with 32 seconds left in the game iced the win for San Francisco. Neither team moved the ball well in this game, but a short punt gave New Orleans great field position at the 49ers' 44-yard line with 1:16 left. On fourth-and-8, Saints' quarterback Jim Everett threw an errant pass right to Sanders. "Prime Time" had come to San Francisco, flash and all.

New Orleans owner Tom Benson had called the 49ers "a Mickey Mouse organization" for their handling of the Sanders signing. Sanders turned down a far more lucrative offer from the Saints to sign with San Francisco. Quipped 49ers safety Tim McDonald after the game, "This is about as tough as it gets and our guys rose to the challenge. If Mickey Mouse clubs can win like this every week, then I'm going to Mickey Mouse land."

Oct. 2nd PHILADELPHIA 40, 49ERS 8 AT SAN FRANCISCO

The Eagles drubbed the 49ers in San Francisco's worst regular-season loss since a 59–14 defeat by Dallas on October 12, 1980. It was their worst loss at home since losing 45–3 to Detroit on October 29, 1967.

The bigger news was Steve Young being pulled from the game while in the huddle in the third quarter. At first, Young was very angry at being benched and the way it happened. He avoided head coach George Seifert as he came to the sideline and angrily paced back and forth. Young had been hit hard by Eagles defensive end William Fuller on the previous play. As Seifert put it, "Steve took the shot at the end of the second down and I just said to myself, 'The hell with this. I'm not going to leave him in anymore.'

We've got a lot of football ahead of us and Steve Young's a great quarterback. It was obvious to me I should take him out of the ballgame."

It may have been obvious to Seifert, but it wasn't obvious to Young. "If I didn't handle it to everybody's liking, it's because I don't have a lot of experience in this situation," he said. "I sure hope to hell that I don't gain it. . . . I understood it, but as a player who has a high standard, you can't fathom it. I would much rather beat myself to a pulp trying to get back into the game than say, 'Wait till next week.' "

Seifert later admitted that the timing of the move was poor.

Oct. 9th 49ERS 27, DETROIT 21 AT DETROIT

The embarrassing loss to Philadelphia led to Frank Pollack's promotion to starting offensive right tackle, while rookie William Floyd became the starting fullback. This marked the first time in nearly four years that San Francisco had made two changes to its starting lineup in the same week for a reason other than injury.

It looked like the defense would be next for changes after the Lions went 87 and 80 yards on their first two possessions to take a 14–0 lead early in the second quarter. After that, however, Detroit had a much more difficult time moving the ball, particularly on the ground with Barry Sanders. Why? According to 49ers linebacker Gary Plummer, "It was easy. After the first quarter, we knew what they were doing. I'd say probably on half their audibles we knew where they were running the ball. You don't have to be a Rhodes Scholar to figure it out."

New starter Floyd scored the first two touchdowns of his NFL career, but San Francisco still didn't have its running game in gear, gaining just 90 yards rushing, and averaging just 88 yards per game in its last five games.

Oct. 16th 49ERS 42, ATLANTA 3 AT ATLANTA

Two defensive touchdowns helped San Francisco to an easy win. After the 49ers moved 68 yards in 10 plays on their first possession to go up 7–0, San Francisco defensive tackle Bryant Young forced Atlanta's Craig Heyward to fumble on a third-and-inches carry. Safety Tim McDonald returned it 49 yards for a touchdown.

In the second quarter, with Atlanta trailing 21–3 but driving, Deion Sanders intercepted a Jeff George pass and ran it back 93 yards to stretch San Francisco's lead to 28–3 at halftime. That, in essence, was the game. Atlanta outgained San Francisco 146 yards to 9 in the second quarter, but was outscored 14–3.

Steve Young was pulled with nine minutes left in the third quarter, but this time there was no controversy.

Atlanta head coach June Jones said after the game, "I'm embarrassed for myself; I'm embarrassed for the team; I'm embarrassed for the city. There's not too much you can say after that."

Oct. 23rd 49ERS 41, TAMPA BAY 16 AT SAN FRANCISCO

Despite being ill, Ricky Watters had his first 100-yard rushing day of the season, gaining 103 yards on 14 carries and scoring 2 touchdowns. Steve Young had another good day, hitting 20 of 26 passes for 255 yards and 1 touchdown. Since being pulled against the Eagles, Young had completed 54 of 67 passes for 550 yards, 6 touchdowns, and no interceptions.

Nov. 6th 49ERS 37, WASHINGTON 22 AT WASHINGTON

Washington defense coordinator Ron Lynn was worried coming into this game, "With these guys [the 49ers] you've got to be able to cover the whole field and I mean literally every hole.... We don't have a good matchup. I don't know that there is any place we could say, 'We'll take that matchup over this one.'"

Lynn was right. San Francisco made a lot of big plays, and not just on offense, to roll over the Redskins. The 49ers' first touchdown came on a 69-yard pass from Steve Young to Brent Jones, the longest catch of Jones's career. On their next possession, San Francisco moved 78 yards in just four plays—including a short pass that Jerry Rice turned into a 55-yard gain, and a 22-yard run by Ricky Watters—to push their lead to 17–3.

In the third quarter, the 49ers got two more big scoring plays, but neither on offense. Tim McDonald intercepted a Gus Frerotte pass and ran it back 73 yards to make it 24–3. After the Redskins made it 24–6, Dexter Carter ran the kickoff back 96 yards for a touchdown. San Francisco's last score came early in the fourth quarter on another big play, a 28-yard reverse by Jerry Rice.

Nov. 13th 49ERS 21, DALLAS 14 AT SAN FRANCISCO

When Dallas won the Super Bowl in 1992 and 1993, they defeated San Francisco in the NFC Championship Game in both years. Safety Tim McDonald stated the obvious before the game, "I think for us to get to the next level, Dallas is the team we have to go through . . . this year we really believe we have the talent to win and we feel good about ourselves."

Although Dallas had success in the air, Merton Hanks had two of the 49ers' 3 interceptions while Steve Young and the 49ers offense made enough plays to win the game for San Francisco.

A 90-yard completion from Troy Aikman to Alvin Harper set up an Emmitt Smith 4-yard touchdown run with two minutes left in the first quarter to put Dallas on the scoreboard first.

On the next possession, San Francisco drove 74 yards on nine running plays to tie the game. Late in the third quarter, the 49ers went ahead on a 57-yard touchdown pass from Young to Jerry Rice.

Dallas was moving for the tying score midway through the fourth quarter, but Hanks intercepted Aikman near the goal line with a little over six minutes remaining. Led by Young's 5-for-5 passing, San Francisco then moved 87 yards in 11 plays and scored on a pass to Brent Jones with 2:32 left. The Cowboys got a late touchdown to make the final score closer.

San Francisco offensive tackle Harris Barton praised Young's effort, "Our quarterback was unbelievable. He won it himself. Nobody else did. Guys caught the ball and guys ran well, but Steve Young hung in there."

Hanks also played a stellar game. Cornerback Eric Davis said, "Merton was all over the place."

The win left San Francisco and Dallas knotted at 8–2 for the best NFC record. Of course, if both teams finished the season with the same record, this win would be the tiebreaker in favor of the 49ers.

Nov. 20th 49ERS 31, LA RAMS 27 AT SAN FRANCISCO

The game story in the *San Jose Mercury News* began with, "Thank you, LA. Or is that St. Louis? Baltimore? Hartford?" In what indeed turned out to be the last game between the Los Angeles Rams and the 49ers, the Rams came back from a 21–6 halftime deficit to take a 27–24 lead early in the fourth quarter only to have the 49ers score with 1:56 left. A Steve Young to Jerry Rice touchdown capped the 10-play, 67-yard decisive drive. Rice atoned for his earlier fourth-quarter fumble inside the Rams' 25. Referring to the turn of events Rice said, "I was upset with myself, but I was very fortunate to have another opportunity."

Actually, Rice had many opportunities, as he caught 16 passes for 165 yards and 3 touchdowns. The 16 catches were a 49ers' team record and, at the time, the third most in a single game in NFL history. (Terrell Owens broke the San Francisco and NFL record with 20 catches against Chicago on December 17, 2000.)

Young threw 4 touchdowns in all, completing 30 of 44 passes for 325 yards and no interceptions. Ricky Watters added 81 yards rushing. In their last four games, the 49ers averaged 145 rushing yards per game, far superior to their early season production.

Nov. 28th 49ERS 35, NEW ORLEANS 14 AT NEW ORLEANS

San Francisco clinched its eleventh NFC West title since 1981 seasons as the 49ers rolled over the Saints.

The 49ers more than doubled the Saints' total yardage (461 yards to 222) and first downs (28 to 13). San Francisco ran for a season-high 191 yards, led by Ricky Watters's 105. Steve Young threw 4 touchdowns, bringing his season total to 26. He completed 24 of 30 passes for 281 yards and no interceptions. In seven games since the debacle against Philadelphia, Young had completed 135 of 187 passes for 1,630 yards, 17 touchdowns, and 1 interception. That produces a neat 126.6 passing rating.

Dec. 4th 49ERS 50, ATLANTA 14 AT SAN FRANCISCO

The Falcons actually led 7–3 after the first quarter, but even after San Francisco scored the last 33 points of the game, some 49ers expressed discontentment. Harris Barton said, "We kinda struggled." William Floyd said, "Nobody's satisfied with our performance."

Maybe, but no one could say that Steve Young's performance needed improvement. He threw for 294 yards and 3 touchdowns and ran for another 2 TDs. Merton Hanks had 2 interceptions, giving him 7 INTs for the season.

For the second straight week, the 49ers compiled huge advantages in yards gained (476–249) and first downs (28–12). Atlanta head coach June Jones, whose team had been outscored 92–17 in two games against San Francisco, was clearly impressed: "The 49ers are playing awfully well, maybe the best I've ever seen."

Dec. 11th 49ERS 38, SAN DIEGO 15 AT SAN DIEGO

Maybe it's just how great teams keep themselves mentally ready to play, but again some 49ers were not happy with the team's performance despite another easy win. "We came out a little too relaxed," Jerry Rice said. "The game was closer than we wanted it." Tim McDonald said, "Yeah, we won, but we had some ugly moments." Whatever...

In what would turn out to be a Super Bowl preview, the result presaged the Super Bowl outcome as well. Steve Young completed his last 13 passes, including all 11 in the second half, on his way to a 25-of-32, 304-yard, two-touchdown, zero-interception performance. Neither team's running game was overwhelming, but the 49ers did a great job stopping San Diego's Natrone Means, holding him to 50 yards—his second-lowest total of the season—on 18 carries. Means would finish the year with 1,350 yards rushing. In their last four games, San Francisco outgained their opponents 1,813 yards to 1,151.

Dec. 17th 49ERS 42, DENVER 19 AT SAN FRANCISCO

Steve Young torched the Broncos for 350 yards and 3 touchdowns on 20 of 29 passing and Rhett Hall, starting in place of injured defensive tackle Dana Stubblefield, had 3 of San Francisco's 7 sacks as the 49ers clinched home-field advantage throughout the NFC playoffs. Jerry Rice, as always, was a big factor in the passing attack as he caught 9 passes to move his season total to a team record 108. Ricky Watters also made big plays, catching the first and last scores from Young, 12 yards and 65 yards, respectively. Watters added another touchdown on the ground.

The 49ers gained a season high 488 yards of total offense, the fifth consecutive game and seventh time in the last eight games with at least 400 yards. As a reference, in the 2000 season teams gained 400 yards in 18.3 percent of their games, 16.9 percent if the Rams are excluded.

Dec. 26th MINNESOTA 21, 49ERS 14 AT MINNESOTA

Vikings rookie cornerback DeWayne Washington scored his third touchdown of the year—a 17-yard fumble return—to key Minnesota's win. Washington's first-quarter score tied the NFL record for defensive return touchdowns by a rookie. Steve Young and Jerry Rice were taken out of the game in the second quarter.

Divisional Playoff:

Jan. 7th 49ERS 44, CHICAGO 15 AT SAN FRANCISCO

San Francisco could have been complacent coming in as 17-point favorites, but behind what George Seifert called "a pretty darned good performance" (way to go out on a limb, George), the 49ers cruised past the Bears to earn their third straight trip to the NFC Championship Game. Safety Tim McDonald expressed indifference at their next potential opponent: "The Cowboys? Green Bay? Who cares? This is a confident football team."

San Francisco was in control against the Bears throughout. An early turnover led to a Chicago field goal, but the halftime score was 30–3. In one stretch of 51 offensive plays, San Francisco made 25 first downs.

The underrated 49ers' defense forced the issue with the Bears' offense. Chicago gained 247 yards in the game, including only 39 rushing yards, and just 95 yards in the first half. San Francisco defensive tackle Bryant Young said, "I think overall we played pretty well. We stopped the run and made them throw the ball. I'm pretty sure that's not what they wanted to do."

NFC Championship:

Jan. 15th 49ERS 38, DALLAS 28 AT SAN FRANCISCO

Before the game, George Seifert commented on the escalating rumors that, despite the team's stellar record with him as head coach, he would be fired if the 49ers didn't beat Dallas. "I'm aware of it," he said. "It's unfortunate that it's allowed to be a topic, but it is.... If you win the game, the fishing's good, the living's easy, and angels follow you wherever you tread. If you lose... death. There's that sense."

Although Dallas fought hard all the way, this game was really decided in favor of the 49ers and their "beleaguered" head coach early in the first quarter. On the third play of the game, San Francisco's Eric Davis intercepted Troy Aikman and ran it back 44 yards for a touchdown. On the third play of the next series, Davis caused Dallas wide receiver Michael Irvin to fumble; 49ers safety Tim McDonald recovered at the Dallas 39. The 49ers scored on a 29-yard pass from Steve Young to Ricky Watters. On the kickoff, the 49ers' Adam Walker forced a fumble by Kevin Williams that was recovered by kicker Doug Brien at the Dallas 35. Seven plays later, William Floyd scored to make it 21–0 for the 49ers with just 7:33 gone in the game.

Dallas cut the lead to 24–14 near the end of the first half, but Seifert made a bold decision that paid off. The 49ers had the ball at the Dallas 28-yard line with 13 seconds left in the half, but no timeouts. Normally, Seifert would have attempted a field goal. However, tight end Brent Jones talked him into going for it, and Steve Young hit Jerry Rice for a 28-yard touchdown. Cowboys' guard Nate Newton said later, "Watching that play was like falling off Mount Everest."

Dallas never quit, but there was just too much ground to make up and not enough time. Cowboys running back Emmitt Smith commented, "It's like spotting Carl Lewis 20 yards in the 100-yard dash."

Super Bowl XXIX:

Jan. 29th 49ERS 49, SAN DIEGO 26 AT MIAMI

San Francisco scored a minute and 24 seconds into the game when Steve Young hit Jerry Rice for a 44-yard touchdown pass. That set the tone for the day. The Chargers were simply no match for the 49ers and their incredible offense. San Diego defensive coordinator Bill Arnsparger was almost in awe. "It didn't matter what we were in, whether it was man coverage or zone coverage or blitz coverage, they beat us," he said. "They're to be congratulated because they beat us at everything we were in at one time or another. We'd make a good play and they'd make two good plays."

The 49ers scored so quickly, leading 14–0 five minutes into the game, that they took the Chargers out of their game plan to run the ball, control the clock, and keep San Francisco's offense off the field.

For the moment at least, 49ers head coach George Seifert could rest easier. San Francisco became the first team to win five Super Bowls, and the rumors of his firing were a little quieter. His players were gracious after the game. Offensive tackle Steve Wallace said, "All the players knew George was a great coach. He gave us a chance to compete when we didn't have the talent to win a championship." Wallace's linemate Harris Barton said simply, "This is George's team."

It may have been George's team, but this was Steve Young's game. Young set a Super Bowl record with 6 touchdown passes, hitting 24 of 36 attempts for 325 yards and no interceptions. He was also the game's leading rusher with 49 yards on 5 carries. He had the Most Valuable Player Trophy sewed up at halftime, but more importantly, he had the monkey off his back.

Elsewhere Around the NFL:

Oct. 17th On a Monday night, Joe Montana threw a 5-yard touchdown pass to Willie Davis with eight seconds left to give the Chiefs a dramatic 31–28 win over the Broncos, their first win in Denver in 12 years. Montana, who threw for 393 yards and 3 touchdowns, led Kansas City to the winning drive after Denver had scored to take the lead with just 1:29 to go.

Oct. 23rd In a wild game that saw 4 touchdown returns of 90+ yards, New Orleans held off the Rams 37–34. The Saints' Tyrone Hughes set NFL records for kickoff return yardage (304 yards) and combined kick/punt return yards (347 yards) and tied the record with two kick return TDs. LA's Robert Bailey set an NFL record with a 103-yard punt return for a touchdown. Rams rookie Toby Wright ran back a fumble 98 yards for another score.

Nov. 13th Detroit's Barry Sanders ran for 237 yards on 26 carries to lead the Lions to a 14–9 win over Tampa Bay. Sanders did not score either of Detroit's touchdowns in this game, a pattern that persisted for most of this season. Despite carrying the ball 331 times for 1,883 yards, Sanders scored just 7 rushing touchdowns all year, a figure topped by seven NFL players and tied by seven others, including Steve Young.

What Happened the Next Season:

Steve Young missed five games with injuries, but the 49ers won another NFC West title in 1995 with an 11–5 record. Jerry Rice caught 122 passes for a league record 1,848 yards, but the team missed Ricky Watters's production. He had signed with the Eagles as a free agent. In an NFC divisional playoff game, the 49ers were upset at home 27–17 by Green Bay.

The Greatest Offenses of All Time

Damn those 2001 St. Louis Rams. If they were going to go to the trouble of compiling the highest Adjusted Power Index (API; +8.40) and Offense Power Index (OPI; +6.23) since 1950, you'd think they could have at least won the Super Bowl. This article was originally written before the 2001 season even started. The continued success of the Rams' offense forced me into a rewrite.

Before the emergence of the Rams as an offensive powerhouse in 1999, the greatest offense in pro football history was the 1993–94 49ers. You don't believe me? Well, even after you read this list you still might not believe me, but I'm convinced. This is a list of all teams with an Offense Power Index (OPI) of +5.00 or higher in a single season, excluding the 2001 Rams for now. If you've been paying attention, a +5.00 OPI should sound damn good because an overall Power Index of +6.00 or higher is what got teams their own chapters in this book (the overall index is just the sum of the Offense and Defense Power Indexes).

Team	OPI
1993 San Francisco 49ers	+5.52
1981 San Diego Chargers	+5.26
1984 Miami Dolphins	+5.19
1950 Los Angeles Rams	+5.15
1994 San Francisco 49ers	+5.12
2000 St. Louis Rams	+5.04

Like I said, I'm convinced. So are many of the coaches that had to play against the 49ers during that period. Bobby Ross, whose Chargers were routed by San Francisco during the regular season and the Super Bowl, certainly concurred, "I don't know if anybody has stopped them. They have great players. You're not talking about Pro Bowl players—you're talking about potential Hall-of-Fame players." Longtime coach and football broadcaster Hank Stram said, "In all my years in football, it is the most impressive offense I have seen."

The 1993–94 49ers were the first of only two NFL teams to compile a two-year OPI of +10.00 or better. Here are all of the teams with a two-year OPI of +9.00 or better:

Team	OPI
2000–01 St. Louis Rams	+11.27
1993–94 San Francisco 49ers	+10.64
1999–00 St. Louis Rams	+9.89
1992–93 San Francisco 49ers	+9.85
1950–51 Los Angeles Rams	+9.66
1980–81 San Diego Chargers	+9.44

Just six teams and really it's only four, of course, as the 49ers of the early 90s and the Rams of 1999–2001 each show up twice. Since the 49ers and St. Louis Rams are represented in the book, I want to briefly discuss the 1950 (1950–51) Los Angeles Rams and the 1981 (1980–81) Chargers.

The 1950 Rams were coached by Joe Stydahar. His predecessor was Clark Shaughnessy, fired after the 1949 season despite an NFL Western Division title and an 8–2–2 record. It was Shaughnessy and Rams' assistant coach Hampton Pool, both excellent innovators, who came up with the idea that helped made the Rams so difficult to defense. By this time, all NFL teams except the Steelers were using the T-formation on offense, with three backs behind the quarterback. Shaughnessy and Pool devised putting one of those three backs out on the flank of the formation outside the tight end, in essence creating the flanker position.

The Rams were blessed with the talent to make that scheme work. Hall-of-Fame receivers Elroy "Crazy Legs" Hirsch and Tom Fears were difficult enough for defenses to account for, given their speed, elusiveness, and the basic man-to-man coverages of the day. Throw in Glenn Davis, "Mr. Outside" of the famous "Mr. Inside/Mr. Outside" backfield at Army (Doc Blanchard was "Mr. Inside"), and defenses were simply overwhelmed. Of course, it didn't hurt to have two Hall-of-Fame quarterbacks, Norm Van Brocklin and Bob Waterfield, sharing the position. This chart shows all qualifying passers for the 1950 season (100+ pass attempts was the standard in 1950) ranked by today's NFL passer rating:

Rank	Quarterback	Team	Pass Att	Rating
1	Norm Van Brocklin	LA	233	85.1
2	Bob Waterfield	LA	213	71.7
3	Sammy Baugh	WAS	166	68.1
4	Charlie Conerly	NYG	132	67.1
5	Otto Graham	CLE	253	64.7
6	George Ratterman	NYY	294	64.6
7	Bobby Layne	DET	336	62.1
8	Y. A. Tittle	BAL	315	52.9
9	Frankie Albert	SF	306	52.3
10	Frank Tripucka	CHC	108	51.5
11	Harry Gilmer	WAS	141	50.8
12	Jim Hardy	CHC	257	49.7
13	Paul Christman	GB	126	49.2
14	Tommy Thompson	PHI	239	44.4
15	Joe Geri	PIT	113	42.4
16	Johnny Lujack	CHB	254	41.0
17	Adrian Burk	BAL	119	37.4
18	Tobin Rote	GB	224	26.7
	NFL Totals		**4,307**	**52.9**

How about that? Much was made about the fact that Trent Green and Kurt Warner, both of the Rams, finished 2–3 in the NFL in passing rating in 2000. Well, the 1950 Rams went that one better. Van Brocklin's passing rating was an incredible 61 percent and 2.2 standard deviations better than the league average. Legendary coach Sid Gillman coached Van Brocklin in the mid-1950s and had an interesting comment about the strength of his arm and delivery, "Every time Van Brocklin threw the ball, you could hear a little 'zzzt!' as it left his fingertips."

The 1950 Rams didn't run the ball much. They were eighth of 13 NFL teams in rushing attempts, but their running game was effective enough. Glenn Davis, who led the team, was only seventeenth in the league with 416 yards rushing. He did, however, average 4.7 yards per carry.

In 1950, the Rams scored 466 points in just 12 games—their rate of 38.8 points per game is still the NFL record. In back-to-back games against the Colts and Lions, they scored 135 total points! Los Angeles scored 40 or more points in six, or half, of their regular season games. They tied the Bears for the conference title, beat Chicago 24–14 in a playoff, and lost 30–28 to Cleveland in a classic game for the NFL championship.

In 1951, coach Stydahar put in another wrinkle. The team often lined up in the "bull elephant" backfield of Dan Towler, Dick Hoerner, and Paul

"Tank" Younger. Each of them averaged over 6 yards per carry in 1951, making teams pay for overplaying the pass; it also afforded either Van Brocklin or Waterfield excellent protection. Both quarterbacks had excellent seasons again in 1951. Crazy Legs Hirsch had a phenomenal year, catching 66 passes for 1,495 yards and 17 touchdowns in a 12-game season. Hirsch's average touchdown catch was 48 yards.

The "Air Coryell" Chargers of head coach Don Coryell were fun to watch and their offense was at its best in 1981. Star wide receiver John Jefferson was sent to Green Bay that year because of a salary dispute, but the Chargers traded for their second New Orleans import in two seasons, acquiring the brilliant, underrated Wes Chandler to replace him. San Diego had already obtained the services of running back Chuck Muncie the year before in a trade with the Saints. (Meanwhile, Jefferson never again compiled the numbers he had with the Chargers. After catching 36 touchdowns in his three years in San Diego, he had just 11 in four years with the Packers. He never again broke 1,000 yards receiving, a mark he surpassed in each of his three seasons in San Diego.)

With the outstanding passing game of quarterback Dan Fouts and the running of Muncie (and 1981 first-round pick James Brooks), the Chargers' offense was almost impossible to defend. Fouts became the first NFL quarterback to average 300 yards passing per game, and he led the league with 33 touchdown passes. Chandler and Hall-of-Famers Charlie Joiner and Kellen Winslow became the first trio of teammates to gain 1,000 or more yards receiving in the same season. (It might not seem like a big deal that Chandler went over 1,000 yards receiving again in 1982. Well, because of a players strike the '82 season was only nine games. Oh yeah, Chandler didn't play in one of those nine.)

Muncie ran for 1,144 yards, a 4.6 average, and led the league with 19 rushing touchdowns. That was only the fifth time in NFL history, going back to 1933, that the same team had the league leader in both touchdown passes and touchdown runs. In all, San Diego scored 60 offensive touchdowns in 1981; the next best team, Cincinnati, scored 49. The Bengals beat the Chargers in the AFC Championship Game on a day when the wind chill was measured at 59 degrees below zero. (That's the old measurement; the new wind chill measurement wouldn't be quite as extreme. It still wouldn't be conducive to a warm-weather passing team.) Cincinnati also beat San Diego 40–17 during the regular season at San Diego.

The loss to the Bengals came eight days after the best NFL game I've ever seen, San Diego's thrilling 41–38 overtime win against the Dolphins in Miami.

I won't recount the details of the see-saw battle, although I can't imagine anyone who watched it, except for perhaps Dolphins fans, who didn't think it was the best or one of the very best games they had ever seen.

Before the 2001 season, I was convinced that the best offense of all time was the 49ers of the early to mid-'90s. Yes, I was heavily influenced by their ranking in Offense Power Index, but I was also influenced by the fact that their offense stayed so good for so long.

Focusing on 1993–94, San Francisco had an incredibly productive passing game triggered by Steve Young with targets Jerry Rice, John Taylor, Brent Jones, and Ricky Watters. Watters gave them an effective ground game and, of course, Young piled up a lot of rushing yards while frustrating a lot of defenses. Counting the playoffs, the 1993–94 49ers scored 30 or more points in 8 of 16 games against teams with winning records. I thought that was clear enough evidence for me to anoint the 49ers of that era as the greatest offense ever.

For offensive prowess over a long period of time, there's still no doubt that the 49ers dynasty is the best. (See "Year after Year" in the 1989 49ers' chapter.) However, for a two- or three-year period, I'm not so sure, anymore. The 1999–2001 Rams have a great case. Here's a comparison of three-year OPIs:

Team	OPI
1999–2001 Rams	+16.11
1992–1994 49ers	+14.97

These are clearly the two greatest offenses since 1950; no other franchise has a three-year OPI of even +13.00. I have to say that despite their upset loss to the Patriots in Super Bowl XXXVI, I give the nod to the Rams.

The Coach: George Seifert

Coaching Record (with 49ers Only)

	W	L	Pct	
1989	14	2	.875	NFC Western Division title; NFC champs; Super Bowl champs
1990	14	2	.875	NFC Western Division title
1991	10	6	.625	
1992	14	2	.875	NFC Western Division title
1993	10	6	.625	NFC Western Division title
1994	12	4	.750	NFC Western Division title; NFC champs; Super Bowl champs
1995	11	5	.688	NFC Western Division title
1996	12	4	.750	NFC Wild Card
Total	**97**	**31**	**.758**	

As a San Francisco native, George Seifert wanted to be head coach of the 49ers long before he was given the job. Unfortunately for him, he entered an absolute no-win situation due to the incredibly high standards set by the team's previous success on the field, and by their mercurial owner, Eddie DeBartolo.

The 49ers won over three-fourths of their regular-season games in their eight seasons with Seifert as head coach. That is a remarkable achievement. I researched the records for all NFL teams for eight-year periods since 1950, and put together a list of all teams with a regular-season winning percentage of .750 or higher:

Team	W	L	T	Pct
Minnesota Vikings, 1969–76	87	24	1	.781
Green Bay Packers, 1960–67	82	24	4	.764
Pittsburgh Steelers, 1972–79	88	27	1	.763
Cleveland Browns, 1950–57	72	22	2	.760
San Francisco 49ers, 1984–91	96	30	1	.760
Oakland Raiders, 1970–77	82	24	6	.759
San Francisco 49ers, 1989–96	97	31	0	.758
Dallas Cowboys, 1976–83	88	29	0	.752
Dallas Cowboys, 1966–73	83	27	2	.750

Yes, I was surprised that the 1969–76 Vikings were first. What strikes you about the list? If you think about it, the coaches. Grant, Lombardi, Noll,

Brown, Walsh, Madden, Landry...and Seifert. Despite this incredible success, no one has given Seifert the label as a great coach. Maybe he isn't or wasn't, but this list is fact. (San Francisco had the same mark from 1990 to 1997, but I felt it would be duplication to twice list the same general period.)

Think about the other coaches. Bud Grant coached the Vikings until 1983 (and again in 1985). Lombardi could have coached the Packers as long as he lived, but he resigned. Noll coached Pittsburgh until 1991. Paul Brown coached the Browns until 1962. Landry coached Dallas until 1988.

Only the Bay Area teams "forced" out their successful coaches during a great run or shortly thereafter. It must be something in the water. John Madden only coached the Raiders for one more season after his great eight-year run. He retired after a "disappointing" 9-7 season in which Oakland missed the playoffs. Walsh resigned after the 1988 season, and while it may be true that he was "an emotional basket case" by that time, as Glenn Dickey described him, it's also true that Eddie DeBartolo was... Eddie DeBartolo.

Of course, one could make the argument, as I have elsewhere in this book, that even the greatest men can stagnate and become less productive if left in the same situation too long. Dr. Harry Edwards, a noted sociologist who has had a long association with Bay Area sports teams and the 49ers, commented on the team's situation at the end of Seifert's tenure, "After a few years, the veteran players have heard the same message from the coach so many times that they tune out. In George's case, he'd been here as a defensive coordinator before he became head coach, so his message was really getting old. The younger players take their cue from the older players. If the older players aren't listening, the younger players don't either." Still, the timing of Seifert's exit from San Francisco seems a bit odd in the context of the team's success. (He returned to coaching with Carolina in 1999, but a three-year record of 16–32 not only got him fired, it dropped his lofty career winning percentage 109 points.)

In his own right, whether or not one considers him "great," Seifert made major contributions to the 49ers as defensive coordinator as well as head coach. He had coached under Bill Walsh at Stanford, and Walsh hired him in 1980 to coach the secondary for the 49ers; Seifert became defensive coordinator in 1983. Glenn Dickey described Seifert in this way, "He had an innovative defensive mind. More than anybody else, he popularized the use of situation substitution, using defensive specialists at a time when teams were generally making few substitutions.... Seifert was as imaginative with his defensive approach as Bill Walsh was on offense."

Great coach or not, George Seifert was certainly an important figure in what was the NFL's greatest dynasty.

The Quarterback: Steve Young

Year	Team	Att	Comp	Yds	TD	Int	YPA	Rating	Lg Avg	W	L	Pct
1985	TB	138	72	935	3	8	6.78	56.9	73.5	1	4	.200
1986	TB	363	195	2,282	8	13	6.29	65.5	74.1	2	12	.143
1987	SF	69	37	570	10	0	8.26	120.8	75.2	3	0	1.000
1988	SF	101	54	680	3	3	6.73	72.2	72.9	2	1	.667
1989	SF	92	64	1,001	8	3	10.88	120.8	75.6	3	0	1.000
1990	SF	62	38	427	2	0	6.89	92.6	77.3	0	1	.000
1991	SF	279	180	2,517	17	8	9.02	101.8	76.2	5	5	.500
1992	SF	402	268	3,465	25	7	8.62	107.0	75.3	14	2	.875
1993	SF	462	314	4,023	29	16	8.71	101.5	76.7	10	6	.625
1994	SF	461	324	3,969	35	10	8.61	112.8	78.4	13	3	.813
1995	SF	447	299	3,200	20	11	7.16	92.3	79.2	8	3	.727
1996	SF	316	214	2,410	14	6	7.63	97.2	76.9	9	3	.750
1997	SF	356	241	3,029	19	6	8.51	104.7	77.2	12	3	.800
1998	SF	517	322	4,170	36	12	8.07	101.1	78.3	12	3	.800
1999	SF	84	45	446	3	4	5.31	60.9	77.1	2	1	.667
Total		**4,149**	**2,667**	**33,124**	**232**	**107**	**7.98**	**96.8**	**76.3**	**96**	**47**	**.671**
1991–98		3,240	2,162	26,783	195	76	8.27	102.4	77.3	83	28	.748

YPA = Yards Per Pass Attempt
Rating = Passer Rating
Lg Avg = League Passer Rating in that season
W, L, Pct = Team's Record in his starts

Without adjusting for league averages or standard deviations, Steve Young has the most impressive set of passer ratings of any quarterback in NFL history. His 96.8 career rating is the best ever, and his 112.8 rating in 1994 is the best ever for a single season. Young had an incredible six qualifying seasons with a rating of 100.0 or higher, plus two more seasons above 100.0 in limited time. Since 1978, the beginning of the "rules regime" that favors the passing game, there have been 18 seasons where a qualifying passer had a rating of 100.0 or better, which means that by himself Young accounted for one-third of those seasons.

Fortunately for Young, he was still in high school in 1978. That was the year the NFL first adopted rules such as the five-yard zone beyond which a receiver couldn't be touched by a defender, which eliminated bump-and-run coverage. More liberal blocking rules for offensive linemen were instituted to allow them to extend their arms as long as they didn't thrust their hands into the defender's head, face, or neck. These rules, as well as additional rules changes since 1978, have made it easier to pass the football, since receivers could now run relatively unimpeded down the field and quarterbacks receive better pass protection. It was tougher for the average quarterback before then; but Young has never been considered average.

For the entire eight-season period when he was San Francisco's starting quarterback, his rating was over 100.0. No doubt, some of you out there are saying, "So what?" I think it's safe to say that many football fans don't pay attention to passer rating because they either don't understand it or don't think it has much to do with who wins or loses the game. (I could be more critical and say that most fans don't care about passer rating because most fantasy leagues don't use it. I could say that fantasy football is well-named because it bears little or no resemblance to the real thing. I would never do that, though.)

First, one need only look at San Francisco's record with Young as the starter to get some idea of the importance of passer rating. I am not arguing that Steve Young was the only reason the 49ers kept winning or that his productivity was solely a result of his ability. Young's 102.4 rating, however, had a lot to do with his team's 83–28 record with him as the starter.

Second, passer rating actually correlates better with winning than any other passing statistic. That is important because, after all, the object of the game is to win. I looked at all NFL team-seasons since Young became the 49ers' starter in 1991 and generated the correlation between team winning percentage and various team passing statistics. Correlations (more precisely, zero-order correlation coefficients) range from −1 to 1; they are numbers like .33. The higher the absolute value, the stronger the statistical relationship between the two events. Correlations can be negative, numbers like −.45, because two events can move in the opposite direction. For example, as a team throws more interceptions, it tends to win fewer games.

I looked at six key passing statistics and how they correlated with winning percentage for all teams from 1991 to 2000. Another reason it made sense to focus on more recent seasons is that the league average for passer rating increased dramatically from the late 1970s through the early 1990s. That means the same passer rating that would help a team generate a good record in 1979 would not be so good in 1994; that fact could cloud the correlations. Here are the correlations with winning percentage for all teams from 1991 to 2000:

Correlation with Winning Percentage	
Passing Rating	.62
Yards Per Pass Attempt	.56
Touchdown Percentage	.52
Completion Percentage	.47
Interception Percentage	−.36
Sacks Per Pass Attempt	−.36

At a team level, passer rating had the highest correlation with winning of any passing statistic. In a sample of this size (294 team-seasons), these differences between the correlations of the various statistics are meaningful. As an aside, the correlation between interceptions and winning is negative, as one would expect, and the correlation between sacks allowed and winning is also negative.

The point of all this math is to show that passer rating is a "meaningful" statistic because it correlates to winning games better than any other passing statistic. Game situation affects play-calling, and teams that are behind in the latter stages of a game are at a disadvantage because their opponent knows they're going to be throwing the ball; however, it seems apparent that passing rating "causes" winning percentage more than the other way around.

All of this means that Steve Young's six passing titles and high quarterback ratings are not just trivia. A quarterback with a high passing rating is also usually a quarterback on a winning team.

1994 San Francisco 49ers Statistics

Passing

	Att	Comp	Comp Pct	Yds	Yds Per	TD	Int	Rating
S. Young	461	324	70.3%	3,969	8.61	35	10	112.8
Grbac	50	35	70.0%	393	7.86	2	1	98.2
49ers	**511**	**359**	**70.3%**	**4,362**	**8.54**	**37**	**11**	**111.4**
Opponents	583	329	56.4%	3,756	6.44	15	23	68.1
League Average			58.0%		6.77			78.4

49ers' passers were sacked 35 times for 199 yards in losses.
The 49ers sacked their opponents 38 times for 255 yards in losses.

Steve Young's 112.8 passing rating is the highest in NFL history. Sort of. (See "1999 St. Louis Rams Statistics.") This is no knock at Young, who was an outstanding player, but relative to the league a 112.8 passing rating in 1994 would not be as good as a 98.4 rating in 1970. Young's rating was 44 percent better than the league average; a 98.4 rating in 1970 would have been 50 percent better than the league average.

On the other hand, the standard deviation of passing rating has decreased enough so Young would be more standard deviations above the mean than our hypothetical 1970 passer would have been. Using the standard deviation of team passing rating, Young was 3.6 standard deviations better than the league average in 1994. Our hypothetical 1970 passer would have been 2.3 standard deviations better than the league average.

Rushing

	Att	Yds	Avg	Net Yards	TD
Watters	239	877	3.67	−13	6
Floyd	87	305	3.51	−19	6
S. Young	58	293	5.05		7
Logan	33	143	4.33		1
Loville	31	99	3.19		0
Rice	7	93	13.29		2
Walker	13	54	4.15		1
Carter	8	34	4.25		0
Grbac	13	1	0.08		0
Taylor	2	−2	−1.00		0
49ers	**491**	**1,897**	**3.86**	**+70**	**23**
Opponents	375	1,338	3.57	−58	16
League Average			3.72		

Not only did Steve Young lead the league in passing, and set a record, he led his team in rushing touchdowns. Only seven NFL backs had more rushing touchdowns. If you take Young's and Rice's rushing stats out, the 49ers averaged only 3.55 yards per rush. Even if you take Grbac and Taylor out, San Francisco still averaged only 3.68 yards per carry without Young and Rice.

Receiving

	Rec	Yds	Avg	TD
Rice	112	1,499	13.38	13
Watters	66	719	10.89	5
Jones	49	670	13.67	9
Taylor	1	531	12.95	5
Singleton	21	294	14.00	2
Floyd	19	145	7.63	0
Logan	16	97	6.06	1
Popson	13	141	10.85	0
McCaffrey	11	131	11.91	2
Carter	7	99	14.14	0
Loville	2	26	13.00	0
Carolan	2	10	5.00	0
49ers	**359**	**4,362**	**12.15**	**37**
Opponents	329	3,756	11.42	15
League Average			11.66	

For me, Jerry Rice's 1989 season was better than this one. He gained almost as many yards receiving on 30 fewer catches, and he caught more TDs.

This was less of a West Coast offense distribution than in 1989. That year, the two starting running backs caught 122 passes, compared to 85 in 1994. Brent Jones and John Taylor had 90 receptions compared to 100 in 1989. I am purely speculating, but perhaps as Jerry Rice gained seniority and began to approach all-time receiving records, he began to "persuade" the relevant people that he should get the ball more. Of course, getting Rice the ball more often has generally been a good idea.

Ricky Watters was very productive catching the ball out of the backfield in his last year with San Francisco before signing with the Eagles. Of the 45 NFL running backs who caught at least 25 passes in 1994, Watters's average per catch was the best and almost 3 yards per catch better than the average.

The McCaffrey above is the same Ed McCaffrey who went on to star with the Broncos. He signed with Denver after the 1994 season, just like his offensive coordinator, Mike Shanahan, who became the Broncos' head coach. If you were an offensive player who was with San Francisco for many of their glory years, you probably played under an amazing collection of assistant coaches. Shanahan, Mike Holmgren, and Dennis Green were three offensive assistants with the 49ers during their dynasty who went on to be very successful as NFL head coaches.

Kickoff Returns

	Ret	Yds	Avg	TD
Carter	48	1,105	23.02	1
Walker	6	82	13.67	0
Loville	2	34	17.00	0
Singleton	2	23	11.50	0
49ers	**58**	**1,244**	**21.45**	**1**
Opponents	89	1,912	21.48	0
League Average			21.22	

Despite an occasional big play on a return, it can be said without fear of contradiction that Dexter Carter was a first-round pick who didn't pan out. According to Glenn Dickey in his book *49ers,* Carter was picked in 1990 (number 25 overall) despite little sentiment among San Francisco's brass that he should be the selection.

Carter signed with the Jets as a free agent after the 1994 season, didn't even last one full year with New York, and returned to San Francisco before being cut for good after the 1996 season. His biggest drawback was his tendency to fumble. Carter fumbled 33 times in his NFL career on 696 attempts, including punt/kick returns, rushing attempts, and receptions. That percentage–4.7%–is way too high. No one could really make enough big plays to offset that much fumbling.

Punt Returns

	Ret	Yds	Avg	TD
Carter	38	321	8.45	0
Singleton	2	13	6.50	0
49ers	**40**	**334**	**8.35**	**0**
Opponents	28	242	8.64	0
League Average			8.94	

Interceptions

	Int	Yds	Avg	TD
Hanks	7	93	13.29	0
Sanders	6	303	50.50	3
McDonald	2	79	39.50	1
D. Hall	2	0	0.00	0
Cook	1	18	18.00	0
Davis	1	8	8.00	0
Drakeford	1	6	6.00	0
Plummer	1	1	1.00	0
Brown	1	0	0.00	0
Norton	1	0	0.00	0
49ers	**23**	**508**	**22.09**	**4**
Opponents	11	107	9.73	1

I am not a fan of Deion Sanders. I find his self-promoting, showboating, me-first attitude to be, frankly, obscene. I have to admit, however, he made an impact on this team. He played in only 14 games, not signing with the 49ers until after the second week of the season, but he made a lot of big plays. Returning 3 interceptions for touchdowns is hard to ignore; his 303 yards returning interceptions is the second most in a season in NFL history, and then only because the NFL counts all records from the AFL. Charlie McNeil had 349 yards returning interceptions for the Chargers in 1961, when the AFL wasn't on par with the NFL.

Sack Leaders

(Sacks have been an official statistic for individual players only since 1982.)

Stubblefield	8.5
Young, B.	6.0
Hall, R.	4.0

Stubblefield was tenth in the NFC in sacks.

Turnovers

Turnovers Committed:	24
Turnovers Forced:	35
Turnover +/−:	+11

The 49ers were tied for third best in the NFL in turnover margin.

Punting

	No	Avg
Wilmsmeyer	54	41.4
Opponents	77	42.5
League Average		41.7

Kicking

	XP	XPA	XP Pct	FG	FGA	FG Pct
Brien	60	62	96.8%	15	20	5.0%
Opponents	23	23	100.0%	15	21	71.4%
League Average			98.8%			78.9%

Leading Scorer: Doug Brien, 105 Points
Leading Scorer, Non-Kicker: Jerry Rice, 92 Points

1994 San Francisco 49ers Roster

Head Coach	George Seifert
QB	Elvis Grbac
QB	Bill Musgrave
QB	Steve Young
RB/KR/PR	Dexter Carter
RB	William Floyd
RB	Marc Logan
RB	Derek Loville
RB/KR	Adam Walker
RB	Ricky Watters
WR	Ed McCaffrey
WR	Jerry Rice
WR	Nate Singleton
WR	John Taylor
TE	Brett Carolan
TE	Brent Jones
TE	Ted Popson
C	Bart Oates
OG	Brian Bollinger
OG/C	Chris Dalman
OG	Derrick Deese
OG	Rod Milstead
OG/C	Jesse Sapolu
OG	Ralph Tamm
OT	Harris Barton
OT	Harry Boatswain
OT	Frank Pollack
OT	Steve Wallace
K	Doug Brien
P	Klaus Wilmsmeyer
DE	Dennis Brown
DE	Richard Dent
DE/LB	Tim Harris
DE/LB	Rickey Jackson
DE	Todd Kelly
DE	Charles Mann
DE	Mark Thomas
DE	Troy Wilson
DT	Rhett Hall
DT	Dana Stubblefield
DT	Bryant Young
LB	Antonio Goss
LB	Kevin Mitchell
LB	Ken Norton
LB	Anthony Peterson
LB	Gary Plummer
LB	Lee Woodall
DB	Toi Cook
DB	Eric Davis
DB	Dedrick Dodge
DB	Tyrone Drakeford
DB	Dana Hall
DB	Merton Hanks
DB	Tim McDonald
DB	Deion Sanders

Ralph Tamm is listed on two rosters in the book; he played a grand total of three games in those two seasons (he played two games for the 1991 Redskins). This was Charles Mann's last NFL season, and the only year of 12 in the NFL that he didn't play for the Redskins. A Super Bowl win was a nice way to finish.

CHAPTER 12

1996 Green Bay Packers: The Trophy Comes Home

STARTING LINEUP – 1996 PACKERS

Offense		Defense	
SE	Antonio Freeman/Don Beebe	LE	Reggie White
LT	John Michels	LT	Santana Dotson
LG	Aaron Taylor	RT	Gilbert Brown
C	Frank Winters	RE	Sean Jones
RG	Adam Timmerman	LLB	Wayne Simmons
RT	Earl Dotson	MLB	George Koonce
TE	Mark Chmura/Keith Jackson	RLB	Brian Williams
FL*		LCB	Craig Newsome
QB	Brett Favre	RCB	Doug Evans
RB	Edgar Bennett/Dorsey Levens	SS	LeRoy Butler
RB	William Henderson	FS	Eugene Robinson

*Numerous injuries make it difficult to define the starter. Robert Brooks, Terry Mickens, and Andre Rison played there. The Packers also played two tight end sets and sometimes even played Keith Jackson in four WR formation.

In the locker room after their Super Bowl win over the Patriots, Packers' head coach Mike Holmgren held up the Super Bowl trophy and said to his team, "This trophy. This is it. It was named after Vince Lombardi. You play in Green Bay. As important as it is to any other team, any other player, it's more important to us." It's not really clear how many players appreciated what Holmgren said, but I think he made a good point.

The Packers have a unique legacy among NFL teams. Under Curly Lambeau, for whom the Packers' home stadium is named, Green Bay won three straight NFL titles from 1929 to 1931. During the Don Hutson era (1935– 1945), Hutson was a revolutionary talent at wide receiver, the Packers had 11 straight winning seasons and won the NFL title in 1936, 1939, and 1944. Under Vince Lombardi, the Packers won five NFL titles in seven seasons, including three straight from 1965 to 1967, the only team to win three consecutive championships since the league split into divisions in 1933.

Part of the Packers' unique legacy is the team's ownership structure. As you may know, the team is owned primarily by residents of Wisconsin, although shares were sold all over the United States in 1997 and 1998 to help finance the renovations for Lambeau Field. No dividends are ever paid, the stock cannot appreciate in value, and there are no season ticket privileges associated with stock ownership. Shares of stock cannot be resold, except back to the team for a fraction of the original price.

So, Holmgren's words have real meaning. I don't think you have to be a Packers' fan to appreciate the significance of the franchise and its history.

If you can't go over them, go around them . . . most observers thought Dallas was the largest obstacle to Green Bay's winning the NFC title in 1996. The Cowboys had beaten the Packers in the playoffs in each of the previous three seasons by a combined score of 100–63. In all, Dallas had beaten Green Bay seven straight times (counting playoffs), the last six of those in Dallas. The Cowboys outscored the Packers 212–122 in that span.

As it turned out, the Packers still couldn't beat the Cowboys in 1996, at least not in Dallas, but it didn't matter. Green Bay earned home-field advantage throughout the NFC playoffs, and the Cowboys lost to the Carolina Panthers in the playoffs.

Allsport

Reggie White, *right*

Brett Favre had another obstacle to overcome. Although he began the 1996 season by saying, "It's Super Bowl or bust. Don't bet against me," it's easy to understand why some people would have a wait-and-see attitude. Before the season, Favre spent 46 days at the Menninger Clinic in Topeka, Kansas, to fight an addiction to the prescription pain-killer, Vicodin. Favre battled through substance abuse and was the major cog in bringing the Lombardi Trophy back to Green Bay.

Team in a Box

Record: 13–3

The Packers' 13–3 record was the franchise's best since 1966 when Green Bay went 12–2. (The Packers won the first Super Bowl that season.)

From 1968, the year after Vince Lombardi retired as head coach, through 1991, the year before Mike Holmgren took over as head coach, Green Bay's record was 146–201–9. In that time, the team had only five winning seasons.

Against Teams Over .500: 4 3, 188 Points Scored, 127 Points Allowed

The Packers did win the Super Bowl, but they lost all three road games against teams with winning records: at Minnesota, at Kansas City, and at Dallas. (See "Game-by-Game.")

The '96 Packers' point differential against winning teams is padded by their 41–6 win against the Broncos, who had already clinched home-field advantage throughout the AFC playoffs. Bill Musgrave quarterbacked Denver in his first NFL start.

Points Scored/Allowed: 456/210 (1996 NFL Average: 327)

The 1996 Packers were the first team since the 1972 Dolphins to score the most points and allow the fewest. Five teams accomplished that feat between 1950 and 1971.

Yards Gained/Allowed: 5,535/4,156 (1996 NFL Average: 5,062)

The Packers allowed the fewest yards of any team in the NFL in 1996. Since the adoption of the 16-game schedule in 1978, 20 teams have allowed 4,200 or fewer yards in a season.

Opponents' Record: 126–114, .525

(Not counting games against the Packers.)

Adjusted Power Index:

Offense: +3.59
Defense: +3.90
TOTAL: +7.49

The 1996 Packers have the highest API of any team in the book. Yes, that surprised me.

Their Offense Power Index (OPI) ranks in the top 4 percent of all teams since 1950; their Defense Power Index (DPI) ranks in the top 2 percent. I think the similarity and excellence of the two scores display the real strength of the 1996 Packers: balance.

Innovations/What You Should Know:

Star defensive end Reggie White signed with Green Bay as a free agent in 1993. Some people surely giggled at his remark that he would sign where God wanted him to sign and in the end, God told him to sign with Green Bay.

As the late Dick Schaap wrote in *Green Bay Replay,* more earthly persuasion might have helped sway White to sign with the Packers. When White first met with Packers general manager Ron Wolf, the GM told White, "Reggie White is already a great football player. If you come here and play for the Green Bay Packers, you'll become a legend." White was moved by that remark.

White was amused by a message that head coach Mike Holmgren left on White's answering machine. Holmgren said, "Reggie, this is God. I want you to play in Green Bay."

The signing of Reggie White re-established Green Bay as a franchise committed to winning. In White's fourth season with the Packers, Green Bay won the Super Bowl.

Homegrown First-Round Picks:

LB Wayne Simmons, 1993; OG Aaron Taylor, 1994; DB Craig Newsome, 1995; OT John Michels, 199.

While this was a team of the modern salary cap/free agency era, this is a very small number of homegrown first-round picks. The star of the team, NFL MVP quarterback Brett Favre, was acquired in 1992 in a trade with Atlanta (see

"The Quarterback: Brett Favre"). Leading rusher Edgar Bennett was a fourth-round pick in 1992; productive runner Dorsey Levens was a fifth-rounder in 1994; leading receiver Antonio Freeman was picked in the third round in 1995. Reggie White, of course, was "led" to Green Bay as a free agent in 1993. Pro Bowl safety LeRoy Butler was a second-round pick in 1990.

Pro Bowl Players:

DB LeRoy Butler, QB Brett Favre, TE Keith Jackson, DE Reggie White, C Frank Winters.

Another relatively short list, the Packers had "just" five Pro Bowl players—a small total for a Super Bowl champion, not to mention a team that led in both scoring and fewest points allowed.

Game-by-Game:

Sep. 1st PACKERS 34, TAMPA BAY 3 AT TAMPA BAY

The Packers routed the Buccaneers in Tony Dungy's debut as Tampa Bay head coach. The Packers' defense harassed Bucs quarterback Trent Dilfer into a horrible day. He completed just 13 of 30 passes for only 123 yards and 4 interceptions.

Edgar Bennett and Dorsey Levens combined for 110 yards on 25 carries. Brett Favre threw 4 touchdown passes and was 20 of 27 for 247 yards and no interceptions.

Sep. 9th PACKERS 39, PHILADELPHIA 13 AT GREEN BAY

Coaching against two of his former assistants—Eagles head coach Ray Rhodes and offensive coordinator Jon Gruden (who would later become a head coach himself)—Mike Holmgren's Packers opened their home season on a Monday night by throttling Philadelphia.

After missing on his first 5 passes, Brett Favre settled down and roasted the Eagles, completing 17 of his last 26 passes for 261 yards, 3 touchdowns, and no interceptions. Many of the plays did not turn out as scripted, but were nevertheless successful—a trait that made Favre so difficult to defense. Rick Spielman, Detroit's assistant director of pro personnel, had this to say about Favre after watching the game to scout the Packers, "Unbelievable . . . the way he improvises and finds the open receiver . . . he's the best quarterback in the league right now and no one comes close to him."

Sep. 15th PACKERS 42, SAN DIEGO 10 AT GREEN BAY

Green Bay notched its third straight lopsided win to start the season. The Packers outscored their first three opponents 115–6.

After the game, Packers' head coach Mike Holmgren was asked to compare this team to the Lombardi Packers. He replied, "That would be very flattering, but I have always said that that group of men and Coach Lombardi and that era will never be duplicated. Now, if we can approach some of that at some point, great."

Green Bay recorded 5 sacks, including 2 each by Reggie White and Sean Jones. Including the sacks, San Diego gained only 108 passing yards on 40 attempts.

Sep. 22nd MINNESOTA 30, PACKERS 21 AT MINNESOTA

Green Bay lost its fifth consecutive game at the Metrodome and fell a game behind the undefeated Vikings in the NFC Central. The Packers' offensive line couldn't block Minnesota defensive tackle John Randle and his cohorts, as the Vikings got 7 sacks and disrupted Green Bay's passing game. The Minnesota defense also shut down Green Bay's running game: Edgar Bennett and William Henderson gained just 35 yards on 13 attempts.

Sep. 29th PACKERS 31, SEATTLE 10 AT SEATTLE

The Packers forced 5 turnovers, including 4 interceptions, to help Green Bay breeze past the Seahawks. Green Bay had forced 22 turnovers after five games. In 19 games in 1995 (including the playoffs) Packers' opponents committed 22 turnovers. Packers' GM Ron Wolf attributed the increase in turnovers to the faster defense.

The last score of the game was one of those plays that you'll see if you watch enough NFL Films shows. On third-and-goal from the Seattle 5, Favre scrambled to his left and looked like he would try to run it in. Then, as he sucked in a couple of Seahawks' defenders, he flipped the ball, back-handed, to Antonio Freeman for the touchdown. It was Favre's fourth TD pass of the game.

Oct. 6th PACKERS 37, CHICAGO 6 AT CHICAGO

In the 152nd meeting between the Packers and the Bears, this was Green Bay's third-largest margin of victory over Chicago.

The Packers scored 20 points in the second quarter to take a 20–3 halftime lead after a scoreless first quarter. The first touchdown drive was set up when blitzing safety LeRoy Butler tackled Bears running back Rashaan Salaam for a 14-yard loss, forcing the Bears to punt from their end zone.

Three long scoring plays put the game away: a 50-yard pass from Favre to Freeman on a "Hail Mary" pass at the end of the first half, a 90-yard kickoff return by Don Beebe in the third quarter, and a 35-yard pass to Freeman also in the third quarter. Brett Favre threw another 4 touchdown passes, bringing his total to 20 in his first six games.

Oct. 14th PACKERS 23, SAN FRANCISCO 20 (OT) AT GREEN BAY

In a much-anticipated Monday night game, the Packers had to go into overtime to beat the persistent 49ers on a 53-yard field goal by Chris Jacke. San Francisco played without injured quarterback Steve Young, but its defense pressured Brett Favre and shut down the Packers' ground game. Favre threw 61 passes, but completed just 28 and averaged less than 6½ yards per attempt. Green Bay's running backs gained just 44 yards on 20 carries. The 49ers didn't move the ball well against the Packers, either. San Francisco gained just 253 total yards, including 74 rushing yards on 28 attempts.

Packers starting wide receiver Robert Brooks suffered a knee injury on Green Bay's first play from scrimmage, an injury that sidelined him for the rest of the season.

Oct. 27th PACKERS 13, TAMPA BAY 7 AT GREEN BAY

After their bye week, Green Bay's offense looked sluggish and lost another starting wide receiver despite winning. Antonio Freeman broke a bone in his left forearm, causing him to miss four games. Still, the Packers' defense was overwhelming. Tampa Bay head coach Tony Dungy said, "They might be the best defense that I've seen in the last six or seven years."

Nov. 3rd PACKERS 28, DETROIT 18 AT GREEN BAY

Brett Favre's 4 touchdowns passes and 281 yards in the air trumped Barry Sanders's 152 yards rushing as the Packers set a Lambeau Field record with their twelfth consecutive home win. In their last 24 home games, regular season and playoff, Green Bay stood 23–1.

Detroit's defensive line coach John Teerlinck had nothing but praise for the Packers, "They've got a great team here. It's the best Green Bay Packer team in my five years in the division." Teerlinck said of Favre, "You see why he was MVP. He is such a great, great player."

Nov. 10th KANSAS CITY 27, PACKERS 20 AT KANSAS CITY

Led by Greg Hill's 94 rushing yards, Kansas City ran for 182 yards and hit some big pass plays, the Chiefs gained 204 yards passing on just 9 completions, to beat the favored Packers in front of a typically rabid Arrowhead Stadium crowd.

Nov. 18th DALLAS 21, PACKERS 6 AT DALLAS

Green Bay lost its seventh consecutive game at Texas Stadium, and eighth overall to Dallas, getting overmatched on a Monday night. Packers GM Ron Wolf was not pleased, "This is professional football. People have to step up and perform. To me, this was an embarrassing game for the Green Bay Packers."

While Green Bay kept Dallas out of the end zone, the Cowboys' Chris Boniol kicked 7 field goals, the Dallas defense was more effective. The Packers gained just over 250 yards of offense. Brett Favre was constantly under pressure and threw for just 194 yards on 37 attempts. Green Bay punted on their first seven possessions and didn't score until 1:53 left in the game.

Boniol's 7 field goals tied the NFL record for a game, but the last one came when Dallas called a timeout with 24 seconds left. Needless to say, the Packers didn't appreciate it. On the ensuing kickoff, many players from both teams ran onto the field and three players were ejected from the game after the scuffle—not that ejecting a player with 10 seconds left in a game means anything. Packers safety LeRoy Butler said, "I just thought it showed no class. To let the kicker come out with 10 or 15 seconds left and let him get a record shows no class. I had a lot of respect for the organization, but I don't anymore."

Nov. 24th PACKERS 24, ST. LOUIS 9 AT ST. LOUIS

Green Bay bounced back after again falling behind early. The Packers, trailing 9–0 late in the first half, gained 178 of their 243 yards and made 13 of their 15 first downs in the second half. Green Bay's Doug Evans scored a 32-yard interception return on the second play of the second half to give the Packers a lead that they kept the rest of the way.

Dec. 1st PACKERS 28, CHICAGO 17 AT GREEN BAY

Antonio Freeman returned from his injury and caught a career high 10 passes for 156 yards and Desmond Howard broke a 7–7 third quarter tie with a 75-yard touchdown punt return as Green Bay beat Chicago for the sixth straight time. Brett Favre had an efficient game, completing 19 of 27 passes for 231 yards with 1 touchdown and no interceptions.

Packers special teams coach Nolan Cromwell had been telling his players all week that they would break a return for a touchdown. Howard said, "Coach Nolan saw something from day one, because as soon as we had a meeting he was telling us how we're going to score a touchdown."

Dec. 8th PACKERS 41, DENVER 6 AT GREEN BAY

Green Bay's easy win over Denver clinched the NFC Central title for the Packers. Remember that Denver had already clinched home field advantage throughout the AFC playoffs.

Antonio Freeman had another big day wtih 9 catches for 175 yards and 3 touchdowns, and Dorsey Levens gained 86 yards on 14 carries. Green Bay outgained Denver 379 yards to 176 and had a 22 to 9 advantage in first downs.

Dec. 15th PACKERS 31, DETROIT 10 AT DETROIT

Brett Favre threw for 231 yards and 3 touchdowns in the second half in Green Bay's win. The defense kept Barry Sanders in check this time; he gained just 78 yards on 21 attempts. Lions quarterback Scott Mitchell completed 23 of 40 passes, but only for 207 yards. He was also sacked four times, twice by Reggie White who played an outstanding game, and threw an interception.

Desmond Howard broke the NFL single season record for punt return yards when he ran one back 92 yards for a touchdown at the beginning of the second quarter. (See "Redemption for Mr. Heisman.")

Dec. 22nd PACKERS 38, MINNESOTA 10 AT GREEN BAY

In a game with a lot of trash talking and late hits, Green Bay dominated the Vikings to clinch home field advantage.

Vince Lombardi would have been proud of the Packers in this game, as they used a power running attack to gain 233 yards on the ground and hold the ball for 37 minutes. Edgar Bennett ran for 109 yards on just 18 carries, while Dorsey Levens and Travis Jervey ran for 108 yards on 16 rushes.

Brett Favre threw 3 touchdown passes to finish the season with 39. At the time, only Dan Marino had ever thrown more touchdown passes in a season.

Divisional Playoff:

Jan. 4th PACKERS 35, SAN FRANCISCO 14 AT GREEN BAY

Desmond Howard's 71-yard TD punt return 2:15 into the game gave the Packers a lead they would never relinquish at muddy Lambeau Field, although Green Bay did have some scary moments due to two special teams mistakes.

Howard's 46-yard punt return set up the Packers' second touchdown of the first quarter, a 4-yard pass from Brett Favre to Andre Rison, and a Craig Newsome interception set up a short second-quarter touchdown to put Green Bay up 21–0.

Late in the first half, though, a 49ers' punt bounced off the leg of Green Bay's Chris Hayes and San Francisco recovered at the Green Bay 26. The 49ers scored with 24 seconds left in the half.

The next miscue was a weird one. Desmond Howard was late getting out of the locker room to receive the second-half kickoff, so Andre Rison was hastily dispatched for the return while the ball was being kicked. San Francisco's Steve Israel beat Rison to the ball and recovered at the Green Bay 4. (Remember that a kickoff is a free ball once it has traveled 10 yards.) The 49ers scored to cut the Packers' lead to 21–14.

Green Bay then executed a 12-play, 72-yard TD drive, primarily on the ground, but even that drive ended strangely. Edgar Bennett fumbled short of the goal line, but Green Bay's Antonio Freeman recovered the ball in the end zone for the TD.

The Packers' defense put the squeeze on the 49ers the rest of the way. San Francisco lost quarterback Steve Young when his rib injuries proved too severe to continue.

After the game, Bill Walsh said of his former assistant coach Mike Holmgren, "I think he has a complete, fully dimensional team. I think they've got an excellent formula and I'm hopeful they go all the way."

NFC Championship:

Jan. 12th PACKERS 30, CAROLINA 13 AT GREEN BAY

The Panthers scored first, capitalizing on Sam Mills's interception, but the Packers ran over Carolina to earn Green Bay's first Super Bowl trip in 29 years. The Panthers, playing in the conference championship game in just their second season in the league, used 2 turnovers to take a 10–7 second-quarter lead.

The key sequence in the game occurred late in the first half. Green Bay scored with less than a minute left to take the 14–10 lead. The Packers' Tyrone Williams then intercepted Kerry Collins at Green Bay's 38-yard line with 35 seconds left. Two Favre passes of 23 and 25 yards got the Packers in position for a Chris Jacke field goal to extend the lead to 17–10.

In the second half, the Packers pounded away at the Panthers' defense. Carolina linebacker Kevin Greene was surprised by the Packers' dominance, "I would have never guessed we would come in here and have our butts handed to us like we did today. Another thing I never would have believed is that a team could run the ball on us like they did."

Green Bay gained 201 yards rushing, well above their regular-season average of 115 yards. Dorsey Levens had a huge day, running for 88 yards on just 10 carries in addition to 5 catches for 117 yards. Brett Favre was sharp in the freezing weather—the wind chill factor was near zero—completing 19 of 29 passes for 292 yards, 2 touchdowns, and just Mills's early interception.

Super Bow XXXI:

Jan. 26th PACKERS 35, NEW ENGLAND 21 AT NEW ORLEANS

Desmond Howard did it again. His 99-yard kickoff return in the third quarter halted the underdog Patriots' comeback and helped bring the Lombardi Trophy back to Green Bay.

Trailing 27–14 at halftime, the Patriots thrust themselves back in the game with a seven-play, 53-yard touchdown drive capped by Curtis Martin's 18-yard run with 3:27 left in the third quarter. Howard then ran the ensuing kickoff back all the way.

The game started very up-tempo. Green Bay scored on its second play from scrimmage, a 54-yard touchdown pass from Brett Favre to Andre Rison, after Favre called an audible. A Doug Evans interception was later turned into a field goal for a 10–0 lead. New England, however, scored on its next two possessions to go up 14–10 at the end of the first quarter.

The Packers scored just 56 seconds into the second quarter when Antonio Freeman burned Patriots safety Lawyer Milloy for a Super Bowl-record 81-yard touchdown catch. Green Bay got a field goal on its next drive to take a 20–14 lead, then converted a Mike Prior interception into a touchdown on a 74-yard drive for a 27–14 halftime lead.

Once Howard gave the Packers a 14-point lead again, Green Bay's defense took over. Reggie White had 3 sacks in the second half, twice simply tossing aside New England offensive tackle Max Lane to get to Drew Bledsoe. This was White's first football championship of any kind.

Once again, someone asked Packers head coach Mike Holmgren to compare this team to the Lombardi Packers, and whether or not his team could be a dynasty. His answer was, "Oh, my goodness. A dynasty in this day and age, I'm not sure if anyone could ever match what the Packers of the 1960s did."

The Patriots acquitted themselves well. They came back twice after falling behind early. New England head coach Bill Parcells saw one key factor in the game's outcome, "Both teams pressured the quarterbacks fairly well. The difference was special teams. That was the worst we've been outplayed this year."

To that end, Green Bay's Desmond Howard became the first special teams player to be named Super Bowl Most Valuable Player. Besides the kick return touchdown, Howard returned 6 punts for 90 yards and in all compiled 244 return yards. Howard was proud, but not too boastful after the game, "There's an old saying that the cream always rises to the top. I was just another strong link in this very, very strong chain. You have such talent on this team that you just want to contribute. . . . I never would have imagined that I would have won MVP of the Super Bowl."

Elsewhere Around the NFL:

Sep. 1st The NFL made its official return to Baltimore, as the Ravens defeated the Raiders 19–14 at Memorial Stadium in the regular-season opener. I guess this is as good a place to say this as anywhere. To all of the many Ravens bashers in the media and elsewhere: Let it go! Maybe Cleveland didn't "deserve" to lose its team, but Cleveland got a far better deal than Baltimore did after the Colts left. Cleveland was guaranteed the return of a team at a known time, got to keep the name, colors, and history, and the NFL even helped finance the new stadium. Baltimore, and the other cities whose NFL teams left, got nothing.

Nov. 3rd Jerry Rice became the first NFL player to record 1,000 career receptions as San Francisco beat stubborn New Orleans 24–17. Rice's 9-yard catch set up Steve Young's 2-yard touchdown run late in the fourth quarter, which was ultimately the difference in the game.

Nov. 10th Dan Marino became the first NFL player to reach 50,000 career passing yards, as Miami routed Indianapolis 37–13 at Pro Player Stadium. He reached the milestone on a 36-yard pass to O. J. McDuffie in the second quarter and that was a key play in a Dolphins' drive that ended with a Marino touchdown pass to Fred Barnett. For the day, Marino completed 17 of 24 passes for 204 yards and 3 touchdowns.

Dec. 8th Kerry Collins's 3 touchdown passes helped the Carolina Panthers defeat the San Francisco 49ers 30–24 at San Francisco and become the first team to clinch a playoff berth in their second season. This was Carolina's fifth straight win; they would finish the season with seven straight to end the season 12–4 and win the NFC West title. Amazingly, the Panthers and their sophomore brethren, the Jaguars, reached their respective conference title games.

What Happened the Next Season:

The Packers had another very good season in 1997, finishing with a 13–3 record and the NFC Central title for the second consecutive year. Brett Favre threw 35 touchdown passes and won his third straight MVP award, sharing this one with the Lions' Barry Sanders. Antonio Freeman and Robert Brooks both stayed healthy and combined for 141 catches for 2,253 yards and 19 touchdowns. Running back Edgar Bennett missed the entire 1997 season with an Achilles tendon injury, but Dorsey Levens stepped up and had a great year, rushing for 1,435 yards and catching 53 passes.

Green Bay made it back to the Super Bowl as heavy favorites over the Broncos, who made the big game as a Wild Card. In an exciting contest, Denver upset the Packers 31–24 for the first AFC Super Bowl win in 14 years. I guess the oddsmakers who made Green Bay a 12-point favorite never heard of Adjusted Power Index (API). Green Bay's API was good at +4.46; Denver's was very good at +6.43. (You'll recall from the introduction, my rule to only include division champions—so that keeps the Broncos from having their own chapter.)

Redemption for Mr. Heisman

On November 23, 1991, in the annual big game between Michigan and Ohio State, Desmond Howard ran back a punt 93 yards for a touchdown in the Wolverines' 31–3 rout of the Buckeyes. That return would probably not be remembered today by many people, except that Howard struck the Heisman pose in the end zone after he scored. Three weeks later, Howard indeed won the Heisman Trophy. He received 85 percent of the first-place votes, the highest percentage ever, and won with the third-largest margin of victory ever.

It's hard to say that he didn't deserve the award. Howard caught 19 touchdown passes, including a diving, game-winning touchdown against Notre Dame, and scored 23 touchdowns in all. He became the first receiver in Big Ten history to lead the conference in scoring.

Howard's future looked bright. He passed up his last year of eligibility at Michigan to enter the NFL. The Redskins traded up so they could pick him at number 4 in the first round in 1992. Despite a "quiet" rookie season, Washington's confidence in Howard was one of the reasons they didn't make much of an effort to re-sign Gary Clark.

Things didn't exactly work out as the Redskins and Howard had hoped. After two years as a part-time receiver and return man, the Redskins made Howard a starting wide receiver in 1994, taking him out of the return role. Although he had a good average per catch (over 18 yards) on 40 receptions, the Redskins left him exposed in the 1995 expansion draft and Jacksonville selected him. This time, he wasn't a high pick. Howard was the twenty-eighth player taken by the Jaguars and the fifty-sixth overall selection. He lasted one year in Jacksonville before being released.

The Packers invited Howard to training camp in 1996, liked what he showed them, and signed him to a one-year contract at just little over the NFL minimum salary. Finally, things worked out for Howard, at least for one season. In particular, his season as a punt returner was extraordinary. Of course, Howard is more remembered for his 99-yard kickoff return for a touchdown in the Super Bowl, but he was much better returning punts that season.

Howard's 15.09 punt return average led the NFL, and his 875 punt return yards shattered the old record of 692 set by Fulton Walker in 1985. While his average wasn't an NFL record, it was very impressive given that his 58 returns were the third most in a season ever. Comparing his average to the league average and weighting for the number of returns (the same concept I used to calculate "net" rushing yards for running backs), Howard's "net" punt return yardage was +293. To be honest, I didn't feel compelled to calculate the net punt return yards number for every player since 1950, but here are a few of the best punt return seasons of the past 15 years or so, including the net yardage:

Player	Year	Team	Ret	Yds	Avg	Lg Avg	Net Ret Yds
Irving Fryar	1985	NE	37	520	14.05	8.63	+201
Walter Stanley	1989	DET	36	496	13.78	9.11	+168
Mel Gray	1991	DET	25	385	15.40	8.74	+167
Deion Sanders	1998	DAL	24	375	15.63	10.00	+135
Jermaine Lewis	2000	BAR	36	578	16.06	9.98	+219

How about some earlier examples? In 1968 Bob Hayes averaged 20.80 yards per punt return, whereas the league average was just 7.05. Hayes had just 15 punt returns that year (of his team's 30); his net return yardage of +206 is not that close to Howard's +293 in 1996, and not even as high as Jermaine Lewis's 2000 number. Hayes's 1968 season is an extreme example because very few players have averaged 20+ yards per punt return; that year was the last time any NFL player has done it.

One more example: in 1975, Billy "White Shoes" Johnson averaged 15.30 yards per return on 40 punt returns; the league average was 9.19. Johnson's net return yardage was +244, which is excellent, but still about 50 yards short of Desmond Howard in 1996.

Howard's Super Bowl MVP performance came at a good time for him. He was a free agent after the season and he signed a four-year, $6 million contract with the Raiders in 1997. He was later a salary cap casualty and was waived after two seasons in Oakland. He briefly returned to Green Bay in 1999, only to move on to Detroit that year.

Through the 2001 season, Howard had 8 touchdowns on punt returns—tied for second most in NFL history. While he has not been the wide receiver everyone expected him to be, he has achieved a great deal as a punt returner, including his brilliant 1996 season. For one year at least, Howard redeemed himself and made a significant mark in the NFL.

The Coach: Mike Holmgren

Coaching Record (with Packers Only)

	W	L	Pct	
1992	9	7	.563	
1993	9	7	.563	NFC Wild Card
1994	9	7	.563	NFC Wild Card
1995	11	5	.688	NFC Central Division title
1996	13	3	.813	NFC Central Division title; NFC champs; Super Bowl champs
1997	13	3	.813	NFC Central Division title; NFC champs
1998	11	5	.688	NFC Wild Card
Total	**75**	**37**	**.670**	

In 1991, Green Bay was 4–12. In the seven seasons before Holmgren became head coach, the Packers' record was 41–69–1 with just one winning season among the seven.

Continuing the theme of how interconnected pro football history is, Holmgren was the 49ers quarterbacks coach under Bill Walsh from 1986 to 1988, and offensive coordinator under George Seifert from 1989 to 1991. Holmgren was also on the staff of legendary BYU coach Lavell Edwards from 1982 to 1985.

I'll repeat something I once wrote for ESPN.com regarding football coaching and higher education. Holmgren has a bachelors degree. Both Walsh and Seifert have masters degrees. The media generally thinks it's amazing when a baseball manager has a college degree of any kind, but it's not such a big deal in football. Eight of the 31 NFL head coaches (about 26 percent) who started the 2000 season have graduate degrees. According to the Census Bureau, only about 7 percent of all Americans aged 25 or older have graduate degrees. (Please, no George O'Leary jokes.)

It wasn't grade point average that Packers general manager Ron Wolf was concerned with when he started his search for a head coach after the 1991 season. Wolf, on the job only since November 1991, supposedly went after Bill Parcells as his first choice for head coach. Stop me if you've heard this before–Parcells wasn't interested in the job. That's not a knock at Parcells, but it's hard to say that Holmgren wasn't the right man for the job. Wolf hired Holmgren in January 1992 and promised that he would never acquire a player that Holmgren didn't want. About a month later, Wolf had a chance to get a backup second-year quarterback from the Atlanta Falcons. True to his word, he first asked Holmgren if he wanted this player. Holmgren's answer: "He can be a good one." Wolf traded a first-round pick for Brett Favre. Holmgren and Wolf had both been at Favre's pre-draft workout in 1991 at Southern Mississippi, although at the time Wolf was working for the Jets and Holmgren was still with the 49ers.

Despite no head coaching experience at either the collegiate or professional level before Green Bay hired him, Holmgren didn't seem overwhelmed by the position. Gil Haskell, a Holmgren assistant for six years, explained, "My impression is that he has prepared himself to be a head coach. Many people get head coaching jobs that never expected to get them. He didn't; he's been planning this for some time."

In an article about Holmgren on the Packers' web site, Wolf talked about what made him successful, "Mike Holmgren is interested in one thing–and one thing only–and that's winning ball games. He's very special at teaching players how to play and communicating with players. He also has tremendous dignity and character. I think all those qualities come through to our football team. I think that's the reason why the Packers are as successful as they have been under his tenure."

Holmgren left the Packers in 1999 to be become head coach and GM of the Seattle Seahawks. After a disappointing 2000 season and slow start in 2001, there was grumbling that Holmgren's stay in Seattle could be shorter than expected. While it's hard to know if Holmgren's approach changed or if the dual role is too much, former players like Packers safety LeRoy Butler still have confidence in him. As Butler told ESPN's Chris Mortenson, "Why not let him teach you what he taught us here? Mike knows what it takes.

He knows how to coach. He's the one who has the Super Bowl ring. He took us to the big game twice." In a way, Holmgren might be a victim of his past success, as his record in Green Bay no doubt raised expectations in Seattle.

Continuing the Paul Brown/Bill Walsh lineage, many of Holmgren's former assistant coaches are now NFL head coaches. During the 2001 season, six head coaches were former assistants with Holmgren; five of them led their teams to the playoffs. The legacy goes on.

The Quarterback: Brett Favre

Year	Team	Att	Comp	Yds	TD	Int	YPA	Rating	Lg Avg	W	L	Pct
1991	ATL	5	0	0	0	2	0.00	0.0	76.2	0	0	—
1992	GB	471	302	3,227	18	13	6.85	85.3	75.3	8	5	.615
1993	GB	522	318	3,303	19	24	6.33	72.2	76.7	9	7	.563
1994	GB	582	363	3,882	33	14	6.67	90.7	78.4	9	7	.563
1995	GB	570	359	4,413	38	13	7.74	99.5	79.2	11	5	.688
1996	GB	543	325	3,899	39	13	7.18	95.8	76.9	13	3	.813
1997	GB	513	304	3,867	35	16	7.54	92.6	77.2	13	3	.813
1998	GB	551	347	4,212	31	23	7.64	87.8	78.3	11	5	.688
1999	GB	597	342	4,101	22	23	6.87	74.7	77.1	8	8	.500
2000	GB	580	338	3,812	20	16	6.57	78.0	78.1	9	7	.563
2001	GB	510	314	3,921	32	15	7.69	94.1	78.5	12	4	.750
Total		**5,444**	**3,312**	**38,637**	**287**	**172**	**7.10**	**86.8**	**77.4**	**103**	**54**	**.656**
1994–98		2,759	1,698	20,273	176	79	7.35	93.3	78.0	57	23	.713

YPA = Yards Per Pass Attempt
Rating = Passer Rating
Lg Avg = League Passer Rating in that season
W, L, Pct = Team's Record in his starts

As I wrote earlier, Brett Favre was not originally drafted by Green Bay. He was drafted by Atlanta in the second round in 1991. If you're wondering how a player like Favre could slip to the second round, drafted after 32 other players, including two quarterbacks (would you believe Dan McGwire and Todd Marinovich?), bear in mind that even with all of the testing and measuring of players' skills, scouting football players is an inexact science. Remember Joe Montana? There were also some health concerns about Favre. He had recently undergone shoulder surgery, and he was involved in a serious car accident the summer before his senior year in college—30 inches of intestine were surgically removed because of the accident. He had the surgery on August 8, 1990, and started for Southern Mississippi exactly a month later against Alabama. The Golden Eagles beat the Crimson Tide, the first time they had beaten Alabama in 15 years.

Then there's the question of how the Falcons could have traded Favre in February 1992. Atlanta received a first-round draft choice for him (it wasn't even Green Bay's pick, it was Philadelphia's; the Packers had acquired that draft choice in a trade in April 1991), but the Falcons sent the pick to Dallas in another trade. When the dust settled, Atlanta had two first-round picks in 1992, which they used on Bob Whitfield and Tony Smith. Smith, a college teammate of Brett Favre's, turned out to be a major bust.

To be fair, the Falcons had a good quarterback at the time in Chris Miller, a former first-round pick. Miller had led Atlanta into the playoffs in 1991 and was one of only five NFL quarterbacks with at least 20 touchdown passes that year. An ironic twist to all this is that while Miller's career faded with a string of concussions, Favre became the most durable quarterback in NFL history, not to mention a three-time league MVP and the cornerstone of one of the best teams in history.

As impressive as Favre's numbers are, I think they would be "better" if he didn't try to make the impossible play, the impossible throw every now and then. I'm talking primarily about his passer rating. I'm not necessarily saying that he would be a better or more effective quarterback; I just believe he wouldn't throw quite as many interceptions and that he would complete a higher percentage of his passes (which would also affect his average gain per attempt) if he didn't take so many chances throwing the ball.

On the other hand, it's that willingness to go for the high-risk/high-reward play that enables Favre to make so many big plays. I also think that attitude earns him the respect and admiration of his teammates, which makes Favre a more effective leader.

There's no doubt that Favre leaves a powerful subjective impression on those who watch him play. During Green Bay's championship 1996 season, former Packers quarterback Bart Starr said of Favre, "I've never seen a quarterback who possessed so much talent at this stage of his career." Recently, Cincinnati Bengals' scouting director Jim Lippincott said, "You don't want to play against him. I think he's the kind of guy who you can jump on his back and he can carry you to victory."

Former foe (as a Chicago Bear) and current teammate Jim Flanigan remarked, "When you've got a player like that, you've always got a chance to win and you're never out of a game. It just gives the whole team a tremendous sense of confidence. That's what I noticed coming into this locker room. Brett's a guy who players look up to constantly." Vikings linebacker Kailee Wong commented, "You just know that he can get hot. When he gets hot, he goes really quickly. It only really takes one play for him to get going, and that whole team is energized."

As Norman Chad of *The Washington Post* noted, "Brett Favre is most enduring in our minds because of his infectious style–the way he bounces around the field like a kid, the way he thrives in freezing weather, the way he pretends to fake a handoff by then throwing a ball he does not have."

People like me, who use numbers more than most to look at sports, are often accused of knowing the cost of everything and the value of nothing (borrowing the cliché that critcizes financial types). When it comes down to it, I enjoy just watching sports. To me, enjoying the game and making objective analysis are not mutually exclusive. One of the reasons I like watching football is a player like Brett Favre. I marvel at his ability to throw the ball with accuracy and velocity, with touch when he needs to, or his ability to scramble just long enough to find an open receiver. I relish Favre's overt enthusiasm. I think that Favre is one of those rare players who transcends his numbers, who brings something to the game that can't be quantified.

1996 Green Bay Packers Statistics

Passing

	Att	Comp	Comp Pct	Yds	Yds Per	TD	Int	Rating
Favre	543	325	59.9%	3,899	7.18	39	13	95.8
McMahon	4	3	75.0%	39	9.75	0	0	105.2
Hentrich	1	0	0.0%	0	0.00	0	0	39.6
Packers	**548**	**328**	**59.9%**	**3,938**	**7.19**	**39**	**13**	**95.7**
Opponents	544	283	52.0%	2,942	5.41	12	26	55.4
League Average			57.6%		6.68			76.9

Packers' passers were sacked 40 times for 241 yards in losses.
The Packers sacked their opponents 37 times for 202 yards in losses.

Brett Favre was edged out by Steve Young for the NFL passing title in 1996; Young posted a 97.2 rating. (I'm sure Young would have traded the passing title for the Lombardi Trophy.) In addition, Young missed four games with injuries and threw 227 fewer passes than Favre. Let me see what I can do with this...

1996	Att	Rating	DIFF	PROD 1	REL	PROD 2
Favre	543	95.8	18.9	+10,263	1.25	+676
Young	316	97.2	20.3	+6,415	1.26	+399

The fourth column (DIFF) is the difference between the individual rating and the league rating.
The fifth column (PROD 1) is that difference times the number of pass attempts.
The sixth column (REL) is the individual rating divided by the league average.
The seventh column (PROD 2) is that ratio times the number of attempts.

To me, it seems like common sense that, all other things being equal, a quarterback with an above average passing rating is more valuable the more passes he throws. If a baseball player has a .600 slugging percentage, he would be more valuable to his team if he had 500 at bats than if he had 300. The intendment of all of this mathematical machination (or lunacy, I've heard it before) is to show that Favre's season had more value because he played more. Both of his "products" (PROD 1 and PROD 2) were clearly higher than Young's.

I think this is an important point. Of course, different offensive systems ask their quarterback to do different things, but that doesn't mean that all statistical comparisons are useless. Why do we keep stats then?

As a team, the 1996 Packers led the league in both offensive passing rating and lowest passing rating allowed. They are also one of four teams since 1978, the beginning of the rules regime that tilted the balance in favor of throwing the ball, to have a passing rating at least 40 points higher than their opponents. Who are the other three? The 1989 49ers, the 1994 49ers, and the 1999 Rams. They all won the Super Bowl and they are all in this book.

Rushing

	Att	Yds	Avg	Net Yards	TD
Bennett	222	899	4.05	+45	2
Levens	121	566	4.68	+100	5
Favre	49	136	2.78		2
Henderson	39	130	3.33		0
Jervey	26	106	4.08		0
R. Brooks	4	2	0.50		0
McMahon	4	−1	−0.25		0
Packers	**465**	**1,838**	**3.95**	**+49**	**9**
Opponents	400	1,416	3.54	−123	7
League Average			3.85		

The Packers had the highest ratio of passing touchdowns to rushing touchdowns of any team in the NFL in 1996. Green Bay managed an above average yards per carry despite not having a run longer than 24 yards.

Dorsey Levens had a breakout year; in his two previous seasons he had rushed for a total of 135 yards on 41 carries. He was a nice complement to Edgar Bennett, and Levens's speed helped to stretch opposing defenses on the flanks, which made the Packers' offense more complete and more potent. Levens had a marvelous 1997 season, replacing Bennett, who missed the year with an Achilles tendon injury.

Receiving

	Rec	Yds	Avg	TD
Freeman	56	933	16.66	9
Jackson	40	505	12.63	10
Beebe	39	699	17.92	4

(continued next page)

Receiving *(continued)*

	Rec	Yds	Avg	TD
Levens	31	226	7.29	5
Bennett	31	176	5.68	1
Chmura	28	370	13.21	0
Henderson	27	203	7.52	1
R. Brooks	23	344	14.96	4
Mickens	18	161	8.94	2
Rison	13	135	10.38	1
Howard	13	95	7.31	0
Mayes	6	46	7.67	2
Thomason	3	45	15.00	0
Packers	**328**	**3,938**	**12.01**	**39**
Opponents	283	2,942	10.40	12
League Average			11.60	

A rash of injuries that struck the Packers' receiving corps resulted in the large number of players with 10 or more catches. Wide receiver Robert Brooks suffered a season-ending knee injury in Green Bay's seventh game. Antonio Freeman broke a bone in his arm in the next game and ended up missing four games. Tight end Mark Chmura missed three games, two of those while Freeman was out. Don Beebe did an especially good job picking up the slack, setting a career high for receiving yardage in the process. Antonio Freeman's season looks very good when you factor in the four missing games. Freeman and I have something in common–geographically, at least–we both went to the same high school: Baltimore Polytechnic Institute, or Poly for short. That's where the similarities end.

Kickoff Returns

	Ret	Yds	Avg	TD
Howard	22	460	20.91	0
Beebe	15	403	26.87	1
Levens	5	84	16.80	0
Henderson	2	38	19.00	0
Thomason	1	20	20.00	0
Jervey	1	17	17.00	0
Freeman	1	16	16.00	0
Packers	**47**	**1,038**	**22.09**	**1**
Opponents	76	1,649	21.70	0
League Average			21.97	

Punt Returns

	Ret	Yds	Avg	TD
Howard	58	875	15.09	3
Opponents	29	237	8.17	0
League Average			10.04	

Desmond Howard obliterated the NFL record for punt return yards in a season. Howard led the league in average as well. (See "Redemption for Mr. Heisman.")

Interceptions

	Int	Yds	Avg	TD
E. Robinson	6	107	17.83	0
Butler	5	149	29.80	1
Evans	5	102	20.40	1
Koonce	3	84	28.00	1
Newsome	2	22	11.00	0
White	1	46	46.00	0
Prior	1	7	7.00	0
Dowden	1	5	5.00	0
Hollinquest	1	2	2.00	0
Simmons	1	0	0.00	0
Packers	**26**	**524**	**20.15**	**3**
Opponents	13	98	7.54	0

The Packers tied for the NFC lead (with St. Louis) in interceptions and finished second in the NFL behind Cincinnati's 34. Not that this has anything to do with the Packers, but the '96 Bengals are one of just four teams since 1990 with 30 or more interceptions in a season.

Sack Leaders

(Sacks have been an official statistic for individual players only since 1982.)

White	8.5
Butler	6.5
Dotson	5.5

It's rare when a safety finishes second on his team in sacks like LeRoy Butler did. Although this was the second time in the past three seasons that Reggie White finished with fewer than ten sacks, it was only the second time in 12 NFL seasons that he failed to reach double-digits. In his first nine years in the NFL, White had 137 sacks in 137 games.

Turnovers

Turnovers Committed:	24
Turnovers Forced:	39
Turnover +/–:	+15

Green Bay committed the second fewest turnovers in the league and was second in turnover margin.

Punting

	No	Avg
Hentrich	68	42.4
Opponents	90	43.1
League Average		42.9

Kicking

	XP	XPA	XP Pct	FG	FGA	FG Pct
Jacke	51	53	96.2%	21	27	77.8%
Opponents	17	17	100.0%	25	27	92.6%
League Average			98.6%			80.0%

Leading Scorer: Chris Jacke, 114 Points
Leading Scorer, Non-Kicker: Keith Jackson and Dorsey Levens, 60 Points

After eight years as Green Bay's kicker, Chris Jacke did not return in 1997. (The Packers picked Brett Conway in the third round of the 1997 draft, but Ryan Longwell ended up as their kicker.) Maybe Mike Holmgren saw that the other team's kickers almost never missed and wanted that for his team.

1996 Green Bay Packers Roster

Head Coach	Mike Holmgren
QB	Brett Favre
QB	Jim McMahon
QB	Doug Pederson
RB	Edgar Bennett
RB	William Henderson
RB	Travis Jervey
RB	Calvin Jones
RB	Dorsey Levens
RB	Brian Satterfield
WR/KR	Don Beebe
WR	Robert Brooks
WR	Antonio Freeman
WR/PR/KR	Desmond Howard
WR	Derrick Mayes
WR	Terry Mickens
WR	Anthony Morgan
WR	Andre Rison
TE	Mark Chmura
TE	Keith Jackson
TE	Kevin Smith
TE	Jeff Thomason
C	Mike Arthur
C/OT	Jeff Dellenbach
C	Gene McGuire
C	Frank Winters
OG/OT	Lindsay Knapp
OG	Marco Rivera
OG	Aaron Taylor
OG	Adam Timmerman
OT	Gary Brown
OT	Earl Dotson
OT	John Michels
OT	Ken Ruettgers
OT	Bruce Wilkerson
K	Chris Jacke
P	Craig Hentrich
DE	Shannon Clavelle
DE	Sean Jones
DE/LB	Keith McKenzie
DE	Reggie White
DE	Gabe Wilkins
DT	Gilbert Brown
DT	Santana Dotson
DT	Darius Holland
DT	Bob Kuberski
LB	Ron Cox
LB	Bernardo Harris
LB	Lamont Hollinquest
LB	George Koonce
LB	Wayne Simmons
LB	Brian Williams
DB	LeRoy Butler
DB	Corey Dowden
DB	Doug Evans
DB	Chris Hayes
DB	Roderick Mullen
DB	Craig Newsome
DB	Mike Prior
DB	Eugene Robinson
DB	Michael Robinson
DB	Tyrone Williams

CHAPTER 13

1999 St. Louis Rams: The New Look of the NFL

STARTING LINEUP – 1999 RAMS

Offense		Defense	
SE	Torry Holt	LE	Kevin Carter
LT	Orlando Pace	LT	Ray Agnew
LG	Tom Nutten	RT	D'Marco Farr
C	Mike Gruttadauria	RE	Grant Wistrom
RG	Adam Timmerman	LLB	Mike Jones
RT	Fred Miller	MLB	London Fletcher
TE	Roland Williams	RLB	Todd Collins
FL	Isaac Bruce	LCB	Todd Lyght
QB	Kurt Warner	RCB	Dexter McCleon
RB	Marshall Faulk	SS	Billy Jenkins
RB	Robert Holcombe	FS	Keith Lyle/Devin Bush

The 1999 Rams Super Bowl championship season is a microcosm of the modern NFL. In 1998, the Rams were 4–12. From 1994 through 1998, they were 26–54. The salary cap and true free agency, instituted in 1993, prevent any team from hoarding talent for a long period of time, so that gives unsuccessful teams a meaningful opportunity to improve. It seems unlikely now that a team could have 20 consecutive winning seasons like the Cowboys did from 1966 through 1985.

As further representations of the way NFL football is played today, consider these points:

- The Rams won in a manner perceived as "untraditional" by football purists, with an aggressive passing attack as the core of their team. That approach would have been unusual, to say the least, in an earlier era, particularly before rules changes designed to help the passing game began to be implemented in the late 1970s.
- The two 1999 Super Bowl teams were franchises who had changed venue. Before Al Davis's lawsuit against the NFL in the early 1980s, teams seldom moved. Since then, six franchises have moved including Davis's Raiders who have moved twice.

- The flipside of the new NFL is that the standings have almost become too volatile, that rosters are almost too fluid. It can be hard to know if a team is really good or just a one-year wonder. Accelerated player movement can make it difficult for fans to know who's playing for whom. Accelerated franchise movement can make it impossible for fans to root for anybody.

Almost nothing in life is all good or all bad. I suspect the new NFL will continue to be the king of American sports.

In the wake of another dismal season in a dismal decade of football, the Rams made some changes after the 1998 season in an effort to jumpstart the franchise. Changes included Mike Martz's return to the Rams, now as offensive coordinator, and the signing of free agents such as quarterback Trent Green, guard Adam Timmerman, and linebacker Todd Collins. Of course, no mention of the offseason changes would be complete without including the trade for Marshall Faulk. The Rams gave up two draft picks, their 1999 second- and fifth-round picks, to acquire Faulk from the Colts.

Green injured his knee in the 1999 preseason, opening the door for an unknown quarterback named Kurt Warner. Toss in two top-notch wide receivers—finally healthy Isaac Bruce and 1999 first-round pick Torry Holt—to the aforementioned additions, and presto, you've got a Super Bowl title. The retooled Rams' offense has been terrorizing the NFL ever since.

Team in a Box

Record: 13–3

From 1990 through 1998, the Rams' record was a miserable 45–99 with no winning seasons and thousands of disinterested fans in two cities. In their first four years in St. Louis (1995–98), their record was 22–42.

The Rams began the 1999 season with six consecutive lopsided wins; they outscored their opponents 217–63 in the six games with 17 points as the smallest margin of victory. (See "Game-by-Game.") Those six wins were more than the season total in six of the Rams' previous nine seasons.

None of the Rams' 13 regular season wins was by fewer than 13 points.

Against Teams Over .500: 0–1, 21 Points Scored, 24 Points Allowed

Obviously, this is unimpressive, both in terms of results and in the number of games. Of all the teams in the book, the 1999 Rams have the least imposing credentials against winning teams.

The only game against a winning team during the regular season was against the Tennessee Titans, a team that the Rams would play again in a slightly more important game.

Points Scored/Allowed: 526/242 (1999 NFL Average: 333)

Among all teams since 1950, and that's over 1,000 team-seasons, the 1999 Rams' +17.8 per-game point differential is the third best. Yes, their schedule wasn't very tough (see "Opponents' Record"), but at least they blew out the patsies.

A tremendous point differential has two components. Although the Rams' defense kind of got lost in 1999 amidst all the accolades for the offense, it did its job well. Not only did the Rams allow fewer points (and fewer yards) than the league average, but the defense scored 8 touchdowns, including 7 interception returns for scores.

Yards Gained/Allowed: 6,412/4,698 (1999 NFL Average: 5,100)

Only 14 other teams since 1950 averaged at least 400 yards of offense per game. No NFL team between 1955 and 1979, inclusive, is among this group.

The Rams are one of the six teams in the book to rank among the top 20 since 1950 in average yards per-game differential. I have mentioned this with all of the relevant teams without revealing the best. Believe it or not, the 1953 Philadelphia Eagles had the best yards per-game differential at +151.1. The Rams rank eighteenth (+107.1).

Opponents' Record: 90–150, .375

(Not counting games against the Rams.)

How easy was the Rams' schedule in 1999? It was the second easiest since 1950. Who had the easiest schedule? See "The Long and Short of Schedules" in "Football Hodgepodge."

Adjusted Power Index:

Offense: +4.84
Defense: +2.07
TOTAL: +6.91

The distribution of the Rams' Power Indexes should come as no surprise. Their Offense Power Index ranks eighth among all teams since 1950; their Defense Power Index ranks in the top 15 percent, which isn't too bad, either.

I mentioned this in the "Greatest Offenses of All Time" article in the 1994 49ers chapter, but in case you haven't read that: the 2001 Rams had the highest Offense Power Index (+6.23) and the highest Adjusted Power Index (+8.40) of any team since 1950.

Innovations/What You Should Know:

It seems to me that the 1999–2001 Rams offense is at least as innovative in attitude as in tactics. At its core is the belief that an offense can take what it wants from a defense and that an offense can play at breakneck speed without self-destructing. For many years, NFL coaches believed in controlled offenses and taking what the defense would give them. The Rams' success makes me wonder if some other team (or teams) could have successfully adopted the same style before the Rams, if only they had possessed the courage to do so.

In chronological order, here are the teams that have averaged at least 8.50 yards per pass attempt since 1978:

Year	Team	Yards per Pass
1983	Green Bay Packers	8.91
1984	Miami Dolphins	9.00
1988	Cincinnati Bengals	9.16
1989	San Francisco 49ers	9.49
1990	Los Angeles Raiders	8.59
1993	San Francisco 49ers	8.55
1994	San Francisco 49ers	8.54
1998	Atlanta Falcons	8.83
1999	St. Louis Rams	8.64
2000	St. Louis Rams	9.36
2001	St. Louis Rams	8.90

These 11 teams had a combined 134–42 record; they played in seven Super Bowls and won three.

Homegrown First-Round Picks:

DB Todd Lyght, 1991; DE Kevin Carter, 1995; OT Orlando Pace, 1997; DE Grant Wistrom, 1998; WR Torry Holt, 1999.

This is not a large number of homegrown first-rounders. The two keys to the offense were Kurt Warner and Marshall Faulk; Warner was signed as a free agent in 1997 while Faulk, a former first-round pick of the Colts, was acquired by trade before the 1999 season. For example, all three starting linebackers were signed as free agents; outside linebackers Todd Collins and Mike Jones as unrestricted free agents from other teams and middle linebacker London Fletcher as an undrafted free agent.

Pro Bowl Players:

WR Isaac Bruce, DE Kevin Carter, DT D'Marco Farr, RB Marshall Faulk, DB Todd Lyght, OT Orlando Pace, G Adam Timmerman, QB Kurt Warner.

St. Louis had five Pro Bowl players who were not first-round Rams' draft picks. The Rams drafted Isaac Bruce (second round, 1994), traded for Marshall Faulk (Colts, 1999), signed Adam Timmerman as an unrestricted free agent (Packers, 1999), signed D'Marco Farr as an undrafted free agent in 1994, and signed Kurt Warner in December 1997, more than three years after he had been released by the Packers.

It's interesting to note that of the Rams' eight Pro Bowl players, three were on defense.

Game-by-Game:

Sep. 12th RAMS 27, BALTIMORE 10 AT ST. LOUIS

It sounds melodramatic, but this may have been the most important game of the Rams' season. The Rams had signed Trent Green as a free agent to be their starting quarterback. Green suffered a season-ending knee injury in the third exhibition game, leaving untested Kurt Warner as the quarterback. Warner had never started an NFL game, and had thrown a total of 11 regular season passes in the NFL before the 1999 season. Against a team whose defense would end up as the second-ranked defense in 1999, Warner threw for 316 yards and 3 touchdowns.

The season opening win was a team effort. The Rams' defense held the Ravens to 223 total yards and had 5 sacks of Scott Mitchell. This game showed that they could win with Warner, but the Rams would have doubters all the way until the last play of the Super Bowl.

Sep. 26th RAMS 35, ATLANTA 7 AT ST. LOUIS

After their bye week, the Rams crushed the defending NFC champion Falcons, who fell to 0–3 on their way to a disappointing 5–11 season. Rams head coach Dick Vermeil sounded clairvoyant after this game when he said, "I don't think I've been around a team as good as this one may end up being."

Oct. 3rd RAMS 38, CINCINNATI 10 AT CINCINNATI

Az-Zahir Hakim scored 4 touchdowns, including one on a scintillating 84-yard punt return, and Kurt Warner compiled a perfect passing rating of 158.3 (17-of-21 for 310 yards, 3 touchdowns and no interceptions) in the team's first road game.

Oct. 10th RAMS 42, SAN FRANCISCO 20 AT ST. LOUIS

The Rams ended their 17-game losing streak against the 49ers. After the game, Rams' defensive tackle D'Marco Farr said, "I've been waiting all my career to watch my quarterback take a knee to beat this team." Farr, then in his sixth NFL season, had played in 10 of the 17 straight losses. Kurt Warner had another amazing day: 20–of–23 for 323 yards, 5 touchdowns, and just 1 interception.

During Dick Vermeil's postgame press conference, former 49ers coach and then-49ers GM Bill Walsh entered the room, hugged Vermeil and told him, "You're going all the way, Dick."

Oct. 17th RAMS 41, ATLANTA 13 AT ATLANTA

Marshall Faulk ran for a season high 181 yards on just 18 carries and the Rams got two long return touchdowns (Tony Horne 101-yard kickoff return, Grant Wistrom 91-yard interception return) in the second quarter to complete a season sweep of the Falcons.

Despite all the points, St. Louis gained less than 300 yards. Warner had his least productive day of the season (13-of-20, 111 yards), but between Faulk's big day, the long touchdown returns, and a defense that held Atlanta to 41 yards rushing on 19 carries, the Rams moved to 5–0.

Oct. 24th RAMS 34, CLEVELAND 3 AT ST. LOUIS

St. Louis took a 14–0 lead before the Browns even ran a play en route to an easy win over the first-year team. The Rams scored on their first possession, recovered Ronnie Powell's fumble of the ensuing kickoff, and scored on Kurt Warner's second short touchdown pass of the game.

Marshall Faulk ran for 133 yards on 16 carries and had 9 catches for 67 yards; 200 yards and another day at the office for Mr. Faulk. (See "The Kings of Versatility.")

Oct. 31st TENNESSEE 24, RAMS 21 AT TENNESSEE

The Rams could not recover from three first-quarter Titans' touchdowns. After Tennessee scored on the opening drive of the game, Kurt Warner fumbled in his own territory on back-to-back possessions, and the Titans turned both turnovers into scores.

The Rams fought back and had a chance to send the game into overtime, but Jeff Wilkins missed a 38-yard field-goal attempt with five seconds left. St. Louis had more first downs than Tennessee (23–17) and more total yards (415–281).

Nov. 7th DETROIT 31, RAMS 27 AT DETROIT

Detroit won as Gus Frerotte, subbing for injured Lions quarterback Charlie Batch, completed a 57-yard pass to Germane Crowell on fourth-and-26 from his own 21-yard line with a minute left and then threw the winning touchdown pass to Johnnie Morton with 28 seconds left. Detroit held Marshall Faulk to 15 yards rushing on 11 carries.

St. Louis cornerback Dexter McCleon was a stand-up guy after the game, "I take full responsibility [for the pass to Crowell]. I just got caught looking back at the quarterback and I lost sight of him. I should have been a lot deeper than I was."

Nov. 14th RAMS 35, CAROLINA 10 AT ST. LOUIS

Rams tight end Roland Williams was clear on what decided this game, "Our defense basically won the game for us. They were making a lot of plays and just shined." Todd Lyght intercepted a Steve Beurlein pass and ran 57 yards unmolested for a touchdown with 15 seconds left in the first quarter to give St. Louis a 14–7 lead. Mike Jones picked up Wesley Walls's fumble and ran 35 yards for a score with a little over three minutes left in the third quarter to extend the Rams' lead to 28-10 and, for all intents and purposes, end the game.

Nov. 21st RAMS 23, SAN FRANCISCO 7 AT SAN FRANCISCO

The Rams completed their first season sweep of the 49ers since 1980. St. Louis wasn't able to throw down the field, but Marshall Faulk ran for 126 yards on 21 carries, and the Rams' defense held the 49ers to 251 yards of offense.

St. Louis wide receiver Isaac Bruce talked about the win in San Francisco, "This means a lot. I went through a lot of torment trying to win games here. It's usually over in the first quarter. . . . There have been a lot of changes."

Nov. 28th RAMS 43, NEW ORLEANS 12 AT ST. LOUIS

Kurt Warner and the Rams shook off a sluggish first half and ran away from the Saints outscoring them 28–0 in the second half. Marshall Faulk set a career high with his fifth 100-yard rushing game.

Warner completed only 5 of 15 passes for 60 yards in the first half, but was 10 for 12 for 153 yards in the second half. Rams center Mike Gruttadauria was impressed by Warner, "He was very poised. His demeanor was the same."

In the postgame press conference, someone asked third-year Saints head coach Mike Ditka if he was the right man for the job. He was not calm when he answered, "Did I do anything wrong out there? Did I drop the ball? Did I miss the field goal? Did I miss the tackles? I'm not sure, did I throw the interception?" Saints' management answered the questions after the season; they fired Ditka.

Dec. 5th RAMS 34, CAROLINA 21 AT CAROLINA

The Rams clinched the NFC West title and moved to 10–2, their first double-digit win total since 1989. Kurt Warner threw for 351 yards on 22 of 31 attempts and 3 touchdown passes, setting a Rams' single-season record with 32. Warner said of the mark, "The records are nice, but we want something that can never be taken away from us. We want that little ring."

Isaac Bruce and Az Hakim each had over 100 yards receiving; Hakim had 122 yards on four catches, including 2 touchdowns from Warner (48 and 49 yards), while Bruce had 6 receptions for 111 yards.

An emotional Dick Vermeil said after the game, "It's an unbelievable feeling, it really is. I thought with the right kind of people around me that we could do it again. Winning isn't complicated, people complicate it."

Dec. 12th RAMS 30, NEW ORLEANS 14 AT NEW ORLEANS

The Rams became the first team in NFL history to go undefeated in their division the year after not winning a divisional game. They outscored their divisional foes 283–104.

Kurt Warner threw for 346 yards (21 of 31, 2 touchdowns, 1 interception) and Marshall Faulk ran for 154 yards on 29 attempts. Isaac Bruce went over the 1,000-yard mark in receptions, catching 4 passes for 102 yards. They outgained the Saints 492 yards to 210.

Dec. 19th RAMS 31, NEW YORK GIANTS 10 AT ST. LOUIS

The Rams clinched home-field advantage throughout the NFC playoffs with this win. The defense scored 2 touchdowns—Devin Bush's 45-yard third-quarter interception return and Mike Jones's 22-yard fourth-quarter fumble return—bringing the season total to 7.

Warner addressed those who downplayed the Rams' success because of their schedule, "This team [the Giants] was playing well and we beat them soundly. If this doesn't quiet the critics, who knows? They can continue to doubt us all the way to the Super Bowl if they want."

Dec. 26th RAMS 34, CHICAGO 12 AT ST. LOUIS

Marshall Faulk had 204 yards receiving on 12 receptions and joined Roger Craig as the only players to compile 1,000 yards rushing and 1,000 yards receiving in the same season. Bears defensive tackle Mike Wells said, "We knew it was coming, we called it out, but he [Faulk] still kept getting the ball. He killed us."

Jan. 2nd PHILADELPHIA 38, RAMS 31 AT PHILADELPHIA

Neither Kurt Warner nor Marshall Faulk finished this essentially meaningless game. The Rams committed 7 turnovers, including 2 interceptions that the Eagles ran back for touchdowns, and Philadelphia came back from a 14–3 second-quarter deficit to win.

Divisional Playoff:

Jan. 16th RAMS 49, MINNESOTA 37 AT ST. LOUIS

In a game that both was and was not as close as the final score, the Rams won the first home playoff game in St. Louis's NFL history.

St. Louis trailed at halftime (17–14) at home for the first time all season. Sparked by Tony Horne's 95-yard touchdown return of the second-half kickoff, the Rams scored 5 touchdowns in 22 minutes to put the game away at 49–17. The Vikings then scored 3 touchdowns in the last five minutes to make the final score closer.

Although the Vikings did contain Marshall Faulk in the running game (11 carries for 21 yards), he had 5 catches for 80 yards including a 41-yard touchdown on a tremendous run after a short pass. Warner completed 27 of 33 passes for 391 yards and 5 touchdowns. Isaac Bruce, who finished the regular season tied for second in the NFL with 12 touchdown catches, had 4 receptions for 133 yards, including a 77-yard touchdown pass on the Rams' first play from scrimmage.

It's easy to understand why Kurt Warner would say after this game, "I don't think anybody can stop this offense. I haven't seen a defense do it so far." Warner would be proven wrong a week later.

NFC Championship:

Jan. 23rd RAMS 11, TAMPA BAY 6 AT ST. LOUIS

Although it wasn't easy and they were somewhat lucky to win, the Rams squeezed by the Buccaneers to earn a Super Bowl berth. Kurt Warner threw a 30-yard touchdown pass to Ricky Proehl, who made an excellent one-handed catch in the end zone, with 4:44 left in the game for what turned out to be the winning score. Proehl had 33 receptions during the regular season, which only ranked fifth on the team, and had not caught a touchdown pass. In this game, he had 6 receptions for 100 yards.

The Buccaneers' defense played an inspired game, and held the Rams in check all day. Bucs All-Pro defensive tackle Warren Sapp summed it up well when he said, "We brought them into our zone, we brought them into our misery..." The Rams gained just 309 yards, nearly 100 below their season average. Marshall Faulk gained only 49 yards from scrimmage, more than 100 below his per-game season average.

The Bucs' offense did next to nothing, gaining just 203 yards and failing to take advantage of opportunities to put points on the board. Dre Bly's interception of Tampa Bay quarterback Shawn King with eight minutes left set up the Rams' game-winning score.

Whether it was the ineptitude of the Tampa Bay offense or the play of the St. Louis defense, the Buccaneers' inability to move the ball cost them the game. Rams defensive tackle D'Marco Farr thought St. Louis deserved credit: "I think we showed the NFL and the world something today. The Bucs thought their defense was going to come in here and walk all over us. We held them without a touchdown and proved that we are a pretty good defensive team." Of course, the Bucs' defense did its job well. It's not clear if this game proved the Rams had a good defense, but St. Louis earned a trip to the Super Bowl.

Super Bowl XXXIV:

Jan. 30th RAMS 23, TENNESSEE 16 AT ATLANTA

The Rams became the first team to blow a 16-point lead in the Super Bowl, but won anyway when Isaac Bruce made a nice adjustment on an underthrown pass by Kurt Warner and turned the play into a 73-yard touchdown pass with 1:54 left in the game. Oh yeah, Rams' linebacker Mike Jones tackled Titans wide receiver Kevin Dyson at the Rams' 1-yard line as time ran out.

St. Louis had a chance to put the game away in the first half as they reached the red zone (inside the opponents' 20-yard line) on each of their five first-half possessions. The Rams only came away with nine points on three field goals. On their first possession, the snap on the field-goal attempt was mishandled. Jeff Wilkins, who had been suffering from tendinitis in his non-kicking knee, missed a field-goal try on another possession. There was also a dropped pass by Torry Holt in the end zone. St. Louis outgained Tennessee 294 yards to 89 in the first half, but had only the 9–0 lead.

The Rams finally reached the end zone on their first possession of the second half to make the score 16–0. The Titans' defense started to shut down the Rams and the offense put together two long touchdown drives to cut the lead to 16–13 (they missed a two-point conversion) with about seven minutes left in the game. Tennessee forced St. Louis to punt and the Titans tied the game at 16 on Al Del Greco's field goal with 2:12 left. On the first play after the kickoff, Warner and Bruce hooked up on the game-winning touchdown.

The Titans drove downfield, but despite heroics by Steve McNair, the lack of a timeout ultimately doomed their chances.

Kurt Warner was named MVP and set a Super Bowl record with 414 yards passing. Although the Titans did pressure Warner at times, particularly in the second half, he was only sacked once.

Marshall Faulk gained only 17 yards rushing on 11 carries. Almost everyone seems to talk about how important it is to establish the running game. In their three postseason games, the Rams gained a total of 1,150 yards. What was the run/pass distribution? The Rams had 111 yards rushing and 1,039 yards passing.

Elsewhere Around the NFL:

Sep. 12th In their first regular-season game since the retirement of Barry Sanders, Detroit defeated Seattle 28–20 at the Kingdome behind 3 touchdown passes by Charlie Batch. After a 6–2 start, the Lions finished at only 8–8, but that was good enough for an NFC Wild-Card berth. Dallas also made the playoffs at 8–8. In the AFC, six teams with records of 8–8 or better did not make the playoffs.

Oct. 17th In a "rematch" of Super Bowl XXXII (that's 32 for you who never learned Roman numerals), the Bronco's throttled Green Bay 31–10 at Denver. The Broncos held the Packers to just five first downs, had an amazing 45:14–14:46 advantage in time of possession and a nearly as amazing 514–133 superiority in yards gained.

In the 1990s, the Broncos were 60–20 at home and 34–46 on the road during the regular season. Denver was undefeated at home for three consecutive seasons, 1996–98, the only team to do so since the adoption of the 16-game schedule, and the first team to do so under any circumstances since the 1972–74 Miami Dolphins.

Dec. 9th Baltimore's Qadry Ismail caught 3 touchdown passes of 50+ yards *in the third quarter* as the Ravens defeated the Steelers 31–24. Baltimore quarterback Tony Banks completed just 8 of 26 passes, but in an extreme example of the importance of yards per attempt and the lack of relevance for completion percentage, he threw for 268 yards to help the Ravens to victory.

Jan. 8th	In the "Music City Miracle," Tennessee's Kevin Dyson scored a touchdown on a lateral during a kickoff return with three seconds left to lead the Titans to an improbable 22–6 playoff win over the Buffalo Bills. Three Titans handled the ball on the play: Lorenzo Neal, who fielded the kickoff; Frank Wycheck, who received a handoff from Neal; and Dyson, who received a lateral from Wycheck and went 75 yards untouched to the end zone.

What Happened the Next Season:

The Rams' offense remained just as potent in 2000, even though Kurt Warner missed five games with a thumb injury. The defense went putrid, however, allowing an amazing 471 points that limited the Rams to a 10–6 record, "only" a Wild-Card berth, and ultimately a first-round playoff loss at New Orleans, the 2000 NFC West champion.

The Rams scored more points and gained more yards in 2000 than in 1999, and their Offense Power Index of +5.04 in 2000 made them one of only seven teams since 1950 with an OPI of +5.00 or higher. The Defense Power Index went into the toilet: from +2.07 in 1999 to *minus* 2.65 in 2000. As you might imagine, that is one of the 10 worst year-to-year declines for Defense Power Index since 1950. (See "The Dam Burst.")

Rams	Points	Yards	OPI	DPI	Record
1999	526	6,412	+4.84	+2.07	13–3 Super Bowl champs
2000	540	7,075	+5.04	−2.65	10–6 First-Round Playoff loss

The Kings of Versatility

Although he didn't gain many yards rushing in the 1999 postseason, much was made (and deservedly so) of the Rams' Marshall Faulk becoming the second player in NFL history to attain 1,000 yards rushing and 1,000 yards receiving in the same season. Faulk's single-season record for yards from scrimmage was also mentioned frequently.

Is there a way to combine rushing yards and receiving yards in a way that rewards balance in addition to overall total? The answer is yes. Bill James, noted baseball author, created a way to combine a player's home run and stolen base totals in just such a manner. (He called it the Power/Speed number. Sounds like a football stat, doesn't it?) I decided to apply James's method to rushing/receiving yards totals back to 1950.

Let me quickly say that I don't think this is the be-all and end-all way to rate running backs. I am aware that different systems use running backs in different ways. Obviously, the quality of the team plays a large role in the production of any given player. A back's efficiency is also significant. If one running back gains 1,100 yards on 300 carries did he really have a better year than a back who gained 1,000 yards on 200 carries?

The actual formula is relatively simple:

$$\frac{2 \times \text{Yards Rushing} \times \text{Yards Receiving}}{\text{Yards Rushing} + \text{Yards Receiving}}$$

Using Faulk as our example, in 1999 he gained 1,381 yards rushing and 1,048 yards receiving. Faulk's "versatility" number, or as I've named it, his Lenny Moore number, is as follows:

$$\frac{2 \times 1{,}381 \times 1{,}048}{1{,}381 + 1{,}048} = \frac{2{,}894{,}576}{2{,}429} = 1191.7$$

A hypothetical running back who had 1,881 yards rushing and 548 yards receiving, the same total yards from scrimmage as Faulk, would have a Lenny Moore number of 848.7. This method rewards balance and quantity of performance. Faulk's 1191.7 is the best number in NFL history.

His number is also the best when adjusting for length of schedule. The NFL schedule hasn't always been 16 games. In order to attempt historical comparisons, I divided a player's Lenny Moore number by the appropriate length of schedule: 12 games from 1950 through 1960, 14 games from 1961 through 1977, and 16 games since 1978. (I did not calculate numbers for the two strike years of 1982 and 1987.) While adjusting for length of schedule, here are the best marks in each decade when since 1950:

Player	Year	Team	Yards Rushing	Yards Receiving	Lenny Moore Number	Per Game
Lenny Moore	1958	BAL	598	938	730.4	60.9
Charley Taylor	1964	WAS	755	814	783.4	56.0
Chuck Foreman	1975	MIN	1,070	691	839.7	60.0
Roger Craig	1985	SF	1,050	1,016	1,032.7	64.5
Marshall Faulk	1999	STL	1,381	1,048	1,191.7	74.5

Marshall Faulk

Allsport

The 1999 season was the third straight time that Faulk led the NFL in Lenny Moore number. Before the 2000 season, Thurman Thomas was the only player to lead the league four straight years (1989 through 1992). Faulk led the league in 2000 with Lenny Moore numbers of 1,030.6/64.4 and again in 2001, for a "record" fifth straight time (984.8/61.6), despite missing two games. The list of players who have led the NFL in Lenny Moore number is very impressive. Besides the players already mentioned, Ollie Matson, Jim Brown, Gale Sayers, Walter Payton, Billy Sims, and William Andrews have all led the league.

Here are the top 10 marks since 1950:

Player	Year	Team	Yards Rushing	Yards Receiving	Lenny Moore Number	Per Game
Marshall Faulk	1999	STL	1,381	1,048	1,191.7	74.5
Marshall Faulk	1998	IND	1,319	908	1,075.6	67.2
Roger Craig	1985	SF	1,050	1,016	1,032.7	64.5
Marshall Faulk	2000	STL	1,359	830	1,030.6	64.4
Marshall Faulk	2001	STL	1,382	765	984.8	61.6
Lenny Moore	1958	BAL	598	938	730.4	60.9
Chuck Foreman	1975	MIN	1,070	691	839.7	60.0
James Wilder	1984	TB	1,544	685	949.0	59.3
William Andrews	1981	ATL	1,301	735	939.3	58.7
Frank Gifford	1956	NYG	819	603	694.6	57.9

Obviously, that's a pretty good list of players. Like I said before, I'm not touting the Lenny Moore number as the only way to evaluate running backs, but it is a good way to measure their versatility. It also shows just how productive Marshall Faulk has been.

The Dam Burst

The Rams' defense really went down the tubes in 2000, the year after they won the Super Bowl. The magnitude of their decline can be shown in any number of ways, but as you might imagine I am going to look at their Power Index.

In 1999, the Rams had a fine Defense Power Index (DPI) of +2.07. In 2000, their DPI was −2.65. That decrease (4.72) is the ninth-largest one-season decline since 1950. The strange thing is that the Rams defensive personnel didn't really change; they just seemed to forget how to play defense. Many observers thought the defense simply lost a step. From a purely subjective standpoint, I thought that the 2000 Rams were one of the two or three worst tackling NFL teams I've ever seen.

Some placed much of the blame on defensive end Kevin Carter. He was supposedly disturbed by the lack of negotiations for a new contract, especially since many of his teammates had received new deals in the off-season after the Super Bowl win. Carter's sack output fell from a league-leading 17 in 1999 to 10 1/2 in 2000, with just 3 1/2 sacks in the first half of the season. During an interview with KFNS Radio in St. Louis, Carter admitted that the contract situation affected his play. Common sense should tell us, however, that one player could not create a decline in performance the magnitude of the 2000 Rams' defense.

Great drop-offs, like remarkable turnarounds, are group efforts in the NFL. I've put together the 10 worst year-to-year declines in Defense Power Index since 1950:

Team, Seasons	Season 1 W-L/DPI	Season 2 W-L/DPI	Decline
1. Chicago Bears, 1963–64	11–1–2/+3.92	5–9/−2.37	6.29
2. Arizona Cardinals, 1994–95	8–8/+2.79	4–12/−2.91	5.70
3. Oakland Raiders, 1996–97	7–9/+1.29	4–12/−4.40	5.69
4. Chicago Bears, 1988–89	12–4/+3.97	6–10/−1.72	5.68
5. Baltimore Colts, 1977–78	10–4/+0.35	5–11/−4.84	5.19
6. New York Jets, 1985–86	11–5/+2.19	10–6/−2.94	5.13

Ten worst year-to-year declines in Defense Power Index since 1950: *(continued)*

	Team, Seasons	Season 1 W-L/DPI	Season 2 W-L/DPI	Decline
7.	Denver Broncos, 1989–90	11–5/+3.49	5–11/−1.58	5.07
8.	Baltimore Colts, 1971–72	10–4/+4.79	5–9/−0.02	4.81
9.	St. Louis Rams, 1999–2000	13–3/+2.07	10–6/−2.65	4.72
10.	Cleveland Browns, 1989-90	9–6–1/+2.09	3–13/−2.62	4.71

1. Chicago Bears, 1963–64

   The Bears rode their defense to the NFL title in 1963. The defensive unit suffered numerous injuries in 1964, but the Bears' season was probably lost when running back Willie Galimore and wide receiver Bo Farrington were killed in a car accident during training camp. Perhaps understandably, after that the Bears never really recovered.

2. Arizona Cardinals, 1994–95

   This decline led to the firing of Buddy Ryan. The Cards' run defense really disappeared; after allowing just 1,370 yards and a 3.3 average per rush in 1994, Arizona allowed 2,249 yards and a 4.5 average per rush in 1995.

3. Oakland Raiders, 1996–97

   Like the Cardinals, this decline led to the ouster of head coach Joe Bugel, who, ironically, had been replaced by Buddy Ryan in Arizona. The Raiders' 4–12 record was their worst showing since their 1–13 record in 1962. It's amazing when an above-average defense turns into one of the 10 worst of the past 50 years, at least as measured by Power Index, in just one season.

4. Chicago Bears, 1988–89

   Jim McMahon had been traded before the season started, but the offense played well all year and the Bears began the 1989 season 4–0. Although I still don't believe that one player can make that much of a difference, defensive tackle Dan Hampton was lost for the year to have surgery on both knees. After allowing 15 points per game in their first four games, the Bears allowed 26 points per game over their last 12 games, and lost 10 times.

5. Baltimore Colts, 1977–78

   This team also suffered one of the 10 worst single-season declines in offensive performance. Unlike the offensive decline, however, the defensive players didn't really change. Maybe when a team's morale is undercut for whatever reason (like the 1964 Bears), it affects the defense because of the intensity needed on that side of the ball. In the case of the 1978 Colts, the trades of several key offensive players for salary reasons helped destroy the team's morale. There's little doubt in my mind that the 1978 Colts were the worst 5–11 team in history.

6. New York Jets, 1985–86

   Like the 1978 Colts were the worst 5–11 team in history, the 1986 Jets were the worst 10–6 team in history. Since the schedule expanded to 16 games in 1978, 67 teams compiled 10–6 records through the 2000 season; 62 teams had positive Power Indexes, and four of the five teams with negative Power Indexes were no worse than −0.86. The 1986 Jets were −2.01. They made the playoffs as a Wild Card and lost to the favored Browns into double overtime 23–20 (no surprise the Jets' defense blew a 10-point fourth-quarter lead).

   Jets' fans defend this team by saying they started 10–1 and only collapsed under the weight of several injuries. Their point differential in their first 11 games, 303 points scored/203 points allowed, projects to an 8–3 record, so I think they were pretty lucky to be 10–1 in the first place. Over their final five games, the Jets were outscored 183–61.

7. Denver Broncos, 1989–90

   Starting with their 55–10 thrashing at the hands of the 49ers in the Super Bowl in January, nothing went right for the Broncos in 1990. Head coach Dan Reeves had heart surgery, defensive end Alfonso Carreker missed the entire season with a knee injury, running back Bobby Humphrey was hampered by a sprained ankle for the last two-thirds of the season, and the defense suffered in-season injuries to key players such as cornerback Tyrone Braxton and linebacker Marc Munford.

8. Baltimore Colts, 1971–72

   The 1971 Colts are the great forgotten defensive unit in pro football history. They allowed just 2,852 yards in 14 regular-season games, the third best total among the 345 14-game NFL team-seasons. Their points allowed total, 140, was sixth-best among the same group. More important to me, their Defensive Power Index was the second-best among *all teams* since 1950.

   The 1972 season was a transition season for the Colts' franchise as it marked the beginning of the Robert Irsay era and the end of the Johnny Unitas era. Many players who had started for the successful Colts' teams of the late '60s and early '70s were traded or coaxed into retirement.

9. St. Louis Rams, 1999–2000
10. Cleveland Browns, 1989–90

    Both participants in the 1989 AFC Championship game suffered through disappointing 1990 seasons. The season, the worst in Browns' history at the time, started in disarray due to numerous training-camp holdouts caused by the large contract given to Plan B free agent Raymond Clayborn. Head coach Bud Carson was fired after nine games. The Browns allowed 30 or more points in half of their games, including a 58–14 humiliation at the hands of the Houston Oilers on December 9.

Mike Martz

Mike Martz has made an infinite leap, if you will. After 18 years as an assistant coach at the junior college and college levels, he began his NFL coaching career in 1992 as an *unpaid* offensive assistant. By 2000 he became the head coach of the defending Super Bowl champions. Before the 1999 season, Martz was basically unknown; he came back to the Rams that year as offensive coordinator after spending two seasons as quarterbacks coach for the Redskins.

Martz's appointment as offensive coordinator was just one of many changes in the offseason between 1998 and 1999 that transformed the Rams' offense into one of the best in NFL history. Trading for Marshall Faulk was obviously an important move. Signing free agent Adam Timmerman, who had a Pro Bowl season, helped solidify the offensive line. Drafting Torry Holt was important because it gave the offense another credible weapon. Even with these player moves, bringing Martz to St. Louis was one of the franchise's most significant decisions. His approach gave the team an identity.

Although he is soft-spoken, Martz has an "in your face" coaching style. Tight ends coach Lynn Stiles said about Martz, "I've never been around a guy that took a more aggressive approach to the game." Pro Bowl wide receiver Isaac Bruce echoes that sentiment, "He [Martz] goes for the jugular and we love him for it. We don't adjust to anyone." Writer Bernie Miklasz believes that Martz's confident, aggressive attitude helped to create that kind of attitude for the entire team.

I tried to devise a way to show the amazing effectiveness of the Rams' passing game in 1999–2001. As I've often repeated, yards per attempt is the most important passing statistic; the Rams easily led the NFL in the category all three seasons. In 1999, St. Louis averaged 8.64 yards per pass attempt; the league average was 6.76 and only one other team was above 8.00. In 2000, the Rams averaged 9.36 yards per attempt; the league average was 6.75 and only one other team was above 8.00. In 2001, the Rams averaged 8.90 yards per attempt; the league average was 6.78 and the second-best team was more than a yard per attempt behind (7.69).

The Rams were also unique because they combined yards per completion and completion percentage beyond the NFL norm. As one might guess, there is a slight negative correlation between yards per completion and completion percentage. That is, as teams try longer passes their completion percentage gets worse. (Understandably, yards after the catch plays a role in yards per completion.) In 1999, the Rams were second in the league in yards per completion and first in completion percentage. In 2000, St. Louis led the NFL in both categories. In 2001, the Rams were first in completion percentage and second in yards per completion. That combination is unusual. Except for the 1998–2000 Vikings, no team since 1990 has finished in the top two in the league in yards per completion and ranked higher than eleventh in completion percentage. Over the past 12 seasons, on average, teams that finished in the top two in yards per completion ranked sixteenth in completion percentage (seventeenth if the Rams are excluded.)

In the two seasons before Martz became offensive coordinator, the Rams were fifteenth and twenty-sixth in the NFL in yards per attempt, twenty-eighth and eighteenth in completion percentage, second and twenty-seventh in yards per completion. I am not suggesting that Martz is the only reason for the dramatic improvement, Kurt Warner and company had much to do with it, but based on reports from on-the-scene observers, I believe that Martz's tactics and his attitude laid the foundation. That's not bad for a guy who started his NFL career as an unpaid volunteer.

The Coach: Dick Vermeil

Coaching Record

Year	Team	W	L	Pct	
1976	PHI	4	10	.286	
1977	PHI	5	9	.357	
1978	PHI	9	7	.563	NFC Wild Card
1979	PHI	11	5	.688	NFC Wild Card
1980	PHI	12	4	.750	NFC Eastern Division title, NFC champs
1981	PHI	10	6	.625	NFC Wild Card
1982	PHI	3	6	.333	
Total PHI		**54**	**47**	**.535**	
1997	STL	5	11	.313	
1998	STL	4	12	.250	
1999	STL	13	3	.813	NFC Western Division title; NFC champs; Super Bowl champs
Total STL		**22**	**26**	**.458**	
2001	KC	6	10	.375	
Career		**82**	**83**	**.497**	

Normally, I haven't shown the head coach's record with a franchise other than the one profiled, but Vermeil spent such a short period with the Rams that I thought I should show his record with the Eagles (and the Chiefs, while I was at it). I also wanted to show, in black and white, just how long he was away from coaching.

One time, when Vermeil was asked why he returned to coaching after 15 years, he answered, "I missed the leadership role. I thought I could do it better the second time around. And I just felt the risk of not going back was greater in the long run than the risk in going back."

Vermeil's recent "flip-flop" concerning his retirement was not the first seemingly abrupt move in his career. He first joined the major college ranks as an assistant coach with Stanford in 1965. (Bill Walsh was also on that staff.) In 1969, Vermeil got his first NFL coaching job with the Rams. In 1970, Vermeil was the offensive coordinator at UCLA. From 1971 to 1973, Vermeil was back with the Rams as the quarterbacks coach. He was then head coach at UCLA in 1974 and 1975 before taking the Eagles' head coaching job in 1976.

Vermeil's overall NFL coaching record is impressive, if one considers the context. The Eagles had not had a winning season since 1966 and had not been in the postseason since 1960. Yeah, that last fact is misleading because of the proliferation of playoff berths.

Philadelphia's winning percentage improved for four consecutive seasons, 1977–80. Only four other teams have matched that feat since 1950: Green Bay (under Vince Lombardi) from 1959 through 1962, San Diego (first by Tommy Prothro, then Don Coryell) from 1976 through 1979, Buffalo (primarily under Chuck Knox) from 1977 through 1980, and Kansas City (under Marv Levy) from 1978 through 1981. That puts Vermeil in some pretty good company.

The Rams had been horrible for a decade until their Super Bowl title. They had gone since 1989 without a winning season or playoff appearance and their last division title came in 1985. In terms of a one-year change in winning percentage, the 1999 Rams had the fourth best improvement of any team since 1950, behind only the 1999 Colts, the 1975 Colts, and the 1976 Patriots.

Vermeil changed his tactics after his first two years in St. Louis. At the urging of assistant coaches like former Vermeil players John Bunting and Wilbert Montgomery as well as newly hired offensive coordinator Mike Martz, Vermeil eased up on his team. He shortened practices and reduced the amount of contact in practice. He began to understand how much players had changed physically since he had coached the Eagles. Average players of the late 1990s were often more gifted athletically than the great players of the early 1980s. In an interview just before the Super Bowl Vermeil said, "When I got back here and I had been away from the game for 14 years and they all look good to me because they are all bigger and faster and stronger than the guys I used to coach. My biggest player on my Super Bowl team [in Philadelphia] was 276 pounds, Stan Walter. We don't have anybody in the offensive line under 295. I had to raise my standards of evaluation of what I call a good football player."

I won't dive into the controversy surrounding Vermeil's retirement after the Super Bowl win and his "un-retirement" a year later to coach the Chiefs; people have the right to change their mind. Some people are turned off by Vermeil's overt emotionalism and he did almost "lose" his team in rebellion in 1998 because of his practice philosophy. I like to look at the facts, at the bottom line. Vermeil was the head coach of two franchises that made historically significant improvements. I think he deserves more than a little credit for that.

The Quarterback: Kurt Warner

Year	Team	Att	Comp	Yds	TD	Int	YPA	Rating	Lg Avg	W	L	Pct
1998	STL	11	4	39	0	0	3.55	47.2	78.3	0	0	—
1999	STL	499	325	4,353	41	13	8.72	109.2	77.1	13	3	.813
2000	STL	347	235	3,429	21	18	9.88	98.3	78.1	8	3	.727
2001	STL	546	375	4,830	36	22	8.85	101.4	78.5	14	2	.875
Total		**1,403**	**939**	**12,651**	**98**	**53**	**9.02**	**103.0**	**78.0**	**35**	**8**	**.814**

YPA = Yards Per Pass Attempt
Rating = Passer Rating
Lg Avg = League Passer Rating in that season
W, L, Pct = Team's Record in his starts

- Kurt Warner's league-leading 101.4 passer rating in 2001 *lowered* his career mark from 104.0.

St. Louis Post-Dispatch writer and fellow native Baltimorean Bernie Miklasz has written about some similarities between the careers of Kurt Warner and Johnny Unitas. Both attended Catholic high schools. They both entered the NFL unheralded–Warner was signed by the Packers as an undrafted free agent, while Unitas was drafted by the Steelers in the ninth round. Both were released by the first NFL team that signed them. Both played in "minor" leagues after being cut, Warner with the Iowa Barnstormers of the Arena League, and Unitas with the Bloomfield Rams in a semi-pro league. After signing with their second NFL team, both got chances to play due to an injury to the starting quarterback (Trent Green with the Rams, George Shaw with the Colts). In Warner's first NFL title game (Super Bowl XXXIV), his team won 23–16 with the game being decided on the last play. In Unitas's first NFL title game (the 1958 NFL Championship Game), his team won 23–17 with the game being decided on the last play.

Although few of them would probably admit it, Warner's amazing success must be an embarrassment to NFL scouts, personnel directors, and general managers. Nine quarterbacks were drafted in 1994, the year that Warner signed with Green Bay. Here are the nine, where they were taken, and who drafted them:

Player	Team	Round	Selection
Heath Shuler	WAS	Round 1	3rd overall
Trent Dilfer	TB	Round 1	6th overall
Perry Klein	ATL	Round 4	111th overall
Doug Nussmeier	NO	Round 4	116th overall
Jim Miller	PIT	Round 6	178th overall
Gus Frerotte	WAS	Round 7	197th overall

Player	Team	Round	Selection
Jay Walker	NE	Round 7	198th overall
Steve Matthews	KC	Round 7	199th overall
Glenn Foley	NYJ	Round 7	208th overall

So let's see . . . only two quarterbacks "worth" taking in the top 100 picks, four of the nine quarterbacks hung around until the last round, and somehow everyone missed Kurt Warner. Warner didn't start in college until he was a fifth-year senior and he didn't play in a big program (Northern Iowa) or conference (Gateway); both those facts partly explain the lack of interest, even in a thin year for quarterbacks. How do I know that's a "thin" crowd for quarterbacks? Indulge me for a minute with this chart:

Year	Total Drafted	1st Round	Top 100 Picks	Last Round
1994 (Warner's Year)	9	2	2	4
1995	14	2	7	1
1996	8	0	3	2
1997	11	1	3	5
1998	8	2	5	1
1999	13	5	7	3
2000	12	1	3	3
2001	11	1	4	0
Average	**10.8**	**1.8**	**4.3**	**2.4**

See? Of the eight drafts from 1994 to 2001, the 1994 draft had the fewest quarterbacks taken in the first 100 picks, the second-most taken in the last round, and a below-average total drafted. Relatively speaking, that's a thin year for quarterbacks.

One of the most important things I have learned in my 15-plus years working for major league baseball teams is that very often the only difference between a "major league" player and a "minor league" player is a meaningful opportunity to play in the major leagues. Kurt Warner feels the same way about football players, "I think there are a lot of guys out there that just don't get the opportunity to play and get the opportunity to be successful. You just never know what a player is all about until he gets in there and gets a chance to play." It is entirely possible that without the injury to Trent Green, we may have never known what Kurt Warner can do.

1999 St. Louis Rams Statistics

Passing

	Att	Comp	Comp Pct	Yds	Yds Per	TD	Int	Rating
Warner	499	325	65.1%	4,353	8.72	41	13	109.2
Germaine	16	9	56.3%	136	8.50	1	2	65.6
Justin	14	9	64.3%	91	6.50	0	0	82.7
Rams	**530**	**343**	**64.7%**	**4,580**	**8.64**	**42**	**15**	**106.6**
Opponents	596	319	53.5%	3,867	6.49	19	29	64.1
League Average			57.1%		6.76			77.1

Rams' passers were sacked 33 times for 227 yards in losses.
The Rams sacked their opponents 57 times for 358 yards in losses.

The 1999 Rams were one of 12 teams since 1978 to average at least two more yards per pass attempt than their opponents.

What can I say that hasn't already been said about Kurt Warner's amazing 1999 season? I'll try some trivia (some might say minutia). Officially, his 109.2 passing rating is the fifth-highest in NFL history. Actually, it is sixth. You see, the NFL passer rating system has a maximum point total that a player can achieve. For example, if a player were to complete more than 77.5 percent of his passes, he would be treated as if he completed 77.5 percent because that is set as the maximum in completion percentage. Normally, these limits are not a problem (although the system should be open ended). However, in 1943 Sid Luckman threw 28 touchdown passes in just 202 attempts, a 13.9 touchdown percentage. The NFL system maxes out at 11.875 percent. If Luckman's rating is recalculated giving him "full" credit for his TD percentage, then his rating would be 114.2 which would be the highest of all time and which would push everyone else down one notch. One can argue that Luckman had his great season during World War II and in a much different era, but his rating is less than it otherwise would be because of an arbitrarily set cap.

Rushing

	Att	Yds	Avg	Net Yards	TD
Faulk	253	1,381	5.46	+395	7
Holcombe	78	294	3.77	−10	4
Watson	47	179	3.81		0

	Att	Yds	Avg	Net Yards	TD
Warner	23	92	4.00		1
Hakim	4	44	11.00		0
Bruce	5	32	6.40		0
Holt	3	25	8.33		0
Hodgins	7	10	1.43		1
Lee	3	3	1.00		0
Germaine	3	0	0.00		0
Justin	5	−1	−0.20		0
Rams	**431**	**2,059**	**4.78**	**+379**	**13**
Opponents	338	1,189	3.52	−128	4
League Average			3.90		

It should go without saying that Marshall Faulk had an amazing season. If you think comparing a back's average per carry to the overall league average instead of the average of the league's busiest running backs is invalid, the 41 NFL backs with 100+ carries in 1999 averaged 3.91 yards per carry. I won't bicker over the more subtle argument that a back's productivity is a function of his teammates' talent and the system as well as his own ability.

The Rams allowed the fewest rushing yards in the league. No surprise that the run defense was so effective because the Rams were usually ahead late in the game by big margins and the other team had no choice but to throw the ball. Opponents attempted more passes, including sacks, against the Rams than against any other team in the league in 1999. As a result, Rams' opponents had the fewest rushing attempts in the league.

Receiving

	Rec	Yds	Avg	TD
Faulk	87	1,048	12.05	5
Bruce	77	1,165	15.13	12
Holt	52	788	15.15	6
Hakim	36	677	18.81	8
Proehl	33	349	10.58	0
Williams, R	25	226	9.04	6
Holcombe	14	163	11.64	1
Robinson	6	76	12.67	2
Hodgins	6	35	5.83	0
Lee	3	22	7.33	1
Lewis	1	12	12.00	0

(continued next page)

Receiving *(continued)*

	Rec	Yds	Avg	TD
Conwell	1	11	11.00	0
Thomas	1	6	6.00	0
Tucker	1	2	2.00	1
Rams	**343**	**4,580**	**13.35**	**42**
Opponents	319	3,867	12.12	19
League Average			11.84	

It wasn't just that Marshall Faulk led all backs with 87 receptions, good for eighth-most in the NFL. His average per reception was phenomenal. The 37 NFL running backs/fullbacks with 25+ receptions in 1999 averaged 8.41 yards per catch—8.19 if you exclude Faulk.

The return of Isaac Bruce to full strength was an important reason for the Rams' offensive explosion. In 1997–98 Bruce missed 15 games, almost the equivalent of one season. In 1996 Bruce had led the NFL with 1,338 receiving yards and in 1995 he had 119 receptions for 1,781 yards and 13 touchdowns.

Kickoff Returns

	Ret	Yds	Avg	TD
Horne	30	892	29.73	2
Carpenter	16	406	25.38	0
Hakim	2	35	17.50	0
Fletcher	2	13	6.50	0
Hodgins	2	4	2.00	0
McCollum	1	3	3.00	0
Bly	1	1	1.00	0
Rams	**54**	**1,354**	**25.07**	**2**
Opponents	85	2,115	24.88	0
League Average			21.23	

Tony Horne led the NFL in kickoff return average and tied with Michael Bates of the Panthers for the league lead in touchdown returns.

Punt Returns

	Ret	Yds	Avg	TD
Hakim	44	461	10.48	1
Horne	5	22	4.40	0
Holt	3	15	5.00	0
Rams	**52**	**498**	**9.58**	**1**
Opponents	23	155	6.74	0
League Average			9.35	

Interceptions

	Int	Yds	Avg	TD
Lyght	6	112	18.67	1
Jones, M.	4	96	24.00	2
McCleon	4	17	4.33	0
Bly	3	53	17.67	1
Wistrom	2	131	65.50	2
Allen	2	76	38.00	0
Bush	2	45	22.50	1
Jenkins	2	16	8.00	0
Lyle	2	10	5.00	0
Coady	1	11	11.00	0
Clemons	1	0	0.00	0
Rams	**29**	**567**	**19.55**	**7**
Opponents	15	266	17.73	2

The Rams' 7 touchdowns on interception returns is the third-highest total in NFL history. In 1999, 17 of the 31 NFL teams had one or fewer touchdowns on interception returns.

Sack Leaders

(Sacks have been an official statistic for individual players only since 1982.)

Carter	17.0
Farr	8.5
Wistrom	6.5

Kevin Carter led the NFL in sacks in 1999.

Turnovers

Turnovers Committed:	31
Turnovers Forced:	36
Turnover +/–:	+5

Punting

	No	Avg
Tuten	32	42.5
Horan	26	40.3
Wilkins	2	28.5
Rams	**60**	**41.1**
Opponents	86	42.7
League Average		41.7

Kicking

	XP	XPA	XP Pct	FG	FGA	FG Pct
Wilkins	64	64	100.0%	20	28	71.4%
Opponents	22	23	95.7%	20	26	76.9%
League Average			98.9%			77.7%

Leading Scorer:	Jeff Wilkins, 124 Points
Leading Scorer, Non-Kicker:	Isaac Bruce & Marshall Faulk, 74 Points

1999 St. Louis Rams Roster

Head Coach	Dick Vermeil
QB	Joe Germaine
QB	Paul Justin
QB	Kurt Warner
RB	Marshall Faulk
RB	Derrick Harris
RB	James Hodgins
RB	Robert Holcombe
RB	Amp Lee
RB	Justin Watson
WR	Isaac Bruce
WR	Az-Zahir Hakim
WR	Torry Holt
WR	Tony Horne
WR	Ricky Proehl
WR	Chris Thomas
TE	Ernie Conwell
TE	Chad Lewis
TE	Jeff Robinson
TE	Roland Williams
C	Mike Gruttadauria
C/OT	Ryan Tucker
OG	Andy McCollum
OG	Tom Nutten
OG	Cameron Spikes
OG	Adam Timmerman
OT	Fred Miller
OT	Orlando Pace
K	Jeff Wilkins
P	Mike Horan
P	Rick Tuten
DE	Lionel Barnes
DE	Kevin Carter
DE	Jay Williams
DE	Grant Wistrom
DT	Ray Agnew
DT	D'Marco Farr
DT	Nate Hobgood-Chittick
DT	Gaylon Hyder
DT	Jeff Zgonina
LB	Charlie Clemons
LB	Todd Collins
LB	London Fletcher
LB	Mike Jones
LB/DE	Leonard Little
LB	Mike Morton
LB	Troy Pelshak
LB	Lorenzo Styles
DB	Taje Allen
DB	Dre Bly
DB	Devin Bush
DB	Ron Carpenter
DB	Rich Coady
DB	Clifton Crosby
DB	Billy Jenkins
DB	Todd Lyght
DB	Keith Lyle
DB	Dexter McCleon

CHAPTER 14

Drum Roll, Please

Maybe some of you came here first to see how I ranked the teams. I can tell you how I didn't rank them; I didn't rank them with a mathematical formula. Whatever criteria I wanted to use, devising a purely mathematical scheme would have been arbitrary. Assigning weights to this number or to that accomplishment would have been nothing more than an educated guess and probably not even that.

Without combining them mathematically, my most important criteria for me in ranking the teams were, and not necessarily in this order:

1. Regular season record,
2. Adjusted Power Index (API),
3. Regular season performance against teams with winning records, and
4. Playoff performance.

Other factors were also considered. For example, I believe that the ability to win on the road is a sign of a great team. It's strictly my opinion, but let's say two teams each have a 12–4 record; if one is 8–0 at home and 4–4 on the road, while the other is 6–2 both home and road, then the latter team's 12–4 is more impressive.

(In case you came here first and don't know what Adjusted Power Index is, it is a measure of how much a team outperformed the other teams in the league in a given season. It measures how far above the league average they were in certain categories, factors in how team performances were distributed, and is adjusted for strength of schedule.)

I allowed a tiny subjective component. I can't tell you how many different rankings I came up with (in particular, trying to rank the teams from number two through number seven) and if a team just didn't look right where it was, then I may have moved it a notch or two.

Please remember that I am ranking these teams on the basis of the one season in the book. If I haven't ranked the '79 Steelers or either 49ers' team high enough for their fans, it's not because I believe they didn't have tremendous dynasties.

Let me say that picking the number one team was relatively easy, and that as I tried to construct the rest of the list, it got more and more difficult. Starting backwards, since I have to keep you in suspense a little bit...

11. (TIE) 1955 Cleveland Browns and 1958 Baltimore Colts

OK, so I copped out. The regular-season records of the two teams are comparable and closer to the bottom of this "Dirty Dozen." The Colts lost two games after they clinched the conference title, but the Browns had a better balance of home and road records. (Of course, the Colts' two "meaningless" losses were on the road.) The Browns had a better API—both teams' API's rank in the bottom third of the 12—but in context, the Colts had a better performance against teams with winning records. Since these two teams and the 1962 Packers played only one playoff game, it was hard to rank them against the three playoff games played by the other nine teams.

10. 1999 St. Louis Rams

The Rams' API was, surprisingly, the third best among the 12 teams, but their total lack of a resume against teams with winning records during the regular season as well as their less than dominating playoff performance led me to place them here. Hey, it's no insult to be called the tenth-best team of all time.

9. 1971 Dallas Cowboys

Nine and eight could have easily been flip-flopped, but in the end I felt that the Cowboys' two fewer games played and their ordinary point differential against winning opponents was a good reason to place them here.

8. 1994 San Francisco 49ers

I ranked this team a little higher than their record and API might suggest. Their dominating playoff run gave them the benefit of the doubt.

7. **1972 Miami Dolphins**

The members of the '72 Dolphins would see this ranking and probably utter some version of Rodney Dangerfield's signature line about not getting any respect. Well, their record is impeccable, of course. Still, their API is middle-of-the-pack, they had a very easy schedule, and they hardly overwhelmed their playoff opponents. If they had gone 12–2 instead of 14–0, they wouldn't be ranked this high.

6. **1996 Green Bay Packers**

I couldn't get over the fact that they lost all three road games against teams with winning records during the regular season, but they did have the best API of all the teams in the book, and I figured that meant they could rank no worse than the last slot of the top half.

5. **1989 San Francisco 49ers**

OK, so maybe I'm placing too much emphasis on playoff performance. Maybe I'm buying too much into the Montana mystique. Not that I used a mathematical formula, but the 1989 49ers had the fourth-best record in the group (granting that the distinctions among teams here are very small) and the tenth-best API (ditto). That would be an "average" rank of seventh. Given their 126–26 point differential in the playoffs, I think fifth is an appropriate spot. The fact that they were 8–0 on the road was another factor that I felt merited a top-five rank.

4. **1962 Green Bay Packers**

For many years, I thought this was clearly the best team in NFL history, even after the '72 Dolphins went undefeated. The '62 Packers were one of only three teams in the group who lost one game or less and their API was in the middle. Green Bay had a good point differential against teams with winning records with the caveat that they only played two such teams, but played them twice each. Their dominating 10–0 start swayed me somewhat, as well as my tremendous respect for Vince Lombardi.

3. **1979 Pittsburgh Steelers**

Does this mean I think that Joe Gibbs's Redskins of the '80s and '90s were better in the aggregate than the '70s Steelers? No, no, no, a thousand times no. Subjectively, I might just as soon pick this team over any other in history. Their regular-season record holds them back just slightly. The 1979 Steelers lost four games, including one to a pathetic Bengals team, and they were just 4–4 on the road. So, despite the fact that I mentally added something to their API because fumbling 47 times and losing 26 of them is basically just bad luck (no matter what coaches tell you), I couldn't put this team any higher than number three. Again, that is hardly an insult.

2. **1991 Washington Redskins**

Their two losses were by a total of five points, and one came in the last game of the season after they had clinched home-field advantage. Their API is fourth-best among the 12 teams. Counting the playoffs, they were 9–2 against teams with winning records, with a 338–157 point differential. I was forced to conclude that for one year this was the second-best team ever; trust me, that was a very tough thing for this Baltimore boy to do.

1. **1985 Chicago Bears**

Like I wrote earlier, picking this team number one was the easiest selection of the bunch. Only the '72 Dolphins had a better record, only the '96 Packers had a better API (and at +7.25 the Bears were way over the "magic" +6.00 threshold), and no team in history had a more dominating performance against good competition, both regular season and playoffs, than the 1985 Bears.

As you can imagine, I couldn't resist a few summary statistics. The teams I ranked 1–6 had an average API of +6.88; the teams at 7–12 had an average API of +6.48. The combined regular season record for the "top" half was 81–13, the "bottom" half was 69–14–1. The top half went 31–12 in the regular season against teams with winning records with a 1,191-684 point differential; the bottom half was 13–7–1 with a 533–386 differential. Here is a summary table:

	Record	API	Record, Point Difference Against Winning Teams		Playoff Point Difference
1985 CHI	15–1	+7.25	5–1,	180/71	91/10
1991 WAS	14–2	+6.89	6–2,	236/116	102/41
1979 PIT	12–4	+6.69	7–3,	270/174	92/46
1962 GB	13–1	+6.67	3–1,	110/40	16/7*
1989 SF	14–2	+6.29	6–2,	207/156	126/26
1996 GB	13–3	+7.49	4–3,	188/127	100/48

(continued next page)

*Only one playoff game; all other teams played three.

Summary table: *(continued)*

	Record	API	Record, Point Difference Against Winning Teams	Playoff Point Difference
1972 MIA	14–0	+6.63	2–0, 43/23	55/38
1994 SF	13–3	+6.27	4–2, 161/109	131/69
1971 DAL	11–3	+6.61	2–1, 57/41	58/18
1999 STL	13–3	+6.91	0–1, 21/24	83/59
1955 CLE	9–2–1	+6.41	2–1–1, 100/90	38/14*
1958 BAL	9–3	+6.02	3–2, 151/99	23/17*

I am not claiming that my list, my methods, or my book are the final words on this subject. I just don't want to hear, "The Redskins suck," or "You just hate the Dolphins." I am trying to move the discussion past blind team loyalties or football "dogma" as perpetuated by coaches, players, or the media. I was as objective as I could be and I look forward to someone else picking up the thread.

About the Author

EDDIE EPSTEIN is a baseball and football author and analyst who has worked for the Baltimore Orioles and San Diego Padres, as well as a number of other sports enterprises. He is the coauthor of *Baseball Dynasties: The Greatest Teams of All Time.* He is currently the president of EBC, Inc., a consulting service for professional sports teams and organizations. He has served as a commentator for ESPN Radio and ESPN.com. He and his wife, Vikki, live in the Dallas area.